W9-CTW-119

The
RIDDLE
of
POWER

*Presidential Leadership
from Truman to Bush*

by Robert Shogan

A DUTTON BOOK

DUTTON
Published by the Penguin Group
Penguin Books USA Inc., 375 Hudson Street, New York, New York 10014, U.S.A.
Penguin Books Ltd, 27 Wrights Lane, London W8 5TZ, England
Penguin Books Australia Ltd, Ringwood, Victoria, Australia
Penguin Books Canada Ltd, 2801 John Street, Markham, Ontario, Canada L3R 1B4
Penguin Books (N.Z.) Ltd, 182–190 Wairau Road, Auckland 10, New Zealand

Penguin Books Ltd, Registered Offices: Harmondsworth, Middlesex, England

First published by Dutton, an imprint of New American Library,
a division of Penguin Books USA Inc.
Distributed in Canada by McClelland & Stewart Inc.

First Printing, March, 1991
10 9 8 7 6 5 4 3 2 1

 REGISTERED TRADEMARK—MARCA REGISTRADA

LIBRARY OF CONGRESS CATALOGING IN PUBLICATION DATA:

Shogan, Robert.
    The riddle of power : presidential leadership from Truman to Bush / by Robert Shogan.
        p.   cm.
        1. Presidents—United States.   United States—Politics and government—1945–
    I. Title.
    JK516.S47   1991
    353.03′23′0922—dc20   90-46611
                                                                              CIP

Printed in the United States of America
Set in Century Expanded
Designed by Eve L. Kirch

For My Mother

CONTENTS

AUTHOR'S NOTE

This book was written in blocks of time spread out over eighteen months in 1989 and 1990. In a larger sense, though, it represents experience and insights gained during more than three decades of learning about American politics as a reporter and editor. I alone am responsible for efforts in judgment or fact. But the end product has benefited immeasurably from the contributions of a great many people. *Los Angeles Times* colleagues Don Irwin and Joel Havemann and John Robert Greene of Cazenovia College took on the heroic task of reading most of the manuscript in draft form and commenting in detail. Larry Berman of University of California, Davis, read the initial proposal and offered encouragement at an important time. And he, along with Ken Bode of the Center for Contemporary Media at DePauw University, Alonzo Hamby of Ohio University, Bruce Jentelson of the Brookings Institution, James Reichley also of Brookings, Larry Sabato of the University of Virginia, and Richard Williamson, who served in the Reagan White House, gave valuable counsel on individual chapters.

David Horrocks, chief archivist at the Gerald R. Ford Library, and Michael L. Gillette, chief of oral history at the Lyndon B. Johnson Library, took pains to help me make optimum use of these facilities as did other staff members at both libraries and also at the Harry S Truman library. Christopher Kline found draft versions of Nixon's "silent majority" speech at the Nixon Presidential Materials Project of the National Archives, and Jody McPhillips, of the *Providence Journal Bulletin*, spent a Saturday night in her newspaper's library gathering clips on Eisenhower's visit to Newport.

Among those who provided a range of advice and information when it was greatly needed were Tom Allen, Lou Cannon, Ron Goldfarb, Erwin Hargrove, Stanley Kutler, Harry McPherson, John Milligan, Richard Moe, Charles Moskos, Doyle McManus, Rick Meyer, Norman Ornstein, Maralee Schwartz, Larry Smith, and Brooks Yeager. Amelia Ford Shogan performed exceptionally meritorious service, researching the original proposal for this book, locating badly needed source material in the Owl bookstore at Bryn Mawr College and scanning these chapters with a discerning eye.

For financial support that helped me carry on the research required for an understanding of nine presidents, I am grateful to Charles Wolff and Public Policy Associates, Benedict K. Zobrist and the Harry S Truman Library Institute, and Frank Mackaman and the Gerald R. Ford Foundation and the Lyndon Baines Johnson Foundation.

I would like to salute Hofstra University for conducting a series of conferences on each of the modern presidents, the published output of which I have found to be a rich source of material.

The editors of the *Los Angeles Times*, particularly national editor Mike Miller, Washington bureau chief Jack Nelson, and his deputy Richard Cooper, made it possible for me to start work on the book. Without the cheerful assistance of Aleta Embrey, chief librarian of the *Times* Washington bureau and her assistants, Abebe Gessesse and Pat Welch, I could not have finished it. Phil Ruiz kept my computer on line.

My agent, Carl Brandt, and his associate, Gail Hochman, were both there when I needed them. Arnold Dolin, who edited my two previous books, again helped me find ways to improve my early drafts, and John Paine, his associate, taught me a great deal about economy of language. My wife, Ellen, and our daughters, Cynthia and Amelia, have been constant in their support and encouragement, helping me to feel, as they have in the past, that the end result of this venture would be worth our mutual efforts.

The
RIDDLE
of
POWER

CHAPTER 1

To Be As Big a Man
As He Can Be

Autumn reds and golds burnished the West Virginia countryside along Teddy Kennedy's path as he won warm greetings from city and mountain folk alike. Many who cheered him also shouted reminders of his brothers, John and Robert, who had both campaigned in the state years before in pursuit of the presidency. Ostensibly the surviving Kennedy brother had made the trip on this crisp October day in 1978 to solicit support for the re-election of the state's senior Democratic senator, Jennings Randolph. But in reality, this was a reconnaissance mission aimed at assessing the support Kennedy might find should he decide, as he ultimately did, to challenge Jimmy Carter for the presidency in 1980.

On this day Kennedy's prospects for the White House appeared as bright as the fall colors and as strong as his family's legacy. At a tumultuous open-air rally that night, following a torchlight parade, Kennedy recalled his brother John's momentous victory in the state's presidential primary in 1960. That success, as everyone gathered there well knew, had all but assured Jack Kennedy of becoming his party's presidential standard bearer. "No member of my family has ever felt a stranger in the hills and hollows and the mines and the cities of West Virginia," Kennedy declared. "My brothers came here, so did my sisters and my mother. It's good to be home again."

The West Virginians roared their approval, and after his oration was finished, they surged around the platform. Kennedy worked the crowd for a while, then with a grin urged me to help him out. "It's easy," he said. "All you have to do is shake their hands and wave at them, and they elect you president."

1

As Kennedy would later find out, along with many others who have sought that office, neither running for president nor serving as chief executive is anywhere near that easy.

Our recent presidents, of both parties, have led us down a road pitted with broken promises and misguided endeavors. Their combined performances have forced us to wonder what it takes to achieve success in the White House and how we should go about choosing a chief executive to lead the nation through the twilight years of this century and prepare it for the next millennium.

With George Bush finishing his second fitful year in the White House as this is written, those questions still beg answers. At the beginning of the 1980s, after a series of failed presidencies, *Newsweek* magazine asked in an article timed to coincide with the inauguration of Ronald Reagan, "The Presidency: Can Anyone Do the Job?" As the decade was drawing to an end, near the conclusion of Bush's first year in the White House, *Time* published an article that provided a disturbing answer to that question. Called "The Can't Do Government," it asserted: "Paralyzed by special interests and shortsightedness, Washington no longer seems capable of responding to its growing challenges."

During three decades, covering a half-dozen presidential campaigns and administrations, I have examined presidents and would-be presidents from a reporter's vantage point. At first hand I have watched politicians as they struggled to gain power, and then later on as some of them struggled even harder to exercise it in the face of adverse fortune and their own shortcomings. What I have learned I believe can aid in unlocking the riddle of power now surrounding the presidency, a conundrum that confounds scholars and politicians as well as ordinary citizens and casts a long shadow over the prospects for the incumbent chief executive.

History's verdict on George Bush's presidency is many years in the offing. In the meanwhile, though, this book offers a set of standards for understanding the modern presidency and the challenges of presidential leadership.

It will define the critical elements of leadership that determine how presidents perform in the White House, what goals they set, and how they go about achieving them. To trace the development of these elements, the book will look back at the formative years of each of the nine chief executives who have followed Franklin Roosevelt, the founder of the modern presidency. Then, president by president, the book will analyze their responses to events that challenged their leadership.

These challenges will be drawn from the wide variety of experiences that have shaped the modern presidency. We will see Harry Truman battling for his political life and for his party's future in the 1948 election and Dwight Eisenhower confronting the American dilemma of race relations at Little Rock in 1957. The 1962 Cuban missile crisis compelled John Kennedy to make life and death decisions for much of humankind; then Lyndon Johnson strove to lead a social revolution at home while waging a divisive war in Indochina. In the face of impassioned opposition, Richard Nixon determined to carry on the same war, until he could end it in his own way. The first unelected president, Gerald Ford, had to deal with the aftermath of the nation's darkest political scandal, by deciding the fate of his predecessor. Confronted by political forces he did not fully comprehend, Jimmy Carter struggled to rescue his imperiled presidency; next, with the economy in chaos Ronald Reagan seized the moment to launch a conservative counterrevolution. Now, Bush has brought us to the brink of war in the Middle East.

In each case, by examining the president's performance, the book will demonstrate how the key elements of leadership interact to contribute to his success or failure. Finally, this book will draw conclusions from these episodes that will help readers to make their own appraisals not only of the forty-first president, but also of his predecessors, and, more important in practical terms, of his successors.

Clearly, we need all the help we can get in this regard. Presidential campaigns in theory are supposed to provide us with enough information on the candidates to make intelligent choices. In fact, however, they have deteriorated to the point where even politicians concede these failings. As the country began to look ahead to the 1992 election, Republican John Danforth of Missouri gave pungent expression to a view widely shared by leaders of both parties when he declared during a Senate debate on campaign reforms: "Political campaigns turn the stomach of the average voter." Certainly they do nothing for the mind.

As the election of George Bush in 1988 demonstrated only too well, presidential campaigns have become a vicious, empty competition, dominated by mudslinging, evasion, and deceit. The substantive value of that election can be judged by what is best remembered now: from the Republican side, Bush's mindless and ultimately hollow injunction to read his lips, and from the Democratic side, Lloyd Bentsen's disparaging suggestion to J. Danforth Quayle that he was not John Kennedy.

As bad as the present campaign system is, we have learned not to expect improvement from reform measures such as those debated by Senator Danforth and his colleagues. Once these proposals have been twisted to protect the various interests who participate in their design, they generally create new problems as bad as or worse than the old. If we are to gain a clearer idea of what to expect from presidential contenders and incumbents we are very much on our own. It is hard work, but there is ample incentive.

Understanding the presidency represents far more than fulfillment of a civic responsibility. In the nuclear age it is a matter of life and death. Even if the threat of doomsday weaponry is set aside, knowledge of presidential candidates that casts light on how they will act in office can aid in weathering the turbulence of modern American society. By and large, Americans pay little heed to most politicians or to the political process. But the president, whoever he—or someday no doubt she—happens to be, cannot be safely ignored. The president bestrides our political world like a contemporary Caesar, reaching into the nooks and crannies of our everyday existence. He can lead us into war, or economic ruin, or set us against each other. Or he can help us resolve our differences and generate fresh confidence and hope.

The many possible outcomes of presidential policies scattered along the spectrum between good and evil are all the consequences of what the presidency has become in little more than a half century, since the time of Franklin Roosevelt. It was in the process of leading the nation out of the Great Depression and into World War II that FDR invented the modern presidency, with all its potential for shaping our lives.

My experience with the modern presidency began in childhood, in the midst of the Great Depression. I did not suffer from this bleak decade, nor was I even much aware of it at its low point, but later on, I heard a great deal about those hard times from my parents. What I remember being told was that Franklin Roosevelt, the president, had managed to rescue us from the Depression—and that the day Franklin Roosevelt stopped being president was very likely to be the day that marked the onset of the next depression.

Years later, after I left home for college, I learned to take a broader, more balanced view of Roosevelt's achievements. But buried beneath the idolatry and exaggeration of those childhood impressions, an important truth was embedded: a president can make a difference in the lives of ordinary people. Roosevelt was a living example of the maxim propounded by one of his predecessors: "The President is at liberty, both in law and conscience, to be as big a man as he can," Woodrow Wilson wrote years before he himself entered the White House, if only he can get "the nation behind him."

Few presidents have been as successful as Roosevelt in getting the nation behind them, but all of Roosevelt's successors have had a dramatic influence, for better or worse, on the lives of the citizens they were chosen to serve. Consciousness of this impact has engendered vast expectations for the use of presidential power. What is often forgotten, though—and what makes life difficult for presidents—is that this power exists only as a potential. Leadership is the means by which the president can exploit that potential. This is no easy task. He must contend with the constitutional checks on his power devised by the Founding Fathers, with the resistance of his political opponents, and with crises he can neither foresee nor control.

One major reason for the riddle surrounding the uses of presidential power is that it is generally thought of too narrowly, defined only in purely political terms—the authority derived from the Constitution and statutes and from the president's role as head of his party and the spokesman for an ideology, a set of political beliefs which define his goals in office. This limited focus contributes to what British journalist Godfrey Hodgson called the paradox of the presidency: "Never has any one office had so much power as the president of the United States possesses. Never has so powerful a leader been so impotent to do what he wants to do, and what he is pledged to do, what he is expected to do, and what he knows he must do."

In a similar vein, in the preface to a revised edition of his classic 1960 study of the post-Roosevelt presidency, Richard Neustadt wrote: "Presidential weakness was the underlying theme of *Presidential Power*." And after twenty years, "This remains my theme. . . . Weakness is still what I see."

Such judgments are easy to understand. Starting with the New Deal, the executive branch of government has steadily expanded in size, which gives the outward appearance of increased power for the presidency. But all these agencies, like the president himself, must still answer to Congress, and their growth has made it that much harder for the president to keep control of the federal bureaucracy.

In a sense, the sole significant addition to the president's *political* power since FDR's day has been the authority he now has in his role as commander-in-chief to touch off a nuclear holocaust, a prerogative too apocalyptic to be constructive. "The only power I have is nuclear and I can't use that," Lyndon Johnson once grumbled.

Nevertheless, as presidents have come to understand, some better than others, political power is only one dimension of the president's potential authority. It is the most important. But a president cannot lead with political power alone. If he is to have a reasonable chance of success he must use the two other formidable arrows in his quiver—the power of morality and the power of his personality.

These two forms of presidential power have been vastly expanded by the social and technological change of the past half century. The collapse of social standards and the fragmentation of traditional institutions have created previously unimagined opportunities for presidents to thrust their morals and personalities to the forefront. Moreover, all this has occurred just as the stunning expansion of the power of mass media, mainly through television, provided the means for exploiting these opportunities.

Recognition of this breadth of presidential power is the underpinning of my formula for presidential leadership. Most studies have concentrated on the political aspect of presidential power. This book will demonstrate that presidential performance can best be understood by examining all three elements of presidential power in conjunction with each other. They are so closely linked that they sometimes overlap, yet each has its own distinctive role to play in relation to the others.

Ideology. This is the basis on which the president attempts to exercise his political power. The absence of distinct social classes in this country, and the conflict between the fundamental national beliefs in opportunity on one hand and equality on the other, tend to blur ideology in U.S. politics. Indeed, sometimes it seems nonexistent. Our politicians are generally uncomfortable talking about ideology to the point of denying they have one. Thus the 1988 Democratic standard bearer, Michael Dukakis, launched his drive to gain the White House by declaring: "This election isn't about ideology. It's about competence." Nevertheless ideology lives in American politics; it just requires an expanded definition—one that includes means as well as ends. The content of the president's political beliefs is the end of ideology. Just as important, however, is his overall strategy for implementing these beliefs, which establishes the means of ideology. For ideology to be an instrument of leadership the president must not only have a broad philosophical framework for deciding which policy goals matter most, but he must also have a realistic approach to the political system, a strategy that allows him to achieve these goals. Because ideological beliefs in our politics are often ill defined, ideological strategy frequently becomes salient.

Values. Providing the foundation for the president's moral power, these principles and beliefs are grouped outside of ideology because they are more personal and emotional than intellectual. Presidential values are both private and public. Presidents rely on private values to guide their own conduct. I will show that Lyndon Johnson was driven by the ethic of Horatio Alger, Dwight Eisenhower by the principle of teamwork, while for Gerald Ford loyalty was a prime motivator. Presidents also use public values to inspire support. Richard Nixon invoked such middle-class icons as rugged individualism and the sanctity of the family; similarly, Harry Truman identified himself with the spirit of the underdog. For effective leadership these values must be as important to citizens in a symbolic sense as the president's political goals are in a tangible sense. Shortly before the revelation of his extramarital affairs destroyed Gary Hart's initial candidacy for the presidency in 1988, he argued that private values should not be imposed on dissenting members of society, nor inferentially on presidential candidates. "This nation from Jefferson on has always believed that," Hart told me. As Hart found out, though, while Jeffersonian tolerance may be well and good for the average citizen, stricter standards prevail for a candidate for president. Such episodes serve as reminders that presidents, potentially at least, are our ultimate heroes, and by our choice of heroes we define our values.

Character. This is, of course, the source of the president's personal power. The term character is a way of describing the president's temperament and inclinations, the visceral drives that motive him. Character is the catalyst that melds a president's ideology and values into his vision for the country, which is the expression of his leadership. For the president to lead successfully this vision must be compelling and persuasive and must be supported by his character. No one understood this better than FDR, whose temperament was so well tuned to the Oval Office that one spellbound associate said of him: "He must have been psychoanalyzed by God." There is no one formula for successful presidential character. Just as Roosevelt's regal bearing bolstered his leadership, Truman's appeal owed much to his lack of pretension. On one occasion, after banging out old favorites on the White House piano, he told his guests that if he had not entered politics, he would have made "a helluva good piano player in a whorehouse." On the flip side, character has also been a source of serious vulnerabilities, personal insecurity, for example. Desperate to project himself more favorably to the public, Lyndon Johnson experimented during one televised press conference with a more informal style, stepping away from the podium, taking off his glasses, and clapping his hands for emphasis. His aides applauded the result, but Johnson abandoned the technique; his self-doubts about his suitability for the presidency made him fear that the informal approach would cause him to be perceived as lacking in presidential dignity.

The importance of all three factors—ideology, values, and character—in determining the success or failure of presidential leadership has never been driven home to me more graphically than in the case of Edward Kennedy. As I barnstormed with the senior senator from Massachusetts on that heady swing through West Virginia in 1978, he appeared to be the answer to his party's and his country's prayers.

Kennedy then confronted the threshold challenge of presidential leadership—getting elected to the office. Nearly every circumstance seemed to favor him. His was a commanding presence, fostered by his family legend but also strengthened by his own achievements as a leading gladiator for the causes around which Roosevelt had forged the old New Deal coalition. He was the acknowledged leader and foremost advocate of the still powerful liberal wing of the Democratic party. In that role Kennedy certainly possessed the ideological framework that is the first criterion for presidential leadership.

What any appraisal based solely on this overlooked, however, was that Kennedy sorely lacked the other key ingredients for leadership— moral underpinning for his values and a strong, consistent character. Memories of his family stirred deep emotions and lofty aspirations not only in West Virginia but nearly everywhere else. But Kennedy himself, by the all too conspicuous evidence of his flawed personal life—his behavior at Chappaquiddick, his shattered marriage—could hardly hold himself out as exemplifying the standards for character and values that the public had associated with John and Robert Kennedy.

When Kennedy, with the cheers from West Virginia and elsewhere ringing in his ears, made the mistake of challenging Jimmy Carter, the incumbent president was quick to strike at Kennedy's weaknesses. One Carter campaign commercial boasted about the president: "Husband, father, president—he's doing all three jobs with distinction." Another television spot pointedly asserted: "A man brings two things to the presidential ballot. He brings his record and he brings himself. Who he is is frequently more important than what he's done." Kennedy's ideology could not protect him against this assault, and his ambitions were crushed.

Kennedy's defeat demonstrated that ideology alone cannot produce leadership success. But as the following chapters will show, the challenges of presidential leadership offer many other ways to fail—and at least as many ways to succeed. The complex interaction of the three elements of leadership, plus the varying demands of different challenges and different political settings, rule out the possibility of constructing one model of leadership that delivers success in every circumstance. Nevertheless, one broad principle does emerge from the episodes recounted here: the outcome of any leadership challenge depends mainly on the president's ability to combine his ideology, values, and character to get "the nation behind him."

Take, for example, the case of Jimmy Carter, who turned back Kennedy's challenge for the Democratic nomination in 1980. Carter did not have the glaring character and moral defects that plagued the youngest of the Kennedy brothers. Indeed, as a born-again Christian and inveterate Sunday school teacher, Carter seemed morally superior not only to Kennedy but also to most other American politicians. But he had other problems.

His main challenge as president was to forge a new political alliance for his party to replace the timeworn New Deal coalition and to help him achieve the difficult goals—from energy independence to welfare reform—that he had set for himself. But when early in his presidency I asked Carter how he planned to do this, he could only refer me to his speeches. "There's an amazing consistency in my speeches," he told me. "I'd say basic morality is there—not that I'm better than other people," he added quickly. "It's hard for me to describe because it's part of my consciousness."

That Carter was almost tongue-tied when asked about his beliefs showed not a lack of intelligence but rather a lack of interest in ideology. His values and his character could not offset this weakness, which crippled his efforts to mobilize support.

By contrast, the anti-government ideology of Carter's successor, Ronald Reagan, came across loud and clear, reinforced by his values, which were based on his reverence for the American past. On a campaign swing through Massachusetts in 1980, Reagan's motorcade halted to permit him to inspect Plymouth Rock, and when he returned to the press bus he managed to epiphanize the import of the Pilgrim fathers' voyage on the *Mayflower* in one rhetorical question:

"If they could come all that way in that little boat, how dare we be afraid of anything?"

Those words, addressed to only a handful of reporters, demonstrated Reagan's skill at fusing his ideology and his values. That ability helped him greatly to get public backing when he confronted his main presidential challenge—repairing the damage done to the nation's economy and self-confidence during Carter's stewardship.

Reagan's early success in the White House stirred optimism about a revival of confidence in the institution of the presidency as a force for leadership, after a series of failures in the Oval Office. But his strong ideology and values could not offset a weakness in his character—his tendency toward overdependence on others—that led him to become ensnared in the Iran-Contra episode, revealing patterns of behavior sharply out of keeping with what he had taught the country to expect from him.

Thanks in large measure to his personal charm, Reagan left the White House with remarkably high poll ratings. But the disclosure after he left office that his own advisers feared that the Iran-Contra revelations had made him vulnerable to impeachment put the polls and the Reagan presidency in sobering perspective.

As Reagan's embarrassment demonstrated, leadership success is hard to sustain from one presidential challenge to another. One reason for this concerns the presidents themselves. In some cases, flaws in their leadership that may be masked during one challenge turn out be damaging in the next. Reagan's characteristic inclination to delegate many of his burdens did not prevent him from winning approval for his economic policies, though it did help bring on the Iran-Contra fiasco.

Another obstacle to following one success with another is the influence of events that a president cannot anticipate or prevent. Thus, after winning his brilliant victory in the 1948 election Harry Truman found himself stymied in his second term in the White House largely because of the outbreak of the Korean War, which drained resources from his domestic programs.

Still, gifted leadership can achieve enduring results. John Kennedy, with the rational approach shaped by his ideology, values, and character, was able to exploit his success in the Cuban missile crisis to gain a nuclear test ban treaty. Kennedy's reasoned response to the threat of nuclear war allowed his successor to take office in a safer world.

The benefits of successful leadership are underlined when contrasted with the stark impact of failure. For example, this book argues that Dwight Eisenhower's combination of leadership elements led to a passive response to the civil rights revolution and made an already grave dilemma more divisive.

Although presidential performance has often been disappointing and success incomplete, even the partial victories of the past offer hope. A fuller solution to the riddle of power awaits a president and a public willing to learn from these lessons of leadership and to apply them to the challenges confronting us in the future.

The need is great. The hard truth is that we have lost our sense of national direction. Without purpose or discipline, we have stumbled for more than a decade from crisis to crisis, from Carter's malaise to Reagan's binge of greed, from the humiliation of the Iranian embassy hostages to the fiasco of Iran-Contra, from the economic devastation inflicted by astronomical inflation to the social corrosion wrought by the rampant drug trade.

Underlying these symptoms is a collapse of faith in two of the critical areas of presidential leadership, ideology and values. The ideological crisis has its roots in the steady debilitation of the New Deal credo that dominated American politics from Franklin Roosevelt's time to the onset of Ronald Reagan—and in the subsequent failure of Reagan to provide a satisfactory substitute. As a consequence, American politics is drifting without any philosophical moorings.

Just as significant is the turmoil surrounding our value structure. The nation has been shaken by a series of jolts challenging standards of behavior: the AIDS epidemic, which mocked the sexual permissiveness of the sixties; the Wall Street scandals, which stained the glorified image of the Reagan era's acquisitive entrepreneurs; the revelations of sordid self-indulgence by the television evangelists who had set themselves up as guardians of the public's mores; and the flood of malefactions committed by our elected and appointed officials, local and federal, Democrat and Republican.

As threatening as the turbulence shaking our institutions and beliefs may seem, it also has created an opportunity rare in our history. This turmoil gives to the president, either George Bush or his successor, a once-in-a-generation opening to redefine the national agenda by framing a vision that will capture the loyalty of a new, enduring majority.

Much of the information in this book is drawn from the public record. But most of the judgments are shaped by my own observations and reactions over the years. Therefore, I have chosen in this book to break the first commandment of journalism: "Keep yourself out of the story." Instead I have inserted myself here and there so that readers can better understand and judge my arguments.

My interest in journalism was rooted in the turbulent times of my childhood—the 1930s. My family took these events very personally, and nearly every family gathering turned into a heated discussion concerning the public controversies then raging—from the AFL versus the CIO to the Spanish Loyalist versus Franco's Fascists.

Understanding little of this at first, I nevertheless found the discussions exciting. Meanwhile I began reading newspapers, at first just the sports news, but after the start of World War II, I became absorbed by the struggle against the Axis, which I reluctantly recognized was more consequential than the American League pennant race. I even kept a scrapbook crammed with clippings recording the progress of the Allied armies.

It may have been inevitable for anyone whose early consciousness was as dominated by newspapers as mine to want to work for them. At any rate, that was what I made up my mind to do. I did not think I could change the world, but I wanted to be close to great personages and events so that I could understand them better, and this I thought journalism would allow me to do. These experiences I have shared in this book.

Working for newspapers has given me a license to ask questions. After more than thirty years of covering the police beat and city hall, Congress and the White House, I have learned that what is important is to ask the right questions. This is what I have tried to do in these pages.

CHAPTER 2

Truman: The Underdog

The occasion was the annual Jefferson-Jackson Day dinner, the most time-honored of all the Democratic party's ritual feasts. On this February evening in 1948, the 2,100 guests filled the grand ballrooms of two of Washington's biggest hotels, the Statler and Mayflower, for the guest of honor was no less than the president of the United States.

Yet Harry S Truman could have taken little personal satisfaction from the size of the crowd. He had been around Washington long enough to know that presidential prestige and power can be depended upon to fill a hall, regardless of the president's personal standing. In the case of this president, as Truman knew as well as anyone else, his standing was scraping the bottom of the political barrel.

The party faithful in attendance that night put up a brave front, washing down their breast of capon with copious champagne, but many of them privately felt that with Truman at the Democratic helm, the party's prospects were bleaker than at any time since Al Smith's candidacy in 1928.

Truman did little that evening to alter this gloomy perception. "This is a year of challenge," the sixty-three-year-old president declared. "I propose that we meet that challenge head on." But his tone was flat, his rhetoric pedestrian, and his voice rasping. His presentation served to remind Democrats once again of the contrast between Truman's drab presidential style and the eloquent discourse and commanding presence of Franklin Roosevelt.

With Roosevelt gone, the grand coalition he had assembled appeared

12

to be crumbling on all sides. On the left, Henry A. Wallace, charging that Truman's hard line with the Soviet Union would lead to war, had announced in December of 1947 that he would run for president as head of the newly formed Progressive party. Wallace had been Truman's predecessor as Roosevelt's vice-president, and many liberals considered him the true legatee of FDR's New Deal.

On the right flank, Southern conservatives were indignant over Truman's approach to civil rights. That very month Truman had sent to Congress a bold legislative program asking for federal action against lynching, the poll tax, and job discrimination. Southern governors meeting in Florida issued a warning that Truman faced "a full-fledged revolt" in the long solid South if he persisted in this heresy. To drive that point home at the Jefferson-Jackson dinner, one Southern senator, Olin Johnston of South Carolina, reserved an entire table in a conspicuous section of the hall, then sent an aide to make sure the seats remained symbolically vacant.

No one had planned for Harry Truman to be president of the United States, least of all Truman himself. And now that he had held the office for nearly three years, it seemed that no one wanted him to keep it. No one, that is, but Harry S. Truman. He was determined to hang on for dear life, and the months ahead would measure his determination and test the three-key attributes—ideology, values, and character—that would define his presidential leadership.

IDEOLOGY

In his nearly eight years as president, Truman embodied the interest-group liberalism that FDR had preached—the use of government to redress the inequities of constituents in rough proportion to their political power. Because Truman shunned rhetorical flourishes and theoretical debates, at first glance he did not seem deeply imbued with any ideology. One biographer called him "a practical, not an ordained New Dealer." Truman himself claimed that his ties to the liberal doctrines Roosevelt promulgated ran deep. "I was a New Dealer from the start," he wrote of his outlook when he first arrived in the Senate in 1934. "In fact I had been a New Dealer back in Jackson County and there was no need for me to change." Truman was set apart from a good many other New Dealers, however, by the fact that his zeal for liberal ends had been seasoned by hardheaded experience with the means that government needed to use.

Two historical traditions, conflicting with but also complementing each other, contributed to his convictions. One was the Yankee Protestant belief that politics ought to be governed by righteous principles rather than selfish concerns. Placing great emphasis on government as a moral force, this credo, as Richard Hofstadter noted, "demanded the constant disinterested activity of the citizen in public affairs." For all its stress on high-mindedness, this approach was firmly practical; as it evolved over the years, it focused on how the machinery of government actually worked day in and day out. This mindset found roots in the states of the Middle Border, and influenced Truman's early career as a county administrator, helping him gain a reputation for efficiency and honesty that would serve him well throughout his career.

But for the immigrants who poured in to man the mines and mills of the burgeoning American economy, and found themselves overwhelmed by its avarice and cutthroat ethics, this selfless faith offered no immediate benefit. They turned instead to Progressivism, which had evolved from the more militant movement of the times, Populism, to help relieve the harsh conditions they faced in the turmoil of industrializing America. The passions and energy they generated helped to energize the big-city machines that in time provided the undergirding for the modern Democratic party.

It was one such machine, based in Kansas City and headed by Tom Pendergast, among the most potent big-city bosses of the era, which launched Truman's political career. His recruitment in 1922 as a candidate for district judge, which was really a managerial post, began what was to be a long and mutually beneficial relationship between Truman and the Pendergast organization. Pendergast's satraps made the machine's formidable organizational and financial resources available to the fledgling politician. For his part, Truman brought to Pendergast a host of personal contacts through his family and his service as a National Guard captain in World War I. The fact that Truman was a Baptist and increasingly prominent as a Mason also helped the Pendergast organization, which was dominated by Irish Catholics.

As he began his political career, the populist strain in his ideological makeup was clear. Raised by highly partisan parents, he had from an early age been attuned to the muckraking cadences of Progressivism and the militancy of Populism, and had grown up revering William Jennings Bryan and Woodrow Wilson as champions of the people against the special interests.

His populist outlook was reflected and reinforced by his response to the failure of the haberdashery store he had launched after his return from World War I service in France. Truman blamed this on economic conditions, specifically on tight money and the Republicans. "In 1921, after the Republicans took over . . . Andrew Mellon was made Secretary of the Treasury. . . . He immediately started a 'wringing out' process, which put farm prices down to an all-time low, raised interest rates and put labor in its place."

Actually, Truman's own faulty business judgment contributed to the demise of the store. But whatever Truman's limits as entrepreneur, his business reverses occurred against the backdrop of a general farm depression in the early 1920s. Much of the drastic downturn was due to circumstances beyond the control of the individual farmer, who since 1914 had seen himself as the underdog of the U.S. economy. Wheat was selling for $2.15 a bushel in late 1919 when Truman and his friend Eddie Jacobson opened their shop in downtown Kansas City. Within a year it had fallen to $1.44, only the beginning of a long slide that was to devastate the farm belt. Truman clearly saw that the Republican policies of presidents Harding and Coolidge did precious little to help conditions. This was a legacy Truman was to carry with him to the White House and out on the hustings in 1948.

Over the long run, Populism would be the most important influence on Truman's ideology. For the time being, though, while he was serving as a newly elected district judge, his populist inclinations were not as relevant to his career as his commitment to integrity and efficiency. Tarnished by graft and corruption as it was—Tom Pendergast was ultimately jailed for income tax evasion—the Pendergast machine was a highly imperfect instrument. Nevertheless, during his years of managing county affairs, Truman earned a reputation as an apostle of honest and efficient public service. Working closely with the Kansas City Public Service Institute, a nonpartisan advocate of the managerial approach to local government, Truman promoted road improvements, zoning regulation, and fairer tax assessments, "all administered," wrote one biographer, "in as efficient and as politically neutral a fashion as possible."

Truman's adherence to this approach helped shield him from most of the less savory practices of the Pendergast machine and ultimately helped him to rise above it. One day in 1928, according to a story Truman liked to tell, he was summoned to Pendergast's office, where he found a group of "crooked contractors." As Truman recalled the circumstances, Pendergast said, "These boys tell me that you won't give them contracts."

"They can get them," Truman replied evenly, "if they are low bidders."

Whereupon Pendergast supposedly turned to the contractors and remarked, "Didn't I tell you boys he's the contrariest cuss in Missouri?"

As self-serving as this anecdote seems, there is reason to believe that it was not merely apocryphal. Jonathan Daniels, who served both Roosevelt and Truman, points out that Pendergast regarded himself not as a crooked politician but an ambitious businessman skilled in the art of "honest graft." By promising that he would award road contracts on a low-bid basis, Truman had overcome voter resistance to construction bond issues, the cost of which had often been inflated by corruption. Pendergast certainly would have preferred road contracts to go to his friends and allies. But as a businessman as well as a politician, he was shrewd enough to understand that low-bid road building was better for business and for politics than no building at all.

It was also good for Truman's reputation. Though he was clearly Pendergast's candidate for the Democratic Senate nomination in 1934, the anti-Pendergast *Kansas City Star* described him as "a capable and honest public official" and "a man of unimpeachable character and integrity." Thus, Truman established himself as relatively independent from Pendergast. This status would help him withstand the sneers he faced in the Senate, where detractors referred to him as "the Senator from Pendergast" because of his early ties and political debts to the machine.

From the time Truman entered the Senate in 1935, he was a reliable supporter of Roosevelt's New Deal policies. More than that, he was a vocal proponent of the ideas that had been part of his populist heritage. The opportunity to translate those beliefs into action came through a friendship that developed with Montana Senator Burton K. Wheeler, an inveterate foe of the Eastern monied interests and chairman of the Interstate Commerce Committee. Wheeler saw to it that Truman was put in charge of a subcommittee probe into the depredation of the Rock Island and Missouri Pacific railroads by unscrupulous holding companies. As Truman put it to his fellow senators:

> The first railroad robbery was committed on the Rock Island back in 1873 just east of Council Bluffs, Iowa. The man who committed that robbery used a gun and a horse and got up early in the morning. He and his gang took a chance on being killed and eventually most were. That railroad robber's name was Jesse James. The same Jesse James held up the Missouri Pacific in 1876 and took the paltry sum of $17,000 from the express car. About thirty years after the Council Bluffs holdup, the Rock Island went through a looting by some gentlemen known as the tin plate millionaires. They used no guns, but they ruined the railroad and got away with $70,000,000 or more. They did it by means of holding companies. Senators can see what pikers Mr. James and his crowd were alongside of some real artists.

Truman did more than just fulminate at the railroads. The product of the probe conducted by himself and Wheeler was the Truman-Wheeler Transportation Act of 1940, which imposed stringent new regulations to prevent financial manipulators from plundering railroads and from duping the public into investing in their worthless enterprises.

But what distinguished his Senate career and transformed him from "the Senator from Pendergast" into a national figure deemed suitable to be FDR's running mate was his role as chairman of the Senate War Investigating Committee. There his work embodied his commitment to the good-government ethic as well as to Populism.

During the course of an informal inspection tour that laid the foundation for the committee's creation, Truman found a plentitude of shoddy workmanship and graft. He conducted the probe in a remarkably even-handed and disciplined style, faithful to the good-government creed. But his motivation was at least in part a populist reaction to the unfairness in the way the early defense buildup was being administered. As Truman later wrote, explaining the need for the committee investigations, "The big manufacturers were getting bigger all the time, and the smaller companies were being threatened with going out of business or starving to death."

On reaching the presidency, Truman was still stirred by the populist battle cries of his youth, and sought to express them in the modern idiom of the New Deal. In his first major statement on domestic policy after Roosevelt's death, on September 6, 1945, Truman assumed the mantle not only of manager of the New Deal but of its prophet. His twenty-one-point message made clear his intention not just to maintain the New Deal but to expand it in the postwar era. The date of its delivery, Truman wrote later, "symbolizes for me the assumption of the office of president in my own right." He added, "Some of my more conservative associates advised me against this definite commitment to such liberal measures." Indeed, Southern Democrats and Republicans sharply criticized the address, with House Republican leader Joe Martin complaining: "Not even President Roosevelt ever asked so much at one sitting. It is just a case of out New Dealing the New Deal."

The speech showed the development in Truman's thinking in his five months in the White House and the direction in which Truman wanted to take the country, but the reaction also made clear the obstacles he would face along the way. What made Truman's commitment to liberalism particularly striking was the fact that it was much harder to get popular and congressional support for such measures in the postwar era than it had been in the grim Depression days of the 1930s.

Postwar conditions both at home and abroad made it hard for him to retain the loyalty of the forces that had made the New Deal reforms possible. Among the most serious of the domestic problems was the discontent of organized labor, a key component of the alliance Roosevelt had constructed. Having been handcuffed by wage controls during the war, the unions struggled to make up for the ravages of postwar inflation.

One of the first confrontations was with the railroad brotherhoods, who called a nationwide strike in May 1946, paralyzing the nation's transportation system. Truman went before a joint session of Congress and demanded the right to draft strikers into the army. The strike was settled even as Truman was speaking, but the episode infuriated his labor supporters, of whom the rail unions had been among the most faithful.

Continued labor trouble in auto plants and other major industries—steel, meat packing, and electric appliances—drove up prices and fired public resentment. All this helped inspire the Republican-controlled Congress to pass the Taft-Hartley Act, aimed at cutting back some of the power labor had gained during the New Deal era. The bill outlawed the closed shop and allowed states to ban the union shop through so-called right-to-work laws. Truman vetoed the bill, but his veto was overridden, with many Democrats joining the Republican majorities.

Just as the war had roiled the economy, it had also greatly intensified racial tensions. Civil rights leaders were becoming increasingly militant in the early months of the Truman presidency. The war against Nazi Germany with its racist policies underscored for Negroes,* and some whites, their country's neglected commitment to equality. In addition, the vast influx of Southern Negroes into the industrial North to work in the booming munitions factories had aggravated racial resentments in the nation's great urban centers.

Truman's initial thinking on civil rights as a senator had reflected both the need to cater to the traditional attitudes of his own border state, where segregation was the order of the day, and the conflicting concern about the demands of black voters, who made up a significant constituency in Missouri. Personal factors complicated his position: his instinct for the value of fairness was juxtaposed with a certain ingrained bigotry.

All these forces continued to shape his policies in this area as president, with political considerations gradually moving him toward the side of the Negro. In the spring of 1945, Truman threw his support behind a proposal to make permanent a Fair Employment Practices Committee (FEPC) to protect the rights of Negroes seeking work in the war plants. But early the next year, faced with unrest from Southern leaders of his party, he backed off the issue, a decision that assured the end of the agency.

On the other hand, he did establish the President's Committee on Civil Rights, whose landmark report paved the way for civil rights leg-

---

* The terms "Negro" and "black" are used throughout to correspond to prevailing usage of the time.

islation. Then, in February 1948, as the election approached, Truman sought to counter the appeal of third-party candidate Henry A. Wallace to Negro voters by sending Congress a special message on civil rights, calling for an anti-lynching law, an anti-poll tax law, and reviving the idea of a permanent FEPC.

From this and later actions, it seems clear that during his years in the White House, his thinking broadened significantly. When all was said and done, he became the first chief executive since Lincoln to actually improve the condition of Negro Americans.

Abroad, Truman also faced a sea of troubles. The wartime alliance with the Soviet Union had turned into a bitter rivalry threatening a new world conflict and causing political tensions at home. Truman was charged alternately with caving in to the Soviets and with war mongering. In March 1947, with Greece torn by civil war and Turkey in economic difficulty, the president proclaimed the Truman Doctrine, pledging economic and military aid to those two countries and any other nations threatened by communism. In June of that year, the promise of military support was followed up with the unveiling of the Marshall plan, which formalized U.S. backing for the economic regeneration of the nations most imperiled by the Red Army or subversion.

In sum, dramatically changed conditions had made it impossible for Truman to merely follow the course laid down by his predecessor. He was forced instead to sail into uncharted ideological seas. This was by no means a smooth passage either for the ship of state or for its new captain. At times Truman seemed to overreact, as when he pressed his proposal to conscript the rail workers even after they had agreed to return to their jobs.* Facing certain controversies, he equivocated, as when he asked Congress for an extension of wartime price controls but failed to put his full prestige behind the idea. The result was that controls lapsed and prices soared.

By and large, however, his was an impressive performance. He managed to keep faith with the principles of his progressive legacy and of the New Deal and at the same time to adjust these ideological principles to the changing conditions of the postwar world. When the tactics of organized labor seemed to threaten the common interest, as in the rail strike, Truman resisted and forced the unions back to work. On the other hand, when Truman perceived that the long-term interests of the labor

---

* Truman's proposal passed the House, but died in the Senate when Republicans balked. The episode must have been especially embarrassing for Truman because he was charged with unfairness to labor by Republican Senator Robert A. Taft of Ohio, considered by organized labor to be one of its archenemies. "It seems to me," said Taft of Truman's proposal, "that it violates every principle of American jurisprudence."

movement were threatened, he fought back and vetoed the Taft-Hartley bill.

He sought not only to maintain the defenses for underdog groups established by Roosevelt, but to extend these protections to Negroes, thus plunging into an arena where FDR had feared to tread.

Similarly, Truman understood as Roosevelt did that advancement of progressive principles at home required a vigorous affirmation of national interests abroad. By acting to meet the Soviet challenge, as Roosevelt had responded to threats from Nazi Germany and imperial Japan, Truman gave his lifelong beliefs added scope and strength to meet the transformed realities of the postwar era.

VALUES

The Populism that dominated Truman's ideology was reinforced by his values, particularly his identification with the underdog—the disadvantaged of society. This attitude was derived in part from the circumstances of his youth, which also shaped his character, and from his later years in politics, during which his ideology also developed.

His poor eyesight was a reason early on for his view of himself as an underdog. Truman was probably close to being legally blind without eyeglasses, and on at least one occasion he referred to his handicap as a "deformity." The thick glasses prescribed for him cut him off from the other children. "Remember, this was in 1889 in farm country," Truman's daughter, Margaret, later pointed out. "Glasses were seldom if ever prescribed for children."

The reaction of other youngsters was predictable. "Of course they called me four eyes," Truman told Merle Miller long afterward. "That's hard on a boy. It makes him lonely and gives him an inferiority complex." His limited vision and his self-consciousness about his glasses led him to avoid the normal rough and tumble of boyhood, and he spent much of his time reading history and studying music. Adding to the boy's distress was his relationship with his father, who favored his younger son, a more rugged and outgoing type than the bookish Harry.

As Truman matured, he outgrew his inferiority complex. His daughter never heard him complain about the painful isolation of his childhood. Instead he talked of how the glasses had made it possible for him to read the books he loved. "I saw things and saw print I'd never seen before," he told her. Yet the experience made a mark on him, and along with later events endowed his value structure with a keen sensitivity to unfairness and inequity.

He and his family were no strangers to hard times. As a boy he had endured the traumas of the farm economy in the early twentieth century. Speculation in grain futures wiped out his father in 1903, about the time young Harry finished high school. Truman was forced to drop out of business school and had to give up the piano lessons he had been taking since childhood. Hoping to get an appointment to either West Point or Annapolis, where tuition was free, he prepped in history and geography. "I was anxious for a higher education and because my father was having financial troubles," he recalled later, ". . . I knew he would not be able to send me." But his poor eyesight ruined his chances for an appointment. As a result, Truman was the only twentieth-century president not to have graduated from college.

Truman's underdog values came into play during his presidency, sometimes offsetting other aspects of his background in shaping his decisions. This was particularly true on the bitter controversies over race that began building during his presidency. In the midst of the 1948 campaign, a group of Southern Democrats promised to subdue a budding Southern revolt against his candidacy if the president would soften his stand on civil rights. Truman's response, related by his daughter, reflected the internal conflicts between his border-state heritage and his values. "My forebears were confederates," he pointed out.

> . . . Every factor and influence on my background—and in my wife's, for that matter—would foster the personal belief that you are right. But my very stomach turned over when I learned that Negro soldiers, just back from overseas, were being dumped out of army trucks in Mississippi and beaten. Whatever my inclinations as a native of Missouri might have been, as president I know this is bad. I shall fight to end evils like this.

From his parents and from his environment in Independence, where his family moved in 1890 when Truman was six, he also acquired the standard values that reflected Midwestern upbringing of that period. He was taught to be honest, to do his duty, and to adhere to the Victorian moral code and the admonitions of the Good Book. Truman practiced these middle-class values all his life. His straightforwardness certainly helped him to overcome the tarnish to his reputation brought by his links to Pendergast. But as he matured as a politician and reached the Senate, his self-identification as an underdog assumed a more important role in influencing his political decisions and his approach to leadership.

As the New Deal gathered momentum in Truman's first term in the Senate, the tactics of the forces opposing the Roosevelt reforms hardened Truman's own natural inclinations to comfort the afflicted and afflict the comfortable. In 1935 he backed the Public Utility Holding Company Act, which he said was designed "to destroy the cartels through which the power trusts were able to maintain exorbitant rates." Massive lobbying operations were launched against the bill, with Truman a prime target. He claimed he paid no attention to these efforts, "knowing I would be the target for many more similar attacks by special interests if I continued to ignore their demands and did what I knew to be right for the majority of people."

Ideological pressures aside, the rocky course of Truman's early career in the Senate reinforced his view of himself as an underdog. This was largely because Roosevelt repaid Truman's support by treating the new senator shabbily. Truman had campaigned, as he said, "heart and soul" for Roosevelt in 1934. But because of his pedestrian style and background, plus his links to the Pendergast machine, FDR and his circle treated him with disdain. Far from making him submissive, though, this seemed to stiffen his backbone. At one point, after Tom Pendergast phoned him to say that he had been told by the White House to order him to change his vote in a hotly fought contest to pick a new Senate leader, Truman not only refused but defiantly called Steve Early, Roosevelt's press secretary. "I've got a message for the president," he said. "Tell him to stop treating me like an office boy." Of more practical concern, Truman got no help from FDR when he faced a major challenge for his party's renomination in 1940. Indeed, the president seemed to be trying to ease Truman out of office by offering him an appointment on the Interstate Commerce Commission if he would back out of the race. Truman's response to the aide who passed on the proposal: "Tell them to go to hell." The beleaguered Truman felt, he later wrote, like a battered old legal document that looked as if it "had been through hell three times with its hat off."

Even when he became FDR's choice for the office that would soon become the stepping-stone to the presidency, as one Roosevelt scholar notes, "the decision could hardly have been made more grudgingly or inconsiderately." Roosevelt did not make his intentions known to Truman until the last minute at the 1944 Democratic convention in Chicago. And then he did not tell Truman directly but instead had the word passed to him by Democratic National Chairman Robert Hannegan.

"You tell him if he wants to break up the Democratic party in the middle of a war, that's his responsibility," Roosevelt told Hannegan over the phone, loud enough for Truman, who was in Hannegan's hotel room, to hear him. Then he hung up.

Truman, who was reluctant to take the job, asked, "Why the hell didn't he tell me in the first place?"

After the election, the dying Roosevelt continued to ignore his vice-president so much so that the memory pained Truman long afterward. When Merle Miller asked Truman years afterward if Roosevelt might have done more to prepare him for the presidency, Truman's mouth "became a very thin line." He said, "He did all he could. I've explained all about that, and I told you that's all there is to it, and it is."

Moving into the Oval Office did not change Truman's view of himself as an underdog or make him less comfortable in that role, as he once demonstrated when he interrupted his regular morning walk to pay a hospital call on ailing Supreme Court Justice William O. Douglas. As Truman walked over to Douglas's bed, he kicked over a urinal that had been hidden from his view. "A president can't even go to see a Supreme Court justice without getting pissed on," he grumbled.

CHARACTER

When I first met Harry Truman, more than a decade had passed since the Jefferson-Jackson Day dinner of 1948, which marked a low point in his fortunes. He had long since vindicated himself and confounded his critics. But if he seemed a far more forceful and confident figure in 1960 than in the winter of 1948, I do not believe the difference was in Truman; rather, it was that the history he had made, which enhanced understanding of his strengths, transformed him into a much larger man in the eyes of his beholders.

Still brisk and vigorous at seventy-four, he strode into the news room of the *Miami News*, where I was then working as telegraph editor, glared at me in mock resentment, and said, "So you're the fellow who blue pencils all my speeches."

I confessed my sins, invited him to sit down at my desk, gave him a wire-service story—reporting one of his speeches—along with a blue pencil and urged him to edit to his heart's content. He grinned, scribbled for a minute, and withdrew, leaving behind a tic-tac-toe box in the margin.

Later, when he met with some of us to answer questions, he showed he had lost none of his old form. Someone asked him for an evaluation of Richard Nixon, then the all but certain Republican candidate for president. Truman demurred, saying, "There is a lady present."

"Can't you clean it up?" I asked him.

"No," Truman said. "Every time anything is said about him now it just means another headline for him. It gives him a chance to get out on the front page."

That brief encounter served as a start in helping me to better understand how he had managed to stage his stunning victory in 1948, which still ranks as the most remarkable upset in modern American history and, because of the remarkable circumstances of his candidacy, serves as a striking example of successful presidential leadership. Bucking great odds, against the will of many in his own party, Truman almost single-handedly had used his values and character to rally the electorate behind a revival and extension of the New Deal ideology. In the years that followed I came to recognize those traits that had been underappreciated by that dinner audience in 1948, as well as by most other Democrats and Republicans. His mind had a sharp partisan edge, soundly grounded in liberal Democratic beliefs. His natural aggressiveness took on breadth from his values, which strongly championed the underdog. Fully as important, his character helped to advance his political beliefs and his values. He was a man who had come to terms with himself, which gave him the strength and the courage to face obstacles that others thought would overwhelm him.

Years later, when I talked to Senator Joseph Biden about his own ambitions for the presidency, Biden told me he believed such self-knowledge mattered more than any other quality in determining fitness for the presidency. The political leaders most likely to succeed in the White House, Biden said, "are those at peace with themselves. They're the leaders who I think are least likely to let their own insecurities impact on the well-being of the nation. It's the difference between a Harry Truman and a Richard Nixon."

At that time, late in 1987, many thought Biden was the most gifted of all the Democratic candidates. Unfortunately, a few months later, Biden proved his point in reverse. Under the pressures of the campaign, the facile and handsome young senator from Delaware was not sure enough of himself to resist the temptation to plagiarize others and misrepresent his credentials, and he was forced to abandon his candidacy.

Biden's vulnerability underlined Truman's strength. The key to Truman's character was his understanding of his own shortcomings and his ability to be honest with himself. Biographer Alonzo Hamby contends that Truman's success rested on "a dogged determination to shoulder the burdens of responsibility and to achieve goals that he often felt were beyond his personal capabilities." But Truman himself would not have accepted that limited praise. While many of his contemporaries may have believed that the goals Truman set for himself exceeded his abilities, Truman did not share that estimate. His understanding of his own shortcomings did not undermine his own belief in himself and in his ability to accomplish even extremely difficult undertakings.

History made him conscious of the potential of leadership. From his childhood, Truman read history, concentrating on the lives of men who had risen to greatness and focusing on models of behavior that he would later follow. "My debt to history is one which cannot be calculated," he wrote. "I learned from it that a leader is a man who has the ability to get other people to do what they don't want to do, and like it. It takes a leader to put economic, military and government forces to work. . . . I saw that it takes men to make history, or there would be no history."

His sense of history strengthened his faith in himself, which was constantly at war with his sense of insecurity. In the Senate, for example, he was troubled not just by the ill treatment he received from the White House but also by the attitude of colleagues who looked down on him because of his association with Pendergast. Truman complains in his memoirs about "some of the liberals," specifically George Norris and Bronson Cutting, "who looked upon me as a sort of hick politician who did not know what he was supposed to do." Nevertheless, he claimed that "this attitude did not bother me," because he knew it would change.

Truman was remarkably frank in expressing his self-doubts when Roosevelt's death suddenly thrust the awesome responsibilities of the presidency upon him. "Boys, if you ever pray, pray for me now," he told the White House press corps on his first full day in office. "I don't know whether you fellows ever had a load of hay fall on you, but when they told me yesterday what had happened, I felt like the moon, the stars and all the planets had fallen on me." In a similar vein, that same day he told his friend, Senator George Aiken of Vermont, "I'm not big enough, I'm not big enough for this job."

As the shock of his sudden elevation wore off, his confidence increased. In his first few months as chief executive, he was certainly not burdened by self-doubt as he made the decision to drop the first atom bombs, presided over the end of World War II, and met with Winston Churchill and Joseph Stalin on what Truman clearly felt was equal footing. "He gave me a lot of hooey about how great my country is and how he loved Roosevelt and how he intended to love me, etc., etc.," he confided to his diary after his first meeting with the British prime minister. "Well, I gave him as cordial a reception as I could—being naturally (I hope) a polite and agreeable person. I am sure we can get along if he doesn't try to give me too much soft soap."

As president, Truman was constantly frustrated not only by forces he could not control but by his awareness of his own shortcomings. This led to peevishness and outbursts of temper that often made him seem unpresidential. Gallup surveys show that public approval of Truman's performance was lower on the average than for any other modern president except Carter.

Public disapproval might have been even higher if citizens had been aware of the letters Truman wrote and then did not mail. In what Truman himself called "my spasms" he harbored feelings about the press that if expressed publicly would have typed him as a paranoid. The letters show that "Truman considered himself the target of a publishing conspiracy," organized by the lords of the press. He called the big newspaper publishers "the sabotage press," and raged that the "prostitutes of the mind are much more dangerous than the prostitutes of the body." He referred to the "kept press" and considered columnists Westbrook Pegler and Walter Winchell "paid mental whores," kept by the "purveyors of 'Character Assassination.'" Even though he is sometimes remembered more for such outbursts than his accomplishments, what is more significant than his "spasms" was his ability to control them and to channel his anger toward constructive ends. Whatever the unmailed letters tell us about Truman's instincts, the bottom line is that they were not mailed. Instead they served as a harmless outlet for inner outrage that might otherwise have been self-destructive.

There is other evidence that Truman was more troubled by the pressures of politics than his outward behavior indicated. He was admitted to the military hospital at Hot Springs, Arkansas, three times from 1937 to 1943, complaining of nausea, headaches, and general debilitation. As the army doctors noted after his 1937 visit, "He has just finished a term in the Senate with its attendant long hours and nervous strain." Characteristically Truman recognized his need for help and welcomed the medical attention. "Excellent treatment by everyone," he wrote on the army medical report, "remarkable rest and very pleasant environment." And to Bess Truman, he wrote, "They are really feeding me. I was half starved, too, I reckon, but I'm eating all they give me now and it's plenty. It surely is a place to rest and they treat me like a king."

To put this in perspective, it helps to remember that Truman had to contend with obstacles few other presidents have—notably succeeding Franklin Roosevelt in the midst of the greatest war in history, with little chance to prepare himself for that office. This was five years after he had brought his political career back from the graveyard by winning a second Senate term, when he had little money, few allies, and a host of formidable adversaries. If he faced great odds at the start of the 1948 campaign, he had been in that position before. In such circumstances he had demonstrated that by mustering his inner resources, he often prevailed and, just as important, never quit on himself or abandoned the causes in which he believed.

THE CHALLENGE

As the 1948 election campaign approached, Truman seemed a lonely and forlorn figure. Support for his presidential candidacy was hard to find even in his own party, where many leaders were determined to find a substitute standard bearer. Truman's challenge was to overcome the opposition and win the presidency in his own right.

He set about meeting this challenge by accepting and casting himself in the underdog role that others had already chosen for him. He defied his foes and rallied his supporters in much the same way as had Willie Stark, the hero of Robert Penn Warren's *All the King's Men.* "Fellow hicks," Willie Stark shouted at the rednecks who gathered to hear him campaign. "Yeah, that's what you are, and me, I'm one, too. . . . Listen to me you hicks. You are a hick, and nobody ever helped a hick but the hick himself. It is up to you and God, and God helps those who help themselves."

Similarly, Truman in effect was telling the American electorate in 1948: "I am an underdog and so are you. And nobody helps an underdog but the underdog himself."

That was the message of his candidacy to Negroes, to union members, and to farmers. It was the substance of his beliefs, which promised tangible benefits for each of the underdog groups, the concern for underdogs embodied in his values and the strength of his character, which served as an example for the underdogs whose votes he needed, that made possible the success of Truman's political leadership.

For an incumbent to run as an underdog was, of course, a desperate strategy. But then Truman was in desperate straits. His fundamental problem was the colossal economic, social, and diplomatic turmoil brought about by World War II. The postwar dislocations at times seemed more than the new president could handle and at other times forced him to attempt unpopular and difficult solutions.

With Truman preoccupied by such complex and bitter controversies as civil rights and inflation at home, and the containment of communism and the establishment of a Jewish homeland overseas, the Republicans took the initiative on the political front. In the 1946 Congressional elections they rode a wave of postwar discontent to a smashing victory that gave them control of both houses of Congress for the first time since the Hoover Administration.

The election was a blow to the new president's prestige and in practical terms Republican control of the 80th Congress foredoomed his hopes of getting significant measures enacted into law. But Truman was to make his difficulties with Congress into the cornerstone of his re-election battle plan.

Meanwhile, Truman had his hands full with his own party, trying to keep both Southerners angered by his civil rights policies and liberals tempted by the Wallace candidacy in the fold. Even many of those liberals who did not share Henry Wallace's view of the Cold War still resented Truman for replacing Wallace on the ticket in 1944.

With Truman's prospects seeming so dim at the start of the presidential election year, the liberal apathy toward Truman—of being "just mild about Harry," as a current saying had it—turned into outright opposition. This attitude was evidenced around the time of the February Jefferson-Jackson Day dinner when a third-party candidate backed by Wallace drew enough liberal support to win a special congressional election in New York City.

By April, the national board of Americans for Democratic Action repudiated Truman's candidacy and urged instead the selection of either Dwight Eisenhower or Supreme Court Justice William O. Douglas as the nominee. Though Eisenhower had ruled himself out as a candidate earlier, two of Roosevelt's sons, Franklin and Elliott, publicly supported him, and a third, James, California state Democratic chairman, worked behind the scenes to organize an Eisenhower draft.

Whatever Truman lacked in support was more than compensated by the abundant advice he received, nearly all of it unsolicited. After the 1946 elections, a group of relatively lesser known Truman appointees set themselves up as an informal board of strategy and began meeting once a week for dinner at the apartment of Oscar R. Ewing, director of the Federal Security Agency. Their declared goal was to develop liberal campaign tactics, then to persuade Truman to adopt them.

These liberal brainstormers had an elevated view of their own importance in shaping Truman's positions. "We were up against tough competition," said Clark Clifford, the liaison between the group and the White House. Clifford contended that most of Truman's cabinet, along with the Democratic congressional leaders, wanted Truman to "go slow," holding up the image of Republican conservative Senator Robert Taft of Ohio "like a bogeyman," while Clifford and his associates urged boldness. "It was two forces fighting for the mind of the President. I don't think Mr. Truman ever realized it was going on," Clifford claimed.

In reality, Truman seemed firmly in charge of setting his own course. With the exception of civil rights, which confronted him with the most intense social and political controversy of the times, the record offers little evidence that Truman wavered at all on domestic policy. From the

time of his September 1945 address Truman marched in a straight line
with the liberal thrust of the Democratic party and with his own record
in the Senate.

Clark Clifford gained what influence he had because his advice generally coincided with Truman's instincts. When Clifford's suggestions for
such things as public relations gimmickry did not suit Truman's style,
they were rejected. Eben A. Ayers, a veteran newsman who served
Truman as a press aide, questioned "the political acumen" of Clifford.
"Clifford is without much practical experience—if any—and I have
doubted the political wisdom of some of his suggestions and advice in the
past," Ayers wrote in his diary as the campaign was getting under way.
"There are, altogether, I feel, too many amateurs trying to run things."

Much of Clifford's claim to being a major shaper of strategy stems
from a forty-three-page memorandum on "the politics of 1948," which he
disclosed to selected journalists and writers after the campaign.* The
strategy memo provides useful insight into Truman's thinking, which
Clifford well understood. But on its predictions of the future the memorandum got mixed grades. It did forecast that the Republicans would
nominate New York Governor Thomas E. Dewey and that Wallace would
run for president on a third-party ticket, both of which were relatively
easy guesses at that time. But the memorandum totally missed the possibility of the Southern bolt from the party, which almost cost Truman
the election.

In fact, the memo stated: "It is inconceivable that any policies initiated
by the Truman Administration no matter how 'liberal' could so alienate
the South in the next year that it would revolt. As always, the South
can be considered safely Democratic. And in formulating national policy,
it can be safely ignored." Eight months later, rebellious Southern Democrats walked out of the Democratic national convention, held their own
convention in Birmingham, formed the States Rights party, and nominated South Carolina Governor Strom Thurmond for President.

Against this background Truman developed a relatively simple fundamental strategy to which he adhered throughout the campaign: on
domestic issues, particularly the economy and race, he moved left; on
foreign policy and the threat of communist subversion, he moved to the
center, effectively blocking off Republican attack.

Truman had established a foundation for his liberal approach to domestic policy as far back as September 1945, and despite the Republicans'

---

* Actually, the authorship of this memorandum is in doubt. James Rowe, a former
Roosevelt aide who served the Truman Administration as a consultant, claims to have
written most of it and then turned it over to Clifford, who expanded on it slightly and
submitted it to Truman over his signature.

control of Congress after the 1946 elections, a flock of other proposals and actions followed along the same line—notably his Taft-Hartley veto, his civil rights proposals, and a plan for a comprehensive national health insurance. In addition, the president advanced a tax-cut credit scheme, giving $40 for each taxpayer and dependent, and subsequently vetoed what he would call during the campaign the "rich man's tax bill" supported by the Republicans in Congress. Truman realized, of course, that many of his proposals would be buried by the hostile legislature, but he was positioning himself to use the Congress as a populist whipping boy in the 1948 campaign.

In foreign affairs, Truman had no difficulty in justifying in his own mind his hard line against the Soviet Union. "The course of freedom was being challenged again," this time by Moscow, he later wrote. In this country he had seen "many well meaning groups who campaigned for 'peace at any price' while apologizing for the aggressive acts of the Russians. Many respectable Americans espoused such ideas without realizing the danger to which they were subjecting our national security and the freedoms for which we had fought so hard."

Truman established strong credentials in this area by proclaiming the Truman Doctrine and then launching the dramatic Berlin airlift. As the Clifford/Rowe memo pointed out: "There is considerable political advantage to the Administration in its battle with the Kremlin. The nation is already united behind the president on this issue. The worse matters get, up to a fairly certain point—real danger of imminent war—the more there is a sense of crisis. In times of crisis the American citizen tends to back up his president."

Less commendable, though having much the same objective, was Truman's heavy-handed revamping of government loyalty procedures, which set off a government-wide witch hunt that paved the way for McCarthyism. "The president's order did not satisfy conservatives, antagonized liberals and failed to calm the public," Barton J. Bernstein and Allen J. Matusow contend in their comprehensive study of Truman's record. Nevertheless, at the time the president's advisers thought the stress on loyalty served a purpose. "The Republicans have tried to identify the Administration with the domestic Communists," the Rowe/Clifford memorandum stated. "The President adroitly stole their thunder by initiating his own government employee loyalty investigation procedure and the more frank Republicans admit it."

The loyalty program left an indelible stain on Truman's record in civil liberties, though it was certainly no worse than the wholesale violation of the rights of Japanese Americans carried out under the orders of his predecessor during World War II. Moreover, Truman deserves good marks in this area for his veto of the McCarran-Walter Immigration Act of 1952 and the Internal Security Act of 1950, which required so-called communist-front groups to register with the attorney general. Both vetoes were overridden.

By the time the Democratic convention opened in Philadelphia on July 12, the stage had been set for Truman's strategy of matching the perception of himself as an underdog to the populist rhetoric of his stump speeches. The image of the president as an underdog had been firmly stamped in the public mind, and was to be reinforced almost every day of the campaign by a variety of factors.

Politicians in his own party shunned him. One such "bandwagon boy," as Truman called him, was William O'Dwyer, mayor of New York City, the stronghold of the modern Democratic party. In late July Truman wrote in his diary that he had finally met O'Dwyer for "the *first time*" (Truman's italics). Truman noted wryly, "He's either been sick, out of town or too busy before."

Journalists of every stripe regarded Truman's defeat as inevitable. Ernest K. Lindley, respected Washington bureau chief of *Newsweek*, wrote shortly before the Democratic convention: "The cold facts . . . are in many ways unjust to Harry Truman, but they cannot be removed by . . . personal pluck. The . . . best service Truman could render his party right now is to step aside."

The pollsters unanimously forecast his defeat. In fact, one of the most prominent, Elmo Roper, announced on September 9, two months before election day, that he was inclined to stop surveying. Barring a "major convulsion," he said, "Mr. Dewey is just as good as elected."

The blindness of the pollsters was so stunning that a special committee of the Social Science Research Council was appointed after the election to find out what went wrong. The panel concluded that the surveys failed to take account of shifts in opinion late in the campaign. During the campaign, though, the findings reported by Gallup and Roper were so much accepted as gospel, that a Kansas City livestock-feed company which found Truman leading in an informal survey of its customers in six Midwestern farm states called off its poll. "We decided that our results were too improbable," a company official explained.

Events at the Philadelphia convention had served to reinforce these impressions. Democratic dissidents pressed their dump-Truman efforts almost to the eve of the balloting.

Truman's fiery acceptance speech, delivered at 2:00 A.M., roused the delegates who had nominated him, seemingly against their better judgment, out of their collective torpor. "Senator Barkley and I will win this election and make those Republicans like it," the defiant president declared. "Don't you forget that."

Still, few believed him. One additional problem that had developed during the convention was the Southern walkout in protest against the strong civil rights plank adopted by the delegates. Truman's supporters had done all they could to block approval of the plank, which had been submitted as a minority report from the platform committee. But an inspiring speech by Hubert Humphrey, then mayor of Minneapolis, helped carry the day for pro–civil rights forces.

It turned out to be a case of Truman being helped despite himself. Strom Thurmond's States Rights or "Dixiecrat" party, as it came to be called, got only 39 electoral votes, and the rights plank helped Truman in Northern cities in his appeal to blacks, the ultimate underdogs of American society.

In a diary entry written during the convention, Truman described the proposal offered by the civil rights forces as "the crackpot amendment." Later, though, he claimed credit for the strong plank. Despite his hypocrisy the fact remained that his own prior advocacy had helped pave the way for the convention action.

Moreover, some evidence suggests that whatever he thought about the tactics that led to the Southern bolt, his values were in sympathy with the substance of the controversial plan. In a letter to an old army comrade who had appealed to him as a Southerner to soft-pedal the civil rights issue, Truman wrote:

> The main difficulty with the South is that they are living eighty years behind the times and the sooner they come out of it the better it will be for the country and themselves. I am not asking for social equality, because no such thing exists, but I am asking for equality of opportunity for all human beings and, as long as I stay here I am going to continue that fight.

Obviously Truman owed much of his underdog image to factors beyond his control. But these circumstances provided a test of his character, values, and ideology, which demonstrated the mettle of his leadership.

Perhaps his most pervasive problem was the defeatism that surrounded him. "There is much confusion and taut nerves due to the political campaign and the belief that the President is going to be defeated," Eben Ayers noted about a month before the election. "There are few optimists in the place. There are jealousies and undercurrents all through the staff. There is a general feeling that the President is making some progress in his campaign, but few believe he can overcome the lead which his opponent has."

In the midst of this malaise, though, Truman's realistic understanding of his strengths and weaknesses helped him keep his head. Though he understood the problems he faced, he was not impressed by the prognosticators of disaster. "I never saw President Truman, at any point, during the campaign, on the train or at the White House or anyplace else, reveal anything other than confidence that he would win, come election day," George Elsey, an assistant to Clark Clifford, recalled. One day late in the campaign, as Truman's train was on its way to Duluth, Minnesota, he told Elsey he wanted to review the electoral vote count. With Elsey acting as his stenographer, the president reeled off the forty-eight states and their electoral votes, and instructed Elsey in which column to put the figures—his or one of his opponents. The final totals, Elsey said, showed Truman elected, and by a number very close to the actual returns on election day—303 for Truman, 189 for Thomas E. Dewey, and 39 for Strom Thurmond.

"And this was purely private," Elsey pointed out. "He was not putting on a show for anybody. Obviously he wasn't trying to persuade or sell me. This is what the man, himself, believed."

He not only disciplined himself to withstand adversity, he managed to take advantage of it. In Omaha, the turnout for a farm policy speech was so dismal—fewer than two thousand in a hall holding ten thousand—that Truman's aides urged him to cancel to avoid embarrassment. Truman refused. "I don't give a damn whether there's nobody there but you and me," he snapped at one adviser. "That's one of the best things that's happened to me in the whole campaign," Truman later recalled. "It made a martyr out of me."

More broadly, Truman saw the connection between his own status as a candidate and the condition of many segments of the electorate—blacks, small farmers, union members—who had filled the ranks of the New Deal coalition and who saw themselves as socially and economically disadvantaged. He did not seek their sympathy because he knew, as they did, too, that simply feeling sorry would be of little help to either Truman or his constituencies. He demonstrated that while an underdog may win sympathy, it takes a fighting underdog to win votes.

By fighting at a time when most saw his cause as hopeless, Truman evoked not sympathy for his presumed political misfortune but admiration for his character and respect for his beliefs and values, the keys to leadership and in this case to victory.

He attacked the Republicans furiously from start to finish, giving rise to the cries of "Give 'em hell, Harry" that became the hallmark of his campaign. Said Truman, "I have never deliberately given anybody hell. I just tell the truth on the opposition."

No sooner had he been nominated than he seized the initiative, summoning "this last, worst 80th Congress" back into a special session to "pass the laws people need on matters of . . . importance and urgency." As Truman expected, the special session accomplished little, but it gave him more evidence to back up his indictment of the "do-nothing" Congress.

In his celebrated whistle-stop tours across the country, Truman did not plead for support. He demanded it—or else. If the Republicans retain power in Congress, he warned on Labor Day in Detroit's Cadillac Square: "You men of labor can expect to be hit by a steady barrage of blows. And if you stay at home . . . and keep these reactionaries in power you will deserve every blow you get."

Republicans "are obviously getting ready to let the bottom blow out of farm prices," he warned farmers at the National Plowing Match at Dexter, Iowa. "Your best protection is to elect a Democratic Congress that will play fair with the farmer."

Making his arguments all the more effective was a newly developed hard-hitting speaking style. He was at his best, Eben Ayers noted, when he spoke without the hindrance of a prepared text. This was no easy task, as Truman himself acknowledged to his diary that spring after the favorable response to an extemporaneous radio speech: "Returns from the radio on the family life speech are very satisfactory. Looks as if I'm stuck for 'off-the-cuff' radio speeches. It means a lot of hard work, and the head at 64 doesn't work as well as it did at 24."

Nevertheless, he stuck to the new style, on his campaign trail as well as in his radio talks. Though he worked from notes carefully prepared by his staff to focus on specific issues of local concern, his informality and apparent spontaneity helped to reflect his ideology and values, heightening the impression of the chief executive as populist underdog.

Truman played this folksy image for all it was worth. After ten or fifteen minutes of slashing away at the 80th Congress, he would suddenly ask, "Howja like to meet the boss?" Out would come Bess Truman, to warm applause. Then the president would introduce "the boss's boss"— daughter Margaret. More applause and occasionally a long, low whistle. Day after day Truman repeated this performance, wherever his train could stop and a crowd could be gathered. He averaged ten talks a day, and one day he spoke no fewer than sixteen times.

Truman had specific arguments to make to each interest group who shared with him the underdog role.

He warned union workers: "You and I know that the Taft-Hartley is only a foretaste of what you will get if the Republican reaction is allowed to grow."

For the elderly there was this warning: "The Republican 80th Congress actually passed a law not to extend Social Security but to take Social Security away from hundreds of thousands of workers. I vetoed the measure. Ninety-eight percent of the Republicans in Congress voted to override my veto."

Blacks were reminded of the militant language of the civil rights plank forced through at the Philadelphia convention. And although Truman had resisted this strong language at first, it was part of the platform he was running on for president. More important, all the plank did was endorse the language of Truman's own civil rights proposals, which aimed to strike down racial barriers in voting, employment, and the armed forces.

While the thrust of his campaign reflected his inherent Populism, Truman sharpened his attack by drawing on the good-government influence on his ideology. This had given him a ready grasp of the workings, and failures, of the federal machinery.

Thus, he was quick to alert voters in the farm states: "This Republican Congress has already stuck a pitchfork in the farmer's back . . . [by] preventing us from setting up storage bins that you will need in order to get the support price for your grain. When the farmers have to sell their wheat below the support price . . . they can thank this same Republican 80th Congress."

Similarly, he attacked the Congress for delaying construction of transmission lines from federal power projects to protect private power interests. "Who benefits from the building of dams if the government does not also build transmission lines to carry the power from the dams to the people?" Truman asked rhetorically. "Who benefits? The private power interests benefit of course—at your expense."

For all the handicaps Truman labored under, he was fortunate in one important aspect of the campaign—the opponent the Republicans nominated to challenge him. In style and demeanor, Thomas E. Dewey, forty-six-year-old governor of New York, was the perfect foil for Truman. Humorless, smug, overbearing, and cold-blooded, Dewey was the quintessential overdog. At his campaign rallies, one reporter wrote, Dewey arrived on stage "like a man who has been mounted on casters and given a tremendous shove from behind." A Roper poll taken in mid-campaign found that most voters attached words like "dignified" and "efficient" to Dewey, but that they had little idea of how he proposed to deal with the issues that concerned them.

Fairly or not, voters drew some inference as to what the candidate was like as a human being when he excoriated the engineer of his campaign train after it had lurched back a few feet, almost striking a group of Dewey admirers standing on the track behind the rear platform. "He probably should be shot at sunrise," said Dewey of the culprit. Bored reporters covering Dewey made a fuss over the incident, giving Truman the chance to jab: "We've had wonderful train crews all across the country. They are all Democrats."

After his ignominious defeat, Dewey reacted with a grace and humor that would have served him well on the campaign stump. He told supporters that he felt like a man who had woken up in a coffin with a lily in his hand and wondered: "If I am alive, what am I doing here? And if I am dead, why do I have to go to the bathroom?"

With the advantage of hindsight, some Republicans in the bitterness of their defeat suggested that Dewey should have exploited the issue of communism in government, particularly since Whittaker Chambers had just made his public charge of subversion against Alger Hiss. But Truman, who denounced the congressional inquiry as "a red herring," had shielded himself by his own loyalty program. And it was by no means clear at this stage of the Hiss case who was lying about whom.

While Truman was whistle-stopping around the country, I was starting my sophomore year at Syracuse University, where I found myself part of what *Time* later called the "silent generation." Most students had little interest in the campaign, having accepted with apparent apathy the conventional wisdom that Truman had no chance at all.

I certainly had no special insights on that score. At dinner on election night, another student offered to give me twenty to one odds if I would bet on Truman. I told him my parents had worked too hard to help me get through college for me to throw my money away like that.

Later that night in the news room of the student newspaper, I was stunned by the incredible returns that showed that Truman was actually ahead. This was the first election story I had ever written, and probably the most dramatic. Not until the next morning, when California went Democratic by a hair, was the result certain.

Until that night the result of the election seemed so much a foregone conclusion that it was almost as if the campaign was fixed. Even those who had voted against Truman found satisfaction in the evidence that the political process was still open enough for an underdog to prevail. Republican politicians saw the results in personal terms. "You've got to give the little man credit," Republican Senator Arthur Vandenburg of Michigan remarked to his staff on the day following the election. "There he was flat on his back. Everyone had counted him out, but he came up fighting and won the battle. That's the kind of courage the American people admire."

This was all true, but it was only part of the truth. Truman's courage, derived from the self-knowledge that marked his character, did inspire admiration for him personally. Yet this response by itself would not have been sufficient to meet the challenge of leadership and win the election. This required the fusion of his personal qualities with his identification with the underdog, which was implicit in his values and also in his ideology. All this was powerfully projected when Truman promised those whistle-stop audiences that the government he presided over would be on the side of the underdogs.

The immediate impact of Truman's victory was to return the Democrats to the White House and restore them to control of both houses of Congress. It allowed him to proclaim the Fair Deal and to lead the nation into a costly war in Korea only five years after the end of World War II.

Truman was unable during the four years he had won in his own right to gain approval for his domestic agenda, and when he left the White House his standing in the polls was at a nadir. For these reasons many have judged his second term to have been a failure. I believe that judgment overlooks much that he accomplished.

On domestic policy issues, which had been the mainstay of his 1948 election victory, Truman's combative personality, underdog values, and proposals for health care, public housing, expanded Social Security, and civil rights provided a rallying point for the various Democratic constituencies who had followed Franklin Roosevelt. He thus preserved for some time to come FDR's Grand Coalition as what Walter Lippman called "the dominant force in American politics." Not only should Truman be credited with preventing repeal of the New Deal, but as one analysis of his record points out, his "best proposals (civil rights, health care, aid to education) proved to be a form of public education that prepared the way for enactment of similar programs in more favorable times."

Because of the Korean War, though, international affairs dominated Truman's second term. That war represented a leadership challenge that rivaled in difficulty his underdog campaign of 1948, and the conclusion of his presidency can best be understood in terms of his response.

The outbreak of the fighting was an event outside of Truman's control; he did not anticipate the North Korean invasion of the South. But committing U.S. troops to the battlefield was an action taken of his own free will. He later called it the most important decision of his presidency.

In leading the country into war, Truman relied on the same elements of leadership that had won him the presidency. The ideological basis for the war was consistent with the previous commitments by both Roosevelt and himself to a government that took an activist role abroad to advance national interests just as it actively pursued the national interest in domestic affairs. Fighting communist aggression was a logical counterpart to fighting fascist aggression. The defense of a country under attack by an aggressive and better prepared neighbor fit in well with Truman's underdog values. And finally the willingness to act swiftly and decisively reflected the self-certitude that was basic to Truman's character.

Had this been a traditional war, and one concluding in victory like most of those the nation had waged in the past, Truman might well have emerged from it as a hero president. But the limited nature of the conflict, which Truman deemed prudent, made it inevitably an unpopular war that badly damaged his personal standing.

Yet in the midst of controversy Truman refused to pull out. He also refused to raise the stakes, even when General Douglas MacArthur argued otherwise, a disagreement that culminated in Truman's dismissal of the World War II hero, surely one of the most unpopular acts ever taken by a U.S. chief executive.

The ultimate test of leadership is whether a president can mobilize public support for his position. It was a test Truman accepted. "A politician must be in a sense a public relations man," he told an interviewer in the early months of his presidency:

> Most leaders have been such men. They had the faculty of presenting the ideas for which they have stood in such a way that the people have understood them and had confidence in them. If they had not been able to make others see as they did, they would not have been leaders.

Years later, after he had left the White House, he modified that view to give himself the benefit of hindsight. "The question is not whether his [a president's] actions are going to be popular at the time, but whether what he does is right. And if it is right, in the long run it will come out all right."

Based on these criteria Truman gets mixed grades. He could not mobilize public opinion behind the war; under the limitations he imposed for its conduct, this was an all but impossible task. But the value of his leadership was that it kept resistance to the war under control. Critics of Truman's war policies complained long and loud, but they staged no campus riots or draft card burnings as the country would face a decade and a half later. Americans resented war, but they were unwilling to repudiate it.

That view of public opinion was the assessment of Dwight Eisenhower during his successful campaign to succeed Truman in the White House.

In the 1952 campaign speech in which Eisenhower announced that he would go to Korea to seek an end to the fighting, he condemned Truman for failing "to check and turn back communist ambition before it savagely attacked us." But with the decision Truman had made to enter the war, Eisenhower found no fault. The Republican standard bearer called the dispatch of U.S. troops "utterly right and utterly inescapable." He saw "no other way to save honor and self-respect."

It was left to the new president to end the war, with an armistice agreement reached in July 1953, but it was under Truman's leadership that the U.S. had established that it would resist armed aggression by communists, a principle that became a bulwark of the nation's foreign policy. In the long run, as Truman would have argued, it came out all right.

In the short run, the war that had provoked such massive discontent gave the next president an opportunity to achieve an early success by bringing the fighting to a conclusion. This was an accomplishment in which Dwight Eisenhower took great pride, describing it later as "an acceptable solution to a problem that almost defied . . . solution."

But the unfinished business of the Truman presidency also presented Eisenhower with another, even more difficult challenge from another form of conflict. This would be waged not on foreign battlefields but in the hometowns of tens of millions of Americans. It was the struggle over race, pitting the tradition of segregation against the new revolution for civil rights. For Eisenhower this problem, which shadowed most of his presidency, was one that did defy solution.

CHAPTER 3

Eisenhower: Fatal Flaw

Not since the last general to occupy the White House, Ulysses S. Grant, had a president chosen to vacation in Newport. That had been in 1869, when Grant had come to this fashionable spa with his wife, son, daughter, and a private secretary. Having had nearly a century to wait for a return engagement, the citizens of Newport gave Dwight and Mamie Eisenhower, and their much larger entourage, the warmest of New England welcomes when they arrived just after Labor Day in 1957. The *Providence Journal*, which sent no fewer than five photographers to cover the First Family's arrival and would print two full pages of pictures, reported that the Eisenhowers received "an enthusiastic reception at all points they touched in the state of Rhode Island—Quonset Naval Air Station, the city of Newport and finally their vacation spot, Coasters Harbor Island, the 92-acre island near the main Newport Naval base."

At the two-hundred-year-old colonial house in Newport where Mayor John J. Sullivan and the state's senior senator, Theodore Francis Green, turned out to greet him, the president expressed his and his wife's appreciation for "the warmth of cordiality" of their reception. "Never did I feel so good on the first two hours of getting away from Washington . . ." Eisenhower said. "I assure you, we look forward to the time of our lives."

It was easy to understand why the sixty-six-year-old president was delighted to leave the capital. An agonizing and long festering national problem now appeared to be on the verge of eruption. At the heart of the matter was the status of the Negro in American society. Nearly a century after the Civil War, this still remained "the American Dilemma," and in varying degrees it had vexed each of Eisenhower's predecessors in the White House.

But it was Eisenhower's misfortune, as he viewed it, that the issue was forced to a critical point during his presidency. In June 1954, eighteen months after Eisenhower's inauguration, the Supreme Court—led by Eisenhower's own appointee, Chief Justice Earl Warren—overturned nearly sixty years of precedent and unanimously ruled that segregation of public schools could no longer be permitted under the Constitution. Since then the entire nation, but particularly the South, had been caught up in impassioned, bitter controversy.

This was just the sort of situation that Eisenhower abhorred; he preferred politics to be as free from open disagreement as possible. So far the ruling principle guiding his response to the turmoil caused by the court's momentous ruling had been to keep himself and the federal government as far removed from the field of battle as he could manage. But this was becoming increasingly difficult even as he arrived in Newport.

On September 3, the day before Eisenhower left Washington, Governor Orval Faubus of Arkansas, facing a federal court order to desegregate Central High School in the state capital of Little Rock, had deployed the Arkansas National Guard outside the school. Their orders were to prevent the admission of the nine Negro students covered by the court decree.

In keeping with his previous position, Eisenhower made plain to his staff before he left Washington that he did not think the U.S. Justice Department had grounds to intervene. The president did not seem to blame Faubus or other opponents of segregation for the prolonged, bitter dispute over civil rights. Rather he complained, as he often had before publicly and privately, about "these people who believe you are going to reform the human heart by law."

Eisenhower made this point almost every time he faced a civil rights controversy. It was hard to argue against what he said because it was a truism. Yet in the case of the racial tensions deeply embedded in the nation's history, Eisenhower's view ignored a broader truth. From my own experience as a private soldier in the army of which Eisenhower was then commander in chief, I had come to understand what the law can accomplish regardless of what the heart might feel.

The army that I was drafted into in July 1952 was integrated. In basic training in Camp Gordon, Georgia, about half of my company was from the North, half from the South. About two-thirds were white and one-third Negro. No one ever asked or cared what the whites and Negroes felt in their hearts about each other. The law—or, to be more precise, an executive order issued by President Truman in 1949 and carried forward by President Eisenhower—ordered the army to be integrated. And that was that.

After some fifteen years of army integration, Charles Moskos, a University of Northwestern sociology professor, analyzed the results and concluded in the *American Journal of Sociology*: "The transformation of the armed forces from a totally segregated to a fully integrated institution is an impressive achievement in directed social change."

Of course, bigotry was not eliminated, as Moskos pointed out and as I had realized. Integration probably works better in a situation like basic training, where soldiers have little time or energy to do anything but obey the rules. And the military, as Moskos wrote, "has means of coercion not readily available in most civilian pursuits." But schools have their own ways of discipline, teachers have moral authority, and experience has demonstrated that given the support of the law and committed leadership, integration can work in schools, too.

The decision to integrate the armed forces was a political act by President Truman. It was a natural consequence of his campaign promises in 1948, and served as a demonstration of what could be accomplished by political leadership and by the law.

But Eisenhower had a far different view of political leadership and the law than Truman had. He concluded that what Faubus did was none of his business. It was no reason for him to change his plans to vacation in Newport, where he and the First Lady settled into a spacious vacation home with a view of the open sea and a gracious lawn bordered by flower beds. But whether the president was yet ready to acknowledge the fact or not, Orval Faubus had added a wholly new element to the civil rights controversy.

By flatly defying a federal court ruling, the governor had elevated the dispute over segregation into an argument directed at the heart of presidential authority. It could hardly be ignored, and it certainly posed the most serious challenge yet to Eisenhower's determined policy of uninvolvement.

In a broader sense, Faubus's act underlined an equally significant question about the nature of the Eisenhower presidency, and particularly about Eisenhower's political philosophy. The answer to this question would determine to a large degree the legacy he left to Americans of both races and on both sides of the Mason-Dixon line.

Dwight David Eisenhower had come to the White House seemingly possessing everything required for greatness in the presidency. His leadership of the "Crusade in Europe" in World War II had made him a national hero. His character and the values he represented had given him an appeal astonishing in its breadth, and despite occasional setbacks, he had maintained his popularity through his first term in office. Yet even after his landslide re-election victory in 1956, doubt remained about his strength in one crucial aspect of presidential leadership: ideology.

Even many of his admirers had difficulty discerning a consistent system of beliefs underlying the president's approach to political issues. Without such a framework Eisenhower had so far been unable to take advantage of his popularity and prestige in confronting the most severe domestic challenge of his presidency, the explosion of the civil rights revolution.

IDEOLOGY

Eisenhower's reluctance to clarify his political beliefs was not an oversight. Rather it was the inevitable consequence of the hallmark of his presidential leadership: his determination to avoid public controversies. To some extent this was a reflection of his values and character. But in the main, Eisenhower's aversion to controversy was a function of his ideology—that is, his strategy for dealing with political problems in an unpolitical way.

Eisenhower's ideology was derived mainly from his military experience. The military world he inhabited was far more orderly than the unruly sphere of politics. Abstract ideas were shunned, and concrete goals were set. In the chain of command, orders were given or taken. Responsibility was neatly divided and delegated. High-level disagreements were resolved quietly by bargaining and manipulation, not through open debate.

This was the way Eisenhower strove to operate as president. He was not lacking in will or determination to achieve his goals. But it was essential to his overall strategy that his subtle maneuvers be obscured from the public and even his political allies. He often went "to great lengths to conceal the political side of his leadership," and frequently used words "to create smoke screens for his actions," Fred Greenstein observed in *The Hidden Hand Presidency*, his aptly titled analysis of Eisenhower's leadership in the Oval Office.

Though Eisenhower had disciplined himself to go through the exercise of campaigning in order to gain the presidency, his feelings about politics and politicians scarcely changed from those he had held as a soldier. When the first Eisenhower for President boom began in 1945, he wrote a potential supporter: "Nothing could be so distasteful to me as to engage in political activity of any kind." Later he would tell a journalist of his contempt for most politicians because they could not "accept the fact that when you're hopelessly outgunned and outmanned you don't go out and pick a fight."

Eisenhower did not pick political fights, outgunned or no. He went to great lengths to avoid them.

He was prepared to be thought of as ill-informed, even dull-witted, if his ultimate purpose was accomplished. During an uproar over his policy on the threat of Chinese communist aggression in the Formosa Straits, his press secretary, James Hagerty, advised the president to refuse to answer any questions at all on that subject at a forthcoming press conference.

"Don't worry, Jim," Eisenhower replied. "If that question comes up I'll just confuse them."

As his vice-president, Richard Nixon, observed, "An Eisenhower characteristic was never to take direct action requiring his personal participation where indirect methods could accomplish the same result."

As for partisan warfare, Eisenhower chose to leave this to Nixon and his ilk. "He told Nixon and others, including myself, that he was well aware that somebody had to do the hard infighting, and he had no objections to it as long as no one expected *him* to do it," his White House chief of staff, Sherman Adams, later recalled.

Eisenhower's ideological strategy left no room for public debate on great issues, as he himself often made a point of reminding his aides. "Now look, I happen to *know* a little bit about leadership," he would say at times when he became angered about the persistent criticism that he vacillated in dealing with his foes in Congress:

> "I've had to work with a lot of nations, for that matter, at odds with each other. And I tell you this: you do not *lead* by hitting people over the head. Any damn fool can do that, but it's usually called 'assault'—not 'leadership' . . . I'll tell you what leadership is. It's *persuasion* and *conciliation*—and *education*—and *patience*. It's long, slow, tough work. That's the only kind of leadership I know—or believe in—or will practice."

Indeed, so concerned was Eisenhower with avoiding confrontation that he often failed to seize the high ground that would have helped him to develop broad public support for his goals. Though he privately opposed Senator Joseph R. McCarthy and recognized the damage he had done to civil liberties, Eisenhower allowed him to inflict even more damage because he, Eisenhower, would not directly act against him. Ultimately, McCarthy's critics in the Senate and elsewhere rallied the public against McCarthy and he was destroyed. But Eisenhower—who because no rational person would have accused him of disloyalty was better positioned than anyone in public life to oppose McCarthy—contributed next to nothing to this struggle.

Like McCarthyism, civil rights was a moral issue. But morality and politics are closely linked, the former endowing the latter with spirit and purpose. Because no one could question Eisenhower's moral standing, and because he was the president, he was once again in a unique position to speak out in the political arena. Civil rights was a truly presidential challenge, too large in scope to manage for senators or congressmen, who were too tied to their states and districts. The Supreme Court could help but only to a limited degree. The court was not a political institution; it needed to be sheltered from the political storms. Besides, to most Southerners the court was the enemy, an open ally of the Negro. So it was left up to the president, and what he did reflected a set of beliefs that he had developed since his childhood in the American heartland.

Eisenhower, born in 1890, grew up in the same part of the country at roughly the same time as Harry Truman, who was born in 1884. Both families endured hard times. But two important differences in their upbringing influenced their early political views.

Unlike Truman, whose hometown, Independence, was relatively cosmopolitan because of its proximity to Kansas City, Ike's childhood in Abilene, almost 150 miles from Kansas City, was a wholly rural experience, far more conservative both politically and socially.

Then, too, religion played a much larger role in Eisenhower's early life than in Truman's. The Trumans were churchgoing and God-fearing, but their Presbyterian faith was only one part of their life. By contrast, religion had been a mainspring of the Eisenhower family's existence for generations. As members of a Mennonite sect they observed an intensely individualistic faith that recognized no authority higher than the Bible and the individual's own conscience. In one biographer's description, "They were a closely knit community, conservative, pacifist, self-reliant, thrifty, abstinent, strict in their behavior, severe in rearing their children."

These religious beliefs took the place of any strong political convictions in Eisenhower's upbringing. Thus, although Kansas, like Truman's Missouri, was a hotbed of agrarian discontent and populist radicalism, Eisenhower's family was untouched by these forces. Instead their religion, with its strong tone of the Puritan work ethic and its promise that the rewards for the good life lay in Heaven, shaped their view. Though

Dwight and his brothers drifted away from literal interpretation of the church's strict standards as they grew older, the overall ethos had a profound influence on them during their formative years.

Like Harry Truman's father and Truman himself, Dwight Eisenhower's father suffered a disastrous business failure shortly before Dwight was born, due at least in part to economic hard times he could not control. Nevertheless, neither David Eisenhower nor his family reacted to the collapse of his general store with the ideologically colored bitterness of Truman. Their response to hard times, influenced by their religious faith, was to grin and bear it. This willingness to accept adversity became part of Dwight Eisenhower's outlook on the world. Rather than becoming caught up in radical causes, he tended to accept overall conditions and to concentrate his energies on bettering his own circumstances.

In school, young Dwight proved to be an adept if unimaginative student. He was quick to learn facts, but he had little interest in ideas. He was more comfortable with the spatial figures of geometry, a subject in which he excelled, than with the abstract concepts of algebra, in which he got only average grades. "His mind had no natural bent toward generalized speculation, where the terms are altogether abstract and symbolic," one chronicler of his early years concluded. He was fascinated by history, especially military history, which meant mainly the names and dates of battles rather than broader concepts and trends.

"Even to this day, there are many unrelated bits of information about Greece and Rome that stick in my memory," Eisenhower later wrote. "I have a sort of fixation that causes me to interrupt a conversation when the speaker is one year off, or a hundred, in dating an event like Arbela."* Truman, by contrast, read history mostly for lessons about the lives of great men.

From start to finish, Eisenhower's military career reinforced his conservative, antipolitical view of politics in several ways. As a soldier, he was cut off from most of the social and economic forces that dominated civil life and shaped American politics. Moreover, his service life inculcated in him disdain for politics. Soldiers did not vote, and rarely did their officers. In 1915, the year Eisenhower graduated from West Point, an estimated one officer in five hundred had ever cast a ballot. One of his instructors declared, "If any convictions . . . were acquired by the cadet they were generally of contempt for mere politicians and their dishonest principles of action."

It was true that Eisenhower's military career had exposed him to a certain kind of political experience. But this was a much narrower and

---

* Where Alexander the Great defeated the army of Darius III in 331 B.C.

more limited part of the political world than if he had run for office. This generated within him the belief that he genuinely understood politics—an attitude that strongly influenced his presidency.

Eisenhower's fundamental approach to governing in the White House derived from what he understood to be the lessons of the political experience he had received as a military officer. But this experience, with its emphasis on order and discipline, was far different from the freewheeling give-and-take and clash of interests of political life.

Yet rather than viewing himself as a novice who had much to learn from career politicians, Fred Greenstein observed, "Eisenhower felt that being president was an extension of his previous leadership experience." On his inaugural day he wrote in his diary, "This seems like a continuation of all I've been doing since July '41—even before that."

"I have been in politics, the most active sort of politics, most of my adult life," Eisenhower told journalist Merriman Smith after he left the White House. "As a matter of fact I am a better politician than most so-called politicians."

Eisenhower's military career before 1941 had indeed been heavily political, but only in the military meaning of the word. After finishing at the top of his class in Command General Staff school he was sent to Washington, where he served as deputy to the assistant secretary of the army and ultimately as chief aide and speechwriter for Douglas MacArthur, Army Chief of Staff. Eisenhower's political experience had little to do with broad policy questions, but rather was based on his ability to carry out the wishes of a cloistered group of superiors, none of whom was directly answerable to the public.

MacArthur was the army's most politicized general, whose ambitions knew no bounds and certainly included the presidency. But ironically the chief lesson Eisenhower learned from MacArthur was how *not* to handle a sensitive political situation. In the grim Depression-ridden summer of 1932 MacArthur insisted on taking personal command of routing the pitiful Bonus Marchers from the shanties they had maintained in the nation's capital. He rounded off that triumph by then telling reporters that these miserable, unemployed veterans were "animated by the essence of revolution." This embarrassing episode reinforced Eisenhower's natural inclination to steer away from controversy.

Later as assistant to MacArthur, who was then serving as military adviser to the Philippines, Eisenhower helped draft legislation aimed at building up the military strength for the newly established commonwealth government there in advance of independence. Eisenhower's friend Lucius Clay later said, "Eisenhower's exposure to all dimensions of Philippine public policy-making gave him a broader education in the problems of civil government than advising in a large industrial society would have permitted." But this ignores the fact that this was in effect a colonial experience during which Eisenhower was accountable to no one except MacArthur.

What some scholars consider the most relevant aspects of Eisenhower's military career to the presidency was his service first in the War Department planning division for a few months after Pearl Harbor, and then as a leader of the Allied assault in Europe. In helping to shape wartime decisions, such as where the U.S. should commit its forces and what cost it could pay in casualties, Eisenhower did have to consider political factors. But only rarely in military decisions with important political consequences did he have the final say or responsibility. And in no case was he accountable for the decisions. That responsibility, of course, fell upon the political leader and commander-in-chief, Franklin Roosevelt.

VALUES

In Eisenhower's approach to leadership his cardinal value was teamwork. This meant achieving goals by emphasizing collaboration and cooperation with others, often at the expense of his own ego and inclinations, and also accepting organizational authority and discipline, all for the good of the team. The team, at various times in his life, meant his family, the West Point football squad, the army, and, ultimately, the government he headed.

Part of his teamwork ethic, derived from sports, was a sense of fair play and respect for others. As a high school athlete, Eisenhower was self-confident without being egotistical and he readily gave credit to his teammates. These are positive values that tend to foster an activist approach to problems. In political life, however, because of his ideological bent against controversy, this activist aspect was often submerged by the more passive concern with harmony.

As president, though Eisenhower's role was team leader, he preferred to rely on indirection and persuasion rather than to issue direct commands or rally public support to achieve his objectives. His stress on team harmony both reflected and reinforced his ideological bias against controversy, since this was bound to disrupt the accord essential for successful teamwork.

Eisenhower, of course, had other values, too. Respect for hard work had been impressed upon him as a child in Abilene. "Physical work was done by almost every male," he recalled years later. "The capitalists of town were no less immune than the poorest. They spent hours each week in currying horses or greasing the axles of a buggy, in managing a base burner and sifting unburned coal from its ashes."

Out of this experience came a sort of practical egalitarianism. "Because everyone had to put his shoulder to it, there was little social stratification because of a man's job," Eisenhower wrote.

He also became an adherent of rugged individualism. As he later wrote:

> Abilene folk believed in education and its value. But for many I'm afraid it became beyond a certain point fancies and frills. . . . Thirty years after Lincoln, to write a good clear hand, to spell fairly well, to be able to read fine print and long words, to "cipher" accurately was still enough to go with native intelligence and a willingness to work hard. Given those qualities Abilene thought that most anyone could succeed in the American environment.

In 1947, looking back on his boyhood in Abilene, he said his hometown provided "a healthy outdoor existence and a need to work," thereby helping to "maintain a standard of values that placed a premium upon integrity, decency and consideration." But Eisenhower did not spend much time pondering the condition of those who grew up without such a firm foundation. His small-town environment did not encourage larger concerns.

He was a natural product of the Western frontier, which, even though it no longer existed in a physical sense, had created a powerful legacy of rough-hewn customs. For Eisenhower, as biographer Kenneth Davis wrote: "The mind was but the tool of the body, ideas were valid only insofar as they were schemes for immediate practical action." The attitudes prevalent in his overall surroundings were reinforced by his parents. "They lived unquestioning lives and they taught their sons to do the same," notes one biographer. "They emphasized accomplishment rather than intellectual contemplation or a wondering about why things were the way they were and what could be done differently."

Beyond all this, the concept of teamwork was an integral part of Eisenhower's early years. One obvious reason for this was his five brothers. His mother, Eisenhower recalled, "skillfully assigned us to beds in such a pattern as to minimize the incidence of nightly fights." All the boys were given chores—helping with the cooking, dishwashing, laundering—and their duties were rotated so that "each son learned all the responsibilities of running the house and none felt discriminated against."

Moreover, when he was still young enough to be vulnerable to neighborhood bullies, he learned that he could depend on his two older brothers, Edgar and Arthur, to stand between him "and what in those early days was clearly a world of enemies." Eisenhower later recognized that many of these tormentors "were only teasing." Nevertheless, to a small boy "they represented sheer terror."

Athletics, particularly football, which Eisenhower played with tremendous enthusiasm, taught him teamwork in a more tangible sense. He was so taken with sports that when he injured his knee as a teenager and doctors feared they would have to amputate his leg to save his life, he made his brother Edgar promise that under no circumstances would he allow that to happen. "I'd rather be dead than crippled, and not be able to play ball," Dwight said. He eventually recovered his health only after a long illness that forced him to repeat a year of school.

Years after his World War II triumphs, Eisenhower wrote:

> I noted with real satisfaction how well ex-football players seemed to have leadership qualifications and it wasn't sentiment that made it seem so. . . . I believe that football, perhaps more than any other sport, tends to instill in men the feeling that victory comes through hard—almost slavish—work, team play, self-confidence and an enthusiasm that amounts to dedication.

In uniform, Eisenhower learned early in his career that teamwork often meant sacrificing his own ambitions to the demands of military discipline and the goals of the army bureaucracy. During World War I, when he was assigned as a training officer, he made so many requests for overseas assignments that he was officially reprimanded by the War Department. Later he offered to accept a demotion to help his chances of getting a combat assignments, but the war ended with Eisenhower still on the American side of the Atlantic.

The experience was a bitter disappointment, but it helped to teach him what he called "the basic lesson of the military—that the proper place for a soldier is where he is ordered by his superiors."

As president, Eisenhower's faith in teamwork was evidenced by the active consulting role he gave to his cabinet. This was in sharp contrast to Roosevelt and Truman, who paid little attention to the views of their cabinet appointees beyond their specific responsibilities.

Eisenhower made his attitude felt at the first cabinet meeting. "I don't want you to feel that you are coming here just to represent your own department," he announced. "I want you to feel that you are coming here as general advisers to me."

According to one high-level appointee, Arthur Flemming, the president was as good as his word. He maintained a formal agenda and took an active part himself in the discussion, "but never in such a way as to convey . . . the feeling that he had made a decision and therefore there wasn't any point to a member of the cabinet expressing himself. . . . Quite the contrary. He participated in such a way as to encourage the persons sitting around the cabinet table to become involved in the discussion."

Much as this practice may have pleased his cabinet members, Eisenhower's reliance on teamwork frustrated other members of the administration who wanted the president to act more quickly and decisively. Eisenhower speech writer Emmet John Hughes later complained:

> The cabinet provided perhaps the supreme occasion both practical and symbolic for the voicing and the enactment of Eisenhower's concept of government. . . . Above all it expressed the President's basic assumption that many heads are always better than one—especially one's humble own. A historian of a decade hence, however, reviewing an exhaustible film strip with sound track of all the years of deliberations by Eisenhower Cabinets, would find that narrative punctuated with remarkably few decisions.

CHARACTER

Raised in extreme poverty, Eisenhower was torn by the tension between his drive to succeed and his fear of failure if he set his goals too high. He reconciled this conflict by striving to make his way by making people like him rather than by challenging them directly. This compromise, which helped to define his life and his career, allowed him to make maximum use of his substantial but not spectacular gifts.

British biographer Piers Brendon refers to the "calculating dexterity with which [Eisenhower] promoted himself while retaining the protective coloration of good fellowship." This character trait, reinforcing his ideology and values, influenced the way he handled such controversial issues as McCarthyism and civil rights, inclining him against forceful action, even in defense of his professed convictions, to avoid placing his cherished popularity at risk.

Early on in life Eisenhower realized he had serious handicaps to overcome if he was to advance in the world. When his parents came to live in Abilene with three small children, shortly after his birth, they could afford little more than a shack just south of the railroad tracks, with no indoor plumbing. They lived there for seven years while three more sons were born, then moved into a bigger house in which they were still jammed together. Cash was short, the boys had to wear hand-me-downs, and they peddled groceries door to door.

Years later, Dwight sought to gloss over the harsh realities of his youth. "If we were poor—and I'm not sure that we were by the standards of the day—we were unaware of it." But that rosy recollection is contradicted by brother Edgar's more candid one. "They made us feel like beggars," he said of the better-off citizens of Abilene. "It was always us against the odds. We developed a sort of feudal feeling."

Yet in spite of this feeling, or perhaps because of it, all were determined to succeed, as all indeed did.*

As he grew into his teens, Eisenhower was certainly not lacking in confidence in his physical and mental abilities and he enjoyed roughhousing with other youths. But he learned that ingratiation was often the better part of valor for a poor boy trying to make his way in the world. "I think his grin saved Ike a lot of trouble," one friend said of him when he was nineteen.

At West Point, cadet Eisenhower showed some rebelliousness, but he broke mostly minor rules, such as card playing or smuggling in food. He even kidded himself about his petty defiance. "Oh, I just know I'm awfully tough," he wrote a young woman friend. He took out most of his aggressions on the football field. And his fundamental acceptance of the academy code was reflected in his decision to become a cheerleader after his knee injury sidelined him from football, an experience that was one of the most devastating of his life.

Once graduated, the young officer remained just as determined, but just as controlled, in his response to disappointment. Chafing at the boredom of the pre–World War I infantry, he applied for transfer to the army's infant aviation section, then in the signal corps. But his wealthy in-laws objected to the danger—he had just recently married Mamie—and he reluctantly abandoned the idea. The episode, Eisenhower later recalled, "brought me face to face with myself and caused me to make a decision that I have never recanted or regretted. The decision was to perform every duty given me in the Army to the best of my ability and to do the best I could to make a creditable record, no matter what the nature of

---

* Arthur, the oldest brother, became a banker, and Edgar, who was next in line, was a successful lawyer and businessman. Of Dwight Eisenhower's three younger brothers, Roy ran a thriving small-town pharmacy, Earl owned a radio station, and Milton, the youngest, was president of Johns Hopkins University. When the brothers had a reunion in 1926, Dwight, then a major in the peacetime army, discovered that each of his siblings was earning more money than he and seemed to have a brighter future.

the duty." He had decided that he would not fight the system, whether it was represented by his in-laws or the army.

His ability to avoid intensifying friction in difficult situations was a key factor in his rise to the pinnacle of the U.S. World War II military machine. Far more important than combat experience, which Eisenhower lacked, was his instinct for getting along with U.S. allies. His insistence conveyed to one and all that he was just a regular fellow got the response he wanted. It was no accident that "I Like Ike" became one of the most potent political slogans of all time. He obviously liked to be liked.

On the other hand, as one former aide, William Bragg Ewald, Jr., writes, he could not stand *not* to be liked. "If Eisenhower did have a tragic flaw it was sensitivity to personal attack"—from Democrats such as Harry Truman, Adlai Stevenson, John Kennedy, and particularly from former speech writer Emmet John Hughes. Ewald suggested that Eisenhower's resentment of Hughes's critical books* led him to favor Richard Nixon over Nelson Rockefeller for the Republican presidential nomination in 1968—Hughes was writing speeches for Rockefeller.

Ewald, himself a White House speech writer for Eisenhower who later helped the former president write his memoirs, also offered insight into how Eisenhower must have seen himself—or at least what characteristics he wanted others to see in him—by contrasting Eisenhower with his former commander-in-chief, Franklin Roosevelt. "Both knew how to rule men and get exactly what they wanted, though one used balance of power and one used cooperation. . . . One saw himself as superior, one as high average in a superior position."

THE CHALLENGE

Orval Faubus's defiant defense of segregation in September 1957 presented Eisenhower with a historic opportunity for drawing on the combined resources of his ideology, values, and character to lead the way to a long-lasting resolution of racial conflict.

The stakes were high. At issue were not only the constitutional rights of Negro school children and the mores of the white South but the impact of the racial issue on the political future of both national political parties. For nearly a century, with only occasional interruption, the Democratic party and the South had been linked by the bonds of segregation. Now those bonds were dissolving. Clearly the Republican party had its best

---

* *America the Vincible*, 1959, and *The Ordeal of Power*, 1963.

chance since the Civil War to stake a claim on Dixie. But the Democrats were certainly not prepared to surrender the ground they had held so long. Both parties would have to consider whether they could conquer the South without splintering their own ranks and dividing the nation. And this partisan struggle would have fateful consequences, determining how both parties dealt with the politics of race, in campaigns and in government, and thus how the public viewed relations between the races.

So the confrontation with Faubus touched on the weightiest issues on the national agenda—the meaning of the Constitution, relations between the races and the political order of battle. In its way this was a more complex challenge than even the supreme commander of Overlord had faced before.

The complications arose because Little Rock was the latest outbreak of a storm that had been building steadily for more than a decade, driven largely by forces unleashed by World War II. Domestically, the economic boom the war triggered created dramatic new opportunities for Negroes in the cities of the North, where their increased migration swelled the ranks of Democratic political machines and made them an increasingly potent cohort of the electorate.

Meanwhile, the struggle against Nazism and its racist doctrines forced white America to become more conscious of the bright promises implied by the nation's historic commitment to equality and freedom. Progress in redeeming that pledge was slow. U.S. armed forces supposedly battling against racism were strictly segregated. During the Battle of the Bulge, when reinforcements were critically needed to stop Hitler's last desperate drive, Eisenhower at first offered to assign Negro volunteers to white combat units. But under pressure from his indignant aides, he reneged. Negro volunteers were assigned to segregated units, with white officers.

Nevertheless, the wartime rhetoric did create an environment for change in race relations in the postwar era. Adding to the impetus for change was the Cold War. U.S. leaders engaged in competition with communist powers for the support of the emerging Third World nations of the world, made up almost entirely of people of color, sought to ease racial barriers.

Not content to fight moral and political battles, Negroes took their demands for equal rights to the courts. They made segregated schools their principal target, determined to overturn the "separate but equal" doctrine laid down by the Supreme Court in 1896. Begun in the early 1950s, this assault led to the challenge that Little Rock represented for Eisenhower. The confrontation with Orval Faubus embodied all the principal elements of a wide-ranging conflict that pitted North against South, Negro against white, change against tradition. The test for the president was to resolve the crisis at Little Rock in such a way as to improve prospects for a constructive resolution of the broader struggle.

Although the complex issues of civil rights were about to explode on the national scene at the time of the 1952 presidential campaign, both parties studiously skirted the issue. For their part, Republicans saw no need to deal with civil rights. They were convinced that the country was weary of sixteen years of Democratic rule and that with the popular Eisenhower as their candidate they had a sure-fire winner. Once nominated, Eisenhower was counseled that any effort to win the support of Northern Negroes would cost him the support of Southern whites, advice that he took to heart in the campaign and for the next eight years. The GOP platform reflected its standard bearer's own views on race, conceding primary authority to the states—that is, to the status quo.

On the Democratic side, mindful of the Dixiecrat defection in 1948, and overlooking the Negro support that helped carry Truman to victory, the convention, which nominated Illinois Governor Adlai Stevenson, approved a bland document designed not to offend the South.

In the general election, Eisenhower assiduously courted Southern voters. His decision to campaign in the South "was flatly opposed by men far more politically experienced than I," he later wrote. But he went ahead anyway because he had "lived for years among the Southern people and liked them." By contrast, he did little to woo Negro voters. On the stump, candidate Eisenhower made plain his opposition to a strong Fair Employment Practices Commission, one of the major Negro objectives, and for the most part ignored civil rights.

His efforts were richly rewarded on election day when he carried Texas, Florida, Virginia, and Tennessee. He was the first Republican nominee to win those states since the election of 1928, when Democratic nominee Al Smith's Catholicism ruined him in Dixie.

The new president's personal views of Negroes, and of the proper relationship between Negroes and whites were reflective of his times and background. Which is to say, he rarely thought about the subject at all, and when he did, his views were informed at best by a benign paternalism—as reflected in the epigraph for the chapter on civil rights in his memoirs, a quote from Booker T. Washington: "The highest test of a race is its willingness to extend a helping hand to the less fortunate."

By the standards of his period, Eisenhower was no racist. In fact, his Democratic predecessor, Harry Truman, was more given to racial epithets, once in a staff meeting calling the irascible Adam Clayton Powell "that damn nigger preacher." Some contend that Ike never used the word "nigger" in the White House, though he did use similar if less offensive terms in private. Writing to his son from North Africa in 1943, he boasted that "a group of darkies takes gorgeous care of me." A year before in an official bulletin the War Department had banned the word "darkey."

Eisenhower's personal views mattered a great deal. In Truman's case, the electoral imperatives of the Democratic party, his own grasp of political realities, and his everyday values generally overrode his visceral prejudices. But Eisenhower had no such ideological framework, except that provided by his military background, which inclined him toward caution. In this intellectual vacuum the personal attitudes Ike had absorbed during his lifetime were a major factor in shaping racial policy.

"Since boyhood I had accepted without qualification the right to equality before the law of all citizens of this country, whatever their race or color or creed," Eisenhower wrote in his memoirs. But in fact, either because of circumstance or choice he had not often dealt directly with racial discrimination.

There were scarcely any Negroes in Abilene when Eisenhower grew up there, but two contrasting anecdotes show the positive and negative sides of young Eisenhower's understanding of race and of the prevailing racial attitudes in his environment.

As one story has it, young Eisenhower's teammates on the Abilene high football squad refused to play across the line from the Negro center of an opposing team. By his own account Eisenhower volunteered to play center that day, and shook the Negro's hand before and after the game. "Rest of the team was ashamed of themselves," Eisenhower later wrote. This anecdote illustrates Eisenhower's inclination to good sportsmanship and fair play.

Another tale, however, shows Eisenhower much more in tune with the racial attitudes of his hometown. Returning home for summer leave in 1913 after a year at West Point, Eisenhower, who had a reputation as a boxer, was urged by his pals to challenge "a lad in town who needed taking down a bit." His name was Dirk Tyler, "a Negro of magnificent physique," who had thrashed all the local competition in boxing matches. Now the losers complained that "Dirk had become a bully who went around with a chip on his shoulder." Reluctant at first, Ike took on the white man's burden and finished off Tyler with three punches. Later on folks in Abilene agreed among themselves that this was good for Dirk— who became a "nice guy" again.

These two incidents are not as incongruent as they might seem. Both fit the Booker Washington epigraph. In the case of the "less fortunate" Negro football player, Eisenhower was glad to offer a helping hand. To Dirk Tyler, who appeared far from helpless, he extended a right uppercut. Eisenhower hardly made a habit of punching out assertive Negroes, but he had difficulty accepting them on their own terms throughout his life.*

His military career further hampered tolerance because of the predominance of military posts in the South and of Southerners in the officer corps. Eisenhower saw no Negroes at all at West Point (from the Civil War to World War II, only thirteen were admitted to the academy, and only three graduated).

Soon after getting his second lieutenant's gold bars, he was assigned as an instructor to a black National Guard unit in Illinois. Their poor performance made him "ashamed and embarrassed," and by his own account affected his overall judgment of Negroes. Years later he told E. Frederic Morrow, the only black on his White House staff, that it had not occurred to him that these men had been poorly trained and led.

In 1948, after he had left the army for the presidency of Columbia University, Eisenhower testified at a congressional hearing in favor of assigning Negroes to units no larger than platoons, but opposed full-scale integration, a step Truman would later initiate and Eisenhower would complete. Eisenhower told the congressional committee that "the Negro is less well educated than his brother citizen" and would not get promotions under full-scale integration. "I do believe that if we attempt merely by passing a lot of laws to force someone to like someone else, we are just going to get into trouble." Eisenhower later told Morrow that his views on integration were based on the opinions of his field commanders. And only later did he realize that nearly all of the field commanders were from the South. Eisenhower then asked Morrow for forgiveness.

In the White House, Eisenhower's lack of an ideological framework for dealing with racial issues was reflected in the equivocation that characterized his civil rights policies. He proclaimed his personal commitment to the principles of equality and considered himself to be a supporter of civil rights. "I believe with all my heart that our vigilant guarding of these [civil] rights is a sacred obligation binding upon every citizen," he declared in his State of the Union speech in February 1953.

Yet Eisenhower saw no political advantage in aiding the Negro cause. Thus, there was little to prod the president into acting decisively in the burgeoning civil rights crisis. By contrast, his vice-president showed a better grasp of the political implications of the issue, and saw an opportunity for gaining Negro support while holding on to moderate and liberal

---

* See E. Frederic Morrow's *Black Man in the White House*, a poignant account of his frustrating career as an Eisenhower aide. Morrow wrote: "At no time had [Eisenhower] made an overt gesture that would encourage Negroes to believe that he sympathized with, or believed in, their crusade for complete and immediate citizenship."

white voters. "There is insufficient emphasis on the Negroes," Nixon told one his advisers as the 1956 election approached, adding that "the large Negro voting groups in states with heavy electoral votes can be most important." Moreover, what Nixon said in private he backed up in public statements calling for support of fair employment and other goals of the civil rights movement.

Nixon was speaking as a seasoned student and practitioner of electoral politics. Eisenhower, lacking that background, drawing solely on his personal experience, was mainly concerned with what would be lost to the GOP by antagonizing Southerners. His attitude was illustrated on the eve of the 1956 Republican convention by the threat he had conveyed to Republican Senator Prescott Bush, father of the forty-first president and then chairman of the convention platform committee. Unless the words "Eisenhower Administration" were deleted from a phrase in the platform connecting it with support for the Supreme Court's desegregation rulings, Eisenhower warned, he would refuse to attend the convention.

In acting to extend civil rights, Eisenhower restricted himself to areas—the armed forces, the District of Columbia, federal employment— that offered the advantages of being under his direct control and also of having relatively little impact on the lives of most Americans. Therefore, public controversy, which Eisenhower always sought to avoid, was likely to be limited. Yet, even in these fields progress was slow.

At any rate, these actions were overshadowed by the historic decision in *Brown* v. *the Board of Education* in May 1954. Ironically, the most positive step the Eisenhower Administration had taken before the Brown decision was unintentional—in fact, Eisenhower later called it a mistake: the appointment of Earl Warren as chief justice.* Warren had been promised the next vacancy on the court as a reward for his support for the Eisenhower forces at the 1952 Republican convention. The vacancy was created by the death of Chief Justice Fred Vinson in September 1953. Vinson had been viewed by some as an obstacle to the court's reaching a just and consistent decision on segregation cases. In deed, Justice Felix Frankfurter remarked upon his passing: "This is the first indication I have ever had that there is a God."

Eisenhower had little thought of Warren's views on civil rights when he appointed him, though shortly afterward, in February 1954, the pres-

---

* In 1961, Eisenhower told author and former aide William Ewald that he regarded his choice of Warren as one of "the two worst appointments I ever made," the other being the man he picked to head the Justice Department's anti-trust division. In 1965, when historian Stephen Ambrose asked him what had been his biggest mistake, Eisenhower replied, "The appointment of that s.o.b. Earl Warren."

ident tried to impress the new chief with the merits of the Southern side in the school case. A resentful Warren not only complained to his family and to friends that Eisenhower had seated him next to the lawyer for the segregationist cause, John W. Davis, but also praised Davis in Warren's presence. What was worse, Eisenhower reiterated one of the emotional arguments made by foes of integration. "These are not bad people," he said of them. "All they are concerned about is to see that their sweet little girls are not required to sit in school alongside some big overgrown Negroes."

The Supreme Court's unanimous opinion was written by the Republican chief justice Eisenhower had himself appointed, and Warren was joined by Southerners Hugo Black of Alabama and Stanley Reed of Kentucky. Here was a historic opportunity for Eisenhower to rally the nation behind the court's ruling and to begin healing racial wounds that went back to colonial days. Instead, with his characteristic determination to avoid controversy, he sought to maintain a sort of neutrality between the court and the opponents of the decision, a posture that inevitably fostered resistance to the ruling.

Asked for advice to the South in his first press conference after the *Brown* decision, Eisenhower said he had none to offer, adding, as if through gritted teeth, that he would obey his oath to "uphold the Constitutional process in this country." During his remaining six years in office he never went any further in backing this or later Court rulings in civil rights. In his memoirs he explained that he felt if he gave his view of one Supreme Court decision, he would be expected to do likewise on many others and might eventually encounter one he disagreed with.

This was disingenuous: presidents often give their views on Court decisions. And in this instance, because of the enormous importance of the ruling, Eisenhower's silence spoke volumes. In one of his most revealing statements on the issue, made in private, he later told Brownell that he was of the "firm conviction" that because of the Supreme Court ruling "the whole issue had been set back badly."

Eisenhower's reaction to the Court's ruling reflected his leadership traits. The controversy stirred by the Court contravened not only his ideological outlook, but also his principal values and character traits. It threatened the accord necessary for the teamwork Eisenhower wanted his administration to practice and threatened his high personal regard with the public.

Not only did Eisenhower refuse to act on his own initiative, he rejected a proposal made by Florida's moderate Democratic Governor LeRoy Collins in early 1956 to meet with Southern governors and attorneys general, contending that such a meeting would only fuel the controversy. He thus passed up a chance to help build moderate political support for compliance with the high court's desegregation decrees.

Determined to avoid controversy, Eisenhower did not publicly distinguish between defenders of segregation who flouted the law, sometimes violently, and Negroes and their supporters who wanted the Court's decision implemented. In the fall of 1956, in the face of threatened violence from a mob protesting school desegregation in Mansfield, Texas, Governor Shivers dispatched Texas Rangers to remove black students from the schools. Eisenhower's response was to condemn "extremists on both sides," thus giving tacit approval to what Shivers had done.

The president's attitude may well have been influenced by his campaign for re-election, then in full swing. Stumping in the South, Eisenhower took pains to reassure Southerners that he believed racial disputes should be handled locally. But in addressing campaign rallies in the North, Eisenhower claimed credit for progress against segregation in the military, in government employment, and in the nation's capital.

On the morning after election day, the usually frosty Sherman Adams, Eisenhower's chief of staff, gave Frederic Morrow, Eisenhower's Negro aide, a big smile and said, "A job well done, son." Adams's pleasure was understandable. Running against Adlai Stevenson again, Eisenhower had gotten nearly forty percent of the black vote—the biggest percentage for any Republican presidential candidate since the New Deal.

Eisenhower did well with white Southerners, too, carrying six Southern states—adding Kentucky and Louisiana to the four he had carried in 1952. In other words, he managed to have it both ways, gaining ground among Southern whites and more dramatically among Negroes in the North. Much of this had to do with his overall personal popularity and the recent crises in the Middle East and Hungary, which tended to overshadow other issues. Beyond that, Eisenhower had plainly convinced whites that the court decision was not his fault and that he would not force that issue. Negroes, on the other hand, could find hope in the simple fact of a Republican president who stated at least his nominal willingness to support the Brown decision.

Eisenhower's second term, however, offered little to sustain those hopes. His policies were still governed by his military orientation against controversy, his faith in the value of teamwork, and his determination to preserve his popularity. His statements on civil rights still often seemed ill-informed and ill-considered, none more so than during a press conference in July 1957. Responding to a question, Eisenhower said he was aware that since Reconstruction days a president had had authority to use military force to implement integration. But he went on, "I can't imagine any set of circumstances that would ever induce me to send Federal troops into . . . any area to enforce the orders of a Federal court." Those were words that in the weeks to come, he would have good reason to regret.

That Little Rock was the site of the climactic civil rights confrontation of the Eisenhower presidency amounted to a significant paradox. The capital city and its state both had a reputation for moderation in civil rights. In 1948, before any other state in Dixie, Arkansas admitted Negro students to its state university. And immediately after the *Brown* decision, the city's school board unveiled a plan for gradual desegregation; this plan was intended to begin with the desegregation of Central High School in September 1957. In such an environment, relatively receptive to desegregation, a prompt, vigorous response by Eisenhower to Governor Faubus's defiance of the federal court order would have had a good chance of forcing the governor to back down.

This did not happen. Just as Eisenhower set the stage for the confrontation by his overall approach to civil rights and by his statement ruling out the use of troops in such a situation, he allowed the struggle to drag on unnecessarily, making its impact more harmful.

First came his decision to go ahead with his plans for a vacation in Newport and then to stay on there in the midst of the crisis, resisting suggestions even from old friends such as General Alfred M. Gruenther that he go back to the White House. If he returned, the president wrote Gruenther, it "would be a confession that a change of scenery is truly a 'vacation' for the President and is not merely a change of his working locale."

This was blatant humbug. The president took every opportunity to go down to the dock of Coasters Harbor Island, where he was staying, and board a boat for the Newport Country Club to play golf. On September 11, with the situation in Little Rock approaching crisis, light rain almost forced him to cancel his customary eighteen holes of golf (in the afternoon the skies cleared and the president managed to get in thirteen). Two days later, on the eve of an ill-conceived, ill-fated meeting with Faubus, the *Providence Journal* reported his schedule thus: "Morning—Golf, Newport Country Club. Afternoon—Lobstering off Newport."

Eisenhower was entitled to a vacation, even if he preferred not to admit he was taking one. More troublesome was the other reason he gave Gruenther for staying in Rhode Island. "I do not want to exaggerate the significance of the admittedly serious situation in Arkansas," he wrote his old comrade-in-arms. "The great need is to act calmly, deliberately and give every offender opportunity to cease his defiance." In actuality, though, the perception Eisenhower inevitably created was that he did not regard Faubus's offense as grave enough to require his urgent attention.

Another strategic mistake was Eisenhower's response to Faubus's request for a meeting. The governor, who faced a hearing before the federal court judge whose order he had defied, sent word through an emissary that he "would like to find a way out of the situation in which he has gotten." Meanwhile, a report reached the White House through Democratic Senator Richard Russell of Georgia that "Faubus was going to try to force a court decision which would be conciliatory to the problems of the South, which would serve as sort of a bellwether in future cases."

Faubus's behavior was hard to fathom. He seemed eager to make what political capital he could of the drama he had created. Yet he was clearly fearful of pushing the president too hard.

While these events unfolded, I was on the rewrite desk of the *Detroit Free Press*, where—because of the Motor City's explosive population mix of blacks, Poles, and Southern white migrants—the confrontation in Little Rock commanded particular interest. As Faubus was trying to wangle a meeting with the president, I was handling a story phoned in by the *Free Press*'s correspondent on the scene, revealing that Faubus's cronies believed that the governor was under such tension that he was taking heavy doses of tranquilizers.

Such reports should have cautioned the president against meeting with Faubus. So also should the advice of Attorney General Brownell, who believed that Faubus had "soiled" himself by his disobedience of the law and should pay the price for it. Besides, Brownell pointed out to Eisenhower, previous attempts by other political leaders to negotiate with Faubus had all failed. But Eisenhower, bent on avoiding confrontation, disregarded his attorney general's counsel and agreed to receive the governor.

At their brief meeting on September 14 in the Newport naval base, Eisenhower told Faubus, as he later recalled in his diary, that he did not believe it to anyone's benefit "to have a trial of strength" between himself and Faubus. In such a contest, he said, "there could be only one outcome— that is, the state would lose, and I did not want to see any governor humiliated."

He suggested to Faubus a way out of the predicament. Instead of using the Guard to prevent the Negro youngsters from entering the school, Eisenhower proposed, tell the Guardsmen just to keep the peace while the students go to school. If Faubus went along with that idea,

Eisenhower would try to get the governor excused from the court hearing he faced.

Though Faubus left Eisenhower with the impression that he was going to accept the proposition, he had no such intention. He continued to use the Guard to keep out the Negro students while Eisenhower continued to delay action. Finally on September 20, under pressure of an injunction from the federal court, Faubus pulled out the Guard, but reiterated his opposition to desegregation and disclaimed any responsibility for preserving order.

A racist mob surrounded the high school, threatening the Negro students. On September 24 Little Rock Mayor Woodrow Wilson Mann wired the White House pleading for help. "The situation is out of control and police cannot disperse the mob," he warned.

Now Eisenhower could delay no longer. He dispatched five hundred men of the 101st Airborne and federalized the Arkansas Guard. Then he flew back to Washington to address the nation.*

The president still showed sensitivity about the criticism that he had stayed overlong in Newport. "I could have spoken from Rhode Island . . ." he declared. "But I felt that in speaking from the house of Lincoln, of Jackson and of Wilson my words would better convey both the sadness I feel in the action I was compelled today to take and the firmness with which I intend to pursue this course."

Stressing that he was sending in troops only to enforce the law, not because he favored desegregation, Eisenhower contended that "personal opinions" on the Supreme Court's ruling had no relevance. He lamented that "our enemies," presumably the Soviet Union and its allies, "are gloating over this incident and using it everywhere to misrepresent our nation." He made no mention, however, of the indignities and the terror inflicted upon the Negro schoolchildren in Little Rock, or of their right to an equal education.

The president clearly wanted to appeal to Southern whites. These were, after all, the people whom he had lived among for years and liked. At the least, he could have talked of values shared by most Americans, and certainly by Eisenhower—of fair play and of the importance of a good education for all children. But to raise these points in this context would have stirred resentment and involved risks. That would have been contrary to Eisenhower's characteristic desire to be liked and to his ideological distaste for controversy. His attempt at conciliation was a

* After the speech he returned to Newport, where he spent the rest of the month. He had previously interrupted his vacation for two other brief trips to the capital.

bloodless, legalistic appeal. His words did little to cool anger in the South or elsewhere in the country. And his actions did little to help Negroes, who faced prolonged white resistance to their demands for equal rights.

Two days after Eisenhower's speech, Senator Russell wired the president, protesting the "highhanded and illegal methods" being used by the troops the president had sent to the scene "to mix the races in the public schools of Little Rock."

In Detroit, a sensitive barometer of racial unrest, the *Free Press* switchboard was flooded with outraged calls from the Southern whites who had come there to work in the auto industry. As time wore on, the tones of the callers became ugly. "Why is the president sending soldiers to fight for the niggers?" I remember one irate auto worker from Dixie demanding.

The Little Rock school controversy dragged on and on. For his remaining three years in office, Eisenhower had to contend with numerous other civil rights controversies in a broad range of areas, and so, of course, did his successors.

Nevertheless, the confrontation at Central High School in the fall of 1957 was a watershed event. It had great impact on the country because it dramatized and personalized the fierce conflicts involved in civil rights, with Eisenhower, Faubus, the Negro schoolchildren, and the white mob each playing out compelling roles.

Tension spread across the country. In Detroit I watched the hostility between blacks and whites mount steadily in the wake of Little Rock, adding to the already sharp divisions in that racially troubled city. I had written my first book about the Detroit Race Riot in 1943, when thirty-four persons were killed and Roosevelt had to send in the army to preserve order. Ten years after Little Rock, Detroit erupted again, in an even worse riot. Once again federal troops had to be summoned. This time the death toll was forty-three, and Henry Ford II called it "the greatest internal violence since the Civil War." That same summer riots broke out in more than one hundred other cities around the country.

Many factors contributed to this violence and hate and to the racial antagonism that continues to distort American politics. But Little Rock was a transforming event in this chain because it permanently sealed off avenues for constructive leadership and locked American politics and society on a divisive and violent course that shaped the ensuing three decades. Eisenhower's handling of this challenge permanently polarized the issue of civil rights and assured that the Republican party would become the party of the white South, leaving the Democrats the vast majority of blacks. Because the Democrats have gotten a majority of white votes for president only once since Eisenhower's time, in 1964, they have won the presidency only once since that election. But Republican failure to get support from more than a slim minority of blacks has contributed to their inability to control Congress most of the time and to become a true majority party.

Yet this polarity did not necessarily have to take shape. Once again, in striking contrast with Eisenhower, no less a political realist than Richard Nixon saw the political opportunities for Republicans from the civil rights issue, even after Little Rock.

In responding to Southern Republicans who wrote to him to protest against Eisenhower's actions, Nixon admitted that the GOP cause had suffered "a temporary setback," but told his correspondents: "You and other Republican leaders in the South can do much to help provide a rallying point for those men and women of moderate and conservative inclinations who are opposed to extremism in any form."

As one of the most popular presidents in our history, Eisenhower was uniquely positioned to take advantage of the opportunity Nixon envisaged and to avoid the hardening of racial and political lines. Of course, he could not have brushed aside Southern resentment about the march of integration. What he could have done, and what he failed to attempt, was to use his prestige, and vast store of goodwill, to reassure whites on one hand—and on the other hand, to make them realize they had no choice but to accept change.

That would have required him to overcome his strongest character traits, the values he had acquired over a lifetime and his approach to ideology. Eisenhower's determination to be liked, his faith in teamwork, his fundamental aversion to public debate and controversy, all combined to incline him against actions that might cause discord, challenge established practices and traditions, and cause anger and resentment among the populace.

As time passed, Eisenhower made no effort to mobilize the white Southern moderate leadership that Nixon sought to rally behind the cause of civil rights. Moreover, Eisenhower failed to understand the potential for Negro support in the North, which would have helped offset any losses he suffered in the South. After watching a speech by a Negro leader in Detroit boosting his candidacy, during a national telecast of campaign rallies on election eve in 1956, Eisenhower turned to Emmet Hughes and said derisively, *"That* sure will do us a lot of good in Houston."

Meeting with Republican leaders in February 1959, five years after the Brown decision, Eisenhower pointed to his achievements in civil rights—completing the integration of the military, attacking segregation in the District of Columbia, passing the 1957 Civil Rights bill. "It's a funny thing," the president said, "there is no evidence that we have raised any votes with all we've done for the Negroes." Then he added that he was not looking for political support anyway. He had done these "as a matter of decency."

Eisenhower's remarks show how little weight he put on the potential value of Negro votes, despite his impressive Negro support in the 1956 election. Decency, Eisenhower's motive for promoting civil rights—to the extent that he did—is a slender reed. When push came to shove, the weight of decency was offset by the political value Eisenhower saw in Southern white votes.

To create a majority of Negroes and whites would have been difficult even for Eisenhower, of course. But that is not why he did not attempt such a task. He simply did not grasp the need for such a coalition and for what it might accomplish. Eisenhower's handling of Little Rock, argued Emmet Hughes, the speech writer whose criticism had so irritated the president, was more than just "a display of chronic indecision. It amounted to a complex testimony to particular personal beliefs of Dwight D. Eisenhower, beliefs that he embraced, in fact, quite *decisively*" (Hughes's emphasis). Beneath the apparent equivocation, Hughes wrote, "there lay a definite and explicit resolve to try one's patient best—to leave things undone."

The principal lesson to be drawn from Eisenhower's management of the Little Rock crisis is that a major weakness in one element of presidential leadership can undermine the potential strengths of other leadership traits. Eisenhower's primary leadership weakness was his ideology, shaped by his narrow view of politics and his determination to avoid controversy. His values—particularly his sense of fair play linked to his emphasis on teamwork—and his characteristic skill at getting people to like him would have been powerful assets to deploy against Faubus and others who defended segregation in defiance of the Supreme Court. But Eisenhower's fatal flaw, his ideology, nullified these strengths, and his values and character became accomplices to the passive role he chose to play.

The president's passivity in combating Faubus and the forces of bigotry had been foreshadowed by his handling of an earlier domestic challenge of profound importance, the pernicious demagoguery and vigilantism of Senator Joseph McCarthy, which cast a pall over the first two years of Eisenhower's first term. A contest between Eisenhower and McCarthy would have been a quick rout. With the boundless public admiration and respect Eisenhower enjoyed, he would have been invulnerable to McCarthy's savage and sometimes incoherent attacks.

The president, however, was not safe against his own leadership defects. As in the struggle over civil rights, the furor over McCarthyism saw the stronger side of Eisenhower's leadership potential submerged. Eisenhower's adherence to the value of fair play, a principle McCarthy violated at every turn, and his appealing personality, in contrast to McCarthy's abrasive character, never came into play because of his ideological commitment to inaction.

And as it was in the case of the civil rights challenge, Eisenhower's behavior, controlled by his limited approach to ideology, was based more on his personal experiences and inclinations than on any intellectual frame of reference. He retained the same disinterest in ideas he had exhibited as a schoolboy; he disliked McCarthy, but mainly on personal grounds. He was indignant about the harm the senator's reckless charges had done to the reputations of Eisenhower's friends and officials of his administration. But not until late in the game did he realize that McCarthy's tactics, like the communism with which McCarthy was obsessed, threatened not just individuals but the nation's liberties and institutions as well.

The pattern by which Eisenhower chose to deal with McCarthy was established even before he took office, when he was still a candidate for the presidency. Infuriated by McCarthy's attacks on George C. Marshall, Eisenhower's old boss and patron, for allegedly helping to lose China to the communists, Eisenhower decided to strike back; he would make a point of paying tribute to Marshall while stumping in Milwaukee, "right in McCarthy's backyard," as Eisenhower put it.

Speech writer Emmet Hughes drafted an appropriate paragraph, hailing Marshall as a man of "singular selflessness and the profoundest patriotism." But when Wisconsin Republican leaders saw the prepared text of Eisenhower's speech, they protested, arguing that these words would give offense to McCarthy and his supporters, even though McCarthy was not mentioned by name.

That was all Eisenhower, with his ideological aversion to controversy, had to hear. Suppressed was the value of fair play in favor of the value of team harmony. The fact that he could have won any personal popularity contest with McCarthy was overshadowed in Eisenhower's mind by the anxiety that his popularity might be slightly diminished by the resentment of some of McCarthy's ardent supporters. The controversial paragraph was excised from the speech, but only after reporters covering Eisenhower's campaign had read it in the advance text. The net result not only embarrassed Eisenhower but boosted the stature of McCarthy by providing dramatic evidence that even Eisenhower was unwilling to defend those he targeted for his attacks.

Eisenhower did not come that close to challenging McCarthy again

until the waning months of the senator's power, and even then he did
not mention him by name. He rationalized his silence by telling himself
and those who urged him to speak out that it was important to deny
McCarthy publicity. "I really believe that nothing will be so effective in
combating this particular kind of troublemaking as to ignore him," he
wrote in his diary. "This he cannot stand."

But McCarthy didn't mind being ignored by Eisenhower as long as
he gained ample attention elsewhere. Meanwhile, he ran rampant, assaulting the innocent in both parties, among them Eisenhower's own
nominees for high office, obstructing Eisenhower's policies, shaming the
country in the eyes of the world.

"McCarthy makes it so easy to hate Americans," one influential West
German politician told his countrymen, a remark Eisenhower recorded
in his diary with the observation that McCarthy "simply terrifies the
ordinary European statesman." Yet this awareness did not cause Eisenhower to abandon his restraint toward McCarthy.

He did at times maneuver behind the scenes to get others to speak
out against McCarthy or thwart his ambitions. But such sub-rosa tactics
were of small consequence in meeting a challenge whose very essence
was public debate and in which McCarthy was playing his part at the top
of his lungs. The president held his own fire, as Fred Greenstein acknowledges in his admiring study of Eisenhower's leadership, until 1954
when "McCarthy became open to attack by *any* right thinking American."
Even then Eisenhower resorted mainly to generalizations and indirection.

By that time, McCarthy was ripe to fall. He would be censured by
the Senate and finished politically in December of that year. But by then
it was too late to save the reputations of those he had slandered, to avoid
the demoralization of the State Department, the undermining of civil
liberties at home, and the tarnishing of national prestige abroad. That
damage would take years to repair at best, and some of what was lost,
measured in the wasted lives of individuals and the lost opportunities for
public policy, would never be recovered.

Strangely enough, though Eisenhower was acutely sensitive to other
people's approval, Eisenhower seemed unaware of the implications of his
ideological bias against controversy. In a diary entry complaining about
the excessive caution of certain Republican senators, Eisenhower wrote
a scathing critique of passive political behavior, obviously without realizing how closely such criticism applied to his own conduct:

> They do not seem to realize when there arrives that moment at which
> soft speaking should be abandoned and a fight to the end undertaken. Any

man who hopes to exercise this leadership must be ready to meet this requirement face to face when it arrives; unless he is ready to fight when necessary, people will finally begin to ignore him.

Tragically, Eisenhower found it easier to preach this principle in his diary than practice it in public.

Understandably, Eisenhower was more comfortable with foreign policy and national security challenges than with domestic issues, for his background gave him more experience and confidence in such matters. Moreover, by law and tradition the president has a freer rein in foreign affairs, and by invoking his role as commander-in-chief and guardian of the national interest, he can often shield himself against the controversy that Eisenhower was so determined to avoid.

Still, even in meeting challenges on this familiar ground Eisenhower's accomplishments were limited by his leadership shortcomings. Attempting to hold down defense spending in order to reduce the burden on the federal budget, he found himself under attack from Democrats. Desperate to find a weakness in Eisenhower's political armor, they sought to depict him as insensitive to the nation's security needs. Naturally indignant, Eisenhower took the criticism personally.

Asked at a press conference about charges that he was too tightfisted to develop needed weapons, Eisenhower retorted: "If anybody—anybody—believes that I have deliberately misled the American people, I'd like to tell him to his face what I think about him. This is a charge that I think is despicable; I have never made it against anyone in the world."

Personalizing the issue did not silence his critics, though, nor was it enough to build sustained public support for the idea of defense cutbacks. Talking to Republican congressional leaders, Eisenhower blamed military contractors for stimulating public enthusiasm for weaponry. "This seems to be a hysteria that is largely political," he complained.

Of course it *was* political, and a powerful political argument was needed to answer it, one based on more than the president's personal pique or on the need to balance the budget. In eight years of battling Congress and defense contractors, Eisenhower did manage to hold back the rising tide of defense expenditures. But he failed to develop a broad constituency in support of his position, which would have made possible deeper and more enduring reductions.

To accomplish this, he needed to make just the sort of ideological argument that was alien to his nature. He could, for example, have linked defense cutbacks not only to fiscal objectives, but also to the more urgent cause of slowing the arms race with the Soviet Union, another challenge that Eisenhower undertook with frustrating results.

Eisenhower might also have pointed out the dangerous implications for American society of sustained military spending, a point he made so eloquently in his justly celebrated farewell address. In that speech he pointed out that the development of "an immense military establishment and a large arms industry" was unprecedented in this country, adding this warning: "In the councils of government, we must guard against the acquisition of unwarranted influence, whether sought or unsought, by the military industrial complex. The potential for the disastrous rise of misplaced power exists and will persist."

Of all his presidential utterances, this was the most widely praised and best remembered. But because it was delivered when Eisenhower had only three days left in the White House, it had no direct effect on the public debate over defense spending. Had he made it earlier in his tenure, it would have forced his critics on the defensive and could have led to dramatic change in national priorities. But it certainly would have stirred just the sort of controversy Eisenhower had spent his presidency trying to avoid. At the end of his political career, as at the beginning, Eisenhower preferred the role of revered statesman to embattled politician.

In his farewell address Eisenhower also chose to deal with the dashing of his hopes for a slowdown in the nuclear arms race, partly because the downing of the U-2 spy plane piloted by Francis Gary Powers in May 1960 had wrecked his plans for a summit conference with Soviet leader Nikita Khrushchev. The president confessed to his countrymen "a definite sense of disappointment" that he had not been more successful. And he used the occasion to emphasize that disarmament "is a continuing imperative."

As he left the presidency, the old soldier could take credit for avoiding war. But now his young successor, with the threat of nuclear catastrophe unabated, would be severely challenged to keep the peace.

CHAPTER 4

Kennedy: Rules of Reason

One of the ironies of John Kennedy's legacy is that most Americans have more compelling memories of his assassination than of the Cuban missile crisis, which threatened nuclear catastrophe and became instead the gateway to improved hopes for peace. But my wife and I have one vivid personal recollection of those fateful days, tied to a telephone call we received from an old friend, Barney Collier.

We had just finished dinner in our home in Maplewood, New Jersey, whence I commuted to my job as an editor on the *Wall Street Journal*. It was Friday night, and four nights earlier, on October 22, 1962, President Kennedy had gone on television to tell the world that the Soviet Union had installed nuclear missiles on Cuba, only ninety miles away from the United States, and to proclaim a naval blockade of the island ruled by Fidel Castro.

This was why Barney had phoned. We had known each other from *Detroit Free Press* and *Miami News* days, and he now worked for *Time* in New York. This was no social call; Barney was worried about the missiles. He wanted to send his wife and their two young sons out of Manhattan to spend the weekend with us. "Our Washington bureau tells us that the Russian missiles are aimed right at Manhattan," he said.

His family was welcome anytime and so was he, I said. "But how safe are they going to be in Maplewood?"

"At least they'll be twenty-three miles from ground zero," Barney said.

As I related Barney's call to my wife, I began to worry myself. I had known in an intellectual sense for four days that we were closer to nuclear war than ever before. But for some reason I just discounted the idea that this would come to pass. Now I had to wonder if I had taken the crisis seriously enough.

It occurred to me suddenly that our lives—those of my family and Barney's family and every other family in the country—were in the hands of one man, John Kennedy. His judgment would determine our fate. I remembered a conversation earlier in the week with a *Journal* colleague. He had been rereading the book about Kennedy's exploits as a PT boat skipper in World War II and was worried. "That guy took a lot of chances," he said. "What kind of person is he, anyhow?"

In the days and months to come, we were all to learn more about Kennedy, who was then only forty-five. The Cuban missile crisis was a severe test of Kennedy's presidential leadership. Only eighteen months before, the young president had been confronted with another test over Cuba and he had failed. The abortive invasion of the Bay of Pigs had been a humiliation for the country and particularly for Kennedy. As the new danger loomed, many feared that he would seek to vindicate himself for that setback by some brash and risky action.

A wide range of circumstances shaped Kennedy's response to the discovery of Soviet missiles in Fidel Castro's Cuba. Some were out of his control, such as the imperatives facing the Soviet Union and its leader, Nikita Khrushchev. But of the factors directly linked to Kennedy himself, it was his pragmatic ideology, his emphasis on the value of rationality, and his characteristic intellectual self-discipline that governed his response. These strengths enabled John Kennedy to expand his ideological horizons to assess the changing realities of his times and his country's place in the world.

As a result of his maturation in office, Kennedy was able to do with Cuba what Eisenhower had failed to do with Little Rock—use a particular crisis to make progress on a broader problem. By his response to the threat of Soviet missiles near the Florida Keys, Kennedy opened the way for agreement on a nuclear test ban that at least for a time eased the tensions caused by the nuclear rivalry between the United States and the Soviet Union.

The importance of that treaty in diplomatic and strategic terms is easy to comprehend. But to understand its full significance as an achievement of political leadership, it is necessary to understand Kennedy himself.

IDEOLOGY

Kennedy's ideological outlook was more activist and intellectual than Eisenhower's, more skeptical than Truman's. His critics and also his sometime allies, particularly in areas such as civil rights, complained of what they called his detachment, lack of conviction, or sheer cold-bloodedness. Certainly he was not as passionate as some of the traditional liberals of his day, Hubert Humphrey, for example. As much as John Kennedy feared anything he feared being committed to illusion—that is, to beliefs he could not persuade his constituents to share. But when he was convinced of the political merits and soundness of an idea, he showed himself to be a formidable champion of principle. Unlike Eisenhower, who viewed politics with disdain, Kennedy had a healthy appreciation of the political process. He learned to master it and in the process began to develop what amounted to his own ideological approach.

Kennedy's skepticism was in part a result of his background. Though he was a member of a wealthy and powerful family, certain circumstances of his upbringing made him think of himself as an outsider. Begin with his Irish-Catholic heritage. Like other immigrant groups low on the socio-economic ladder, the Irish looked to political organizations at the local level and to government at all levels for support. Natural fodder for the new Democratic party that began to emerge in the late 1920s under the leadership of Irish-Catholic Al Smith, they were quick to rally behind such bread-and-butter goals as higher wages, shorter hours, and better working conditions.

Just as economic need drove the Irish to the political left, though, their ties to the Holy Mother church and their other traditional values had led them to oppose such threats to their way of life as women's rights and public schools. Thus the Irish were divided on what most people thought of as liberalism, and this division complicated the careers of Irish politicians like Jack Kennedy.

In Massachusetts, an Irish politician needed the backing of the liberal reformers—Yankees, intellectuals, Jews—for programs of social improvement. But the reformers were a step or two above the Irish economically and socially. Moreover, over the years they had mainly been concerned with the sort of high-principled issues—religious freedom, civil rights, curbs on gambling and liquor—that were remote to the Irish masses, and in some cases flew in the face of their faith and culture. As a result, James MacGregor Burns points out, many of the Irish were cut off "from the whole Western Liberal heritage of civil liberty, tolerance, intellectual freedom, social equality and philosophical rationalism and pragmatism."

But these were the sort of ideas that attracted young John Kennedy as he was getting into politics. As repugnant as they were to the hard-working Irish families in Kennedy's hometown, they were watch words in the Yankee elite schools—Choate and Harvard—to which his father sent him. Moreover, and this became increasingly important later in Kennedy's career, these ideas were the foundation of the national ideology of his political party. He could not hope for national advancement without subscribing to them.

Kennedy could not or would not repudiate completely either the reformer or the Irish traditions. Neither could he fully resolve the conflict between them. So he tried to choose a neutral ground between the two camps.

Greatly adding to the complexities of Kennedy's background was the role in his life of Joseph P. Kennedy, Sr., a domineering yet thwarted figure: tycoon, diplomat, politician, philanderer, and last, but certainly not least, father. Indeed, he seemed at times more father than his sons could handle.

In the 1960 presidential campaign, after John and Robert Kennedy had interceded with Southern authorities on behalf of the imprisoned Martin Luther King, Jr., King's father announced that he had been planning to vote for Richard Nixon because of Kennedy's Catholic faith, but would now vote for John Kennedy. "Imagine Martin Luther King having a bigot for a father," Kennedy remarked to an aide, but then added with notable irony: "Well, we all have fathers, don't we?"

Many did indeed judge Joseph Kennedy to be a bigot, and there was no shortage of evidence to support that suspicion. Some of his attitudes inevitably shaped the thinking of John and his brothers as they came of age. To their credit, they managed to outgrow most of their father's darkest prejudices. But this was not easy; old Joe was a believer and a hater of outsize proportions and the possessor of an iron will. Jack Kennedy's struggle to establish his own ideological identity in the face of this force left its mark and was another reason why he usually was found standing apart from the rest.

Whatever price they paid, though, Joe Kennedy's sons got from him a legacy of intellectual activism and curiosity. "At an early age we were sent on trips," Robert Kennedy recalled. "We embarked on study programs under teachers or political leaders who held views quite different from his." A prime example was British socialist thinker Harold Laski. The elder Kennedy, though he regarded Laski as "a nut and a crank," nevertheless arranged to have him teach his two eldest sons.

When John Kennedy entered Harvard in 1936, Hitler was already on the march in Europe and the New Deal at its peak. Harvard Square was seething with intellectual ferment and political and social protest. But the young student remained remote from all this. His grades were poor in his freshman year and he did not even bother to sign up with the Young Democrats, though he did take enough interest in campus life to join the *Harvard Crimson.* "The fact of the matter is," he later told his aide and confidant, Theodore Sorensen, "I fiddled around at Choate and really didn't become interested until the end of my sophomore year at Harvard."*

But even as he became more serious about his studies, Kennedy remained ideologically uncommitted. One of his political science professors, Arthur Holcombe, observed: "He had no interest in causes, his approach was that of a young scientist in a laboratory." When in his junior year he wrote a paper on a politician, he chose as his subject an obscure New York Republican and outspoken foe of the New Deal, one Bertrand H. Snell, whose career he analyzed with clinical objectivity.

The most conspicuous evidence of young Kennedy's intellectual invigoration was his senior thesis at Harvard, which analyzed the reasons for England's failure to prepare itself against Hitler. The work reflected the twenty-three-year-old author's by now characteristic detachment; he criticized those who had been overemotional in reacting to Munich. With his father's encouragement and vigorous assistance, the thesis was transformed into a book. One of Joe Kennedy's friends, Arthur Krock of the *New York Times*, gave the young author tips on rewriting and a catchy title: *Why England Slept*; another prominent friend, Henry Luce, wrote the foreword. *Why England Slept* made the best-seller list, but managed to avoid taking a clear position on U.S. aid to Britain.

His political career started down the same non-ideological path. When he made his maiden run for Congress in 1946, voters seemingly had "had enough" with the New Deal, as the Republican campaign slogan contended, and the young candidate was taking no chances. While promising to bring his district the benefits of government activism—housing, Social Security, and medical care—he nevertheless termed himself "a fighting conservative."

Ideology did not matter as much as Kennedy's own resources in winning that contest. First he made good use of his renown as a war hero, having survived the sinking of the PT 109, the torpedo boat he had commanded in the Pacific. In addition, he used his family's myriad con-

---

* Sorensen notes: "Some might say he fiddled around as a Congressman and really didn't become interested until his sophomore year in the Senate."

tacts in the Boston political world, lavishly dispensed his father's wealth, and profited from the energy of the friends and relatives who campaigned for him.

In the longer term, though, what was significant about that election was unspoken at the time. By running as a Democrat, Kennedy had made a commitment to the party and to its long tradition of government activism. "There is a straight and logical stream in the party from William Jennings Bryan through Woodrow Wilson to Franklin Roosevelt and Harry Truman," Leon H. Keyserling, a New Deal economist who served both Roosevelt and Truman, has pointed out. Now Kennedy had joined that line and as he climbed to the top of the political ladder, he would adapt that tradition in his own way.

These broader interests took time to develop, though. In his early years in the House, Kennedy was primarily concerned with solidifying his hold on his seat so he could make plans for a run for the Senate.

On domestic policy, the young Congressman followed the Democratic White House on most issues, opposing cuts in school lunches and supporting broader Social Security benefits. In foreign affairs, Kennedy, reflecting the feelings of his constituents and the influence of his father, was intensely concerned with the menace of communism. He took the House floor to denounce Truman for the loss of China. And at an informal Harvard seminar in 1950 he voiced both his admiration for Senator Joseph McCarthy and his satisfaction with Richard Nixon's victory over Senator Helen Gahagan Douglas, whom Nixon's supporters had dubbed "the pink lady."

To some liberals the young Congressman sounded ominously like his father. After serving FDR as the first chairman of the Securities and Exchange Commission and later as wartime ambassador to Britain, Joseph Kennedy, Sr., had broken with the New Deal at the end of Roosevelt's second term and moved to the right.

Actually, though, John Kennedy's views were so scattered he was hard to categorize, an ambiguity he took advantage of when he challenged Republican Senator Henry Cabot Lodge in 1952. Lodge, the scion of two of Boston's most prominent Brahmin families, the paragon of a moderate Yankee Republican elitist, and a prime mover behind the Eisenhower candidacy, was already a national figure and thought to be close to invincible in his home state. Kennedy attacked this eminent incumbent from both the left and the right. With his New Dealish-Fair Dealish record, he was able to hold on to the Democratic vote while drawing support from conservative Republicans who resented Lodge for his championship of Eisenhower over their hero, Robert Taft.

Money and personality also contributed heavily to Kennedy's victory in the Senate race, as in the initial House contest six years before. "We're going to sell Jack like soap flakes," his father vowed, and he was as good as his word. Meanwhile, the candidate, his brothers, his sisters, and particularly his mother stumped the state, providing a celebrity attraction to match what one of Kennedy's managers, Lawrence O'Brien, called "the snob appeal" of his Yankee aristocrat opponent. Amid an Eisenhower-led Republican landslide elsewhere in the country, Kennedy toppled Lodge.

Just as the House was a springboard for the Senate, the Senate was a launching pad for the White House. For the first time Kennedy began to deepen his ideological views. These metamorphoses reflected in part political calculation—he wanted the support of liberals and intellectuals for his incipient presidential candidacy—and in part changing times. The menace of communism began fading with Eisenhower's election, allowing Kennedy to soften his once strident attacks on communism.

Beyond that, though, Kennedy showed signs of what impressed Harris Wofford, a liberal lawyer and civil rights advocate who was recruited to help prepare Kennedy for his White House drive, as a "capacity for growth." In 1957 he delivered a much heralded Senate speech calling on the French to negotiate an end to the rebellion then raging in Algeria and urging the U.S. to stop supporting the French effort to crush the revolt. In what was considered bold language at the time, Kennedy warned the Western powers against "abandoning African nationalism to the anti-Western agitators and Soviet agents who hope to capture its leadership."

Kennedy's views on Algeria drew criticism from the Eisenhower Administration, but won him attention and the support of Democratic liberals. It also helped answer the criticism of his Senate record as insubstantial that Kennedy knew would be made when he sought the presidency. Kennedy followed that up with an article in *Foreign Affairs*, in which he called for more balanced U.S. policies in dealing with nationalist demands of the emerging nations and the interests of U.S. allies.

But under pressure from his father, a good friend of Joe McCarthy, he did not attack the Wisconsin senator, and he was the one senator whose vote was not recorded on the Senate roll call to censure him. Later on, Kennedy explained that his reluctance to go on record was because his brother Robert worked for McCarthy and described it "as a personal problem." Whatever the actual reason, it was evidence that on the issue of McCarthyism, one of the most sensitive controversies of the time, Kennedy had not yet mastered the conflicting forces that would shape his ideological stance.

As he mounted his presidential campaign, after his whopping Senate re-election victory in 1958, Kennedy's intelligence and ambition attracted intellectuals to his side, even though his views on many issues were still taking form. In this regard he found use for a potent new political instrument—his religion.

Kennedy and his partisans professed to view his Catholicism as a negative, creating an extra burden in addition to his youth and relative inexperience. And to a degree this was true, particularly among the Catholic leadership of the Democratic party, who, remembering the disastrous 1928 defeat of Al Smith, the first Catholic presidential candidate, feared that another debacle would be a severe blow to their own prestige and power.

Nonetheless, Catholicism was also a potential asset for Kennedy and not just because he would be able to count on massive support from Catholic voters. Perhaps just as important, his religion gave his candidacy a special identity that Kennedy himself felt he badly needed. "I can't afford to sound just like any Senator," he told Theodore Sorensen. The issue of his religion provided that vital difference Kennedy sought; as such, it was a surrogate for the ideological distinction Kennedy had not yet established. What's more, it reached at the hearts of the very liberals who were inclined to mistrust him because of his alleged lack of conviction.

In the general election, Kennedy defeated Nixon much as he had conquered Lodge. He attacked him from the left on domestic issues, and from the right on foreign policy. Shortly after his nomination, Kennedy went back to his hitherto neglected roots in the nourishing liberal earth of the Democratic party. "This contest is not between the vice-president and myself," he declared. "This contest is between the Democratic Party and the Republican Party and in that regard there is no contest." Time and again he declared, proudly quoting Franklin Roosevelt: "Better the occasional faults of a government living in the spirit of charity than the consistent omissions of a government frozen in the ice of its own indifference."

Everywhere he went, Kennedy sought to adapt Roosevelt's legacy and use it to spell out the differences between himself and the Democrats on one hand and Nixon on the other. He reminded voters that proposals he had advocated for federal housing aid and for strengthening the minimum wage and Social Security had all been blocked by GOP opposition. "I think we can do better," he declared.

As long as there are 15 million American families who live in substandard housing, as long as the average wage for laundrywomen . . . is 65 cents

. . . as along as 17 million Americans . . . live on an average Social Security check of less than $78 a month . . . as long as there is unfinished business before our country, I think there is need for our party.

Still, because of Kennedy's previous ideological detachment, many voters had difficulty distinguishing between him and Nixon, to the point that Arthur Schlesinger, Jr., a Kennedy supporter and adviser, felt the need to write a book to point up the differences.* At that, his opus turned out to be unconvincing. For two thirds of the book Schlesinger dwelled on the differences of style between the two men, concluding: "The hard fact is that Nixon lacks taste."

Meanwhile the candidate and his advisers were concerned about opinion surveys that showed that foreign policy was their candidate's most serious weakness—both because of Nixon's presumed greater experience and also the Democrats' reputation for being soft on communism. Kennedy responded by blaming the incumbent Republican administration for allowing "a missile gap" to develop,† for permitting Castro to seize power in Cuba, and for not rolling back the Iron Curtain in Europe.

Apart from political expediency, Kennedy was motivated by his belief in the need for government activism of some sort. Abroad, as at home, the promise of his campaign was "to get America moving again."

No matter what he said, many voters found the idea of a Kennedy presidency difficult to accept. His credentials were slim and the fact that he was only forty-three made him seem callow and opportunistic. On the morning after the election, when it finally became clear to us on the *Miami News*, where I was then working, that he had indeed eked out a narrow victory over Nixon, the news editor suggested a headline that would have summed up the widespread doubts about his candidacy and his presidency: "It's a Boy!"

Such scoffing, however, overlooked Kennedy's essential nature as a leader: his capacity for growth which had impressed people like Harris Wofford and was a product of his pragmatic ideology, rational values, and disciplined nature. Kennedy's ideological ripening, which had begun in the Senate and quickened during the general election as he learned to make use of his party's legacy, accelerated even more under the stern pressures of the presidency.

Three principles would emerge as the hallmarks of Kennedy's ideological approach, all of which were evident in his response to the Cuban missile crisis and his drive to gain a nuclear test treaty with the Soviets.

---

* *Kennedy or Nixon: Does It Make Any Difference?* New York: Macmillan, 1960.
† A gap Kennedy acknowledged after the election had never existed. Sorensen claimed the charge had been based on miscalculation.

The first was the definition of an issue in terms that the public readily understood. Second was the establishment of realistic goals, taking into account the position of his adversaries. And finally, the commitment of presidential prestige and popularity to the struggle to attain these goals.

This approach was short on dogma but long on reason. Most important, these principles helped Kennedy, unlike Eisenhower, not only to understand the political realities of the challenges his leadership faced, but to take advantage of them. Much of this was the product of Kennedy's educational background and his ability to absorb information and analyze events. But the young chief executive's ideological development reflected not only his intellect, but also his values and character.

VALUES

Rich and powerful as he was, Joseph Kennedy, Sr., never stopped striving for more wealth and power. This drive for success became one of John Kennedy's principal values. This was tempered, though, by another important value, the respect for civility and rationalism that he acquired from his social relationships and education.

For the Eisenhower family, the drive to succeed was spurred by their mean economic circumstances. For the Kennedy family, money was a subject they did not need to think about and that the elder Kennedy did not even allow to be discussed at the dinner table. Consequently, the Kennedy children grew up with a strange innocence of money; hearing them talk about it, a friend once said, was "like listening to nuns talk about sex."

As he grew older, John Kennedy faced a problem that money did not solve: class snobbery as practiced by Boston Brahmins. When Kennedy was a youngster, the Boston papers had a social section for the Irish that was separate from the one that covered the Yankee upper crust. His father was refused membership in exclusive clubs, snubbed in the state's resort towns, and the local papers—in the city that his father-in-law Honey Fitz had governed as mayor—would not list his daughters among the season's debutantes. Fed up with being called Irish, Joe Kennedy once said, "I was born here. My children were born here. What the hell do I have to do to be an American?" This consciousness of prejudice drove the father and his sons harder to gain the success needed to overcome it.

From the start, Joseph Kennedy insisted that his male offspring rise to the top of whatever field of endeavor they tackled. When his sons raced on Nantucket Sound he followed them in another boat, shouting out their errors on a bullhorn and making notes for later instruction sessions. Like the legendary football coach Vince Lombardi, he believed that "winning isn't everything, it's the only thing" and told his sons, "Second place is failure." When his boys did not meet his expectations, they were banished to the kitchen for their meals.

When Jack, then a senior at Choate, acknowledged in a letter that "I have been bluffing myself about how much real work I have been doing" and resolved to do better, the senior Kennedy responded:

> Now Jack, I don't want to give the impression that I am a nagger, for goodness knows I think that is the worst thing any parent can be. After long experience in sizing up people I definitely know you have the goods and you can go a long way. Now aren't you foolish not to get all there is out of what God has given you. . . . It is very difficult to make up fundamentals that you have neglected when you were very young and that is why I am always urging you to do the best you can.

Like many men of his ilk, Joseph Kennedy was often guilty of stretching the truth, but never further than when he wrote in his 1936 campaign book, *I'm for Roosevelt*: "I have no political ambitions for myself or for my children." As his biographer, Richard Whalen, has written: "Wealth, power and the chance of greatness for his name were the lifelong ambitions of Joseph Patrick Kennedy. The first two goals he achieved to an awesome degree; the last, which came fleetingly within his grasp, eluded him. From early on he saw in his sons a chance to redeem that part of his dream.

Initially his eldest, Joseph P. Kennedy, Jr., was the cynosure of his hopes for political greatness. But after Joe was killed in World War II, his father transferred the mantle to Jack, telling him with characteristic bluntness: "I told [Jack] Joe was dead and that it was his responsibility," he later recalled. John Kennedy himself said later that "wanted" was not strong enough to describe his father's feeling about his second oldest son entering politics: "He demanded it."

In his high-handed, often ruthless determination to achieve wealth, power, and recognition from the American elite, Joe Kennedy often violated the standards to which this group adhered and which had been instilled in John Kennedy. The son had as much ambition as the father could wish, but his father's conduct stiffened his aversion to excessive behavior and encouraged him to restrain his own aggressive instincts. From this was fostered one of his hallmark values, rationality.

Sorensen was struck by Kennedy's ability "to look at his own strengths and weaknesses with utter detachment." For Kennedy detachment was an extension of his rationality. He even viewed his religion with a measure of detachment. "How do you come out on all this?" he once asked a Catholic friend as they were passing a church. The friend said he had not really thought it through, but that generally speaking he was uncertain about the teachings the church presented as eternal verities. That was about how he felt, Kennedy remarked.

Kennedy prided himself on his ability to learn and adjust his thinking. "We all learn from the time you are born to the time you die," he said in 1960. "Events change . . . conditions change and . . . you would be extremely unwise . . . to pursue policies that are unsuccessful."

Indeed, Kennedy was remote to the point that it became a potential liability. James MacGregor Burns, in a generally sympathetic biography, questioned whether the newly elected president had the necessary qualities to inspire and command, contending that "he seemed so dispassionate, so level-headed, indeed so disdainful of dramatics." The most Burns would grant was that "it is by no means so clear that Kennedy lacks commitment."

Though earlier in his career Kennedy did not object to such characterizations, as president he grew weary of the criticism and saw its potential for causing political damage. The new president and the First Lady were both "irritated" by Burns's assessment, noted Sorensen. "Burns seems to feel," Kennedy told Sorensen, "that unless somebody overstates or shouts to the top of their voice they are not concerned about a matter."

In the long run, Kennedy benefited from both his principal values—his drive for success and his rationalism. His ambition impelled him to Congress, to the Senate, and then to the presidency at the earliest age in history. And once he got there, his rationalism, combined with the self-discipline that marked his character, greatly enhanced his ideological outlook and strengthened his leadership.

CHARACTER

The principal feature of Kennedy's character was a self-discipline shaped by his upbringing and also by his chronic bad health. This trait reinforced his adherence to rationality as a value and helped him to control himself and to deal with events beyond anyone's control.

This self-control was conspicuously marred by his sexual promiscuity for most of his life, including the presidential years. Since this behavior was not generally known at the time, it had little impact on his ability to generate support among the citizenry. The reasons for this hidden behavior are not clear, but they are worth exploring for the light they shed on the public man.

The roots of Kennedy's self-discipline are easier to find, starting with his parents. "I grew up in a very strict house," he once said. "There were no free riders and everyone was expected to give their best to what they did. There was a constant drive for self-improvement."

Joe Kennedy did not hit his children. He did not need to. "His eyes would take you right out of the window," a family friend recalled. Even in his absence, his letters kept up the pressure. "Don't let me lose confidence in you again, because it will be pretty nearly an impossible task to restore it," he warned young Jack after the boy had fallen down in his grades at school.

His mother, Rose, was no slouch as a disciplinarian, either. Writing to a daughter-in-law about a grandson, she said: "The reason I am sometimes reluctant about extra goodies for the children is that I read once that youngsters should get used to a few disappointments or jolts when they are young. They thus build up an immunity against them, so that when they encounter life's vicissitudes when they are older . . . they can take them with a smile."

What Jack Kennedy needed immunity against more than disappointment was the physical problems that plagued him throughout his life, including both sports and wartime injuries. At Choate he was absent due to illness more than any boy in his class. At Harvard he cracked a leg bone and ruptured a spinal disk. PT 109's collision with a Japanese destroyer aggravated an old college back injury, and he also developed malaria while he was in the service and his weight dropped to 125 pounds.

After he returned to civilian life he was afflicted by Addison's disease, making him vulnerable to other infections. After he entered the Senate he twice underwent life-threatening back surgery. "At least half the days he spent on this earth were days of constant pain," his brother Robert wrote. "We used to laugh about the risk a mosquito took in biting Jack Kennedy—with some of his blood the mosquito was almost sure to die." The physical suffering and his consciousness of the threat posed to his life combined to produce in Kennedy a disciplined self-confidence and an ability to laugh at himself.

These traits worked to his benefit in politics and in the presidency. They certainly aided his adjustment to the often unreasonable demands of the campaign trail. "He learned the art of swiftly getting down from the speaker's stands into a crowd for handshaking instead of being trapped by a few eager voters behind the head table," recalled Theodore Sorensen of his drive for the presidential nomination. "He learned to pause when trails whistled or airplanes flew over—to laugh when a tray of dishes crashed (or as in one hall, when the flag fell practically on him)—and to shout when the amplifying system broke done (once bellowing into the microphone just as it became operative again)."

As chief executive he was able to control his temper and to respond to provocation with disarming humor and restraint. At his first meeting with Khrushchev in Vienna in June 1961, in the midst of one of the periodic crises over Berlin, he stayed cool in the face of the Soviet ruler's attempt to bully him. Noting the Lenin peace medal that Khrushchev was proudly wearing, Kennedy said, "I hope you get to keep it."

When the two men talked alone in a garden, Kennedy aide David Powers watched from a window and observed Khrushchev stalking around in circles, shaking his finger at Kennedy, while the president seemed unperturbed. Later, Powers asked Kennedy how he managed to remain so calm.

"What did you expect me to do?" Kennedy asked. "Take off one of my shoes and hit him over the head with it?"

As for Kennedy's sexual activity, it may be as his court historian, Arthur Schlesinger, Jr., has contended that the accounts of Kennedy's illicit behavior are greatly exaggerated. "If half the claims were true," Schlesinger wrote in a retrospective on the New Frontier, "he would have had time for little else." In any case, Schlesinger testifies that based on his own experience in the White House, "if anything untoward happened at all, it did not interfere with Kennedy's conduct of the presidency."

But that claim begs a larger issue. The revelations of Kennedy's sexual athleticism in the White House, even Schlesinger admits, created "disappointment edging into bitterness, resentment bordering on rage," among those who had accepted Camelot at face value and had pursued the high-minded causes the Kennedy legend had helped to foster. The macho standards disclosed to have governed Kennedy's life and his presidency contravened the qualities of moralism and idealism that he purported to represent.

More fundamentally, there was a glaring contradiction between the control Kennedy took pride in imposing upon himself and his behavior, which at the least involved the risk of exposure and serious damage to his reputation. The evidence is that the tension between these two modes of conduct was a major force in Kennedy's life before and during his presidency.

Some biographers have suggested that Kennedy's strong sexual drive was intensified by the cortisone shots he received for Addison's disease. Another theory advanced is that Kennedy, having been advised by a British doctor that he would probably die before he reached the age of forty, was determined to make the most of the years remaining to him.

Yet another possible explanation is that Kennedy simply used sex as a distraction from the considerable physical pain he suffered much of the time. This may well have been the case with his most notorious paramour, Judith Campbell, with whom he conducted a steamy affair before he learned of her ties to organized crime. Her visits to Kennedy, by her own account, were concentrated in the summer of 1961 when Kennedy was in great physical discomfort from a back injury he had suffered in the spring as well as a severe viral infection.

In his memoir of the Kennedy presidency, Theodore Sorensen suggested that Kennedy had adopted this rationalization during his first year in the Senate. He wrote:

> Having borne more pain and gloom than he liked to remember, he enjoyed in his bachelor days carefree parties and companions on both sides of the Atlantic Ocean. There was a natural temptation to spend the limited number of days in which he could count on enjoying full health in pursuit of pleasure as well as duty.

In a sense Kennedy's clandestine sexual activities were akin to the public demonstrations of machismo he indulged in as president. For example, shortly after Christmas of 1961 Kennedy was invited to attend a rally of the remnants of the ill-fated Bay of Pigs invasion brigade in Miami's Orange Bowl. Though warned not to attend, Kennedy went anyway and when presented with the combat banner the brigade had borne into combat he incautiously vowed, "This flag will be returned to this brigade."

Even his faithful aide Kenneth O'Donnell conceded afterward that "diplomatically it was the worst possible gesture that a President of the United States could have made at the time."

Nevertheless, O'Donnell added that as the president's brother Robert, who had suggested that he attend the event, expected, "it did John F. Kennedy a lot of internal good. He came back to the White House to start the New Year in a much happier frame of mind."

John and Robert Kennedy might have justified the president's sexual activities on the same grounds as his bellicose rhetoric—that it did him "a lot of internal good."

Sorensen, the president's closest aide, did not advert to Kennedy's womanizing in his memoir, though he must surely have been aware of it. Yet he did write that in 1953 it seemed to him "that an inner struggle was being waged for the spirit of John Kennedy—a struggle between the political dilettante and the statesman, between the lure of luxury and lawmaking."

Of course, as we now know, this contest continued well beyond 1953. But the record suggests that the statesman had the upper hand over the dilettante. There is no evidence that John Kennedy's pursuit of pleasure in the White House interfered with his meeting the obligations of his office, or in any way clouded his judgment when he faced his severest test as president.

THE CHALLENGE

The challenge facing Kennedy was to lessen the danger of nuclear war without weakening the U.S. position in the world.

When Kennedy entered the White House, U.S.–Soviet relations were at a crossroads. The improvement that had begun under President Eisenhower had been halted, if not reversed, as a result of the disclosure of the U-2 flights and the resulting torpedoing of the Paris summit conference in June 1960. Potential flash points for an explosion between the two great powers were spread across the globe, from Indochina to the Congo to Berlin.

No place was more dangerous, though, than Cuba. Castro's proclamation that he was a Marxist-Leninist shortly after his rise to power changed the power balance that had prevailed since the death of Stalin and created an irresistible opportunity for Khrushchev.

Kennedy's attitude toward Moscow was shaped by the conflict between his intellectual grasp of the realities determining relations between the two superpowers and his anticommunist instincts. On one hand, the new president was looking for a way to break away from the stale dialectic that governed Cold War diplomacy. His rationalism rejected the light-versus-darkness view of the conflict reflected in the Eisenhower Administration's policies. The rhetoric of John Foster Dulles, according to Schlesinger, "bored him."

In the campaign, however, Kennedy had taken a hard line, particularly on Cuba. Along with blaming the incumbent GOP administration for a missile gap that he soon had to acknowledge did not really exist, candidate Kennedy had held the Eisenhower Administration responsible for Castro's coming to power. In the campaign debates he taunted Nixon for not taking action against Castro. Those "who say they will stand up to Mr.

Khrushchev," Kennedy declared, "have demonstrated no ability to stand up to Mr. Castro."

On the other side of the Curtain, Khrushchev's views, like Kennedy's, were a mixed bag. The Soviet leader welcomed a change in administrations after the stalemate that had developed after the U-2 episode. On the other hand, Khrushchev clearly saw a chance to score some points against a new and untested adversary.

On January 6, 1961, two weeks before Kennedy was sworn in, Khrushchev gave what the president-elect's advisers regarded as a truculent speech, declaring that Marxists took "a most favorable attitude" toward wars of "national liberation," which he defined as uprisings by colonial peoples against their oppressors.

Kennedy struck back in kind, reverting to the harsh rhetoric of his campaign. In his inaugural speech, he pledged that the U.S. would "pay any price, bear any burden to assure the survival and success of liberty." Ten days later in his first State of the Union address Kennedy issued this ominous warning: "Each day the crises multiply. Each day their solution grows more difficult. Each day we draw nearer the hour of maximum danger."

Soon thereafter, in April 1961, Kennedy faced the first direct challenge to his resolve at the Bay of Pigs. The ensuing failure was made all the more bitter that it was not Khrushchev who had instigated the fiasco, but Kennedy himself, who permitted the insurgent invasion plans hatched in the Eisenhower Administration to go forward with his approval.

The underlying reasons for the debacle were linked to Kennedy's ambivalence about the most effective way to deal with the threat of communism. His campaign rhetoric, reinforced by his inaugural and State of the Union speeches, made calling off the invasion politically difficult. Moreover, he allowed himself to get personally involved, permitting, as Sorensen noted, "his own deep feeling against Castro . . . to overcome his innate suspicions."

He was also absorbed by the opportunity he saw for a victory over communism early in his presidency. "He wanted [the scheme] to work and allowed himself to be persuaded that it would work," McGeorge Bundy, his national security adviser, said later. Then, too, Kennedy's thinking was influenced by the element of macho pride in his character. "I know everybody is grabbing their nuts on this," he told Sorensen beforehand, but he himself, the president said, would not be "chicken."

The lessons Kennedy learned from his blunder reinforced his adherence to reason and logic, which was the greatest strength of his presidency. His key mistake had been to accept the advice of supposed experts, some with narrow points of view, without seriously challenging them.

From then on he realized that a president must seek a broad range of counsel and in the final analysis trust his own judgment.

Still, Kennedy deserved credit—and got it—for taking the blame for the debacle. "There is an old saying that victory has one hundred fathers and defeat is an orphan," he said. "I'm the responsible officer of this government and that is quite obvious." This won him the admiration of the public—his standing in the polls soared—and he gained confidence in his political strength and judgment.

The lessons of the Bay of Pigs appeared not to sink in immediately. For a while the internal conflict continued between Kennedy's inclination toward aggressiveness and his new rationale for dealing with the Soviets that was emerging from his experience. He set in motion Operation Mongoose, the CIA's largest covert operation, designed to harass Castro and undermine his government. Meanwhile the CIA pressed efforts to assassinate Castro, ones that had begun during the Eisenhower presidency and would continue to 1965. Though Robert Kennedy later claimed his brother was unaware of these operations, to some extent at least he bore responsibility.

As time passed and he encountered such danger spots as Berlin and Laos, Kennedy gained a better sense of his foes and his advisers. Gradually he reached the more mature viewpoint he exhibited in the Cuban missile crisis.

The critical element in his handling of this episode was his ability to understand it as mainly a political rather than a military problem. It was thus susceptible to the reasonableness that governed his approach to politics. "The management of the crisis was not primarily nuclear," McGeorge Bundy said later. Instead, he pointed out what was required was "the development of a diplomatic and political position which could be set forth in a presidential speech," which was the course Kennedy followed.

To be sure, the threat of military action was part of Kennedy's political approach to the missile crisis, but the threat never became reality. Kennedy was able to defend and even advance the interests of the United States without resorting to armed conflict, which made his success all the more significant.

The political implications of the missile crisis were far-reaching, extending from the 1962 midterm election campaign, then entering its climactic phase, to the arena of international power politics. In the campaign, Republican strategists had declared that Cuba would be "the dominant issue of the 1962 campaign." In Indiana, right-wing Republican Homer Capehart, seeking another term, called for an immediate invasion. Republican Senator Kenneth Keating of New York, though not up for re-election, dramatized the issue by issuing a series of specific warnings that the Soviets were installing offensive missiles in Cuba, all of which the administration denied. Both houses of Congress passed a joint resolution pledging to use any means, including military force, to keep Cuba from being a threat to the U.S.

Trying to help Democratic candidates fend off the Republican barrage, Kennedy denied the presence of offensive weapons in Cuba. And the president promised to "act" if Cuba should gain the capacity to attack the United States.

All of this served to establish the presence of missiles in Cuba as a national political issue. When Kennedy showed Kenneth O'Donnell the first U-2 photos of the Soviet missile sites, he said bitterly, "We've just elected Capehart in Indiana and Ken Keating will probably be the next President of the United States."

But what was at stake was far more important than the particular number of House and Senate seats and perhaps governorships, too (Richard Nixon was trying to mount a comeback, running for governor of California that fall) that the Democrats stood to lose. "I just don't think there was any choice, if you hadn't acted, you would have been impeached," Robert Kennedy told his brother after the key decisions had been made. Kennedy himself responded: "That's what I think—I would have been impeached."

That may have been an overstatement. But it is no exaggeration to suggest that if the existence of missiles in Cuba had become public knowledge, as it almost certainly would have, and Kennedy had failed to act, then his credibility on national security issues would have been crippled and his potential for leadership undermined.

As far as the global balance of power was concerned, Sorensen acknowledged afterward that it would not have been substantively altered by the presence of the missiles in Cuba. But he added, "That balance would have been altered *in appearance*; and in matters of national will and world leadership, as the president said later, such appearances contribute to reality" (Sorensen's italics). If the Soviets had gotten away with their demarche, as Kennedy later said, it would "materially . . . and politically change the balance of power" between the two great adversary states.

In a broad range of ways Kennedy's response to the Cuban missiles contrasted with his handling of the Bay of Pigs, and reflected the more mature approach to ideological strategy that he had developed—establishing realistic goals, defining the issue in terms the public could understand, and finally committing his prestige to achieving his objective.

Before he made his own decisions as to what the objectives of U.S.

policy should be, he took into consideration the perspective of the Soviets. At the start of the deliberations of the Executive Committee of the National Security Council, or ExCom, Kennedy let his advisers concentrate on developing the strategic options for the U.S. while he himself examined the reasons underlying Soviet actions. While he did not, of course, draw a firm conclusion on Khrushchev's motives, by viewing the crisis from the Russian viewpoint, he gained a far more balanced outlook than he had during the Bay of Pigs.

For example, he agreed when national security adviser Bundy pointed out that Kennedy's warning issued in September that he would act against offensive missiles had come too late for Khrushchev, who probably had made his commitment to Castro in June. "Maybe our mistake was in not saying something *before* this summer," which would have warned the Soviets off, he said (original emphasis).

Another move that helped the president in setting forth U.S. aims in the crisis was his establishment of ExCom itself to provide him with analysis and recommendations. ExCom's fifteen members, some from the State and Defense departments and from the Joint Chiefs of Staff, gave the president far broader input than he had received from the Bay of Pigs advisory team, which represented only the CIA and the Joint Chiefs.

Moreover, by giving this responsibility to such a broad group—reflecting what one Kennedy adviser called "all the different viewpoints, constituencies and centers of expertise"—Kennedy was helping to develop a consensus within the highest ranks of the government and among other influential Washington insiders who shape opinion. Thus he was assured that his actions would have widespread support from the governing elite, which would certainly help in fostering public support.

His willingness to seek the views of others, though, did not mean that anyone ever doubted who was in charge. "I am the responsible officer of this government," Kennedy had said after the Bay of Pigs. In dealing with Castro's missiles, he shouldered that responsibility from the beginning.

"The President was . . . determined to manage the crisis himself—and he did so, in all its exquisite detail," recalled Roger Hilsman, head of intelligence for the State Department. "There was not going to be any possibility for someone down the line to push events any faster or further than he judged necessary."

Though after the first session the president was often absent on other necessary business, his brother Robert was always a strong, persuasive presence. At several points when the ExCom deliberations began heading on a different course from the one Kennedy had charted, he lost no time in curbing that waywardness. But he generally did this in a way that preserved the group's reason for existence and avoided affront to its members.

Thus, when ExCom seemed inclined to endorse a surprise air strike over the idea of a blockade, which Kennedy himself had apparently already decided upon, he simply asked for more discussions and more options. And late in the crisis, when the Soviets shot down a U-2 plane and killed its pilot, Kennedy backed away from a previous pledge to launch a retaliatory air strike.

Leaving on a previously scheduled campaign trip, just before his public address to the nation, Kennedy told his brother, "If you have any trouble [with ExCom members] call me and I'll call off the trip and come back and talk to them." When Kenneth O'Donnell asked what would he do if he could not get a consensus, Kennedy replied, "I'll make my own decision, anyway." Then he recounted the familiar tale about Abraham Lincoln's handling of his cabinet—as the story goes, after the cabinet had voted unanimously in favor of some controversial measure, Lincoln cast a solitary nay and then declared, "The no's have it."

On the final Saturday of the crisis, Robert Kennedy later reported "almost unanimous agreement that we had to attack early the next morning with bombers and fighters and destroy the SAM sites." But the president wanted to give Khrushchev time to deal with his own hardliners. "It isn't the first step that concerns me but both sides escalating to the fourth and fifth step—and we don't want to go to the sixth because there is no one around to do so."

Moreover, Kennedy took upon himself the critical task of defining the crisis for the public—and at the same time put his full prestige behind the goals he had established. After a week of secrecy to ensure time to come to a decision and to preserve the initiative in the confrontation with Khrushchev he made a candid and dramatic address. Setting forth the risks and laying out the U.S. position, he strove to rally support without causing panic or stirring up a jingoist atmosphere he would not be able to control.

First he pointed out the danger: The missiles, capable of striking at Washington or "another city in the southeastern part of the United States," represented "an explicit threat to the peace and security of all the Americas." He stated a clear, specific, and limited objective: "the withdrawal or elimination" of the missiles. Then he laid out his plan for action, including the blockade, the threat of nuclear retaliation against the Soviet Union, but also the use of diplomatic pressure through both the Organization of American States and the United Nations.

Even at this tense moment he left the door open for negotiations with Khrushchev, calling upon the Soviet leader "to join in an historic effort to end the perilous arms race and to transform the history of man."

Finally, realizing that the most effective way of gaining political support for an objective is to enlist the citizenry in the cause, he challenged Americans to respond to the crisis. "This is a difficult and dangerous effort on which we have set out," he said, adding that "many months of sacrifice and self-discipline lie ahead."

That night, October 27, the day after Barney Collier had called our home, his wife and sons were with us in Maplewood, sitting in front of the fireplace, twenty-three miles from ground zero. We tried to relax, but it was difficult to ignore the tension, even though none of us talked about Cuba and missiles. Barney was still at *Time*'s offices in Manhattan. He called once, to talk to his wife, and to tell us that from what he could learn from the Washington bureau, both the Soviets and the U.S. were still hanging tough.

That same night, President Kennedy sent his brother to meet with the Soviet ambassador, Anatoly Dobrynin.

Robert Kennedy told Dobrynin that the president did not want war, but that he wanted the missile bases removed. If the Soviets did not accede, Kennedy said, "we would remove them." The president had just sent Khrushchev a letter, Kennedy added, offering assurances that the U.S. would not invade Cuba if the missiles were withdrawn.

What would the U.S. do about its own Jupiter missile bases in Turkey, which the Soviet Union regarded as a thorn in its side, Dobrynin wanted to know.

Robert Kennedy chose his words carefully. "There could be no quid pro quo or any arrangement made under this sort of pressure," he said. But then he told Dobrynin something quite helpful.

"President Kennedy had been anxious to remove those missiles from Turkey and Italy for a long period of time," Robert Kennedy pointed out. "He had ordered their removal some time ago, and it was our judgment that within a short time after this crisis was over, those missiles would be gone." He returned to the White House to meet with his brother. "The President was not optimistic, nor was I," he recalled.

The president ordered to active duty twenty-four Air Force Reserve troop carrier squadrons. They would be needed for a U.S. invasion of Cuba.

On Sunday morning, keeping a promise to his daughters, Robert Kennedy took them to a horse show at the Washington Armory. It was there, about ten o'clock, that he got word that Khrushchev had agreed to pull the missiles out of Cuba.

In Maplewood, the news came over the radio while we were having a late breakfast. Almost immediately Barney Collier called to tell his wife it was safe for her to return to ground zero.

I took my own daughter for a walk. It was a crisp fall day, and the air had never seemed fresher, the sun never brighter.

I wondered what President Kennedy would do now in his moment of triumph. Just as the missile confrontation itself had been a test of his leadership, so was its successful outcome. It was a famous victory for him, as it would have been for any president. But he made the impact of his success more significant by the way he accepted it.

Instead of humiliating Khrushchev, he was magnanimous, welcoming the Soviet leader's "statesmanlike decision" to withdraw the missiles. Moreover, as one of his advisers recalled, he "cautioned the members of his Administration against any tendency to gloat or claim a victory." This permitted Khrushchev to avoid disgrace, to retain his position at the Kremlin, and eventually to move closer to an agreement on arms.

Despite the general public acclaim for the denouement of the missile crisis, Kennedy still endured criticism from both left and right, which served as reminders of the difficulties in charting a rational course in the Cold War. Liberals charged that Kennedy had unnecessarily risked nuclear war to solve a problem that they argued had more political than military dangers. Some accused him of trying to protect his party in the congressional elections.

Conservatives were more outspoken. Richard Nixon, himself recently defeated in his race for governor of California, said that by not using military might to liberate Cuba, Kennedy "enabled the U.S. to pull defeat out of the jaws of victory." Within Kennedy's own party, hawks such as Dean Acheson contended, "So long as we had the thumbscrew on Khrushchev, we should have given it another turn every day."

Nevertheless, Kennedy now felt freer than before to seek ways to reduce the risk of nuclear collision between the two superpowers. In accord with his ideological strategy he once again began by selecting a realistic goal—a test-ban treaty with the Soviet Union.

Efforts to limit nuclear arms had been politically controversial from the dawn of the nuclear age, but in 1956 Democratic presidential nominee Adlai Stevenson broke new ground by proposing a limited test ban as part of his campaign. The idea survived his unsuccessful candidacy, for in 1960, platforms of both parties called for steps to curb nuclear testing.

A test-ban treaty had been on Kennedy's agenda from the start of his presidency, but early talks with the Soviets at Geneva had foundered.

Nuclear testing, which both sides had suspended for three years, was resumed by the Soviets in September 1961 in the atmosphere and by the U.S. underground soon after that.

After the missile crisis, Khrushchev signaled his interest in curbs on nuclear weaponry in the same statement that announced pullout of the missiles from their Cuban sites. Then on December 19 Khrushchev wrote to Kennedy directly, stating that the "time has come now to put an end once and for all to nuclear tests."

Kennedy was just as eager—and also more mindful than ever of the danger of nuclear war. Commenting to Sorensen on the post–missile crisis installation of a hot line between the White House and the Kremlin, he said, "If he fires his missiles at me it is not going to do any good for me to have a telephone at the Kremlin . . . and ask him whether it is really true."

He now directed his newly created Arms Control Agency to focus on the possibility of a limited rather than a comprehensive ban as something that would "be better than nothing." As off-the-record talks went forward, the issue of the number of on-site inspections became the chief obstruction. Kennedy proceeded to pull out all the stops: he dispatched the government's most senior negotiator, Averell Harriman, to Moscow; sent word of his sincerity with magazine editor Norman Cousins; and teamed up with British Prime Minister Harold Macmillan to press his case. In June 1963, Khrushchev sent word of his readiness to resume talks.

Now Kennedy took on the job of defining the test-ban treaty for public debate and shouldered the responsibility of making the case for the accord he sought. In a memorable address at Washington's American University, he made his most ambitious effort to lead the country beyond the rigid formulas of the Cold War and toward a test-ban agreement. It was an eloquent and carefully wrought document. The president touched all the chords essential both to encourage the Soviets toward an agreement and to rally public opinion.

Kennedy sounded a note of hope: "Our problems are man-made . . . therefore they can be solved by man." He conceded error: "Some say that it is useless to speak of world peace . . . until the leaders of the Soviet Union adopt a more enlightened attitude. I hope they do. . . . But I also believe that we must re-examine our own attitude." He underlined the essential reasonableness of his objective: "I speak of peace therefore as the necessary rational end of rational men. I realize that the pursuit of peace is not as dramatic as pursuit of war . . . but we have no more urgent task."

The president proclaimed "a world safe for diversity" as a new goal for American foreign policy: "Our most basic common link is that we all inhabit this small planet. We all breathe the same air. We all cherish our children's future. And we are all mortal."

The Soviet reaction was enthusiastic. A few weeks after the American University address, Khrushchev accepted the U.S. proposal on the number of inspections required to ensure compliance with the agreement, and the treaty was signed in August. But Kennedy still faced a difficult task.

Foes of the treaty rose on both sides of the aisle, including Cold War liberals such as Democratic Senator Henry M. Jackson of Washington as well as right-wing activists. Not one of the Democratic members of the Senate Armed Services committee was even willing to attend the signing ceremony in Moscow.

Once again Kennedy used his prestige and the prerogatives of his office to build support. Seeking to neutralize potential opponents, Kennedy saw to it that former President Eisenhower was briefed early on. Though Eisenhower later expressed reservations about the treaty, he did not flatly oppose it.

Moreover, on the day the treaty was signed, Kennedy addressed the nation on television, making a forceful but realistic argument for the treaty. "This treaty is not the millennium," he said. "But it is an important first step . . . toward peace, a step toward reason, a step away from war. This treaty is for all of us. It is particularly for our children and our grandchildren, and they have no lobby here in Washington." Within two weeks he sent a vigorous message to the Senate calling for ratification, urged approval at every press conference, and endorsed the treaty in the opening minutes of his televised tax-cut speech. His missionary work helped shift public sentiment on the treaty from about fifty-fifty to overwhelming support. The roll call in the Senate was an overwhelming 80 to 19 vote for the treaty.

Afterward, Sorensen complained that the American press largely underplayed the American University speech, in part because it was overshadowed by Kennedy's dramatic civil rights speech the next night. But that was a shortsighted view. In the long run, the two speeches reinforced each other, both conveying the image of a president willing to break new ground and determined to define the presidency as an office where politics could serve the goals of moral leadership. Indeed, Kennedy included in the American University speech a passage relevant to civil rights: "The quality and spirit of our own society must justify and support our efforts abroad. . . . In too many of our cities today, the peace is not secure because freedom is incomplete."

More fundamentally, civil rights, like the nuclear threat, was a crucible that tested the mettle of Kennedy's strongest character trait, his disciplined intelligence, the key to understanding his leadership in the White House. During the first two and a half years of his presidency, his response to the conflict between Negro demands and white resistance in the South developed in a strikingly similar fashion to his reaction to the Cuban challenges. Just as he had been overly bellicose in his campaign rhetoric on communism, he had promised too much on civil rights. No one had been more biting in criticism of Eisenhower's handling of civil rights, and he had made certain that the 1960 Democratic platform contained a strong civil rights plank, in the spirit of the pledges that had helped elect Truman in 1948. Moreover, Kennedy made a point of arguing that Eisenhower had ignored opportunities to issue executive orders against segregation in areas where he did not need to wait for congressional approval. For example, Kennedy contended, the president had the authority to abolish discrimination in federal housing simply, as Kennedy put it, with "a stroke of the pen."

This phrase was to haunt him for the first two years of his presidency. For despite his bold promises, once in office Kennedy dragged his feet on civil rights. Clearly, he had given no more thought to brokering the complexities of the South's racial problems than he had to the implications of deposing Castro. The fact was, despite his campaign rhetoric, he was not personally committed to civil rights. "We didn't lie awake nights worrying about it," Robert Kennedy said later.

Kennedy had no problem finding excuses for his inaction. For starters, he claimed the narrowness of his margin of victory over Nixon limited his options. In private, Kennedy quoted Thomas Jefferson's counsel: "Great innovations should not be forced on slender majorities." Another excuse was Eisenhower's failure to act, which had encouraged the consolidation of Southern resistance. If Kennedy moved precipitously against the South, his advisers argued, he would forfeit the Southern support he needed to enact other items on his legislative agenda.

At the start of his term, therefore, Kennedy offered none of the bold civil rights proposals the Democratic platform had led blacks to expect. He held off for months that "stroke of the pen" to eliminate the racial barriers in federal housing that he had referred to so often in the campaign. And when he did finally sign it, on Thanksgiving Eve of 1962, he did so when his action was likely to attract minimal attention.

Frustrated by Kennedy's inaction, civil rights advocates mailed pens and ink wells to the White House. But in the streets of the South, where blacks had long since lost patience with the Jim Crow strictures that ruled their existence, the civil rights revolt went far beyond such mild symbolic protests. Sit-ins, "freedom rides," bus boycotts, and mass marches led by Martin Luther King, Jr., who charged Kennedy with "tokenism," captured the nation's imagination, but also brought harsh retaliation. Local police backed up the South's segregationist laws with clubs, fire hoses, and dogs. It was the impact of this brutal response, particularly in Birmingham, which King called the nation's most segregated city, that finally provided the impetus for Kennedy to act.

"The civil rights movement should thank God for Bull Connor," Kennedy often said of the Birmingham police commissioner whose brutality stigmatized the entire white South. "He's helped it as much as Abraham Lincoln."

Even before racism reared its violent head in Birmingham, though, bitter experience had made clear to Kennedy the folly of temporizing with the die-hard Southern segregationist leaders. Most notably, he had attempted to placate Mississippi Governor Ross Barnett in 1962, but the net result was an explosion of mob violence in protest over the court-ordered integration of the University of Mississippi.

Just as the Bay of Pigs had instructed Kennedy in the danger of ill-considered action in foreign policy, his encounter with Barnett and similar frustrating experiences drove home the perils of equivocation on civil rights. And just as Khrushchev's incautious missile gamble in Cuba was the pivotal event that led ultimately to the nuclear test-ban treaty, the violence perpetrated by Connor and his ilk in the South was the catalyst that made possible the development of a far-reaching new civil rights policy, unveiled in Kennedy's speech on June 11, 1963.

First, as he had done in responding to the missile challenge, he established clear goals. In the case of civil rights, it was nothing less than the use of federal power to strike down legal defenses of segregation everywhere they existed—in hotels, lunch counters, schoolrooms, offices, and factories. Then he defined the problem, using the most forceful language ever heard from an American president on the subject of race:

> We are confronted primarily with a moral issue. It is as old as the Scriptures and it as clear as the American Constitution. The heart of the question is whether all Americans are to be afforded equal rights and equal opportunities, whether we are going to treat our fellow Americans as we want to be treated.

Finally, Kennedy used his prestige to mobilize public support and the backing of other national leaders, first through the address itself and then in countless meetings with prominent figures in all walks of life. He also personally negotiated a compromise with congressional leaders that made possible House passage of the proposals in December.

Some critics never forgave Kennedy for his long delay, but Martin Luther King, Jr., saw it differently. By waiting until he could clearly show that "he was responding to mass demand" Kennedy ensured what King and other civil rights proponents viewed as most critical in the long run—a favorable environment for the legal attack on racial barriers.

In any event, Kennedy's civil rights program was difficult to pass even with the support of the president and of many Northern whites indignant over the tactics used by Southerners resisting integration. Not until after Kennedy's assassination did the Senate, prodded by Lyndon Johnson to keep faith with the dead president's legacy, enact those measures into law. Nevertheless, it was Kennedy's leadership that created that legacy.

In both challenges—the Cuban missile crisis and civil rights—Kennedy's response was determined by the combination of his character, values, and ideology. His belief in rationality and his inherent self-discipline helped the hitherto unideological Kennedy fashion a fresh ideological approach to two of the nation's most serious problems.

In both cases also Kennedy had been astute enough to draw on relevant parts of the Democratic party legacy—from Stevenson, the test-ban treaty, from Truman, support for civil rights. Moreover, in a broader sense, the foundation for civil rights advances had been prepared by the New Deal of Franklin Roosevelt, whose condemnation of "a government frozen in the ice of its own indifference" Kennedy had quoted so often during his presidential campaign. Kennedy had synthesized these views from the Democratic past with his own, which had significantly matured since his first political campaign. And he restated these beliefs in terms that were relevant to his own times and bore directly on his own presidency.

"Above all, he was motivated by a deep sense of justice and fair play," Sorensen wrote about his fallen chief in explaining his shift on civil rights. But on close examination, politics, in the best and broadest sense of the word, appears to have been Kennedy's main motivation in this case and also with the missile crisis. Kennedy understood that to have accepted the presence of the missiles in Cuba would have emasculated him politically, and destroyed his chances of achieving the activist role in the White House that was steadily evolving in his mind. Similarly, if he had done nothing more than express sympathy over the mistreatment of Negroes in the South, he would have estranged himself from the liberal core of his political base and surrendered his chance to gain access to the full powers of the presidency.

Both these episodes demonstrate the distinctive quality of Kennedy's leadership—the interplay of the self-discipline that marked his character, the rationality that reflected his values, and finally, his ability to adjust his ideology—which enabled him to learn and grow in stature in the White House. Critics contend that he only reacted to events. But he chose which events to react to and he used them to fulfill his own design for his presidency.

In evaluating liberal causes, Kennedy managed to combine commitment with skepticism. Near the end of his foreshortened presidency, he became interested in mounting a major program to aid the poor—what would ultimately become under his successor the War on Poverty. But Kennedy was also mindful of the political risks such an effort involved. A few days before his assassination, he told his chief economic adviser, Walter Heller, that he was "very much in favor" of some sort of anti-poverty program. "But," Kennedy added, "I also think it's important to make it clear that we're doing something for the middle-income man in the suburbs, etc. But the two are not at all inconsistent."

Judging from their responses to their own leadership challenges, Truman and Eisenhower would have been inclined to deal with Kennedy's challenges far differently than he. Truman's natural tendency would have been to act less reflectively and more instinctively. He might have been sorely tempted to use military force against the missiles almost immediately, risking retaliation by Khrushchev but confident that the Soviet leader would back down. And if he had followed past behavior, Truman would have probably pushed for civil rights legislation early on, gambling that the backing he could mobilize would outweigh a possible white backlash.

As for Eisenhower, it is hard to believe that he would have been any quicker or more decisive in dealing with the likes of Bull Connor than he was contending with Governor Faubus. Nor can one imagine him ever making legislative proposals of the breadth that Kennedy offered. In dealing with the missiles, if he followed his tendencies, Eisenhower would have tried to reach a secret agreement with Khrushchev for withdrawal of the missiles rather than stage a public confrontation. Such a behind-the-scenes arrangement might have made it easier for Khrushchev to pull out his weapons by sparing him embarrassment, but it would not have produced any public momentum for a test-ban treaty.

The acid test of Kennedy's ability to lead was one he never fully confronted—Vietnam. It is possible only to speculate on what he would have done, given what is known about Kennedy's views when he died.

We know that two factors controlled Kennedy's thinking on Vietnam—he believed that the U.S. had a commitment to that country, but he was determined to keep that commitment limited. "He preferred to treat the problem of Vietnam as something other than war," Roger Hilsman wrote, "and to avoid getting American prestige so involved that the United States could not accept a negotiated settlement. . . . President Kennedy made it abundantly clear to me on more than one occasion that what he most wanted was to avoid turning Vietnam into an American war."

Some evidence suggests that Kennedy had come to believe that the U.S. had reached the boundaries of that limited commitment. At the same time that he approved a request from the Joint Chiefs of Staff to increase the number of American advisers to 17,000, he made clear that he would grant no more such requests.

Kennedy was well aware of the political dangers of withdrawal. "If I tried to pull out completely now from Vietnam," he explained to Senator Mike Mansfield, who had made an inspection trip to the battle zone at the president's request, "we would have another Joe McCarthy red scare on our hands, but I can do it after I'm reelected. So we had better make damn sure that I *am* reelected."

After Kennedy's death, his secretary of state, Dean Rusk, claimed that to have removed U.S. troops after the 1964 election "would have been a decision to have Americans in uniform in combat for domestic political reasons. No president can do that and live with it." But war and politics, of course, can never be wholly separated. Indeed, the decision to *keep* U.S. troops in Vietnam had already been influenced by political reasons, as Kennedy's conversation with Mansfield makes clear. For Kennedy not to have withdrawn these men, once he became convinced that continued U.S. support for Vietnam would mean an open-ended commitment for more troops, would have fundamentally contradicted the rational approach to ideology he had developed.

Still, we cannot know for sure how changing circumstances might have altered Kennedy's judgment on Vietnam. History dictated that this test be left to his successor, who was a very different sort of leader.

CHAPTER 5

Johnson: LBJ vs. LBJ

In ordinary times a president attending a meeting of the nation's governors would not have been unusual. But the times in July of 1968 were far from ordinary and Lyndon Baines Johnson was certainly no ordinary president. So I had reason to take note when it was disclosed that the principal speaker at the final banquet of the National Governors Conference in Cincinnati would be none less than the thirty-sixth president of the United States.

I was covering the presidential campaign for *Newsweek* then. Along with a good many other reporters I had come to the conference mainly to talk to Republican governors about their party's national convention, which was to open two weeks later in Miami. But I found little to report on that subject: everyone was confident, correctly as it turned out, that Richard Nixon would be nominated. The president's speech at least offered something different.

It had been quite a while since any reporter had seen this president outside the bounds of the White House. For more than a year Johnson had been a virtual prisoner there, hostage to the threat of violence that had become an everyday fact of life in the country he governed. The president was in danger, or so those responsible for his safety believed, from the growing legion of white middle-class youths who raged against the Vietnam War, chanting as they marched: "Hey, hey, LBJ, how many kids did you kill today?" Also to be feared, it was believed, were the black youths whose fury and frustration at the conditions that ruled their lives had time and again these past two years erupted in violence in ghettos from coast to coast.

Lyndon Johnson, who not so long before had won a precedent-shattering election majority, could no longer safely venture out into the country that had given him that victory. His was a stupendous collapse.

No one since FDR had come to the office burning with such programmatic ambition, and even Roosevelt could not match Johnson for the experience he had gained in statecraft in his years on Capitol Hill. This skill was brilliantly demonstrated as he pushed Congress into enacting first the Kennedy legacy of legislative proposals, and then the first installment of his own Great Society agenda. Politics was in his blood; it was both his vocation and his avocation. On one quiet Sunday afternoon in Camp David, when he was supposed to be relaxing, an aide overheard him phoning an old friend in Texas to discuss a local school board race—just to keep his hand in, so to speak.

Johnson's political makeup was marred by a sizable flaw, though. His philosophy was grounded not on conviction but on the need to avoid open conflict and to seek instead what was for Lyndon Johnson the Holy Grail of politics—consensus. On its face, consensus sounds like an attractive, constructive objective, implying the agreement among diverse groups on common goals. But for Lyndon Johnson, consensus meant agreement on *his* goals. His reason for emphasizing it was to drown out rival political ideas and to rally overwhelming support behind his own policies. Rather than relying on consensus as a means of strengthening the political process, as the word suggests, Johnson used it as a tool to manipulate politics.

Johnson's consecration to consensus was a product of his background in Texas, of his career in the Congress, of his values, and of his convoluted character. It was only to be expected, then, that he would rely on consensus when he had to deal with the most severe challenge of his presidency, the conflict between the Vietnam War and the Great Society. But the economic demands and political tensions caused by Vietnam and by Johnson's broad domestic agenda were too great to be reconciled by consensus, and in consequence Johnson tarnished his proud achievements and wrecked his presidency.

In a very personal sense Johnson, then nearly sixty, had become the enemy of those protesting the war and the unkept promises of the Great Society. As their discontent flared on campuses and in cities around the country, a quiet but bitter battle was waged within the president's official family about where he should be allowed to travel.

On one side was the Secret Service, on the other a group of political advisers desperately trying to build support for Johnson's policies. "I thought he was going down in flames unless he did expose himself to the people," Harry McPherson, a Texan who had been a speech writer and general factotum to Johnson since his Senate days, later recalled. "The Secret Service felt just as strongly that he must not go. On the basis of what happened to him politically, I think I was right. On the basis of the fact that he is alive and might well be dead if he had followed my advice, I think they were right."

Johnson had come to the governors' conference in an attempt to revive, in a small way, the prestige that not so long ago had been his on a vast scale. The Secret Service had been persuaded that the surroundings in Cincinnati's Civic Center presented a readily controlled environment. To lure the president from the White House, his remaining allies among the governors and his own aides had connived to gain approval just the day before of a laudatory resolution. It was a modest manifesto that duly expressed the appreciation of the governors to the president "for all his considerations and many courtesies" and for "establishing the best working relationship that has ever existed" between the White House and the governors.

Honoring Lyndon Johnson in such mundane terms, for the sort of achievement in which some city manager might have taken pride, mocked his real accomplishments. This was, after all, a president who had set out to transform the nation's society and had come closer to bringing that off than most people expected. But faint as it may have been, the praise from the governors was more than the president was receiving from any other quarter in that season of discontent.

In his remarks, Johnson sought to treat the matter with tongue in cheek. "You know so many resolutions are just simply empty rhetoric," he told the governors. "But this one deeply impressed me with its poetry and its accuracy and its very great wisdom."

Then suddenly, caught up by the occasion, Lyndon Johnson became the chieftain of old. He proudly reeled off a list of Great Society statistics—30 million children vaccinated, 1.5 million young people given help to pay college tuition, 80,000 acres of beaches and forest land added for the scenic pleasure of the American people. After that, as had long been his custom, he moved on to talk of what remained to be done—of "more than fifty major bills" awaiting action in Congress "which I believe are essential to the well being of the American people."

It was if he had flipped a light switch, so suddenly did he lose the interest of the governors. They had been willing to be polite while he patted himself on the back for his past accomplishments. But in the summer of 1968 they had neither patience nor tolerance for any more of Lyndon Johnson's programs.

The day before the president spoke, governors in both parties attacked a proposal for more federal spending to help the cities. Dependence on government funding, argued Republican George Romney of Michigan, would stop people from helping themselves. Democratic Governor Charles L. Terry of Delaware said, "Hard core unemployed that won't work must be transferred from the dole to work programs." Terry got a hand from his fellow governors when he added, "They say, 'If you don't give it to us, we'll burn and loot.' But I say, 'Make 'em work for it.' "

It was this feeling of these governors, etched in their faces as Lyndon Johnson spoke, not the empty words in their resolution, that represented the true political judgment on Lyndon Johnson's presidency. He had won a great victory in 1964 as the champion of government and had found more ways to put government to work than any other chief executive in history. But now, I realized in watching the governors turn off as he spoke, his presidency had given government a bad name.

The reasons for this had a great deal to do with Lyndon Johnson's political beliefs. These are hard to track because they were not what he said they were or probably even believed them to be.

IDEOLOGY

In Cincinnati, Johnson reiterated for the governors what he had previously stated to be his political philosophy. "First of all, I want to be a free man," he said. "Second, I want to be an American. Third, I want to be a public servant. . . . Fourth, I want to be a Democrat." This was, however, merely a list of goals and values, not a philosophy that outlined a reasonably consistent approach to political thought and actions.

What served Johnson in place of such a philosophy, as a recipe for the power he sought, was his faith in consensus. This was actually a political strategy rather than a system of substantive beliefs, but it was both the goal and engine of Lyndon Johnson's ideology. The benefit of consensus is that it avoids conflict, but since conflict is an inherent part of democratic politics, Johnson's commitment to consensus inevitably led him to distort the political process.

Johnson's quest for consensus meant that he was not satisfied with mere majorities supporting his goals. He felt compelled instead to achieve almost universal accord, or at least to stifle any significant disagreement. Such objectives imposed enormous, unrealistic burdens on Johnson. Even more serious was the harm his pursuit did to the political system. As David Broder has pointed out, the flaws in the consensus strategy are clear from Johnson's most definitive statement on the subject in a speech at the University of Texas early in his presidency. Declaring that "the real voice of America" is one of unified purpose, Johnson continued:

> It is one of the great tests of political leadership to make our people aware of this voice, aware that they share a fundamental unity of interest, purpose and belief. I am going to try to do this. And on the basis of this unity, I intend to try and achieve a broad national consensus which can end obstruction and paralysis and can liberate the energies of the nation for the future. I want a happy nation, not a harassed people.

The trouble is, on only a very few public problems do most Americans share a "fundamental unity of interest, purpose and belief." Ours is a pluralistic society, and in the political system diverse interests compete for the favors of government. Johnson sought consensus to short-circuit this competition.

In every consensus scenario Johnson was always front and center. "To me," Johnson later explained, "consensus meant, first, deciding what needed to be done, regardless of the political implications and, second, convincing a majority of the Congress and the American people of the necessity for doing those things." Johnson himself did nearly all the deciding and nearly all the convincing. As he said, "I pleaded, I reasoned, I argued, I urged, I warned."

As a result, Johnson's persona became the focus of debate. This pattern developed most dramatically, and disastrously, in his attempt to resolve the conflicts between his aim of a Great Society and his determination to deny a communist victory in Indochina.

Johnson's character contributed to his devotion to consensus, but the most direct influence on his political outlook was his long and intense experience with politics, beginning with his boyhood in the Hill Country of Texas and his initial exposure to Populism.

"The People's Party," as the populists billed themselves, was part of Johnson's heritage. His grandfather, Sam Ealy Johnson, ran on the populist ticket for the state legislature. He himself was defeated, but populist candidates running for state office carried the surrounding districts.

In west central Texas, the Hill Country was a natural ground for Populism. Against its thin, unyielding soil and arid climate farmers faced a desperate struggle for survival. Whereas farmers elsewhere complained about the high tariffs charged by railroads and the high interest charged by banks, Hill Country farmers like Sam Johnson had no railroads at all and its banks had precious little money to loan at any rate. Its agrarian base was crushed under the heel of America's rising industrial power before the new century dawned, but its demands for regulation of "the interests" and for government help in redressing the inequities that pervaded the lives of its citizens echoed through the years.

Johnson's father, Sam Ealy, Jr., followed in his father's path to the legislature and still carried the populist torch high when he arrived there in 1918. This was not so with Sam Ealy's grandson—in part because his father's later financial failure led the son to repudiate his principles, in part because Lyndon Johnson was inflamed with ambition on a far grander scale than his forebears.

Still, his populist legacy was to serve Johnson well in the years to come; it provided him with a common political grammar for communicating first with his House constituents and then with broader interest groups. One element of Populism that he embraced wholeheartedly was the use of government to aid people, a concept that the New Deal put vigorously into practice. The coming of the New Deal coincided with the beginnings of Johnson's rise to power in Washington, where he started as a congressional secretary. Even in that lowly post he demonstrated a natural skill at taking advantage of New Deal programs for the benefit of his boss's constituents.

But the other tenets of Populism, which defined democracy in terms of citizens having an active voice in the decisions of government, were always alien to Johnson's fundamental method of operation as it developed during the next three decades in the legislative and executive branches. More important than Populism in shaping Johnson's consensus approach were the tactics required for success by the one-party politics of Texas. Though when convenient to do so Johnson styled himself as a Westerner, his native state was solidly Southern as far as the dominant role of the Democratic party was concerned.

In Texas, as in any part of the Old Confederacy, victory in the Democratic party primary was tantamount to election. When Lyndon Johnson entered politics, and for a good many years after that, the Republican party was of no consequence in the state. This did not mean there were not disagreements and factions in Texas politics. They abounded—between populists and conservatives, ranchers and farmers, oil barons and factory workers. But it served the interests of Johnson and other Democratic party leaders to keep these factions within their own party. That way their differences could be brokered in back rooms rather than fought out publicly in a two-party election.

Thus Johnson learned early in his career to minimize and overlook genuine political disagreements in the interests of keeping all sides within the Democratic party and keeping the Democratic party dominant. For instance, in 1960 the Texas Democratic convention that endorsed Johnson's ill-fated presidential candidacy included a sizable contingent of delegates wearing Nixon for President buttons. No one objected to their presence, and in the 1964 election many of them helped Johnson carry Texas.

In Texas politics, Johnson's own personality and political skills, the driving force behind his consensus, overshadowed disputes over issues. Johnson knew the key party leaders, could convince them that he shared their objectives, and that he was the most able of the competing candidates to achieve them. It made it easier for him that the minorities in Texas as yet lacked the organization and leadership needed to make them a factor in the state's political equation.

By contrast, the limits of consensus were demonstrated by Johnson's unsuccessful run for the presidency in 1960. Minorities and other interest groups who did not matter much in Texas—such as blacks and labor unions—were active and potent in the Democratic presidential nominating process. Moreover, they were concerned with issues that were by their nature divisive rather than with Johnson's achievements.

In this personality-dominated politics the decisive factor was not what a man believed but whom he knew and who owed him favors. The reliance on personal contacts was an important corollary to Johnson's consensus strategy, because it allowed him to avoid open debate on issues that would have marred the appearance of harmony.

The use of personal contacts played a large role in Johnson's rise in Congress, from the beginning of his career in the House in 1937, when a vacancy in the Texas congressional delegation gave him the chance to move up from his assistant's role to a seat of his own. The key to his victory—he defeated six other candidates, several of them far better known than he—was his decision to tie his candidacy to Franklin Roosevelt's policies. Only a few months after FDR won his landslide victory in 1936 over Alf Landon, his prestige had been battered by the negative reaction to his court-packing plan, and several of Johnson's rivals for the House seat were anti-Roosevelt. By going all out for FDR—"A vote for Johnson is a vote for Roosevelt's program," Johnson's campaign posters proclaimed—he established a special identity for his obscure candidacy. His pro–New Deal battle cry struck just the right note in the backwaters and byways of the Hill Country, where support for FDR was overwhelming.

Johnson's campaign tactics not only earned him a House seat, they also gained him a personal relationship with FDR, who helped him get a choice assignment on the House Naval Affairs committee. In addition, the president also opened doors to him among the movers and shakers of the New Deal, from high-ranking officials like Harold Ickes and Harry Hopkins to young lions like Abe Fortas and Jim Rowe. Those contacts and Johnson's own furious energies opened a cornucopia of federal largess for his district—water, electricity, highway credits, and other benefits from a score of New Deal programs.

On the great issues of the time, though, Johnson's performance was a far cry from the promises of his campaign. Though he had based his candidacy around FDR's court-packing scheme, once the election was over he never again voiced his support for the plan. By and large, Johnson made himself into what Rowland Evans and Robert Novak described as "a shadowy, unmemorable figure" in the House. He shied away from introducing or even speaking out for national legislation, thus avoiding the controversy such measures cause.

While other House members inveighed against the "economic royalists" whom Johnson's patron, Roosevelt, had identified as the enemy, Johnson himself was silent. With his eye already fixed on higher goals that required broader backing, Johnson cultivated the consensus support that he would always seek and depend on. He carefully ingratiated himself with colleagues across the ideological spectrum. "We agreed on so many of the big issues," liberal California Democrat Helen Gahagan Douglas told an interviewer. "He basically agreed with the liberals." But his views also jibed with those of right-wing New York Republican Sterling Cole, or so Cole believed. "Politically, if we disagreed, it wasn't apparent to me," he said.

Meanwhile, restless and frustrated by the seniority-dominated House power structure, which he knew would postpone significant advancement for years to come, Johnson pounced on the first Senate vacancy that developed in 1941, but lost a close race. While he waited for another opportunity he shifted his political ground, distancing himself from elements of the New Deal program that had first brought him to elective office. In a December 1942 speech, Johnson ridiculed the New Deal agencies as "old domestic museum pieces" and called for an end to "overstaffed, over-stuffed government that worries along like a centipede."

As the Texas economy changed with the end of World War II, shifting away from its debt-ridden reliance on cotton to the much richer revenues from the booming oil and gas industries, the state shifted to the right and so did Johnson. He established alliances with politically active businessmen and contractors, thereby enhancing his personal financial status. Aided by Lady Bird Johnson's inheritance, he acquired an interest in an Austin radio station which became the foundation of an economic empire that grew at the rate of about $500,000 a year over the next two decades and was estimated at $14 million by the time he entered the White House.

When Roosevelt died, Johnson, after expressing his grief, made a point of underlining his independence from his longtime hero and champion: "Never once in my five terms did he ever ask me to vote a certain way or even suggest it. And when I voted against him—as I have plenty of times—he never said a word." With the far less potent figure of Truman in the White House, Johnson's independence was plain for all to see. He voted for Taft-Hartley and against the president's ensuing veto. And when Johnson jumped into the 1948 Senate race, he attacked Truman's civil rights program, arguing that this was something Congress should not "try to cram down the throats of Southern states."

In his battle for the Senate seat, Johnson waged a campaign that matched the amorphous context of Texas Democratic politics. His opponent in the Democratic primary, Texas Governor Coke Stevenson, was an ultraconservative, actually far to the right of Johnson. But Johnson was able to depict himself as more anti-labor than Stevenson, largely because Stevenson had been endorsed by the AFL-CIO. The labor federation had done this to get even with Johnson because he had voted for the Taft-Hartley law, which labor bitterly opposed.

The outcome was desperately close; Johnson with the help of some high-powered legal finagling won by only 87 votes, earning him the nickname of "landslide Johnson." All that mattered, though, was that he had found his way to the Senate, and had blurred substantive debate in his campaign sufficiently so that he felt free to pursue the politics of consensus.

Johnson's approach was well suited to the political environment in the Senate, helping him move ahead swiftly—to Democratic whip by 1951, to Democratic leader by 1953, and Senate majority leader by 1955. Control of the Senate was exercised by a handful of men, all conservatives, most of them Southern Democrats, who could generally count on the backing of a group of conservative Republicans. Most of the Southerners had an abiding belief in racial segregation. Johnson, raised in a different racial setting from the Deep South, was much more open-minded on the issue. However, in his 1948 campaign, he had already found it politically convenient to move toward the Deep South's position, when he attacked Truman's civil rights program. And on one of his early Senate roll calls he allied himself with the Deep South troops in voting down the latest liberal attempt to change Senate rules to make it easier to shut down filibusters, the South's chief weapon against civil rights measures.

Yet if the rules of consensus politics dictated that Johnson move to the right in the Senate, these same rules and his ambition for higher office made him want to avoid seeming overly rigid on racial issues. In a mild gesture of independence Johnson announced that unlike the twenty-one other Southern senators, he would not attend meetings of the Southern Caucus, where strategy to block civil rights legislation was planned. But having hedged his position, Johnson hedged the hedge; instead of *formal* membership in the caucus, he accepted an *informal* membership.

Johnson's ability to establish a seeming balance on civil rights, an issue that became increasingly explosive during his tenure as majority leader, helped him transform that position into one of the most powerful in government. A key test of his consensus leadership came on the 1957 civil rights law, which Southerners viewed as a threat and Northern liberals complained was not strong enough.

Johnson feared, he later explained in words that graphically defined his stake in consensus, that unless the Senate took some sort of action, "extremists" on both sides would dominate the debate, a prospect that would of course undermine his own power. "I knew that if I failed to produce on this one, my leadership would be broken into a hundred pieces; everything I built up over the years would be completely undone."

On the one hand, he sought to win the support of liberals by arguing that this bill was the strongest measure that the Senate would pass. On the other hand, he labored to persuade Southerners to agree not to filibuster by promising them that if they allowed the measure to go forward he would see to it that its provisions were drastically weakened.*

As Congress debated, Johnson worked both sides of the fence frantically. "I heard him at one end of the cloakroom talking to Paul Douglas one day, saying, 'Paul, the amendment to the Civil Rights Bill is coming up and I need your support,' " Harry McPherson recalled. "And he went to the other end of the room and was talking to Sam Rayburn, and said, 'Sam, why don't y'all let this nigger bill pass?' "

In this fashion, consensus was preserved.

On a less substantive but tactically important issue, he persuaded the Southern grandees to ease seniority rules enough to allow new senators posts on key committees that would strengthen them at home. The advantage of the change for Johnson was that it gave him additional leverage in mustering support for his Senate leadership irrespective of the issues that senators stood for or against.

In many ways Johnson's consensus leadership in the Senate foreshadowed his approach to the presidency, particularly his aversion to

---

* Johnson kept his word. By the time the bill became law, its most potent section, Title III, which would have authorized the Justice Department to file suit for civil rights injunctions in school desegregation cases, had been eliminated. And an amendment requiring jury trials for conviction on contempt charges had been added.

debate on foreign policy. As Democratic Senate leader he was unquestioning in his support for President Eisenhower's foreign policies. "People said to me, 'Why don't you get up and criticize?' " he later recalled. "I replied, 'We ought not to do anything that might be misunderstood by foreign countries: He is the only president we have, and I am going to support that president, because if I make him weaker I make America weaker.' "

He revered bipartisanship in foreign policy—actually in domestic policy, too, though he felt restrained from saying so explicitly—because it conformed to consensus. "The more the two parties could agree," Johnson later explained, "the smaller the area of conflict shown to the American public and the less I worried about the public's tendency to go off on a jag, paralyzing itself in the endless debate or stampeding us in panic." Not too long after he left the Senate, the destructive potential of this attitude would become painfully obvious to the country and the world.

VALUES

For all his family's populist heritage, it was Horatio Alger and the Protestant work ethic that from the start defined Johnson's value structure and his ambitions. The Johnsons were middle-class strivers who saw themselves as country gentry. The keynote in the Johnson household, as in most other middle-class homes in the early twentieth century, was the potential for what one associate called "the triumph of character, determination and will over all adversity."

Johnson's father, who took the side of the downtrodden in the legislature, tried hard to rise in the business world but failed because of bad luck and bad judgment. The son seemed destined to fulfill the unsatisfied dreams of his father for material success. "With Lyndon there was an incentive that was born in him to advance and keep advancing," a childhood neighbor of the family recalled. "Sam had that. But he didn't have it anywhere near like Lyndon did."

From infancy he was quick, bright, and restless. His mother spurred her firstborn's drive, teaching him the alphabet from blocks when he was two and Mother Goose and Tennyson by the time he was three. At ten he liked to analyze current affairs for the crowd at the barbershop, where he also established a shoe shine stand, to his father's mortification. He started school at four, and at fifteen he graduated from high school, prompting his classmates to prophesy that he would rise to become the governor one day.

"Restless, energetic, purposeful, it is ambition that makes of the creature a real man," he wrote as a student editor at Southwest Texas State Teachers College at San Marcos. "It is direction behind force that makes power. . . . If one wishes to make something of his life he must have steadfast purpose, subordinate all other hopes to its accomplishment and adhere to it through all trials and reverses."

At San Marcos and elsewhere, Johnson practiced what he preached. He dominated campus politics at college, gaining enough confidence so that he could tell a fellow student: "Politics is a science, and if you work hard enough at it, you can be president. I'm going to be president."

He attacked every task with the full force of his being. In his first teaching job, at a tiny school for Mexican children, the janitor remembered many years later the lanky Anglo instructor who "seemed to have a passion to see that everything was done that should be done—and that it was done right." In his next teaching post, at a Houston high school, Johnson coached the debating team into the state championships and made his speech course the most popular in the school.

In his first job in Washington, as a congressional aide, he transformed a lifeless group of other Capitol Hill clerks like himself into a dynamic organization that attracted the attention of House members and the press, and became known as "the boss of the Little Congress."

This driving ambition, which reflected his value structure, reinforced his faith in consensus as a political philosophy. For in any Johnson consensus, Johnson himself was the central figure, persuading, deciding, and enforcing. It was Johnson's own performance that was the key to consensus and to his political advancement.

CHARACTER

When Lyndon Johnson first came to Washington, he was enraptured by Huey Long. The young congressional secretary made special arrangements whenever the Louisiana Kingfish was due to take the Senate floor so he could be certain not to miss one of Long's celebrated stemwinders. "For leading the masses and illustrating your point humanly," Johnson believed, "Huey Long couldn't be beat."

Despite his admiration for Long, Johnson himself avoided such appeals to passion as a public speaker. "I never wanted to demagogue against business," he told an interviewer. "I wanted a minimum of rhetoric that would inflame or incite against either businessmen, management or labor." Johnson's unwillingness to use heated rhetoric, though he recognized its effectiveness, was a reflection of his own inner turmoil. "Beneath the expressed belief that politics required reasonable discussion not rhetorical speeches," wrote Doris Kearns, who spent four revealing years working with Johnson on his memoirs, "lay a deep characterological fear of direct and open conflict, a lifelong tendency to withdraw from confrontation."

At the podium, as in many other situations, Lyndon Johnson was a man at war with himself, driven by inner tensions that he fought to restrain in a never-ending battle. This struggle to gain control of himself, and to alleviate the additional pressures imposed on him by the outside world, intensified his commitment to consensus as a political strategy.

Johnson's personality conflicts were rooted in the traumas of his early years. His mother was a woman with strong cultural interests, in contrast to his father. As a child Johnson was caught between his mother's emphasis on intellectual and artistic attainments and his father's rejection of such pursuits as unseemly for a young man. "My mother soon discovered that my daddy was not a man to discuss higher things. To her mind his life was vulgar and ignorant," Johnson later said. "She felt very much alone. Then I came along and suddenly everything was all right again. I could do all the things she never did."

But Rebekah Johnson aggravated young Lyndon's anxieties by seeming to make her love for her son dependent on his measuring up to the goals she set for him. Thus, when he quit taking the violin and dancing lessons she had arranged, she retaliated by in effect "pretending I was dead . . . and . . . being especially nice to my father and sisters," Johnson remembered.

Adding to these emotional difficulties were the economic reverses suffered by his father after he overinvested in Hill Country ranch land. Sam Johnson owed money to banks and storekeepers that he could not pay and would remain in debt for the rest of his life. His family had to struggle to get by. Making all this even more painful was the fact that Sam Johnson had cut an expansive, self-confident figure in Johnson City, buying big cars, even hiring a chauffeur to drive them, boasting of imminent deals that would make him rich. From a respected and envied leader of the community, Sam Johnson became a despised and ridiculed figure, a circumstance that fell heavily on his children.

Johnson's reactions to the turmoil of his childhood went in two different directions—one aggressive, one conciliatory. On one hand, he was spurred to assure himself of power and control. By nature, perhaps by what biographer Robert Caro calls a "powerful inherited strain" transmitted over several generations, Johnson was possessed of more than ordinary aggressiveness and drive. Though he was evidently brighter than average, he was unwilling to rest on this natural superiority. Instead he pushed himself relentlessly to take full advantage of his abilities.

"Everything was competition with Lyndon," recalled his cousin Ava. "He had to win."

As a ten-year-old, Lyndon became so enamored of money that he consented to let other boys grab one of his earlobes and yank it—ear popping, as it was called then, being a popular pastime—in return for money. The going rate was a nickel for five pulls and Johnson, who even then had very large ears, made a choice victim. Later his friends would remember young Lyndon submitting to the yanking, with tears streaming down his face at the pain, determined to earn his five cents. It was not the last time Johnson's intensity would cause him pain.

In part Johnson's drives reflected his value structure—with its principal goal of success. But Johnson's determination to dominate the circumstances of his life had another incentive. By controlling his environment at home he stood a better chance of putting to rest the conflicts and insecurities stemming from his relationships with his parents and theirs with each other.

This would have a long-range impact on him. As Johnson matured, he learned that establishing command of a situation was the first step toward establishing the consensus he always sought. Often he resorted to bullying and intimidation. When Secretary of State Dean Rusk was asked about the furor Johnson had caused by picking up his pet beagle by the ears, Rusk replied, "That's nothing. You ought to see how he treats his cabinet."

On the other hand, because he could not dominate every situation, Johnson developed conciliatory stratagems for getting his way. And these also became part of the underpinning for consensus.

One such gambit was adopting a father figure. Throughout his career Johnson made a point of attaching himself to a senior man who was in a position to advance his career. These surrogate fathers shielded him from the threats he would otherwise have faced from rivals among his peers.

He first established this pattern as a financially hard-pressed freshman at San Marcos College. By fawning on the college president, considered a remote personage by most students, he managed to get a part-time job specially created by the president in his own office. In Washington, the special rapport he established with Roosevelt helped him get off to a fast start. Meanwhile he began an assiduous courtship of a venerable fellow Texan, Speaker of the House Sam Rayburn. Johnson assuaged bachelor Rayburn's loneliness with invitations to the Johnson apartment, where Lady Bird served Mr. Sam his favorites: black-eyed peas, corn bread, and peach ice cream. Before long Rayburn became another potent figure who eagerly assumed the role of shepherd to Johnson's burgeoning ambition.

Of all these foster fathers, none was more important to Johnson's career than Senator Richard Russell. This was because of the nature of the Senate, where the controlling factor in shaping the careers of members was the Senate network of personal relationships—particularly relationships with the ruling clique, most particularly, Russell of Georgia, the most puissant of the Senate lords. A courtly, dignified figure, Russell was very different from the rowdy Johnson. But Johnson adapted; instead of barging into Russell's office, as was his habit with other senators, he first sent a note politely expressing his interest in dropping in for a visit. Moreover, he always took pains to refer to him as *Senator* Russell. When Johnson was ready to make his climb on the Senate leadership ladder, Richard Russell could be found at his side, lending a helping hand. And once having achieved the leadership, if Johnson needed an extra vote or two on a crucial roll call, he knew he could always count on the support of *Senator* Russell.

Another Johnson tactic was to ensure the loyalty of followers by providing them with ample rewards. "He was the best Congressman for a district that *ever was*," Tommy Corcoran, one of the many New Deal operatives Johnson came to know and use, said of Johnson's ability to get government benefits for his House constituents. Members of Johnson's Senate network might have said much the same thing about Johnson's practice of showering them with committee posts and other legislative favors.

The tactic, another reflection of Johnson's chronic insecurity, was an attempt to guarantee the approval and support of others that his psyche desperately craved. As president, he applied this principle of rewards on a massive scale, striving to distribute benefits to nearly every significant segment of the populace through the largess of the Great Society. This would be the ultimate insurance policy for the president who wanted "a happy nation." He would make himself so valuable to so many people that no one would have reason to challenge him or his consensus.

Yet even at the height of his powers the personal approval he desperately sought was denied him. Once he asked Dean Rusk why he was not better liked by the American public. "You are not a very likeable man," Rusk told him.

History and circumstance seemed to mock his every effort. Johnson struggled all his adult life to overcome what he believed to be the lasting marks left by the hardships of his childhood, but his succession to the presidency as a result of Kennedy's assassination intensified his internal struggle and aggravated the flaws in his character.

He was continually tormented by the endless comparisons with his more stylish predecessor. Kennedy had gone to Harvard; Johnson had gone to Southwest Texas State Teachers College at San Marcos, an institution whose degree, as former aide Robert Hardesty wryly observed, "wasn't honored very highly."

As president he was wildly suspicious of anyone who had been close to John Kennedy. When Harry McPherson, one of Johnson's trusted aides, sent him a memorandum suggesting that he be more willing to use former Kennedy people, the president responded by suggesting that McPherson transfer to another job outside the White House.

The special nature of the presidency minimized his strengths and exaggerated his faults. A powerfully persuasive figure in small groups, he was transformed by self-doubt into an unctuous bore on television. "He was enormously preoccupied with the press," observed Douglass Cater, one of his speech writers. He lavished attention and flattery on reporters and was almost invariably dissatisfied with the results.

At times, when he was on his way up and seemingly confident of success, the depth of his insecurities was matched by the height of his arrogance. When he was running for the Senate in 1948 and a young aide suggested it would be unwise for him to campaign in the Texas hustings wearing a Countess Marà tie, a monogrammed shirt, and french cuffs, Johnson retorted, "Son, they take me like I am or they find themselves another boy."

But for all his bluster, campaigns were an ordeal for him. Prior to his stunning withdrawal from the 1968 presidential campaign, he had drafted statements taking himself out of two other critical races—for the Senate in 1948 and for the presidency in 1964—and then had torn them up. In the midst of his unsuccessful 1941 Senate campaign Johnson had to be hospitalized for nervous exhaustion. For him politics was a never-ending dilemma. He was driven to seek public office to gain power and control. Yet he feared these tests before the electorate precisely because he could not control them and also because they forced him to confront controversy.

THE CHALLENGE

The supreme challenge of Lyndon Johnson's presidency was how to promote his dream of a Great Society while meeting what he regarded as the threat of communist aggression in Indochina. Choosing between the two was a challenge Johnson did not want to face because whatever choice he made was bound to cause controversy which would threaten his cherished goal of consensus. As a result, his response was marked by evasion of reality and concealment of the truth, which doomed his chances of gaining public support for his policies.

Before he confronted this dilemma, Johnson's confidence in his leadership skills had been bolstered by his successful response to his first two major challenges in the White House—his succession to the presidency in 1963 and his election to the office in his own right in 1964. In both cases Johnson's approach was shaped by the three key elements of presidential leadership. His actions were driven by the ambition which reflected his values, by the tensions which shaped his character, and finally, by his political experience in Texas that contributed to his ideological strategy of consensus. But these challenges were not rigorous tests of his leadership; in both instances, factors which he did not control, though he fully exploited them, helped to determine favorable outcomes.

In the case of his succession after Kennedy's assassination, the shock from that tragedy unified the country to a degree not seen since Pearl Harbor, creating a receptive climate for consensus. Johnson was quick to take advantage of the situation. By pledging himself to carry out the slain man's public testament, he elevated both himself and Kennedy to a moral level neither could have otherwise reached. His purpose, Johnson later explained in a phrase that might have been drawn from Shakespearean tragedy, was to "take a dead man's program and turn it into a martyr's cause."

Johnson used the mood of the times to help him gain the support of political leaders as well as the backing of the public. A few days after the assassination he called Senate Republican Leader Everett Dirksen and asked him to persuade his fellow Republicans "that it was essential to forget partisan politics, so that we could weather the national crisis in which we were involved and unite our people."

Under the circumstances Dirksen, an old Johnson crony, could hardly say no.

Johnson had many other similar conversations. As he later boasted: "I brought people together who under ordinary circumstances would have fled at the sight of each other." With them all he stressed his basic consensus theme: "People must put aside their selfish aims in the larger cause of the nation's interest."

Yet the resolution of these so-called selfish aims was actually supposed to be the task of political process, whose normal workings had been muzzled by consensus. In these circumstances it seemed left to Lyndon Johnson alone to define the nation's interest. Thus did Lyndon Johnson make his succession a triumph for consensus.

He managed to achieve the same result in the 1964 election campaign, thanks in no small measure to the nomination of Barry Goldwater as the

Republican standard bearer. By selecting a candidate so far right of what was then considered to be the mainstream of his own party, the GOP convention eliminated any danger that Johnson would be seriously challenged on matters of substance. A more moderate Republican candidate could have pressed Johnson to explain his policies on the two most crucial issues of the day, civil rights and Vietnam. Goldwater was in no position to do that, and indeed, was apparently leery of even trying. At the onset of the campaign he met with Johnson in the White House, and, as he later told the story, he pledged not to raise either of these issues in the campaign in the interest of national unity.

That worked out splendidly for Johnson. While a special section of his campaign ground out material depicting Goldwater as a threat to Social Security, TV, and world peace, the president was free to spend his days on the stump defending motherhood and the flag. "I just want to tell you this," he assured a crowd in Providence, Rhode Island, "we're for a lot of things and we're against mighty few."

Brandishing a poll that showed him winning favorable ratings from liberals, middle-of-the-roaders, and conservatives, he boasted to White House visitors: "They all think I'm on their side."

In the interest of preserving that belief, Johnson sought to avoid as much as possible the controversial subject of Vietnam. By getting the Congress to pass the Tonkin Gulf resolution, granting him free rein in Southeast Asia, Johnson appeared to have defused the issue. And his staff advised him to risk reviving it. In a memorandum to the president, Bill Moyers argued against the idea of Defense Secretary Robert McNamara making an inspection trip to Vietnam just before the election. "It would only tend to *increase* public attention and concern about the situation out there," Moyers wrote. "We ought to be hoping that public discussion of Vietnam could be kept to a minimum."

On election day, not only did Lyndon Johnson himself win the presidency in his own right by more than fifteen million votes, but the Democrats gained the biggest advantage they had enjoyed in Congress since the heyday of Johnson's early hero, Franklin Roosevelt. Mindful of his far-reaching Great Society legislative objectives, Johnson rushed to take advantage of what he regarded as a golden opportunity, but also a fleeting one.

"I have watched the Congress from either the inside or the outside, man and boy, for more than forty years," Johnson told his administration's lobbyists assembled in the White House only a few weeks after this great victory. "And I've never seen a Congress that didn't eventually take the measure of the president it was dealing with. I was just elected president by the biggest popular margin in the history of the country, fifteen million votes," he reminded his listeners. But he calculated that he had already lost about two million as the voters recovered from their panic over Goldwater. And he warned, if he got into a battle with Congress, or escalated the war in Vietnam (as he would decide to do only a few months later), "I may be down to eight million [votes] by summer."

Eight million must have sounded like a large number at the time. But as it turned out this was an underestimation of the toll Vietnam took of Lyndon Johnson's presidency.

Johnson's response to the challenge of Vietnam developed over a period of nearly a year, beginning with the August 1964 attack on U.S. warships in the Tonkin Gulf and culminating with his July 1965 announcement that he was sending 50,000 more troops to South Vietnam. During that period, even as he dealt with Indochina, at home he won a great election victory, established the agenda for the Great Society and saw its first legislative seeds come to fruition.

By the time he was sworn in for his elected term, he had already achieved impressive legislative results, notably the enactment of the Kennedy civil rights program and the initial measures in his own war on poverty. But these turned out to be only appetizers on the far-reaching menu of demands he now placed before Congress.

Consensus required something for nearly every national interest of consequence. Medicare for the elderly and federal aid to education for young middle-class families were the major components of the Great Society blueprint; they headed a laundry list of other programs in areas ranging from arts to Appalachia, from water pollution to weather forecasting.

An added and momentous starter was voting rights. After gaining enactment of the 1964 law striking down segregation in public accommodations, further action on civil rights was the last thing on Lyndon Johnson's mind. But the voting-rights issue took on a life of its own, as a result of Negro demonstrations in the South and violent attempts by local authorities to suppress them. The proposed legislative response—federal voting registrars to ensure the access of Negroes to the ballot—was an idea that Johnson had blocked when it came before the Senate in 1960 and he was majority leader. But now he was president and what was at stake was not just the Negro's right to vote but Johnson's own cherished consensus, which was threatened by the swelling controversy over the issue.

Johnson reacted with alacrity; he did not merely support the legislation, he made the Negro cause and its stirring battle cry his own. "We shall overcome," he declared in a memorable address to both sessions of Congress, and voting rights became another Johnson legislative accomplishment.

Still Johnson pushed the Congress for more laws, including many that lacked the constitutional and moral imperative of voting rights. To maintain the pressure, in Lyndon Johnson's ship of state, all hands were always required to be on deck. After he was unable to reach his domestic policy chief, Joseph Califano, at a critical moment, the president ordered that a phone be installed in Califano's office lavatory. Just as the needs of consensus did not permit time for individual privacy, they certainly offered no opportunity, as Johnson saw things, to establish priorities or to build public support for costly and controversial new ventures.

This glut of success inevitably led to trouble that was a reflection of the shortcomings of consensus as a strategy for presidential leadership. One problem stemmed from Johnson's failure during the 1964 campaign to assemble a coalition of public support for his legislative agenda. To do so would have risked controversy, which Johnson was determined to avoid. In many areas outside of Medicare and voting rights, which clearly met widely felt concerns, his programs suffered from hasty preparation and lack of public understanding. To a troublesome degree they reflected Johnson's own will and ego, not needs perceived by the public.

By the end of 1965, the Congress had passed 84 of the 87 major bills Johnson had submitted, a record that in some ways surpassed what Johnson's former patron Franklin Roosevelt had accomplished when the New Deal was at its zenith. But in the process the president who wanted "a happy nation" had created enormous expectations which he would have difficulty meeting.

To overcome these developing problems, Johnson had hoped to rely on the tactics that had served him so well in the Senate and in his early months in the White House. But altered circumstances created obstacles. With the memory of the assassination fading and Goldwater eliminated as an opponent and as a threat, Johnson found his old methods did not always work. He was forced to modify the techniques he had used in the Senate, where his success had been fostered by his ability to reward his friends. The need to play Lord Bountiful led him to elevate results to an importance that made the means employed to achieve them irrelevant. "He doesn't believe that the end justifies any means," Harry McPherson argued. But he acknowledged, "He believes it justifies quite a few means."

As president, though, Johnson had to deploy his resources in a much broader arena. As the stakes increased and the battlefield expanded, so did the difficulties of maintaining the control that was the lifeblood of Johnson's consensus. "This was a man who . . . had found [that] total mastery of the communications system in a confined environment of Congress was essential to the kind of job he was capable of doing," Douglass Cater said. "When it got on the presidential level it was no longer possible."

The celebrated "Johnson treatment"—the nose-to-nose, hand-to-lapel administering of persuasion and bullyragging that won him countless triumphs in the Senate cloakrooms—could not be brought to bear on Ho Chi Minh, or even on Martin Luther King, Jr.

To enact the mind-boggling domestic agenda he proposed, Johnson could no longer count on winning support with something as minor as a post on a key committee. He had to deliver rewards to one after another of the many diverse groups he needed to bring into his ever-widening tent. Success with one group meant that he had to find at least a comparable reward for another. This, of course, soon proved to be impossible; unlike Johnson's ambitions, the total of federal revenues was finite. In other words, as he nailed each new coonskin to the wall, Johnson was competing with himself and this was a game he was bound to lose.

Whereas in the Senate he had exploited his relationships with his colleagues, now as president he developed friendships with the influential leaders of key interest groups to help expedite approval of his proposals.

He liked to tell the story of a prominent Baptist who called the White House to grumble that Johnson's proposal for federal aid to education unfairly favored Roman Catholic schoolchildren. The aide taking the call mentioned that at that very moment the president was relaxing in the White House pool with none other than the Reverend Billy Graham.

The caller paused, then asked, "Is that *our* Billy?"

Indeed it was, he was told. Did he want the president to call him back?

"Oh no," the mollified caller said. "Just give the president my very warm regards."

Such poolside hospitality was consistent with the practice of consensus that made Johnson's persona rather than his policies the center of his strategy. But later, as many of the policies could not produce the results Johnson had promised and Johnson himself became less popular, these leaders could not deliver the support of their own rank and file. This weakened the political backing for the Great Society at a time when Johnson's policies on Vietnam were also being seriously challenged.

And Vietnam, of course, was the greatest threat to the Great Society. The war halfway around the globe confronted Johnson with a terrible dilemma.

"I knew from the start," Johnson would say later, "that if I left the woman I really loved—the Great Society—in order to get involved with that bitch of a war on the other side of the world, then I would lose everything at home. All my programs."

War has always been the enemy of domestic reform, a rule Johnson well knew and one that even Franklin Roosevelt had to respect. When, during World War II, he sidelined "Dr. New Deal" in favor of "Dr. Win the War." War not only took funds away from domestic programs but hardened the mood of the country, making the public less accepting of the social goals Johnson had set.

But if Johnson could not afford to go to war, he felt he also could not afford to make peace. He was convinced that the Great Society would be doomed because its progenitor would lose credibility if he appeared to abandon the anti-communist cause in Indochina.

This was a dilemma serious enough that one way or another it touched the lives of nearly all Americans. One possible course for the president would have been to lay the problem out in the open for the electorate and the Congress to debate. But to do that would have inevitably exposed fissures in American society that threatened the accord he had gained from his huge election victory.

Instead he chose to follow policies that would minimize debate. Searching in his own past experience for clues, he decided that he had found the answer in the example of Roosevelt, who during World War II had enjoyed just the sort of consensus backing for which Johnson yearned. But Roosevelt had been unable to gain that wide support until Pearl Harbor. Meanwhile, his warnings went largely unheeded.

The lesson Johnson chose to read from that chapter of history was that appeasement inevitably begets aggression. Likening himself to FDR, he analogized the North Vietnamese leaders to Hitler and his cohorts.

"Our policy in Vietnam . . . springs from every lesson that we have learned in this century," he declared in an address in Chicago, the same city, where as he pointedly recalled, Roosevelt in 1937 had issued his famous call to quarantine the aggressors. "The country heard him but did not listen. The country failed to back him in that trying hour. And then we saw what happened when the aggressors felt confident that they could win while we sat by."

Just as the Roosevelt model inclined Johnson to a military answer to Vietnam as a way to preserve consensus, so did his concern about his party's unfortunate reputation in foreign affairs. Though Communist China had been "lost" more than a decade earlier and the supposedly infamous agreements of Yalta were now twenty years old, the Democratic party still carried a heavy burden to demonstrate that it was sufficiently hard on communism.

"Liberal Democrats were suspect on the Communist issue," Harry McPherson later pointed out. "If they were 'soft' on Communists at home or abroad, they would find their legislative programs stopped cold by charges of complicity." Horace Busby believed that Johnson was "very much afraid" that if he pulled out of Vietnam, "the Republicans would say this man is just like Truman and Acheson; he's selling out in Asia."

That sort of uproar would have certainly ruined the prospects for Johnson's consensus. Yet Johnson feared that open pursuit of a hard-line military policy was bound to cause controversy, too.

He had good reason for concern on this score. For one thing, while depicting Goldwater as a warmonger during the campaign, he had pledged time and again not to send "American boys to do what Asian boys ought to be doing." In the closing hours of the campaign he declared, "There can be and will be as long as I am President, peace for all Americans." Those pledges, he well knew, could come back to haunt him.

Already, as he began moving toward stepped-up military involvement in Vietnam in late 1964, opposition to the war was mounting. Resistance came from the campuses and also from liberal academics and foreign-policy specialists who regarded Johnson's policies as simplistic and based on outmoded ideas. Though their numbers were not large, their influence in the media and among activists in the Democratic party was great. If Johnson turned Vietnam into a full-scale war, he knew these critics would raise a storm that could wreck his chances for maintaining consensus and with it his hopes for a Great Society.

This was the nature of the dilemma that confronted Lyndon Johnson during the months he took over the White House from Kennedy, made plans for his legislative program and the election campaign, and then for his first full term in office. Reasonable men could disagree about a solution, but Johnson's response was not to make any choice at all. Indeed, he claimed that no choice was necessary.

On the domestic front, with all his might and main he pushed Congress to enact his Great Society into law. In Vietnam, he made war, but in a peculiarly circumscribed way that served his short-term purpose of protecting his consensus. In the long run, however, it damaged his presidency beyond repair.

His strategy was based on a series of dissemblances. It began to unfold in August 1964, following the attack by North Vietnamese torpedo boats on U.S. destroyers in the Tonkin Gulf. Johnson used the attack to preempt Congressional opposition to the war—to smother it with consensus before it got started.

This had been part of Johnson's plan from the start. "I was determined from the time I became President to seek the fullest support of Congress for any major action that I took, whether in foreign affairs or in the domestic field," Johnson later wrote. He "repeatedly told" Rusk and McNamara that any proposal for action needed to be accompanied by a proposal for getting congressional backing.

Ordinarily that would require taking the lawmakers into his confidence and submitting his policies to debate. But Johnson had no intention of doing that. Instead he used the murky circumstances of the Tonkin Gulf incident to stampede Congress into adopting a resolution giving approval in advance for "all necessary measures to repel any armed attack against the forces of the United States and to prevent further aggression." It amounted to a blank check for Johnson in Southeast Asia.

Not only did the administration exaggerate the seriousness of the attack, more fundamentally, the president distorted the purpose of the resolution. Initially Johnson told Senator Fulbright, who guided the resolution through the Senate, that its adoption was necessary to show the North Vietnamese "a united front" on policy in Indochina. The incident occurred in the midst of the presidential campaign, and many who supported it feared that unless Johnson showed his toughness in Southeast Asia, the supposedly irresponsible Goldwater would revive the dread charge of "soft on communism" against Johnson and his Democrats.

"The way [Johnson] presented it made me believe, and I think others share that [belief], that he wasn't intending to enlarge the war," Fulbright later complained.

But that was exactly what Johnson did. The resolution became the legal charter for the broad escalation of the next three years.

The next milestone on the road to escalation was a result of the ground war in Vietnam. Communist forces had been undeterred by the symbolic display of unity embodied in the Tonkin Gulf resolution and by the increased military support for the South Vietnamese. From the White House the situation looked grim. In January 1965 McGeorge Bundy and Robert McNamara wrote the president calling for the U.S. "to use our military power in the Far East to force a change of Communist policy."

Within two weeks, the Vietcong attacked the U.S. barracks in Pleiku, killing nine Americans. The president launched a sustained campaign of "tit-for-tat" bombing raids against the North. Addressing the nation in phrases presumably deliberately reminiscent of his predecessor's inaugural speech, Johnson declared, "We love peace . . . But we love liberty the more and we shall take up any challenge, we shall answer any threat. We shall pay any price to make certain that freedom shall not perish from the earth."

Johnson's action was fundamentally disingenuous. Once again, as with the Tonkin Gulf resolution, he had seized upon the fortuitous circumstances of war to provide justification for a policy he wanted to carry out anyway. Although communist forces had taken American lives at Pleiku, those same Americans were in South Vietnam to help kill Communists.

But even as he acted, Johnson avoided sending in troops, which would have alarmed the public. Casualties to ground troops was not part of the price Johnson was willing to impose to ensure "that freedom shall not perish." At least not yet.

Meanwhile, as criticism mounted of the increasing U.S. military involvement in Indochina, Johnson decided to make a dramatic gesture in the direction of a peaceful settlement, and to bring his skill at personal persuasion to bear on the problem. In April 1965 he drafted a proposal for a consortium of Asian nations to join the U.S. in a sweeping program of economic aid to Indochina, including a sort of TVA on the Mekong River. The U.S. participation would be planned by "a special team of outstanding, patriotic, distinguished Americans."

A few hours before he was to make the proposal public, Johnson put through a call to Eugene R. Black, former head of the World Bank, and asked him to lead the U.S. planning team. Black, who was lunching with Henry Ford II, said he was sorry, but he already had too much to do. Johnson persisted. To make sure Black understood the importance of the post, he decided to read him the entire speech text.

Finally Ford convinced Black that the only way he could get off the phone and finish lunch was to say yes. Proudly the president announced his appointment the next day.

Unfortunately, Johnson's methods worked better on Black than on the North Vietnamese. Despite the bombing, the war continued to go badly for the U.S. and its South Vietnam ally. Though the increased bombing was intended as a substitute for sending U.S. ground troops into combat, it gradually caused just what it had been designed to avoid. First U.S. ground troops were sent to help defend the air bases used for the bombing. Then more troops were sent to help defend the defenders. Then U.S. troops were sent into combat to help out the South Vietnamese. By June 1965 they were going into combat on their own. Without benefit of a formal declaration, the U.S. had gone to war.

At the time, I was working as a Peace Corps evaluator, interviewing volunteers in Malawi. I found these young Americans, who were supposed to be helping to strengthen the U.S. abroad, disillusioned about what their president was doing at home.

"What is that guy Johnson doing in Vietnam?" one young man from Ohio wanted to know. "Last November was my first vote for president. I voted for LBJ because he was against the war. Who is he trying to kid?"

It was a refrain I heard time and again during my month in Africa. Many of the volunteers said they had joined up because they believed what John Kennedy had said about "ask what you can do for your country." Now they felt that Lyndon Johnson had betrayed Kennedy and themselves.

The mood among my colleagues in Peace Corps headquarters was as bitter as that among the volunteers. Our offices were on H Street, across Lafayette Square from the White House. One Friday afternoon in July my friend David Gellman and I watched Lyndon Johnson's helicopter soar into the sky from the south lawn, headed for Camp David and another series of meetings on Vietnam.

Gellman told me the latest gag about Johnson's credibility gap.

"When he pulls his ear, you know he's telling the truth. When he scratches his nose, you know he's telling the truth. Do you know the only time he lies?"

"Go ahead, tell me," I said.

"When he moves his lips."

That same month Robert McNamara was sent to Vietnam for another in a series of inspection trips. On his return he offered the president three choices—withdrawal, keeping the status quo, or escalation. Johnson decided to escalate. But his decision was so blurred by his concern with protecting his consensus that its ultimate effect was not much different than if he had chosen to maintain the status quo—except for the increasing toll that would be taken in the coming months of lives, dollars, and of the president's credibility.

Most of his advisers wanted Johnson to sound a more certain trumpet—to put the economy on a war footing, activate the reserves, and ask Congress for a tax increase to finance the war effort. They wanted this not just for the practical results but for political reasons, in the best sense of the word, in hopes of rallying the country behind the effort in Vietnam.

Johnson did no such thing. Instead of delivering a prime-time television address to rouse the country, he broke the news at an afternoon press conference, guaranteeing a much smaller audience. Instead of calling up the reserves, he talked only of increasing draft calls and enlistments. Instead of the 200,000 men he had secretly promised to send to

General William Westmoreland in Vietnam, he mentioned only an immediate increase of 50,000. Instead of proposing a tax hike, he asked only for a $1.8 billion raise in defense spending.

Would the country have to choose between guns and butter? he was asked. He could not foresee the future, the president said, but he added, "At the moment we enjoy the good fortune of having an unparalleled period of prosperity with us, and this Government is going to do all it can to see it continue."

So Johnson would not "bug out," as he himself would have put it. Instead, as Professor Larry Berman writes, "the decision was made to lose Vietnam slowly."

Lyndon Johnson's failure was not that he made the wrong decision. Rather it was that he did not make any honest decision at all. As a result he divided his country and his party, causing wounds that more than two decades after his presidency have not entirely healed.

Some have argued that Johnson was the victim of his advisers, but by and large a president gets the sort of advice he is looking for. Hubert Humphrey found that out when he sent Johnson a memo questioning the wisdom of the bombing. He was then shut out from future foreign policy meetings.

Harry McPherson recalls drafting what he thought was "a damned conclusive memorandum" to the president opposing the bombing of North Vietnam.

"I started to send it in and realized that it would very likely mean the end of my participation in matters with Vietnam," he said. "So I appended a paragraph saying, 'This is the way doves feel about the bombing,' or something, without saying whether I felt that way or not."

The deliberations that the president conducted that fateful summer of 1965 had some aspects of a charade. When Johnson's top advisers met to discuss McNamara's memo, it did not seem to William Bundy "that this was where the decision was made in all honesty." Bundy believed McNamara had already made his report to Johnson earlier in the day and gotten the only vote that counted, the president's. "As for the discussion, you felt," Bundy said, "that it had been staged to a degree."

Indeed, his brother, McGeorge Bundy, believed that in a sense McNamara's entire report had been staged to conform to Johnson's preconceived decision. When Johnson sent McNamara to Saigon, Bundy later wrote, "his purpose was to build a consensus on what needed to be done to turn the tide, not cover a retreat. . . . His own priority was to get agreement on the lowest level of intensity he could on a course that would meet the present need in Vietnam and not derail his legislative calendar."

Under Secretary of State George Ball seems to have been given special license to question the president's policies, but even as designated dissenter he had to meet a heavy burden of proof. When Ball resisted the idea of escalation and recommended that the U.S. withdraw and "take our losses," Johnson pressed him:

"But I want to know, can we make a case for your thoughts? Can you discuss it fully?"

At this point Ball gave up. "We have discussed it. I have had my day in court."

Finally the meetings reached their denouement: Johnson asserted his preference for the McNamara option, in effect to go to war without asking Congress or the public for wartime measures. Then he turned to the chairman of Joint Chiefs of Staff, General Earle Wheeler, and asked, "Do you, General Wheeler, agree?"

Wheeler wanted an unequivocal U.S. commitment, not the partial war Johnson had decided on. But having no other real option except to start an argument with the president that he could not win, the general nodded his head. Johnson had his consensus.

Vietnam offered Johnson and the U.S. no easy choice. But the courses favored by Ball and Wheeler, opposing ones though they were, had the advantage of honestly addressing the problem.

If he had taken Ball's advice, Johnson could have pulled out of Vietnam after telling the public this was a struggle the U.S. could not win, except at a price it could not afford to pay. He could have drawn a distinction between communist aggression against another country—that is, North Korea's attack on South Korea—and the civil war in Vietnam. The best American answer to Communism around the world, the president could have argued, would be to build a Great Society here at home and maintain an economy strong enough to help our friends around the world.

If he had followed the course Wheeler preferred, Johnson would have had a natural political base on which to build. As late as 1967 polls showed a majority of Americans favored the U.S. taking tougher military measures against the communists. Of course, a full-scale war effort would have meant that sacrifices could not be avoided, but at least Johnson would have been able to offer a clear and tangible goal.

"The central fact of [Johnson's] time was the convergence of war and social revolution," wrote Walt Rostow, a combination that immensely complicated the task facing any president. The presidency itself, though, was a significant institutional asset. Johnson could have used it to make a case to the country if he had been able to preserve his own credibility. Asked at the press conference in which he announced the dispatch of 50,000 troops to Vietnam about the choice between guns and butter, Johnson said that he believed Americans "will do whatever is necessary."

Evidence from past wars supported that proposition, and Johnson would have served his country's interest and his own far better if he had operated as if he himself believed in it.

In the end Johnson failed to reconcile Vietnam and the war on poverty because of the contradictions of his leadership. He had been able to succeed at earlier challenges as president despite these conflicts because special circumstances had warded off public pressures normal in the political world. In assuming the presidency he had benefited from the emotional response to Kennedy's death; in the 1964 election he had been aided by the distraction of Goldwater's candidacy.

But with frustration over Vietnam and skepticism over the Great Society both mounting, starting in 1965, Johnson himself became the main focus of public criticism for which he was ill equipped as a personality and a politician to bear. This was an unavoidable result of his consensus strategy, which demanded that Johnson dominate the political landscape. Under this scrutiny the contradictions in his leadership approach became apparent.

On one hand, Johnson's character, with its internal tensions, along with his early political background in Texas, caused him to rely on the strategy of consensus that inherently sought to muzzle disagreement. Yet on the other, Johnson's ambition, which was at the heart of his value system, combined with the populist thrust of the political party he led, compelled him to be an activist president—to generate social change at home and wage war overseas. This inevitably triggered the disagreement consensus sought to avoid. The harder Johnson tried to act as if this disagreement did not exist, the faster his credibility drained away, and with it his access to presidential power.

Johnson's consensus strategy resembled Eisenhower's ideological approach in that both men wanted to avoid controversy. But Eisenhower had a generally passive view of the presidency. He generally seemed glad, as Emmett Hughes observed, "to leave things undone" while Johnson was determined to get as much done as possible.

In another comparison, both Johnson and Truman waged unpopular wars. But Truman confronted the economic cost of the Korean War head-on. "In the months ahead the government must give priority to activities that are urgent, like military procurement and atomic energy and power development," he warned in his 1951 State of the Union address, six months after the fighting in Korea had begun. "It must practice rigid economy in its non-defense activities." To fund the war without generating the inflation that afflicted Americans in the closing years of Johnson's presidency, Truman sacrificed his domestic programs, imposed wage and price controls, and pushed three tax hikes through Congress. He paid a price in popularity, but so ultimately did Johnson. Meanwhile, though, the country's economy was on sounder footing and its citizens had a clearer understanding of what their government was doing under Truman.

Johnson committed his prestige to the political process. So did Kennedy. But for Kennedy presidential prestige was a means toward achieving a larger end. In the case of Johnson, because the substance of debate was submerged by the strategy of consensus, the president's power became not just the means, but the end.

Johnson tried to meet the challenge of Vietnam by avoiding controversy and failed. In facing the same challenge, the next president, whose career was wedded to controversy, would actively seek it out as the handmaiden of leadership.

CHAPTER 6

Nixon: Us Against Them

It was probably inevitable that when Richard Nixon was inaugurated as president, amid due pomp and circumstance, protestors against the Vietnam War mounted a "counter-inauguration." By January 1969, when the fifty-six-year-old Nixon began his first term in the White House, the Vietnam protest movement was so widespread that its leaders had begun to establish their own set of moral and political symbols. Their overall motif, as evidenced by the counter-inaugural, was to mock and challenge the middle-class beliefs that dominated the rest of the country and that countenanced the continuation of the fighting in Indochina.

On January 20, Nixon's inaugural parade would move east to west from the Capitol, where the president would take the oath of office, to the White House. By contrast, on the day before, the five thousand or so counter-inaugural marchers plodded in the opposite direction, from west to east. Since I had been assigned by *Newsweek* to cover the counter-inaugural activities, I walked along with the marchers, jotting down notes on their signs and slogans.

Several signs reviled Nixon, who would shortly become the commander-in-chief, as the "Number One War Criminal," a crude play on his campaign slogan of "Nixon's the one." The chant I heard most often as we strode down Pennsylvania Avenue was the marchers' salute to the leader of the enemy forces: "Ho, Ho, Ho Chi Minh, the N.L.F. is going to win."

As the parade neared its end, a handful of the marchers spotted the American flag flying in front of the Health, Education, and Welfare building. Breaking ranks, they charged over to the flagpole, with the idea of tearing down Old Glory. This was the first sign of disorder and I rushed over for a close-up view. But before I had a chance to question the group assaulting the flag, a larger group of marchers intervened to stop them.

"You'll make us all look like traitors," one of them shouted at the militants. A scuffle ensued and police arrived to safeguard the flag and haul off some of the more aggressive demonstrators.

The episode at the flagpole reflected an inner conflict that was widely evident at the counter-inaugural. For all the trappings of rebelliousness that the protestors proudly displayed—their long hair, their seedy pea jackets and jeans, their raucous slogans—the vast majority were children of the middle class. They found it as hard to tear down their country's flag as it would have been to undo the expensive orthodontic work in their mouths.

"Maintain a sense of dignity along with militancy," the folk singer Phil Ochs had admonished the marchers at a rally before the parade. "The country is degenerating, but there is no sense in our joining them."

"Wall Street's War System Must Be Smashed" posters at the counter-inaugural headquarters, which I visited later that day, declared. But these kids had no knives, clubs, or bombs. After the parade some stones were thrown, landing harmlessly in front of the police. For most of the demonstrators, though, the weapons of choice were safely metaphorical: the $1 plastic Nixon masks that they were instructed to wear "to reflect Nixon's facade back at Nixon."

Richard Nixon had not been in the White House for very long before I began to realize how the conflict that motivated the counter-inaugural protestors helped illuminate his approach to presidential leadership. The demonstrators were torn between the values that had been integral to their upbringing and their revulsion against the war. As a result, their rebellion often seemed like a middle-class masquerade. Without intending to, they demonstrated the strength of the forces that had shaped their upbringing, which still governed the lives of their parents and which Richard Nixon would use against them. This was the heart of Nixon's ideology, the core of his values, and the cause that had carried him to the presidency—the defense of the middle class.

The protestors against the war had helped to drive Lyndon Johnson from office, but their effectiveness was blunted against Nixon. Indeed, for the first term of his presidency, the chief political significance of the protest movement was as a rallying point for Nixon to rouse a large and potent constituency—the "silent majority," as he would call it—behind his policies on the war. For all the ambivalence the protestors felt, their anger was real enough and their symbols jarring enough that Nixon could make them into a menace.

The lesson I learned at the counter-inauguration, amplified by Nixon's presidency, was that Nixon and the demonstrators needed each other and used each other. But for a long while it was Nixon who got the better of the bargain.

Confronted with the most unpopular war in modern American history, Nixon sought political support to allow him to attempt settlement of the war in his own time and on his own terms. Combining his commitment to middle-class economic interests and his identification with middle-class values, driven by his unyielding determination, Nixon relied on a polarizing strategy to win that support. He used the protest movement to dramatize both the threat to middle-class citizens and his role as their champion.

Nixon's triumph turned out to be transitory. His tragedy was miscalculating the advantage his political support at home gave him confronting his adversaries abroad. He prolonged the end of the war to a point where the gains did not justify the cost. In the face of continuing attack from his opponents, the force of will that marked his character and had contributed to his triumph betrayed him. The consequence was disgrace and the downfall of his presidency.

IDEOLOGY

The foundation of Nixon's political beliefs was his championship of the middle class against a range of threats, real and perceived, that developed from the transformation of this country and its role in the world in the middle decades of the twentieth century. He gained prominence in his role by polarizing the electorate as a strategy for gaining support for his convictions. But with each successive polarized success, Nixon himself became the focal point of divisiveness, straining his rapport with his middle-class base.

Dwight Eisenhower, Nixon's chief for eight years, also had close ties to the middle class. But Stephen Ambrose, a biographer of both presidents, points out that Eisenhower took a more sanguine view of the middle-class condition, emphasizing what the middle class had gained. By contrast, Nixon stressed what it had lost or was in danger of losing. For example, during one White House meeting considering a proposal for a tax exemption for tuition payments to private schools, Nixon warned that "what's involved is the whole erosion of the middle class," adding that "the middle class is shrinking." Eisenhower's view was that the middle class was growing, not eroding, as more working-class families moved up the ladder.

In part this difference in outlook reflects the two different periods in which the two men were raised. In the late nineteenth century, when Eisenhower grew up, most Americans still took the chance for advancement for granted. Born more than twenty years later, in 1913, Nixon matured at a time when economic and technological change not only made the future less certain but also threatened the gains made in the past.

The contrast between the two periods was heightened by the uneasy environment in Richard Nixon's home state, a land that promised more than it could possibly deliver. The California of Nixon's boyhood was made up of the rhapsodic dreams evoked by real estate brochures and also of such harsh realities as well water unfit to drink. Ambitions for fortunes to be made in citrus orchards were undermined by disillusionment with arid soil. This setting was reflected in the conditions faced by Nixon's family, particularly in the difficulties experienced by Nixon's father, Frank.

The elder Nixon had a hard time making a go of it. He was a trolley car conductor until he was fired, then flopped as a carpenter, a farm hand, and a lemon grower before opening a general store that became a fairly dependable source of income. The Nixons still were a long way from easy street, though. Like the rest of the family, Richard had to work hard, hoeing weeds in the lemon grove, getting up before dawn every day to buy produce for the grocery store. "We were poor. We had very little. We had used hand-me-down clothes. . . . We certainly had to learn the value of money," Nixon recalled years later.

The family always had food on the table and a roof over their heads. Yet they were rarely free from anxiety, in part because Frank Nixon had both bad luck and poor judgment.

In 1919 he turned down a fat offer from an oil speculator for property he owned in Yorba Linda that he later sold for less than one-tenth of that amount. When he moved from there in 1922, he chose a location in Whittier instead of a site in Santa Fe Springs, where two years later enough oil was discovered to have made the Nixons rich.

He did manage to make a moderate success of his general store in Whittier. But the Depression, and the long illness of Nixon's brother, Harold, before he died of tuberculosis, cost Frank much of what he had accomplished. During her two years at an Arizona nursing home with the stricken Harold, Hannah Nixon paid the board by scrubbing floors and cooking. Her husband helped meet the bills by selling the land on which his store was built.

Not surprisingly, this succession of setbacks had an impact on Frank Nixon's political outlook, which in turn affected his son Richard. "My father had a deep belief in the 'little man' in America," his son later wrote. "He opposed the vested interests and the political machines that exercised so much control over American life at the beginning of the century."

Though he had been, in his son's phrase, "a hard-line Ohio Republican" most of his life, in the wake of his bad luck in real estate and oil, Frank Nixon "became disenchanted with the stand-pat Republicanism of Harding and Coolidge." He deserted the GOP in 1924 to vote for Robert La Follette, the Progressive party candidate, and "a populist strain entered his thinking." During the Teapot Dome scandal in 1924, Frank Nixon fumed so much about the corrupt politicians that eleven-year-old Richard told his mother, "When I get big I'm going to be a lawyer they can't bribe."

The elder Nixon considered the Standard Oil trust created by John D. Rockefeller to be such "a blight on the American landscape," that he refused to do business with the company and insisted on having his service station supplied by Richfield instead. Worried about the future of his grocery, he "became a vociferous opponent of chain stores," which he feared "would crush the independent operator and the family grocery store."

After casting a Progressive ballot in 1924, Frank voted for Republican Herbert Hoover in 1928 and 1932. But then in 1936, after Harold's costly illness and death, he voted for Franklin Roosevelt's re-election—or so Nixon believed—rather than for Republican Al Landon, whom he considered "a stand patter."

Listening to his father's populist complaints and looking at his family's circumstances, Richard Nixon came to understand how forces beyond an individual's control combined with hard luck could threaten his livelihood and the security of his family. But in the process of being handed down from one generation to the next, the father's populist attacks on the power of "the vested interests" were transmuted into the son's defense of the status of the middle class against the assaults of communism and the intrusions of government.

This change reflected the other circumstances of Richard Nixon's early years. For one thing, his hometown, Whittier, was certainly no hotbed of Populism. It was as solidly Republican as Lyndon Johnson's Hill Country and John Kennedy's Boston were staunchly Democratic. For a young man with political ambitions, which Nixon exhibited early on, Republican was the way to go.

Even the Depression did not shake Richard Nixon's faith in free enterprise. His chief reaction to those years was instead a resentment and suspicion of the burgeoning government apparatus that developed under the New Deal. "We used to argue politics constantly," a young woman Nixon dated regularly at Whittier College later recalled. "He was a Republican. I thought Roosevelt was wonderful and he detested him."

In 1940, Nixon "strongly supported" Wendell Willkie, even campaigned for him, because he opposed Roosevelt's attempt to break the two-term tradition. In 1941 after practicing law in Whittier and before enlisting in the navy, Nixon did an eight-month stint with the Office of Price Administration in wartime Washington. He later claimed that this experience "had an enormous effect" on his political views, though it seems mainly to have reinforced the beliefs he already held and given him ammunition to support them. Nixon's most enduring impression was that some government workers "became obsessed with their own power and seemed to delight in kicking people around, particularly those in the private sector."

Unlike his father, who rebelled against "stand-pat" Republicanism, Nixon had long viewed rebellion as a threat. In a high school speech contest in 1929 on the Bill of Rights, Nixon's opponent called for extending these rights around the world. Nixon wanted to limit them to U.S. citizens, who had demonstrated that they were responsible and therefore deserving of Constitutional protection. The first ten amendments he referred to not as rights but as "our privileges." And the youthful orator warned, in words that foreshadowed the rhetoric of the adult politician:

> There are those who under the pretense of freedom of speech and freedom of the press have incited riots, assailed our patriotism and denounced the Constitution itself. They have used Constitutional privileges to protect the very act by which they wished to destroy the Constitution. Consequently laws have justly been provided for punishing those who abuse their Constitutional privileges.

Nixon's argument reflected the prevailing thinking in Southern California, where union busting and red baiting had long been the order of the day. During the Red Scare that followed World War I, in no area of the country were authorities more vigilant or less inhibited by Constitutional protections in their effort to stamp out the Bolshevik menace. From 1919 to 1921 more than 500 persons were arrested and 264 convicted under California's criminal-syndicalist, red flag, and sedition statutes. These presumably were the laws young Nixon had in mind as designed to punish "those who abuse their Constitutional privilege." The Los Angeles school system banned the *Nation* and *New Republic* from its libraries and fired teachers who dared to discuss such supposedly subversive subjects as public ownership of utilities.

In the next year's speech contest, with the Depression worsening and unrest beginning to build, Nixon spoke on "Americans' dependence on the Constitution," warning that "at the present time, a great wave of indifference to the Constitution's authority, disrespect of its law and opposition to its basic principles threatens its very foundations."

These were the sort of solidly middle-class beliefs that helped launch Nixon's political career after his return from the navy in 1946. His chief backing came from the "Committee of 100" made up of small businessmen, professionals, and ranchers in his hometown. They had long resented Franklin Roosevelt's New Deal, and the regime of Harry Truman and the economic dislocations of the postwar years made them even more determined to rid themselves of the curse of big government, or at least that part of it represented by their Democratic congressman, Jerry Voorhis, seeking a sixth term.

Sensing the mood of these Southern California burghers, Nixon exploited it brilliantly when he sought their endorsement. The country had a choice, he told them, between two contrasting views of the American political system: the New Deal idea of "government control in regulating our lives," and his position, based on faith in "individual freedom and all that initiative can produce." With the committee enthusiastically behind him, Nixon began his career as political polarizer, adroitly linking the postwar discontent to what would be his lifelong theme of the imperiled middle class.

The key to his strategy was attacking Voorhis as a tool of the allegedly communist-tinged CIO Political Action Committee (PAC), which Nixon portrayed as the enemy of all the middle class held dear. Because the PAC had endorsed Voorhis in the past, Nixon claimed it had done so again for the 1946 campaign. Actually this was untrue, because some of Voorhis's positions had irritated the PAC leadership.* But Voorhis was so ineffective in denying the charge and Nixon so aggressive in making it that Voorhis was thrown permanently on the defensive. The PAC charge was the first piece of evidence that would ultimately earn Nixon his reputation as "Tricky Dick," and make his name among Democrats a synonym for deceit.

The PAC charge also helped Nixon exploit what were the prime Republican issues around the land in that first post–World War II campaign—shortages of every product from toasters to T-bones and the

---

* Nixon's case against Voorhis on the CIO-PAC endorsement rested on the fact that the local chapter of the National Citizens Political Action Committee (NC-PAC) had sought to get *its* national leadership to endorse Voorhis. The endorsement was not given. Though both organizations shared some of the same goals and leaders, they were separate and NC-PAC was not communist-dominated. The distinction was lost on most voters.

highest inflation rate of the century. All this was blamed on the Democratic administration, whose follies were made to seem even more outrageous to middle-class voters who heard Nixon's charges of the role of big labor and communism in influencing the administration.

Having won Voorhis's seat with a slashing right-wing attack, Nixon was careful once he got to Washington to take centrist positions on certain issues that he realized were more consistent with his role as a defender of middle-class interests than those of the right wing. These positions were designed to help advance anti-communism, fast becoming the underlying theme of his commitment to the middle class, which felt threatened by Soviet power abroad and subversion at home. In 1947, when many conservative Republicans opposed any foreign aid at all, particularly aid to Europe, Nixon vigorously supported the Marshall Plan as a way to bring stability to Western Europe. When a poll showed that voters in Nixon's district were strongly opposed to it, he took the stump on behalf of the plan, arguing that it was necessary "if we were to save Europe from the twin specters of starvation and communism." He made a good enough case that in the end he claimed his popularity was enhanced.

Meanwhile, on a range of domestic issues he established himself as advocate for middle-class economic interests as defined by the conservative leadership of the Republican party. He voted with a majority of his party 84% of the time in his first year in Congress. By the end of his second term, he could cite positions on a number of key issues as protective of middle-class well-being. Among others, he voted for the Taft-Hartley law, which organized labor opposed, and voted against national health insurance, which Nixon called socialized medicine. By and large, Nixon explained to middle-class voters, he was opposed to the increase of government regulation and wanted instead to "encourage to the fullest extent possible individual opportunity."

But it was anti-communism, rather than any of these economic issues, that propelled Nixon into the national limelight in his very first term in Congress. By his dogged and ultimately successful pursuit of charges that Alger Hiss, who had been a well-connected figure in the Democratic State Department, was a Soviet agent, Nixon gave credence to the darkest suspicions of the middle class that the nation's destiny was being manipulated by a far-reaching communist conspiracy. And he identified himself with that issue for the rest of his career.

The case, resulting in Hiss's conviction for perjury in January 1950, advanced Nixon's polarizing strategy in two ways. Defensively, it allowed him to portray himself as a favorite target for communists, fellow travelers, and left-wingers. This tactic proved useful to him during the 1952 campaign controversy over charges that he was the beneficiary of a "secret fund" established by wealthy businessmen. Fighting for his political life, Nixon was quick to attribute the furor to the animosity of the left. "You folks know I did the work of investigating the Communists in the United States," he said from his campaign train. "Ever since I have done that work, the Communists and the left wingers have been fighting me with every smear they had."

The Hiss case strengthened Nixon offensively, too, helping him to make a broad appeal to middle-class voters in both parties on grounds of his credentials as a prime battler against communism. His first target was Helen Gahagan Douglas, his Democratic opponent in the 1950 California Senate race.

By the time that campaign got under way, the outbreak of the Korean War in June 1950 naturally increased American concern about the threat of communism and made Nixon's status as a top commie fighter even more potent politically. Reflecting the temper of the times, and the contagion of polarization, Douglas attempted some red baiting of her own in the campaign, charging that Nixon had voted with left-wing Representative Vito Marcantonio of New York in cutting aid to Korea.

Nixon easily refuted that charge, and all Douglas accomplished was to focus attention on the issue of communism, on which she was far more vulnerable than Nixon. Nixon's campaign manager called Douglas the "Pink Lady," and Nixon himself in one stump speech declared his opponent was "pink right down to her underwear." Whenever he could, Nixon coupled her with Hiss, and recalling Douglas's opposition to the House Committee on Un-American Activities, Nixon charged, "If she had her way the Communist conspiracy in the U.S. would never have been exposed." Meanwhile Nixon's anti-communist credentials gained him the support of prominent Democrats, contributing to his overwhelming victory. Both candidates were guilty of shoddy campaigning. But Nixon's tactics were more outrageous and more successful.

From precinct captain to presidential nominee, the Republicans clearly saw that Nixon's reputation as an implacable foe of the left was a prime political asset. At the party's 1952 national convention Eisenhower hailed his freshly nominated running mate as a person "with a special talent and an ability to ferret out any kind of subversive influence where it may be found and the strength and persistence to get rid of it."

To Herbert Brownell, one of Eisenhower's chief strategists, "Nixon seemed an almost ideal candidate for vice president. . . . The President could be presented to the country as one who would stand up against the Communists in the international sphere and Nixon would lead the fight in the discussion of the domestic issues."

Eisenhower had in mind an aggressive role for his young running mate, too. Nevertheless, at times Eisenhower had qualms about the way Nixon played his assigned part, and the president's ambivalence created confusion and difficulty for Nixon. His long tenure as vice-president was to demonstrate that his polarizing strategy had disadvantages as well as benefits.

In their first discussion of 1952 campaign strategy, Eisenhower made plain that he "envisioned taking an above-the-battle position, and that whatever hard partisan campaigning was required would be pretty much left to me," Nixon later recalled. As far as the threat of communism was concerned, Nixon remembered Eisenhower saying, "The Hiss case was a text from which I could preach anywhere in the country."

As might be expected, Nixon poured it on, with his invective mounting as the secret fund episode dramatized his candidacy and as the campaign neared its climax. His most notorious speeches came late in October. In one he branded Stevenson, Acheson, and Truman as "traitors to the high principles in which many of the nation's Democrats believe."* In another oration he said that Stevenson had "a Ph.D. degree from Acheson's college of Cowardly Communist Containment."

Eisenhower recognized Nixon's contribution to the campaign as prime antagonist of the Democrats. Yet he also felt that Nixon "was too right wing and irresponsible in his views" and "too strident" in attacking the Democrats. In answer to this somewhat hypocritical disapproval, Nixon later acknowledged, "Some of the rhetoric I used during this campaign was very rough." He went on to state, "Perhaps I was simply carried away by the partisan role Eisenhower had assigned me and the knowledge that someone had to fire up the party faithful."

This pattern of aggressiveness repeated itself in the 1954 congressional campaign. After first urging that Republican campaigners defend Eisenhower's economic policies, Nixon apparently lost faith in his own advice and went on the attack. He charged that the policy of Truman's Secretary of State Dean Acheson "was directly responsible for the loss of China," and therefore for the Korean War and the war in Indochina, which the French were then losing. For this Eisenhower bawled him out, and Nixon had to promise to be more reticent.

In the 1956 re-election campaign, Eisenhower was well out in front from the beginning, and Nixon did adopt a more restrained stance, giving rise to talk of "a new Nixon." But in 1958 with prospects bleak for the GOP, Nixon hammered away again, spreading rancor among Democrats

---

* Truman never forgave Nixon for calling him a "traitor," though Nixon insisted that he had merely accused the thirty-third president of betraying his party, not his country.

and Republicans alike. He lambasted the Democrats for their "sorry record of retreat and appeasement" and "defensive, defeatist, fuzzy-headed thinking" which, Nixon claimed, had resulted in the loss of China and the onset of the Korean War.

Both Eisenhower and Dulles, who relied on Democratic cooperation on foreign policy, criticized him publicly. Nixon responded by saying that it was understandable that the president would want to place himself above the battle, but that the guidelines for a partisan like himself were different. "One of the reasons the Republican Party is in trouble today is because we have allowed people to criticize our policies and we have not stood up and answered effectively," he said. "I intend to continue to answer the attack . . . that's my view of a political campaign."

Nixon was half right. He was wrong in his diagnosis of the Republican party's problems. The party would take a terrific shellacking election day—losing 47 House seats as well as 13 seats in the Senate—not because of foreign policy but because the economy had sunk into a deep recession.

As a reporter in Detroit at that time I remember the despondency that overwhelmed the Motor City as auto-assembly lines shut down and workers were turned out into the streets. In their desperation the auto companies tried to convince Americans that it was their patriotic duty to buy a new car to help get the economy back in high gear. "You auto buy now!" was one typical slogan. But Detroiters scraping by, many of whom still remembered the greed of the auto dealers during the postwar years of shortages and black markets, just jeered and voted Democratic.

What Nixon attempted to do by his furious attacks on Democratic foreign policy was take the voters' minds off jobless gloom and make them worry about the damage Democratic congressmen might cause abroad. It did not work.

Nixon was right, though, in his view of what a political campaign should be like. It should indeed involve give-and-take between Democrats and Republicans. And certainly the Democrats were in a position to give back as good as they got from the vice-president. This was a view alien to Eisenhower because of his narrow understanding of politics and certainly to Dulles who did not even pretend to be a politician. Their concern was with preserving "bipartisanship" in foreign policy not because it necessarily served the highest order of truth but because it was convenient for them to be insulated from criticism of their mistakes from the opposition party.

But Nixon was no longer free to choose between stridency and moderation. By the time the 1958 election ended, the vice-president had carved out an indelible image for himself in the public's mind. To an extent his well-established identity was a plus. Nixon could get his name in the press and on radio and television with ease, an achievement greatly envied by lesser-known politicians. It was harder and harder, though, for him to control how he would be presented and perceived.

Nixon's image was shaped by a range of memories—the Hiss case, the Nixon fund controversy, the slashing attacks of a half-dozen campaigns. And these remembrances were so emotionally charged that in terms of the retention span of the average American voter they were veritable primordial recollections. The impact on Nixon's political fate was clear in the two back-to-back defeats he suffered, running for the presidency in 1960 and for the governorship of California in 1962.

Both setbacks emphasized the problems inherent in Nixon's polarizing strategy to win middle-class support. His strategy depended on an apparent threat to the middle class as a result of national conditions or of his opponent's defects. But in 1960, as the vice-president of the incumbent administration, Nixon could scarcely blame the nation's problems on his opponent, Democrat John Kennedy. Instead it was Kennedy who seized the initiative on Nixon's favorite issue, communism, accusing the Republicans of not being tough enough on communism abroad—by allowing a "missile gap" and by not cracking down on Castro's Cuba. Meanwhile, Nixon's own divisive reputation helped rally Democrats to support Kennedy.

In California in 1962, running against incumbent Democrat Pat Brown, Nixon found himself the dominant issue in the campaign. The speculation that he planned to use the office as stepping-stone to the presidency, as well as a controversial loan made by a defense contractor to his brother Donald, overshadowed his efforts to attack Brown.

The realization of the trap that he had created for himself contributed to the resentment that poured out in his "last press conference." But by declaring, "You won't have Nixon to kick around anymore," Nixon at least returned to a familiar and effective stance. Once again he was an embattled figure, assaulted by foes on all sides but not prepared to yield. In fact, he spent much of his time during the next six years pondering the lessons of these defeats to make certain they would not be repeated.

VALUES

Just as Nixon's identification with middle-class political interests was the core of his ideology, so was his commitment to middle-class standards the foundation of his value structure. Nixon's upbringing fostered a natural affinity for such values as free enterprise, individualism, and the sanctity of the family, and his public discourse was liberally sprinkled with such terms. To advance himself politically, however, he often found it more effective to attack the forces that he contended threatened these values—notably communism and big government. Nixon dramatized these threats, but he did not invent them; they arose from the social and economic ferment that gripped the country in the years between the two world wars.

In 1922, when he was nine, his family moved from Yorba Linda to Whittier, twenty miles east of Los Angeles, and one of the largest Quaker settlements in the U.S. Outwardly a tranquil place, Whittier resembled the sort of small town in Ohio in which Frank Nixon had been raised late in the nineteenth century. "Neatly paved and enlivened with crowds of crisp-looking girls, healthy, fresh and clear as the air itself, and happy in well-starched blouses or clean muslin frocks" was the way the town and surrounding communities were sketched in a contemporary travelogue.

"Three words describe my life in Whittier: family, church and school," Nixon wrote later, citing three bulwarks of middle-class values. He left out a fourth that was equally reflective of the middle class and of his boyhood: business. In the early twenties Whittier, along with most of the rest of the country, was enjoying an economic boom that nurtured ambition and rewarded hard work. When he moved his family to Whittier in 1922 Frank Nixon opened a filling station. Over the next three years, during which the whole family toiled night and day, the enterprise steadily expanded and was transformed into a thriving general store.

Underneath the stable facade, social and economic shifts abetted by technological advances already seemed to be jeopardizing the middle-class values that the Nixons had brought with them to the Pacific shores. The Midwest style of Protestantism was not vigorous enough to satisfy the spiritual needs of bustling Southern Californians, even of Quakers like the Nixons. They often drove to Los Angeles to hear Aimee Semple McPherson, "evangelist of a Four Square Gospel made in California," who held forth in her five-thousand-seat temple. Another attraction for the Nixons was Bob Shuler, who used the power he gained from his vast radio audience to attack such heresies as the teaching of evolution and to threaten the careers of public officials who failed to conform to his moral standards.

One reason the Quakers had chosen to found Whittier in 1887 was because it was removed from the railroad lines. They did not anticipate the development of the automobile and other threats to the tranquility of Whittier, such as the proliferating Hispanic society in its environs and the burgeoning of nearby Hollywood, with its enticements of glamour and make-believe.

This flux and turmoil, though particularly conspicuous in Nixon's California, was only part of a national upheaval in manners and morals that characterized the roaring twenties. One of the most troublesome aspects of these agitated conditions, as social historian Frederick Lewis Allen pointed out, is that it is "not easy to overthrow the moral code and substitute another without confusion and distress." For millions of Americans "the only values they had been trained to understand were being undermined."

As if this were not disturbing enough for middle-class Americans, the economy came thundering down on their heads in the wake of the 1929 stock market crash. As commerce and industry ground to a halt, people's savings vanished and lives were wrecked for reasons that were almost impossible to fathom. Many of the victims of the Great Depression, Allen wrote, "had been brought up to feel that if you worked hard and well and otherwise behaved yourself you would be rewarded by good fortune. Here were failure and defeat visiting the energetic along with the feckless . . . the virtuous along with the irresponsible."

The Nixon family did not escape entirely. Belts had to be tightened and Richard Nixon became a victim of the relative family austerity. "I had dreamed of going to college in the East," he later recalled. He certainly had the qualifications, having graduated third in his class, twice won local oratorical contests, served as student body manager, and been selected by the Harvard Club of California as outstanding all-around student. He did have the possibility of a scholarship to Yale but given the decline in business at the family store due to the Depression and the burden of his brother Harold's illness, the family concluded that Richard would have to stay home and attend Whittier College. He claimed not to have been disappointed, because "the idea of college itself was so exciting that nothing could have dimmed it for me."

Yet being denied the chance to go to Harvard or Yale taught him that the boyhood values he had cherished could not be taken for granted. This lesson would be reinforced by other episodes in his life and would in the long run aid him as a political leader to reflect and exploit the concern of millions of Americans that their traditional middle-class values were eroding.

The success of the New Deal made some in the middle class appreciative of government and resentful of the evils of big business. But once the government had helped to repair the worst of the economic damage, a good many others saw government itself, with its intrusive regulations and burdensome taxes, as posing the greatest threat to their values. Richard Nixon was part of this group.

This was only natural because though he and his family had been hard-pressed at times, he never yielded his identification with the middle class. "It's been said our family was poor, and maybe it was in a way," Nixon once told journalist Stewart Alsop. "But we never thought of ourselves as poor and we never had to depend on anyone else."

What distinguished his family as middle class rather than poor was Frank Nixon's store, which even in the bleak days of the Depression turned a profit. "I remember back in the 1930s how deeply I felt about the plight of those people my own age who used to come into my father's store where they couldn't pay the bill," Nixon once recalled, "because their fathers were out of work and how this seemed to separate them from others in our school."

Nixon himself was clearly among the more fortunate ones. In the depths of the Depression he bought a two-year-old Model A Ford for $325, more than most students spent on a year of college.

So for Nixon, the middle-class values never lost their validity. And when the Depression faded into memory and he entered politics, he identified with them and defended them.

Probably the most memorable of such occasions was his televised speech defending himself during the Nixon fund furor in the 1952 campaign, when his political future was at stake. With his wife, Pat, at his side, Nixon denied that he had benefited personally from the fund established by some of his supporters, and then gave an account of his then modest finances, which, as he later wrote, he "wrapped up this way":

> I should say this, that Pat doesn't have a mink coat. But she does have a respectable Republican cloth coat, and I always tell her that she would look good in anything. One other thing. We did get something, a gift after the nomination. . . . It was a little cocker spaniel dog . . . and our little girl, Tricia, the six-year-old, named it Checkers. And you know, the kids, like all kids, loved the dog, and I just want to say this, right now, that regardless of what they say about it, we are going to keep it.

Nixon captured the sentiments that stir the hearts of middle-class America. His words combined the pride of the solid family man in his wife who would "look good in anything" and in the respectability of her cloth coat, with an undeniable measure of resentment at members of the upper class, who presumably *did* have a mink coat. Also embodied in the Checkers speech, as it came to be called, was the devotion of the family man willing to protect his children's pet and their happiness against the worst that "they," whoever they might be, could say or do.

It was not a subtle performance, and many people found it mawkish and tasteless in the extreme. After watching Nixon in his own living room, Walter Lippmann turned to his guests, the correspondent of the *Times* of London and his wife, and said, "This must be the most demeaning experience my country has ever had to bear." In his column the next day he wrote of the speech that it was "with all the magnification of modern electronics, simply mob law."

But Lippmann and his readers were not the middle-class voters to whom Nixon was speaking. In fact, he had gauged his audience superbly. In response to his plea for support, some 200,000 letters poured into Republican party headquarters in Washington, along with 160,000 telegrams. The verdict in Nixon's favor was roughly 350 to 1.

In addition to defending himself by appealing to middle-class values, Nixon generated support by attacking threats to these values. The most rewarding of these targets was Alger Hiss. Handsome, educated in the best schools, accustomed to holding the best jobs and associating with the best people, Hiss was the epitome of the mid-century American elitist. A Harvard Law School classmate once said of Hiss: "If he were standing at the bar with the British Ambassador and you were told to give a package to the Ambassador's valet, you would give it to the Ambassador before you gave it to Alger."

Wholly apart from any involvement in espionage, Hiss was just the sort of patrician figure who aroused instinctive resentment from many middle-class voters. He had ties not only to prominent Democratic leaders such as Dean Acheson and Adlai Stevenson, but also to such a distinguished Republican as John Foster Dulles, who as chairman of the Carnegie Endowment had hired Hiss as their president. By taking the great risk to his own career of challenging Hiss, Nixon set himself apart from other politicians.

Similarly during the 1952 campaign, Nixon mercilessly attacked Hiss's old colleague, Dean Acheson, who fell into the same category. "His clipped moustache, his British tweeds and his haughty manner made him the perfect foil for my attacks on the snobbish kind of foreign service personality and mentality that had been taken in hook, line and sinker by the Communists," Nixon observed.

On less substantial ground, Nixon went after Harry Truman during his 1960 presidential campaign. When a question about Truman's intemperate language was raised during his third campaign debate with Kennedy in 1960, Nixon said, "When a man's president of the United States, or a former president, he has an obligation not to lose his temper in public. One thing I've noted as I've traveled around the country are the tremendous number of children who come out to see the presidential candidates."

If he won the election, Nixon said he hoped that American parents would be able to look at him, whatever they thought of his policies, and say, "Well, there is a man who maintains the kind of standards personally that I would want my child to follow."

John Kennedy parried with a lighthearted rejoinder: "I really don't think there's anything that I could say to President Truman that's going to cause him, at age seventy-six, to change his particular speaking manner. Perhaps Mrs. Truman can, but I don't think I can."

Nixon continued to take middle-class values seriously after he took office in 1969. As he analyzed the wave of protest against the war, and the overall permissiveness that accompanied it, Nixon decided, as he later wrote, that he was ready "to take a stand on these social and cultural issues. I was anxious to defend the 'square' virtues." On issues such as his opposition to funding abortion and legalizing marijuana and his support for "unabashed patriotism," Nixon claimed that he "would be standing against the prevailing social winds, and that would cause tension." But, he went on to note, "I thought that at least someone in high office should be standing up for what he believed"—and, he might have added, for what the middle-class silent majority also believed.

CHARACTER

"Courage—or putting it more accurately, lack of fear—is a result of discipline," Nixon wrote in *Six Crises*, after losing his first run for the presidency. "Any man who claims never to have known fear is either lying or else he is stupid. But by an act of will, he refuses to think of the reasons for fear and so concentrates entirely on winning the battle." By an act of will Nixon throughout his career was able to shut out not just fear but also pride or shame so that he could contest the endless battles that shaped his career.

It was this will that dominated his character, allowing him to overcome other traits which were handicaps to him in his chosen field of politics. But Nixon's determination to conquer the obstacles he faced was so single-minded that it distorted his view of reality and ultimately left him isolated, beleaguered, and vulnerable to the many enemies he had made.

From his youth Nixon brought to every competition not only the total commitment of his mental and physical energies, but a willingness to bend and break the rules to his advantage and a cunning insight into how best to accomplish this. "Pour it on at this point," or "Play to the judges; they're the ones who decide," he advised his Whittier College teammates in debate contests. "He would always come up with something," one debate colleague recalled. Once the editor of the college newspaper, watching a debate from the gallery, was shocked to observe that the sheet of paper from which Nixon seemed to be reciting figures to support his argument was in fact blank. "It was all against regulations and very cunning," she said.

The deviousness of the college debater evolved into the chicanery of the political candidate. After watching Nixon assault Jerry Voorhis with "half-truths" and "innuendos" about the alleged PAC endorsement during his first congressional campaign, a former college debate partner in his distress confronted Nixon directly. "Why are you doing this?" he asked his old friend.

"Sometimes you have to do this to be a candidate," Nixon replied. "I'm gonna win."

Nixon would later deny that his tactics against Voorhis had exceeded the bounds of vigorous debate. "If some of my rhetoric seems overstated now, it was nonetheless in keeping with the approach that seasoned Republican politicians were using that year," he wrote. It was true that red baiting was rampant in the 1946 campaign. But for most other Republicans this tactic represented nothing more than an occasional indulgence. For Nixon the smears of Voorhis and of later foes were part of a persistent, calculated pattern of negativism and dissembling stemming from the core of his character.

If he was to succeed at politics Nixon needed all the guile and determination he could muster. For he had to overcome not only his opponents but his own brooding, introspective nature and the saturnine impression he created. After watching him debate John Kennedy in the 1960 campaign, Marshall McLuhan said he resembled "the railway lawyer who signs leases that are not in the best interest of the folks in the little town." Norman Mailer likened him to "a church usher, of the variety who would twist a boy's ear after removing him from church."

No other modern president has seemed less comfortable with himself. Nixon's self-consciousness compelled him to close the kitchen blinds in their home in Yorba Linda so he would not be seen doing the evening dishes for his mother. Later on, when it was his task to buy produce for the family grocery store in Whittier, he rose at 4:00 A.M. for the drive to the market in downtown Los Angeles. "He didn't want anybody to see him go get vegetables, so he got up real early and then got back real quick," a cousin who worked with him in the store recalled.

Nixon heaped praise on both his parents publicly. In his 1968 speech accepting the presidential nomination, he lauded his father for having "sacrificed everything" so he could go to college, and in his emotional farewell to the presidency he described his mother as a saint. But it is clear from Nixon's account of his growing up that both were difficult personalities who contributed to his inner tensions.

Frank Nixon had been "discouraged and frustrated" by his early working career, Nixon writes, adding: "It was his temper that impressed me most as a child. . . . He was a strict and stern disciplinarian and I tried to follow my mother's example of not crossing him when he was in a bad mood."

In an attempt at self-analysis, Nixon suggests that the cause of his own "personal aversion to confrontations"—referring to personal, not political encounters—was linked to his father's belligerence. Fawn Brodie, Nixon's psycho-biographer, points out that Nixon also tried to be different from his father. For example, he prided himself on remaining cool and detached instead of hotheaded like his father. Also, Frank Nixon had a reputation as a flirt and a pincher, whereas his son has difficulty displaying any affection at all to women in public, not excepting even his own wife.

Hannah Nixon was a serious, deeply religious person. But she was forced to leave Richard and his father for two years while he was in his teens so she could nurse her older son, Harold, a tuberculosis victim. And when weary of her burdens as wife and mother she made brief visits back to the home of her parents. These absences were hard on Richard, who was particularly dependent on her. "As a youngster Richard seemed to need me more than my other sons did," she later said. He liked to be near her when he did his homework, not because he needed help but rather because, she said, "he just liked to have me around."

Nevertheless, Hannah Nixon was a fearsome scold in her son's recollection. "We dreaded far more than my father's hand, her tongue. . . . She would just sit you down and she would talk very quietly and then when you got through you had been through an emotional experience." He added, "In our family, we would always prefer spanking."

Nixon also was twice subjected to the trauma of sibling death, an experience that often leaves a surviving child with feelings of guilt and depression. In Nixon's case, the death of his younger brother, Arthur, from tubercular meningitis when Richard was twelve and of his older brother, Harold, when Nixon was twenty, affected him deeply. "For weeks after Arthur's funeral there was not a day that I did not think about him and cry," he recalled. As for Harold, Richard "sank into a deep, impenetrable silence." From then on, Hannah Nixon recalled, "It seemed that Richard was trying to be three sons in one . . . to make up to his father and me for our loss."

Shy and intense from childhood, Nixon did not make friends easily.

The novelist Jessamyn West, a cousin of Nixon's, said her brother found him to be at an early age, "serious, introspective, interested in history and politics, and no happy-go-lucky play fellow."

He turned for support to teachers and parents. When he looked back years later on a seventh-grade course he had taken on the Constitution and the political system, what he remembered better than the subject matter was what the teacher had taught him about "the importance of fighting hard all the time and working hard all the time." Similarly, he remembered his father's intense interest in his progress in school. "My biggest thrill in those years," he told an interviewer, "was to see the light in his eyes when I brought home a good report card."

In college, where he was notably successful in his courses and in extracurricular activities, he was generally respected, but some students resented his "almost ruthless cocksureness." And another complained that "there was always this barrier" surrounding him that prevented friendship. By the time Nixon entered law school, he had gained the nickname "Gloomy Gus." A professor said, "He was what today we'd call uptight—there was the suggestion of an intellectual inferiority complex."

Yet his determination helped him to make the most of his strengths and overcome his weaknesses. He suffered his first political defeat in his first campaign, losing the election for president of the Whittier High School student body. He "had to work hard at being a politician," one of his Whittier opponents said. "I don't think he ever did have smooth going—not a naturally glad-handing, extroverted politician." But Nixon persisted, achieving success through sheer doggedness. At Whittier College he was elected class president and then student body president, building his campaign around a promise to lift the college's ban on campus dances, a pledge he kept even though he himself disliked dancing.

Despite his shyness and self-consciousness young Nixon also made himself into a top-notch debater and an accomplished student actor. The Whittier drama coach, Albert Upton, taught Nixon to cry on stage, and years later, when Upton saw a photo of Nixon weeping on the shoulders of Senator William Knowland after he had vindicated himself in the Nixon fund case, he exclaimed, "That's my boy. That's my actor."

Nixon also went all out for college football, even though he was too small and lacked athletic skills. His coach, Wallace "Chief" Newman, whom Nixon idolized, later said, "We used Nixon as a punching bag. If he'd had the physical ability, he'd have been a terror."

"I hardly cut a formidable figure on the field," Nixon himself said later. "But I loved the game—the spirit, the teamwork, the friendship."

Realizing that he needed a scholarship to get into law school, he earned excellent grades in college, though he lacked imagination. One of his favorite teachers said, "Nixon had an analytical mind rather than a philosophical mind. He gave all of what was asked. But he didn't vouchsafe much beyond that." Whatever he lacked in imagination, though, he made up in diligence. Smith gave him straight A's.

The portrait that emerges from these accounts is of a young man whose greatest character strength was that he could make himself do almost anything he felt needed to be done to reach his goals. This pattern carried over into his political career during which he made himself seek confrontations and polarize sentiment because he knew by doing this he could arouse enthusiasm for himself that he could accomplish in no other way. As he turned himself into "a punching bag" for the college football team so he could make the team, he invited attack for three decades in national politics so he could gain power.

THE CHALLENGE

Nixon's challenge was the war in Indochina. When he took office it overshadowed all other concerns and threatened to prevent any accomplishments, foreign or domestic. Nixon's leadership success was in turning the war to his political advantage by using it as a rallying point for his middle-class constituency. Thus he was able to stand his ground against the widespread opposition to the war while pursuing his global strategy.

Nixon wanted the war to end, "but in a manner that would save the South Vietnamese people from military defeat and subjection to the domination of the North Vietnamese Communist regime." Just as important, he wanted the war to conclude in a way that would maintain U.S. credibility as a world power so he could carry out his double-barreled grand strategy—establishing diplomatic relations with Red China and detente with the Soviet Union. "To abandon Vietnam to the Communists," he believed, "would cost us inestimably in our search for a stable, structured and lasting peace."

Nixon was fully mindful of the potential power of the protest movement which had massed in Washington for his inauguration. If the resistance to the war intensified, his freedom of action would be restricted and he would find it just as difficult to govern as Lyndon Johnson had. Indeed, in the fall of 1969, as the Nixon White House braced for the first protests of the new presidency, a former aide to Johnson told Nixon's staff, "Now you guys will see how it feels to be prisoners in the White House."

The new president needed to wind down the war in Indochina—"Vietnamization" was the word he used to describe his goal—but he wanted to do this at his own pace, not in response to the antiwar movement. This required a delicate balancing act for an indefinite period.

Right after his narrow election victory over Hubert Humphrey in November 1968, Nixon promised to "bring us together," a slogan born out of his campaign that implied he would heal the deep divisions over Vietnam. At *Newsweek*, where I was then working, the editors made that pledge the focus of a cover story. I called Henry Kissinger, whom I had gotten to know during the campaign when he had been an adviser to Nelson Rockefeller, to ask him if Nixon could indeed "bring us together."

Kissinger, who had not yet become Nixon's national security adviser, snorted. "If he did, it would be the first positive thing he's done in his whole career," he said.

As it turned out, Nixon made Kissinger into a prophet, and Kissinger, as his principal adviser on Vietnam, helped him do it.

Vietnam certainly offered no easy answers to Nixon any more than to Lyndon Johnson. As Kissinger suggested, trying to unify the nation on this issue would not only have been difficult but also out of character for Nixon. Instead, he resorted to polarization. He resolved to isolate the antiwar movement by rallying a more potent force, the middle-class citizens who came to be known as "the silent majority."

He had set the stage for this presidential strategy during the campaign, not only by what he did say about Vietnam but perhaps more important, what he did not say.

Privately Nixon had made up his mind to end U.S. involvement in the war well before he took office. Though he believed that Johnson had erred by failing to use sufficient force at the start, Nixon had come to realize that the public would not support the steps needed for military victory. In March 1968, eight months before election day, Nixon told his campaign advisers, "I've come to the conclusion that there's no way to win the war." Then he added, "But we can't say that, of course."

His approach to solving the dilemma was to make the Vietnam settlement part of what he viewed as a "global transaction," allowing the U.S. to take advantage of the split between China and the Soviet Union. This historic fissure, Nixon realized, could be of enormous benefit to the U.S. All of this had been discussed with his speech writers more than a year before he took power, and this goal was fundamental to every step he took in dealing with Vietnam for the next four years.

The American public, though, had little inkling of this grand strategy because Nixon held his Vietnam cards close to the vest during the campaign. He realized that he would inevitably benefit from public discontent with the war—"If there's war people will vote for me to end it," he told one of his speech writers—regardless of what he said. Therefore, Nixon said as little as possible. By holding his tongue, he set the stage for the confrontation between the antiwar movement and the middle class which was central to his polarizing strategy.

Meanwhile, he used the campaign to reach out to his middle-class constituency. In his acceptance speech at the Miami convention, he reminded middle-class voters not only of Vietnam but also of the threat domestic violence posed to their security—and to their values. "As we look at America, we see cities enveloped in smoke and flame," Nixon said. "We hear sirens in the night. We see Americans dying on distant battlefields.

"Did we come all this way for this?" he asked. "Did American boys die in Normandy and Korea and Valley Forge for this?" The answers to these questions, he said, came from "a quiet voice in the tumult of the shouting. It is the voice of the great majority of Americans, the forgotten Americans, the non-shouters, the non-demonstrators. . . . They give drive to the spirit of America. They give lift to the American dream."

Candidate Nixon had identified the quiet voices to whom he would listen. As president he would provide the text for their discontent.

Once he was in office, his initial bargaining objective in the war was to get the North Vietnamese to withdraw from South Vietnam as a condition for ending U.S. involvement. Even as he began the phased withdrawal of U.S. forces he had long planned, he sought to wring an agreement from Hanoi through a combination of diplomatic pressure on Russia and of military force in Indochina, such as the secret bombing of communist supply lines in Cambodia.

Nixon's international strategy thus combined diplomatic finesse with military might, and while it focused on Vietnam it also scanned broader horizons in the communist world. Nixon looked to Moscow, where he sought detente, and at the same time looked to Beijing, where he laid the groundwork for a dramatic new relationship.

But underlying Nixon's hopes for making a settlement in Vietnam part of "a global transaction" was his political strategy at home. A major part of this blueprint was using the war protestors for his own purposes. At times he mollified the protestors to make himself appear more reasonable. At other times he defied them to make himself seem stronger. But he never lost sight of his main goal—creating a middle-class constituency for his policy.

The failure of Lyndon Johnson to do this had cost him dearly. He was so furious at the opposition to the war and so frustrated by his own inability to end it that he lost sight of the fact that misgivings about the war were spreading beyond the raucous protestors he saw in the street. "Large numbers of people, suburban families with college age kids and that sort of thing were getting to be troubled about the war," Harry McPherson recalled. They were asking, "What the hell is this all about? Why are we fighting it? And if we are to fight it, why don't we win it?"

Nixon understood the importance of responding to these misgivings. As his strategy unfolded, he kept his middle-class constituency always in mind.

At his first National Security Council meeting to discuss Vietnam in late January, Nixon decided to withdraw troops from Vietnam gradually but unilaterally. Commanders in the field were notified, but Nixon held back public announcement. In fact, when he was asked about the possibility of withdrawals at a March press conference, he rejected the idea outright, stirring a storm of criticism.

As a result of Nixon's refusal to spell out his withdrawal policy, Rowland Evans and Robert Novak later wrote, critics of the war "were pulled prematurely into a posture of opposition [to Nixon's policies] from which it was difficult to withdraw." But Nixon was not troubled about this sort of opposition. Indeed, this was a logical requirement for his polarizing strategy. He had concluded that the enmity of the war protestors would help solidify the support of the middle class.

Meanwhile he set out using the bully pulpit of his office to explain his policy to his constituency in his own way. Four months into his presidency, on May 14, in his first address on Vietnam, he outlined his plans to achieve peace. Emphasizing that he recognized the importance of finding an end to the fighting, he declared, "When Americans are risking their lives in war, it is the responsibility of their leaders to take some risks for peace." Unilateral withdrawal of American troops had been ruled out, Nixon said, because it would strengthen the hand of communist leaders "who scorn negotiation." Then he laid out U.S. peace terms: a mutual withdrawal of forces, followed by free elections under international supervision.

The president was walking a tightrope. Having made plain his peaceful hopes—and having decided to announce the first U.S. troop withdrawals from Vietnam on June 8—he sought to prepare his middle-class constituents for this news by reassuring them of his determination to be strong. Speaking appropriately enough at the Air Force Academy on June 4, Nixon warned that if the U.S. should back away from its world responsibilities, "there would be peace . . . but it would be the kind of peace that suffocated freedom in Czechoslovakia."

With these two speeches Nixon strove to drive a wedge between the middle class and the antiwar demonstrators. This strategy was to culminate in his first showdown with the protest movement and his rallying cry to "the silent majority."

During the first months of Nixon's presidency, the protest movement had been relatively quiescent. But as students returned to campuses in the fall and the end of the war seemed no closer, protest leaders announced a new round of demonstrations—the first on October 15, the next on November 15. Nixon promptly announced that "under no circumstances" would he be affected by the demonstrations.

In his memoirs Nixon claims that he wanted to show the North Vietnamese he meant business about an "ultimatum" he had privately issued that threatened to escalate the war if the North made no concessions. But this turned out to be a pledge Nixon could not keep. The arrival of nearly half a million Americans in Washington to participate in the so-called anti-war moratorium on October 15 "undercut the credibility of the ultimatum," as Nixon grudgingly recognized. The protestors had achieved their purpose better than they knew.

The success of the October moratorium stirred speculation that the president would take some dramatic new step toward peace, something on the order of huge new troop withdrawals or even a cease-fire. But Nixon had no such intentions. He laid out the fundamental line in notes made on October 22: "They can't defeat us militarily in Vietnam. They can't break South Vietnam. . . . They can't break us." Meanwhile, the speculation that he would make concessions served to heighten the dramatic impact of the tough position he would take.

Looking ahead to the November 15 demonstration, Nixon knew he had to establish command over events or be forced to abandon his entire blueprint for a phased retreat from Vietnam that would preserve U.S. prestige and his own credibility. Now he decided to reach out to his middle-class constituency directly with a dramatic speech that changed the course of his presidency.

Nixon scheduled his address for Monday, November 3, in between the two demonstrations, allowing him to claim that he was not reacting to either one. But in reality, the timing gave him the chance to respond to the first demonstration and to undercut the second.

Disappointed that he was not assigned to draft the speech, Nixon speech writer William Safire learned that there were no other ghost writers. Instead, "the President was treating this with the seriousness of an Inaugural or an acceptance address, doing it all himself."

On October 24, Nixon left for Camp David, where he spent the weekend working twelve to fourteen hours a day drafting and redrafting. By the next weekend, after a dozen drafts, he was back at Camp David for pre-delivery scrutiny.

Meeting with Republican congressional leaders before the speech, National Security Adviser Henry Kissinger was asked by Republican Senate Leader Hugh Scott, "What's new in the speech?" Kissinger replied, "What's new is our commitment to end the war through Vietnamization." Then he added, "We have two choices, Senator: to get high grades for ingenuity or for candor. In this case, we have chosen the latter, and the president says to the American people, 'Here is what we have to do.' "

The significance of candor was that it helped Nixon contrast himself with his predecessor, Lyndon Johnson. "One of the reasons for the deep division about Vietnam is that many Americans have lost confidence in what their government has told them about our policy," the president pointed out early in the address. He could not ask for support, Nixon said, unless he told the truth. Whether Nixon would actually do that remained to be seen, of course. But by raising the issue of credibility that had been so damaging to Johnson, Nixon at least gained for himself the opportunity to prove his own.

He got off to a good start, by refusing to yield to the temptation to make the future sound easy. He made clear he would not approve "a precipitate withdrawal," which he said "would be a disaster . . . for the cause of peace."

Drawing another favorable contrast with his predecessor, Nixon flatly committed himself to ending the American role in the war, pledging complete withdrawal of all U.S. combat ground forces according to a scheduled timetable. "In the previous Administration we Americanized the war in Vietnam," Nixon said. "In this Administration, we are Vietnamizing the search for peace."

Nixon's use of the "silent majority" phrase, the key to the speech, evolved during the drafting. On the eleventh page of a sixteen-page draft composed during his first long speech-writing weekend at Camp David, Nixon wrote: "Time for great silent majority to speak up for America— to speak up for end the war and win the peace." In an October 30 draft, he altered the wording: "Time for silent center to speak out." But by Sunday morning, November 2, the phrase reappeared in close to final form: "The support of great silent majority of my fellow Americans."

In the 1968 campaign Nixon had used similar constructions. Besides "the forgotten Americans," he had referred to "the silent center," "the new majority," "quiet Americans," and the "quiet majority." This concept was an underlying theme Nixon had been developing along with his basic political strategy. But it was to have particular impact in this speech because of the context and because of Nixon's rhetorical skill.

Before he actually used the phrase, which does not appear until eight paragraphs from the conclusion, Nixon established rapport with his middle-class constituency by the way he described their mutual foe—the opponents of the war. "The approach to silent America is through young America, or for purposes of a rhetorical antithesis, 'shrill America,' " Professor Herman G. Stelzner wrote in a telling analysis. Nixon first referred to the protestors in seemingly positive terms, paying his respects to their "idealism" and sharing their "concern for peace." But then those positive traits were overshadowed by a grave fault of the protestors— "the bitter hatred" to which their opposition to the war has been transformed.

Along with discrediting the protestors, Nixon distanced himself from them. "I would like to address a word, if I may, to the young people of this nation who are particularly concerned . . . about the war," he said. The coolness and formality of this style of address contrasts with the directness with which Nixon spoke to the middle class: "And so tonight— to you, the great silent majority of my fellow Americans—I ask for your support."

The president reminded his listeners that in his campaign he pledged "to end the war in a way that *we* could win the peace." It was clear that by "we" he meant both himself and the silent majority. Then he defined the role of the silent majority in this partnership: "The more support I can have from the American people," Nixon said, "the sooner that pledge can be redeemed."

In the White House immediately afterward, Chief of Staff H. R. Haldeman took notes on the reaction of other staff members and journalists. Defense Secretary Melvin Laird thought the president had shown "real sincerity" and believed that the speech "got through to people"; Patrick Buchanan told Haldeman that the president had gotten across "a good, solid hard line." Robert Semple, the White House correspondent of the *New York Times*, a voice certainly to be heeded, phoned in his judgment: "It was eloquent"—striking praise indeed, coming from a presumably objective journalist.

By morning, the White House had received the biggest response ever to a presidential speech—more than 50,000 wires and 30,000 letters, nearly all of them favorable. A Gallup poll gave the speech a 77% approval rating, and the next week Nixon's personal approval rating climbed to 68%, the highest mark of his presidency.

Even Seymour Hersh, arch critic of Nixon and the war, later conceded:

"America, it seemed, supported a President who sounded aggressive and sure."

Roger Morris, an aide to Kissinger and later a Nixon biographer, later called the speech "a climactic event in the internal evolution of the Vietnam policy. It was the event that determined in so many ways the war would go on." The speech, Morris wrote, led to the "veritable emasculation of the peace movement which left it unable ever again to mount protests similar to those organized that autumn."

Nixon himself explained the success of the speech better than anyone in a radio address three years later. A leader must be willing to take unpopular stands, he said. "But a leader who insists on imposing on the people his own ideas of how they should live their lives—when those ideas go directly contrary to the values of the people themselves—does not understand the role of a leader in a Democracy." When a leader does take an unpopular stand, Nixon said, "he has an obligation to explain it to the people, solicit their support, and win their approval."

Because Nixon met that obligation, he scored a great success that he described in his memoirs "as both a milestone and a turning point for my Administration. . . .

> Now, for a time at least, the enemy could no longer count on dissent in America to give them the victory they could not win on the battlefield. I had the public support I needed to continue a policy of waging war in Vietnam and negotiating for peace in Paris until we could bring the war to an honorable and successful conclusion."

Nixon used that time and the majority he had won to advance his policies and his country's interests. Standing firm on a highly controversial approach to a divisive issue that had already ruined one presidency, he was nevertheless able to win re-election by a landslide over a Democratic adversary who based his candidacy on opposition to that policy. Nixon believed that a gradual withdrawal from Vietnam was necessary to help him achieve broader aims in foreign policy. He did manage a gradual withdrawal and he did achieve those aims.

Able to deal from strength with the Soviet Union, he reduced tensions with the world's other superpower to the most comfortable point since the 1963 test-ban treaty negotiated by Kennedy and Khrushchev. He furthermore took advantage of that improvement to reach the precedent-setting Strategic Arms Limitation Treaty with Moscow. Meanwhile, ending more than two decades of unrealistic estrangement, Nixon made a dramatic start toward establishing a normal relationship with mainland China and fostering its role as a balance against Soviet ambitions.

Nevertheless, in the long run, Nixon's response to the challenge of Vietnam turned out to demonstrate once again the lesson the Korean War had taught Truman: leadership success is difficult to sustain. Nixon made his point on Vietnam, but then he ran it into the ground. Gaining the power to continue the war yielded benefits for his presidency and for the country. But he let the war go on too long, and for that miscalculation, both Nixon and the country paid a high price.

In a sense, Nixon became a victim of his own success. Because his will and his middle-class values had made his ideological strategy of polarization pay off, he was unwilling to make peace with his enemies for fear he would lose his middle-class supporters. Having gained a majority, he did not try to persuade the minority. They remained dedicated in their dissent. If they could not change Nixon's policy, they could force him into self-destructive acts.

In May 1970, Nixon's decision to "clean out the sanctuaries" of the North Vietnamese in Cambodia inflamed the opposition to the war. The shootings of the Kent State students protesting against the Cambodian invasion followed, and outrage against the war—and at Nixon—mounted.

Opinion polls showed that the president had the silent majority with him, but the pressure of dissent was vexing, particularly on Capitol Hill, where proposals to end the fighting were gaining support. In October 1970, nearly a year after his silent majority address, Nixon appeared ready to make peace in Indochina. He proposed allowing North Vietnamese forces to remain in South Vietnam, an idea he had previously rejected, while U.S. troops made a staged withdrawal. Had this bargain been sealed, Nixon would still have been able to gain the full benefit in prestige from his silent majority success, while the nation would have been spared prolongation of the Vietnam ordeal.

But at this point Nixon had to contend with the incalculable element in the presidential leadership equation—the role of forces outside the president's control—in this case the North Vietnamese. Hanoi rejected Nixon's proposition, demanding that any agreement must include the ouster of Nguyen Van Thieu's South Vietnamese government. Thieu was doomed anyhow, as later events demonstrated, but Nixon was unwilling to accept direct responsibility for his downfall.

A truce was not signed until January 1973, under terms that allowed Thieu to say in power. During the more than two years it took to gain this dubious and short-lived advantage, thousands of American lives were lost and cleavages in the country sharpened, in addition to the terrible havoc wrought by American bombers in North Vietnam.

For Nixon's presidency, Vietnam turned into an institutional disaster. The will that had been the prime strength of his character for most of his life ultimately became self-destructive. As biographer Joan Hoff-Wilson wrote, Nixon's conduct of the ending of the war "established secrecy, wiretapping and capricious personal diplomacy as standard operation procedures in the conduct of foreign policy that ultimately carried over into domestic affairs."

Nixon offered his own self-revealing analysis:

> Once I realized that the Vietnam War could not be ended quickly or easily and that I was going to be up against an anti-war movement that was able to dominate the media with its attitudes and values I was sometimes drawn into the very frame of mind I so despised in the leaders of that movement. They increasingly came to justify almost anything in the name of forcing an immediate end to a war they considered unjustified and immoral. I was similarly driven to preserve the government's ability to conduct foreign policy and to conduct it in the way that I felt would best bring peace.

But it was not only in foreign policy that Nixon adopted this combative stance. In responding to domestic challenges, his characteristic determination, his championship of middle-class values, and his polarization strategy also combined to produce antagonism and division.

His most critical domestic challenge was dealing with the tension between increasing black demands for civil rights expansion and white resistance to those demands, the same problem that in different forms had plagued each of his four predecessors. As Eisenhower's vice-president, Nixon, mindful of the potential of the Negro vote, had suggested that Republican leaders try to rally moderate whites in the South against extremism.* But that had been a decade earlier, before racial divisions had hardened along partisan lines, in part because of Eisenhower's policies, which had created formidable obstacles to any Republican effort to gain votes by appealing to moderation.

In any case, Nixon was no longer interested in such an approach. In winning his party's nomination and the general election, Nixon had made plain as part of his overall appeal to middle-class voters that as president, he would be an ally of white Southerners, sympathetic to their anxieties about the threat of racial integration. As he campaigned in Dixie he chipped away at the federal courts for overreaching their authority, and pledged himself to restore "law and order," a term that most Southerners had no trouble interpreting as meaning putting blacks in their place. "If I am president, I am not going to owe anything to the black community," Nixon told a group of Pennsylvania Republicans.

* See page 65.

The votes of Southern whites helped make Nixon president—he carried seven Southern states—and once in office he sought to solidify their support in much the same way he had rallied the silent majority behind his Vietnam policies. Just as he had used the protest movement against the war to mobilize support to continue the fighting, he used the Supreme Court, and its unyielding opposition to segregation, to rally support to slow the pace of integration.

First he defied the court by having the Justice Department resist its orders. When that approach failed, Nixon sought to change the court, tailoring it to suit the conservative tastes of his Southern supporters. He twice tried to fill a court vacancy with a conservative Southern judge, who presumably would be willing to slow the court-ordered pace of desegregation in Dixie. But each was rejected by the Senate in part because of his views on civil rights. In a public tirade, Nixon then accused the Senate of "malicious character assassination." He called upon "the millions of Americans living in the South" to bear witness to this "act of regional discrimination."

For all of Nixon's fulminations, school desegregation in the South went forward anyway, with the full authority of the high court behind it, as Nixon must have known it would. But he had made clear to the South that the change was none of his doing. In substantive terms his response to the challenge of civil rights accomplished nothing except to delay the inevitable. As an exercise in manipulative politics, though, it could be counted at least a short-term success. By establishing his bona fides with the white South, Nixon consolidated his support there and with the middle class in general. The cost of the divisiveness his polarizing strategy created was a bill that would not come due until later. Meanwhile, his Southern supporters helped him gain his overwhelming majority in 1972, a triumph he was confident would "give the Republican Party the new majority momentum that would give it a new lease on life."

That success, however, did nothing to mellow Nixon's leadership style. Indeed, he seemed more aggressive than ever as he set about responding to his self-designated next challenge—to once and for all break the power of the "liberal establishment" and promote the beliefs of his silent majority. "We will tear up the pea patch," he told his White House staff on the day after his election—and drove that point home by demanding the resignations from all these aides as well as every other political appointee.

Returning to tactics he had used in his first term, he stepped up the bombing of North Vietnam, determined to blast that country into submission, and launched a broad new program of impoundments, refusing to spend money Congress had appropriated for programs Nixon did not approve. Both these actions, in addition to their direct objectives, had the further goal of inciting his adversaries into public opposition that, he believed, would serve to help him rally middle-class support.

Nixon was in the midst of carrying out these stratagems when he was suddenly forced to confront another sort of challenge, which turned out to be the ultimate test of his presidency—the scandal of Watergate. The mysterious burglary of Democratic party headquarters in June 1972 at first had been dismissed as a trivial "caper."

But as gradually became clear the break-in was only the first visible element in a collection of misdeeds which had their roots in Nixon's characteristic determination to prevail at any cost and in his polarizing strategy.

Later on Nixon would seek to justify some of the excesses of Watergate by condemning the malefactions committed by the opposition. "Democratic presidents since FDR had excelled—and reveled—in flexing the formidable political muscle that goes with being the party in the White House," he observed as the 1972 election approached.

> I planned to take no less advantage of it myself. So I ended up keeping the pressure on the people around me to get organized, to get tough, to get information about what the other side was doing. . . . I told my staff we should come up with the kind of imaginative dirty tricks that our Democratic opponents used against us and others so effectively in previous campaigns.

As it turned out, of course, they far outdid the previous machinations of either Democrats or Republicans. In large measure this was because Nixon's re-election campaign took shape not just as a campaign against Democrats but also against the opposition to the war. Nixon had set out to Vietnamize the war in Indochina; now he also Vietnamized his re-election campaign. Figures from the shadowy world of national security and intelligence such as Howard Hunt and Gordon Liddy were recruited for the campaign apparatus, and their minds had little room for distinctions between the interests of national security and the president's re-election prospects.

Consequently Nixon's agents, in addition to engaging in relatively conventional political "dirty tricks" aimed at sowing confusion and discord among their Democratic opponents, also mounted a more ominous campaign against resistance to the war that disregarded the Constitution and included wiretapping and burglary. The reckless aggressiveness of the Nixon White House toward dissent was later described by William Safire as "the political philosophy of the pre-emptive strike which is rooted in an attitude of us against them."

This attitude had long been the underpinning of Nixon's presidential leadership, and it did not change in the midst of the most serious crisis of his turbulent career. As the outcry against him mounted, fed by ever new disclosures of wrongdoing, he lashed out against his foes, hoping to rally his supporters. The decisive moment came in October 1973, when he fired special prosecutor Archibald Cox for insisting that the president turn over tape recordings of his White House conversations. That action, which came to be known as "the Saturday night massacre," brought a storm of public and congressional indignation down on his head, and, it later became clear, effectively ensured that his presidency would be foreshortened.

Still, Nixon fought on as he always had before. On the first day of 1974, which would be the last year of his presidency, he privately pondered whether or not to resign in the face of the growing drive to impeach him. "The *answer*—" he wrote in a note to himself, "*fight*." Later he wrote, "Impeachment was not going to be decided on the basis of the law or historical precedent. Impeachment would be an exercise in public persuasion."

Yet this was a struggle he already sensed he was losing, even if he could not yet admit this to himself. Though he could still attack, his defenses were being shredded. Not only was he accused of managing a cover-up of a political crime, he was also charged with cheating on his income tax by taking huge bogus deductions. Nixon himself tracked his decline in the polls. In 1973, "a majority of the public still believed I was a man of high integrity," he noted later. But by 1974 the charges against him had begun "to undermine the confidence in my integrity."

Through all the months of the Watergate onslaught, Nixon's will remained as strong as ever. His instinct for attack and polarization, the foundation of his ideological strategy, was still keen. What had collapsed was his claim to middle-class values which above all else had made him credible as a political leader. "I am not a crook," the president startled the public by declaring at one point in his ordeal. But the preponderance of evidence suggested otherwise. By his conduct he appeared to have repudiated such prime bulwarks of the middle-class code as respect for law and simple truthfulness.

Over the years Nixon's leadership appeal to middle-class voters had rested on his assertion that he would use political power to protect their interests. Now it appeared he had used that power mainly to advance his own interests and save his own skin and was no longer in a position to be of much help to anyone else.

Just as Nixon lost public favor, he encountered that bane of presidential leadership: unfavorable outside circumstances. The Arab oil embargo in the winter of 1973 cut gasoline supplies and added to the resentment of many voters who believed Nixon was too preoccupied defending himself to manage the country properly.

During the congressional recess in January 1974, I accompanied Angelo Roncallo, a Republican congressman, and his wife, on a walk through his Long Island district to test the mood of his constituents on Nixon.

By his own reckoning, Roncallo talked to more than 250 voters, only two of whom had a positive word for Richard Nixon. Most antagonistic were the motorists waiting for gas in long lines outside every service station we passed.

"How are things going?" Roncallo asked one matron waiting impatiently in her Cadillac.

The woman glared at her congressman. "Angelo," she said, "impeach the son of a bitch."

"How soon people forget the good things a man does," said Mrs. Roncallo.

Even after he resigned to avoid impeachment, Nixon counted on those good things being remembered some day. "History will make the final judgment," he wrote in his memoirs, adding: "It is a judgment I do not fear." But for the time being the verdict on Nixon's presidency that stands is the impeachment resolution voted by the House Judiciary Committee and endorsed by overwhelming public sentiment, which drove him from office in disgrace.

Among his recent predecessors in the White House, in some respects Nixon most resembled his old adversary, Harry Truman. As Nixon himself noted, "Truman thrived on the cut and thrust of politics." So, of course, did Nixon. Both were extreme partisans who were favorite targets for the opposition, and who, up to a point, benefited from being attacked. The chief difference was in how they defined the makeup and interests of the electorate. Truman viewed the voters as underdogs and pledged to use government to act on their behalf. Nixon addressed the electorate as members of the middle class, and promised to defend them against the actions of government, which he argued threatened their well-being.

Like Nixon, Truman was commander-in-chief in the midst of an unpopular war, though the opposition to the Korean War was not as embittered as with Vietnam. Even if it had been, nothing in Truman's past suggested that he would have yielded to it. On the other hand, it is difficult to imagine Truman subverting the Constitution as Nixon did to muzzle the opposition to the war. That conduct was largely a function of Nixon's character; only a thin line separated his single-minded determination from unscrupulousness and lawlessness, and he stepped over that boundary when he felt himself under siege.

Like his immediate predecessor, Lyndon Johnson, Nixon calculated and connived relentlessly, seeking every possible advantage. In strategic terms, though, the two men were polar opposites. Through consensus, Johnson sought political advantage by blurring ideological differences. Nixon, relying on polarization, depended on sharpening disagreements. Both strategies when carried to extremes become self-destructive and damaging to the health of the nation. In Nixon's case the harsh divisions caused by his presidency would remain to confront the next one.

CHAPTER 7

Ford: The Congressman's Congressman

Unpretentious and even tempered, Gerald Ford was generally one of the easiest politicians in Washington for reporters to deal with. But on this pleasant afternoon early in May of 1974, Ford was very much out of character. He was blazing mad.

I found that out when the phone rang at my desk in the *Los Angeles Times* Washington bureau and a secretary told me that Vice-President Ford wanted to talk to me. Before I even had time to say anything more than hello, he started firing away.

"It's my firm recollection we were talking off the record," he said, his voice low, but hard with anger. "Damn it, it just destroys our relationship if what was in my opinion clearly off the record is now going to be used otherwise."

As I frantically scribbled notes trying to keep up with him, I was struck by the fact that Ford had called me to complain bitterly about a story he had not yet read, a story in fact I had not even finished writing. Absurd as it seemed, it was not really hard to understand. This was what it meant to be Richard Nixon's vice-president at the height of the Watergate scandal.

The story that touched off Ford's outburst had its origins the night before aboard *Air Force Two*, the vice-presidential Convair, bringing the sixty-year-old Ford and a handful of reporters, myself included, back from a dinner speech he had delivered to the Economic Club of New York. A few minutes after takeoff Ford had left his private compartment to come back to the press section of the plane. His evening jacket was off, but he was still clad in the dress shirt and trousers he had worn for the black tie dinner.

But it was not the speech, which was routine, that was on the vice-president's mind. Rather, it was a Senate vote earlier in the day on a Nixon Administration proposal for additional military aid for South Vietnam. Ford had delayed his departure for New York so he would be able to cast a tie-breaking vote for the bill if a deadlock developed. But the result was not that close. The administration was beaten, 43 to 38.

Ford made clear to us as he talked that he saw the vote as a sign of how much damage Watergate had done to Nixon's political standing on Capitol Hill and consequently, Ford believed, to Nixon's ability to conduct foreign policy. If Nixon could not persuade the Democratic-controlled Congress to appropriate such monies, Ford told us, the president would be in a poor bargaining position with the Soviets during arms-limitations negotiations.

For the reporters on the plane this was an awkward situation. None of us took notes because of the informality of the setting. But Ford never said the conversation was off the record. At any rate, the fact that the vice-president of the United States was losing confidence in the president of the United States, who was already under an impeachment investigation, was a piece of news that could not be ignored.

After *Air Force Two* landed at Andrews Air Force Base around midnight, we reporters spent a half-hour reconstructing the conversation and discussing how we would use the conversation with Ford to develop stories the next day. We overlooked, however, the linkage between gossip, politics, and journalism, which is an integral part of the Washington environment.

Before I could finish writing my story the next day, little more than twelve hours after *Air Force Two* had landed, word had somehow reached Ford that his after-dinner remarks were going to make headlines. Moreover, the urgency of his comments had been vastly inflated in the retelling. According to the accounts that had been relayed to Ford, he had supposedly said that he had lost all faith in Nixon's ability to manage foreign policy and that he was thinking of resigning the vice-presidency in despair.

I told Ford that the story I was writing was not that dramatic. It simply reported that he was worried about the consequences of the president losing prestige in Congress.

Ford seemed relieved. "There is a difference," he said, "between clout in the Congress right now and clout in the conduct of world affairs." If the story he had heard about were to be published, he said, "I can just see Henry Kissinger blowing his stack."

I never found out what Kissinger's reaction was. But as Ford later revealed in his autobiography, "Nixon was very angry" about what Ford called his "backgrounder for reporters aboard *Air Force Two*."

The incident drove home to me the tensions that Ford faced as vice-president because of Watergate. These problems became even more serious when he succeeded Nixon and was confronted by the dilemma of whether to pardon his predecessor, who had been forced to resign in disgrace. Dealing with the pardon meant coming to grips with Watergate, the most far-reaching political scandal in the nation's history.

This was the first major challenge of Ford's presidency. In responding to it, Ford's values and character, which had aided his rise to party leader in Congress, did not serve him well. Even more of a handicap was his ideology, the limitations of which led him down a path that gravely damaged his presidency and lowered the regard for government of an already cynical electorate.

IDEOLOGY

Gerald Ford was the first man to reach the White House without ever standing in a national election. Almost as unusual—and just as important for his conduct in the office—Ford was the first president in this century to come directly from the House of Representatives, where his service had molded his outlook on politics.

"He was a politician's president, in the best sense of the word," said his longtime friend and White House counsel, Philip Buchen. His was a very limited view of politics, however, focusing inward on the workings of the political system, rather than outward on the nation's fundamental needs and problems. Ford's solidly Republican western Michigan district assured him longevity on the job and reflected and reinforced two main underpinnings of his career—his conservatism and ambition.

His Republican heritage from Grand Rapids was strengthened by his working situation in the House. As a congressman from a safe conservative seat, Ford could devote himself to protecting the status quo in his district and to supporting the majority Republican position in the House. This stance allowed him to satisfy his constituents and at the same time avoid disputes with his Republican colleagues, which might have hindered his climb up the career ladder.

Ford's conservative beliefs opposed government attempts to solve national problems. That outlook jibed with the way the House Republican party worked. This operating system was based mainly on the bargains members struck to help each other, and actions they took to satisfy the short-term interests of their constituents, rather than great national concerns on which conservatives saw little need for government action, anyway. As an insider on Capitol Hill, Ford not only worked through the system, but made it the cornerstone of his actions and beliefs.

The Republican outlook was narrowed not only by the party's conservatism but also by the fact that for nearly all of Ford's service in the House, the Republicans were a minority party. This subordinate status, as Charles Leppert, a longtime House Republican staffer who served on Ford's White House staff pointed out, influenced the way Ford addressed public policy: he reacted rather than initiated. "The majority operates from the perspective that it has the votes to pass programs," Leppert told an interviewer. "Being in the majority means that . . . if members of the minority have amendments they have to seek you out." By contrast, "the minority always deals with things from a largely secondary and reactive standpoint."

The development of Ford's ideology helped bring about his success in Congress. His upbringing in Grand Rapids as the adopted son of a respected local businessman made it easy for him to accept the Republican faith in free enterprise and mistrust in government that prevailed in western Michigan, an acceptance that all but guaranteed his hold on his House seat.

Before World War II, that creed would also have been isolationist in foreign policy. Indeed, Ford had belonged to the militantly anti-interventionist America First Committee during his days at Yale Law School and shared with other young men his age what his old friend Phil Buchen called "a practical pacifism." But then came Pearl Harbor and Ford's service as a navy lieutenant commander in the Pacific. His military experiences gave him "an entirely new perspective," Ford later wrote, and turned him into "an ardent internationalist."

Ford was shrewd enough to realize that for conservatives and Republicans to make political gains, it was not enough to battle big government at home. They must also gird the nation against the threat of communism abroad. In the long run this shift helped solidify Ford's position with Republican internationalists who in the 1950s came to dominate the party and thus aided his advancement in the party's congressional hierarchy. More immediately, the change helped launch his political career.

Ford first sought elective office in 1948, challenging his hometown Republican congressman, Bartel J. Jonkman, a four-term incumbent. Though this seemed to be a long-shot political gamble, Ford had the backstage support of Michigan's senior senator and erstwhile presidential candidate, Arthur Vandenberg, who also came from Grand Rapids.

A bulwark of prewar isolationism, Vandenberg had converted in a dramatic change of heart to internationalism, and in the process he became a mover and shaker in postwar U.S. foreign policy. Jonkman, on the other hand, remained a die-hard isolationist "who spent more time attacking the senior senator than he did other things in Congress." Embarrassed by these assaults by his own congressman, Vandenberg let it be known that he wanted Jonkman replaced.

His allies back home in Grand Rapids quickly settled on Gerald Ford, who felt that "an isolationist like [Jonkman] ought not to go unchallenged." Besides Vandenberg's backing, Ford had on his side the appeal of his youth, and his energetic campaign style was in sharp contrast to the stodgy Jonkman's. Ford won the primary easily, ensuring his election in the rock-ribbed Republican district and the start of his congressional career.

When Ford arrived in Washington in January 1949, the Republican 80th Congress so reviled by Harry Truman had become a footnote to history. With Truman's upset victory over Dewey, the Democrats once again regained the legislative control they had enjoyed during the Roosevelt years. On the minority side, Ford was well down the seniority scale, but as one of the few new Republican congressmen he had also had a small measure of distinction and a large measure of ambition.

Some of Ford's colleagues in his early years in the House, men like John Kennedy and Richard Nixon, were already aiming at the Senate, a goal that would open the way for them to bid for the presidency. But Ford picked a target down the same road on which he was already marching. By the end of his first term he and his aide, John Milanowski, had already begun to talk about reaching the post that they figured was the second most powerful job in Washington—Speaker of the House. "That," Milanowski recalled, "was where all the patronage was, the power."

Meanwhile Ford had taken to heart the advice of his patron, Senator Vandenberg. He had recommended that the new congressman concentrate on two areas—servicing his voters back home and making his mark in committee work, which was where the real business of the House was transacted. His first assignment, on the Public Works committee, proved the value of Vandenberg's counsel and marked the start of Ford's rise in the House. That committee's control over pork-barrel projects gave him an opportunity both to help his constituents and also to do useful favors for his new colleagues.

When New York Representative John Taber, the ranking Republican on the House Appropriations committee, needed information from Public

Works on a particular problem, Ford had his man Milanowski research the issue and draft a full report. The grateful Taber repaid the favor at the start of the next session of Congress by using his seniority to give Ford a choice assignment—a seat on the powerful Appropriations committee. Its control of congressional purse strings gave this committee command of every branch of the far-flung federal bureaucracy, and made its members among the most influential figures in Washington.

Occasionally Ford used his position on Appropriations to protect the interests of his constituency. Thus, as a member of the subcommittee on Defense Department spending, he upbraided the Pentagon for awarding a fat army contract for chairs to a Tennessee company that had never before made any chairs. Unmentioned by Ford, but not overlooked back home, was the fact that Grand Rapids was a great furniture center and home to several of the country's biggest chair factories.

In a broader context, Ford's new post on the defense appropriations panel gave him a chance to demonstrate his commitment to building U.S. military strength in the days of mounting tension with the Soviet Union and Communist China. Not incidentally, his enthusiasm for Pentagon spending bolstered his ties to powerful defense contractors and to colleagues who had military installations or factories in their districts. His support for military outlays was one of the hallmarks of his House career, which helps explain why he was so distressed aboard *Air Force Two* about the Senate's rejection of the Vietnam aid proposal.

Mindful of Vandenberg's counsel that the voters back home "want to hear from you more than they want to read about you," Ford developed such an efficient system for servicing his constituents that his envious colleagues sent their aides to study it. In Ford's office no letter went unanswered, no visitor went without a welcome; for the more prominent guests there was often an invitation for dinner with the congressman or with his vivacious wife, Betty. A Polaroid camera on a tripod became a permanent office fixture, snapping visitors with the congressman if he was in, or seated at his desk if he was not.

Though his job security was protected by the overwhelming Republicanism in his district and his own hard work cultivating grass roots, Ford was not given to taking political risks. In 1954, as he later recalled, Senator Joseph McCarthy "was peddling his charges of treason in high places. People who should have known better tolerated him because they felt *someone* had to alert the nation to the Communist threat." Ford himself considered McCarthy "a professional bully" and "detested him personally," but did not publicly object to him. "In retrospect that was wrong. I should have taken him on. . . . The fact that I didn't speak out against McCarthy is a real regret."

But as Ford noted: "At the time I had no other major regrets." His conscientious attention to the demands of the Republican congressional operating system had secured his base and allowed him to begin looking ahead. "My career was progressing nicely. . . . My seat in the House seemed safe . . . and I dreamed of becoming Speaker of the House."

So safe was his seat, so fond his dream, that he several times shunned the opportunity for higher office. He turned down Michigan Republicans twice, in 1952 and 1954, when they urged him to run for the Senate and a third time in 1956 when they wanted him to seek the governorship. The House was clearly his home.

Ford waited fourteen years before he made his first direct bid for power in the House. He had spent the time using his committee posts to strengthen his position in his district and to make allies among his colleagues. He was not known for his intellect or his imagination or his dynamism. Indeed, outside his own district and the House itself, he was hardly known at all.

For example, Robert Griffin, then a junior Michigan congressman, tells of attending a breakfast meeting in 1959 with Ford and other Michigan House members and a defense manufacturer from the state who was trying to get their support for a Pentagon contract. Ford was then the ranking Republican on the Appropriations committee defense subcommittee.

At one point during breakfast the manufacturer asked Griffin, nodding toward Ford, "Who is that fellow over there? The one with the pipe."

"He's the only guy in this room who could do you any good," Griffin told him. "He's Jerry Ford."

But if Ford did not have high cards, he played the cards he held very well. His long suits were availability and inoffensiveness. A series of Republican reverses helped give him a winning hand.

After losing the presidency in 1960, Republicans suffered another disappointment in 1962 when they failed to improve their minority position in the Congress. It was clear to the "Young Turks" among the Republicans in Congress that their House Leader, Charles Halleck, had to go. Not daring to challenge Halleck directly just yet, they attacked instead one of his lieutenants, Charles Hoeven of Iowa, chairman of the House Republican conference, the third-ranking post in the House leadership. Griffin and New York Congressman Charles Goodell approached Ford to take on the task. "It wasn't as though everybody was wildly enthusiastic about Jerry," Goodell said later. "It was just that most Republicans liked and respected him. He didn't have any enemies."

Reluctant at first, Ford allowed himself to be persuaded to challenge Hoeven and won. "You'd better be careful," Hoeven warned Halleck. "He's just taken my job and the next thing you know he'll be after yours."

Halleck should have taken heed. After the Republicans suffered a landslide defeat in the 1964 election because of the massive repudiation of Barry Goldwater's presidential candidacy, Ford did challenge Halleck. The insurgents at first had a hard time deciding between him and Wisconsin's Mel Laird, who was younger, more aggressive, and more gifted politically. Ford's biggest asset, Griffin recalled, was that unlike Laird he "seemed to have no enemies. Everybody liked him. He was a good guy."

Ford served in the House for more than twenty-five years, the last ten as leader of his party. He cast well over three thousand roll-call votes on legislation and showed himself to be solid in his loyalties to his party and to its presidents. His votes on major issues tended to support his hazy description of his "political philosophy," which he claimed to have formed before he entered Congress and maintained ever since. "On economic policy, I was conservative—and very proud of it. I didn't believe that we could solve problems simply by throwing money at them. On social issues I was a moderate; on questions of foreign policy, a liberal." Along with the voters of the Fifth District, he "tended to agree with Thomas Jefferson's axiom that the best government is the least government."

More important than Jeffersonian philosophy in Ford's view of politics was his understanding of the House Republican system with its foundation of personal favors and alliances. Ford was able to get more loyalty from House members than other leaders "because he worked for it in his campaign speaking trips out in the district of the members," a colleague, Glenn Davis of Wisconsin, later told an interviewer. "He just worked quietly with a whole lot of people and became very effective in fighting rear guard actions. He knew that oratory and flag waving could not stop the steamroller programs of the Great Society."

Instead of oratory or grand ideas, Ford concentrated on the nuts and bolts of government. In 1961, the American Political Science Association gave him an award for distinguished service, hailing him as a "Congressman's Congressman." The citation said Ford "symbolizes the hard working, competent legislator who eschews the more colorful publicity-seeking roles in favor of a solid record of accomplishment in the real work of the House: committee work."

For Ford the most important committee was Appropriations, whose members, according to James Cannon, who headed the Domestic Policy Council in the Ford White House, spend most of their time listening to "the factory managers of the vast federal operation that we call the American government." From this testimony, Cannon contended, and Ford no doubt agreed, "Ford learned the essence of the American federal government system, who spends how much, for what and why, and how effectively is it used."

That is not really the essence of government, though, but merely the essence of bureaucracy. What was missing from these committee sessions was a sense of purpose and direction that should inform government and is necessary for presidential leadership. In remarking on the influence of Ford's years in Congress on his presidency, Phil Buchen later wrote of Ford: "He didn't have a vigorous ideology; he had been through too many arguments and too many fights in Congress to believe that he had an answer for every issue." But Ford's real problem was not lacking all the answers; rather, it was not raising the right questions and not being able to tell which answers mattered.

Ford's ideology was in a state of arrested development. Designed to appeal to his district and help his colleagues appeal to theirs, it provided no broad framework for considering public policy and evaluating national priorities.

Not that Ford lacked convictions. He had come to Washington with a deep-rooted suspicion of the federal government and a recently formed belief that the U.S. must actively combat the spread of communism abroad. He drew on these ideas within the confines of his congressional career, building alliances with other Republicans who shared these attitudes and who ultimately made him their leader. But the contents of these ideas was less important than the bargains he could strike with his allies and adversaries.

Looking at his party's problems at the national level, Ford emphasized not the substance of Republican ideology but the "image" of its congressional leadership. After Republicans took what Ford called "a terrible licking" in the 1958 elections, Ford had no changes in economic policy to recommend. Instead he was convinced that the GOP needed to improve "the old and tired image that the party was projecting." So he helped organize a successful coup that dumped the longtime Republican leader, Joe Martin, whom Ford regarded as "pleasant but ineffective" and replaced him with Charles Halleck, whose "gutfighting" style Ford favored at the time, but whom four years later he would himself replace.

Once Ford gained his seat in the House, his views were never seriously challenged in his safe Grand Rapids district. Since he was interested only in retaining his seat and advancing in the House, he rarely participated in public debate on a national level. He thus never refined his views, expanded his horizons, or strengthened his skills at persuasion. These were ideological deficiencies that in the White House would turn out to be glaring.

VALUES

Wherever Ford went as vice-president, he could not avoid the shadow of Watergate. He had to answer questions about the scandal even from conservative audiences, such as members of the Economic Club of New York prior to his controversial "background session" aboard *Air Force Two*. Ford tried to turn the attention of his listeners away from Watergate and on to the 1974 congressional elections, still some six months away. "If you really want to survive in 1974, you better start talking about the issues and not let this be a referendum on what's going on in Washington," he said.

He hailed Nixon's foreign-policy performance as "the best record on peace and diplomatic negotiation in my lifetime, and maybe in the history of the United States." On domestic policy, he was more modest, claiming only that there were "more pluses than minuses."

Ford warned the club members, "Before you make a moralistic decision in Senatorial and House races, just bear in mind what you faced as businessmen in 1965 and 1966." During those years, when Lyndon Johnson's Democrats controlled Capitol Hill, Ford reminded them, "you had a tough time as business people." They would have a tough time again if the Democrats made big gains in 1974. "So all I'm doing is cautioning my good friends in the business community, don't take out your moralistic attitudes vis-à-vis the executive branch on elected members of the House and Senate."

As Ford spoke that night, the Nixon presidency was crumbling fast and he himself, judging from his conversation later aboard *Air Force Two*, had grave misgivings about Nixon's ability to govern. The voice that advised the Economic Club members to disregard their "moralistic attitudes" was the voice of the political loyalist—loyal to his party, loyal to his president.

Loyalty was one of Ford's two dominant values as a political leader. The other value was integrity, on which was based his reputation for candor. The conflict between these values influenced Ford's use of power all through his career and along with his ideology and character shaped his response to the leadership challenge of Watergate.

The same moralistic attitudes Ford sought to dismiss in his remarks to the Economic Club had been an integral part of his upbringing. The mores of Grand Rapids reflected the rigorous faith of the Dutch Calvinists who had settled western Michigan and remained the dominant cultural force there when Ford was young. They tolerated neither work nor play on the Sabbath, and shunned drinking or even such innocent pleasures as dancing and moviegoing. Though Ford's parents were Episcopalians and did not fully accept all these puritanical tenets, the atmosphere in their home was nevertheless strict. "My parents didn't drink and never kept liquor in the house," Ford recalls. "The environment they created was—you darn well better tell the truth and live an honest life if you don't want to pay a penalty down the road."

Ford's father seems to have been the strongest influence on the boy. Gerald Ford, Sr., "said what he meant and he meant what he said," his son later recalled. "A man of impeccable integrity, he drilled into me . . . the importance of honesty. In fact, he and Mother had three rules: tell the truth, work hard and come to dinner on time—and woe unto any of us who violated those rules."

Ford well understood the political value of cultivating a reputation for straightforwardness. Early in his congressional career he considered putting his wife on his congressional payroll, as many other members did for their wives. "Betty was seeing my constituents and participating in other political activities." Besides, with their family growing, the Fords had decided to buy a home and "had a real need for the income she would deservedly earn."

But John Milanowski talked him out of the idea, telling Ford, "It would be misunderstood in the district" and "contrary to your whole philosophy of public service."

Ford's reputation for rectitude, fostered over the years, was called into question in 1972 by the disclosure that he allowed a noisome Washington lobbyist and political fund-raiser, Robert Winter-Berger, easy access to his office. As Winter-Berger told it, Ford had done him various favors in return for contributions he had arranged for other Republican candidates. But in the end, no one, including the Senate Rules committee probing Ford's qualifications for the vice-presidency, found Ford guilty of anything more than bad judgment.

In his home district as well, the charges were shrugged off. "He would have to actually be caught smuggling heroin into the country or something, he has such an image and believability," said Jean McKee, a Democratic lawyer who challenged Ford's re-election in 1970 and 1972. "I think he's probably as clean as anyone can be."

Appearing before the Senate Rules committee as Nixon's nominee for vice-president, Ford emphasized the importance of honesty to his view of politics. "The president of the United States has been my friend and he has always been truthful to me, as have my good friends in the Congress. I have never misled them when they might have wanted to hear something gentler than the truth and if I change jobs, that is the way I intend to continue." Ford added a favorite aphorism of his: "Truth is the glue on the bond that holds government together, and not only government, but civilization itself."

Despite his testimony, Ford knew even then that Nixon did not always let truth stand in the way of political purpose. At the 1960 Republican convention, when Ford and others were summoned by Nixon to give him their advice on who his running mate should be, Ford learned that Nixon had in fact already decided to select Henry Cabot Lodge. "I didn't go away bitter, but I was very disappointed," he said. "Making up his mind and then pretending that his options were still open—that was a Nixon trait that I'd have occasion to witness again."

In point of fact, as his favorable testimony about Nixon in 1972 demonstrated, Ford himself was not above dissembling at times. Often this was a result of the clash of values between candor and loyalty.

If the truth holds government together, as Ford contended, then loyalty binds politicians to each other. Political loyalty has several levels, including mutual allegiance to shared principles. But on the level on which Ford operated the loyalty that mattered most was loyalty of one politician to another and to his party. It was a political golden rule based on mutual trust and need that served not only to nurture ambition but also to protect against risk and error.

In part Ford's strong sense of loyalty was based on the ethics of sports he had absorbed as a high school and college football player. At Michigan, Ford's loyalty was severely tested when the Georgia Tech football team refused to play the Wolverines unless Willis Ward, a black pass receiver and a good friend of Ford's, was benched. Ford felt this was "morally wrong" and supposedly considered sitting out the game in protest. He claimed he was persuaded to play by Willis, who supposedly told him: "You owe it to the team." Ford played and Michigan won, 9–2. Years later, though, Ward said Ford had never even told him of his dilemma and contended that "dropping me from the lineup for racist reasons" had damaged team morale. Ford clearly chose to honor his loyalty to his team rather than to his friend.

Loyalty was particularly important to Ford because of his natural gregariousness. Well built, with manly features and a direct manner, he got along well with most people and found satisfaction in frequent and widespread contacts.

"He knew everybody in town," according to Niel Weathers, another young lawyer in the Grand Rapids law firm where Ford practiced for a year before entering Congress. "I've never seen a fellow more at ease with all kinds of people."

"I was a compulsive joiner," Ford recalled of this period in Grand Rapids. He signed up for everything from the American Legion and the Veterans of Foreign Wars to the county chapter of the American Red Cross and the local chapter of the National Association for the Advancement of Colored People.

More significant for his political future, when Ford reached Congress, along with Nixon and a number of other young Republican House members he helped to form a social organization called the Chowder & Marching Club. Over the years membership in this group strengthened the personal ties between a number of influential Republicans, most notably the men who would turn out to be the thirty-seventh and thirty-eighth presidents of the United States.*

Ford demonstrated his loyalty to Nixon long before Nixon became president. One of the first occasions followed the revelation of the Nixon "slush fund" in 1952. No sooner had Nixon finished his memorable Checkers speech than Ford wired him: "Fight it to the finish just as you did the smears by the Communists when you were proving charges against Alger Hiss. . . . I will personally welcome you in Grand Rapids or in any other part of Michigan."

Just before the 1956 convention, when Republicans were questioning the wisdom of renominating Nixon as Eisenhower's running mate, Ford joined with other former Nixon House colleagues in deflating the dump-Nixon movement. His efforts gained him several grateful "Dear Jerry" notes from the once and future vice-president.

During Nixon's presidency, Ford could usually be relied on to help fight his fights, even when good judgment dictated otherwise. One notorious example was his ill-conceived effort to impeach Supreme Court Justice William O. Douglas, a staunch member of the high tribunal's liberal bloc. Ford's initial reasons for going after Douglas are unclear. Hartmann claimed it was moral indignation. "Ford disapproved of Douglas the way a Grand Rapids housewife would deplore the behavior of certain movie stars," he explained. "The old man took too many young wives and he seemed to encourage every new fad in youthful rebellion."

* When the club celebrated its twentieth anniversary in 1969, Nixon, who was then president, said, "The Chowder and Marching Society is the most disorderly, badly organized organization I know. It has no charter, no bylaws and no president." Still, the ties of membership were strong enough so that the charter members, Ford among them, commemorated the occasion with a private White House dinner, a banquet for guests, and a golf outing.

Even Hartmann acknowledged, however, that Ford was "manipulated" by Nixon's operatives, who were seeking to gain revenge for the Senate's rejection of two Southern conservative Supreme Court nominees. Ultimately Douglas was cleared of the charges against him, and Ford's future press secretary J. F. terHorst summed up the widely shared judgment in Washington when he called the episode "a dark blot on Ford's Congressional career."

In the immediate aftermath of the Watergate break-in, Ford played a leading role in heading off an investigation planned by Democrat Representative Wright Patman of Texas, chairman of the House Banking committee, into the financing of Nixon's re-election campaign. Such a probe might well have disclosed the financial link between the president's campaign treasury and the Watergate burglary months well in advance of the 1972 presidential election. White House Counsel John Dean later testified that Ford and other Republican leaders had "acted at the request of the White House to block that investigation."

During his confirmation hearings, Ford denied that he had been prompted by the White House. He contended that he and his colleagues were concerned that Patman was "going on a fishing expedition" that "might lead to a precedent." But Ford hardly needed to be told by the White House that Patman's proposed inquiry could be a serious blow to Nixon and the Republicans. And whether Ford acted on his own or not, the motivation was the same—loyalty to the president and his party.

As details of Watergate came to light, the conflict between integrity and loyalty was further complicated. Watergate created another conflict—between loyalty to Nixon personally and loyalty to the Republican party being damaged by the scandal. Typically, it took a development involving Congress—in fact, Ford's own seat there—to awaken him to the seriousness of the trouble. In February 1974, in a special election to fill the Grand Rapids House seat Ford had vacated five months earlier to become vice-president, the Democrats won for the first time in sixty-two years. When Nixon tried to pass off the defeat on the impact of inflation, Ford disagreed. "No, Mr. President, it's Watergate that's responsible," Ford later recalled saying. "This election is a sign that if you don't clear up Watergate soon, we're going to face disaster in November." That was wise advice, and history might have been different had Ford taken his own words to heart.

CHARACTER

The character trait most helpful to Ford's successful career in the House was his ability to make himself liked. This proved to be less suited to the uses of presidential power, though, than it had been to the environment on Capitol Hill.

Moreover, under his cloak of affability Ford harbored emotional tensions that at times made him seem stubborn and insensitive to the point of arrogance. These traits made him resist adjusting his style as a congressman to the demands of his new office and unwilling to respond to influences that could have broadened his approach to presidential leadership, a shortcoming made evident by his handling of the Nixon pardon.

Not since Dwight Eisenhower had there been a president who was so determined to be liked, and who succeeded so well at it. "He didn't keep us together with his intellectual brilliance, persuasion or pressure," said another Michigan House member, Guy Vander Jagt. "He kept us together with his personality."

"I can get tears in my eyes when I think about Jerry Ford," said California's Pete McCloskey, a maverick whose opposition to the Vietnam War led him to challenge Nixon's renomination in 1972. "We love him."

And no one in memory, not even Eisenhower, tried so hard to like people as Ford did. It was part of a creed he consciously adopted as a youngster. "By the time I entered seventh grade, I was becoming aware of the deep emotions that rivalries can stir," he recalled. Concluding that "hating or even disliking people because of their bad qualities was a waste of time," Ford decided that "everyone had more good qualities than bad. If I understood and tried to accentuate those good qualities in others, I could get along much better."

"Ford was an accommodator," Pat O'Donnell, who served him in the White House later, recalled. "His motto when he first came to the White House was: 'We can disagree and still be friends.' "

Ford's gift for getting along with people reflected his secure childhood. He owed much of his solidity both to his mother's ability to remake her life after a stormy, unsuccessful first marriage and to the devotion of her second husband. When Gerald was nearly three, his mother married again, to Gerald R. Ford, Sr., a handsome Grand Rapids bachelor whom she met at a church social. Her new husband subsequently adopted her son, gave him his own name, and proved to be a strong, caring father. Gerald R. Ford, Jr., regarded him as "the only father I ever knew."

The Ford family's life in Grand Rapids in the 1920s typified the stability of middle-class Midwestern America. Both of Ford's parents were active in community life and charity work, particularly his father, who set up a summer camp for poor youngsters and helped run the church Boy Scout troop in which Jerry made eagle scout. The elder Ford did suffer financial reverses during the Depression, but his standing in the community and the business world was such that DuPont kept shipping him supplies for his paint business on credit and he was able to persuade his own workers to accept shrunken pay checks to keep the business afloat until conditions improved. "Neither of my parents could be described as 'secure' economically," Ford wrote later. "But emotionally both were very secure and if I retain that characteristic today, I owe it to them."

Ford built on that security, achieving success that gave him reason for self-confidence. In the Depression days of the 1930s he worked his way through the University of Michigan, waiting on tables and washing dishes, graduating in 1935 with a B average. He was a first-rate center for the football team, good enough so that after his senior year he played for the college all-stars and was recruited by two professional teams.

Then came Yale Law School. Ford's entry there was delayed until 1938 while he earned tuition money as an assistant football coach for the Eli. Yale questioned whether Ford could hold his own against the competition of his classmates—98 out of the 125 law school freshmen had earned Phi Beta Kappa keys. Yet Ford finished in the top quarter of the class even as he kept up his coaching duties, too.

Ford practiced law for only a few months before the U.S. plunged into World War II, and he joined the navy. After nearly four years he came home with the rank of lieutenant commander and ten battle stars earned in the South Pacific.

Ford's coming of age had its unpleasant side, though. Probably his most traumatic experience was encountering his biologic father, Leslie King, a wealthy Omaha businessman who stopped off at the Grand Rapids hamburger stand where Ford was working one day, introduced himself and his second wife, and took his son out to lunch. After an hour of trivial conversation, King, who had come to Michigan mainly to pick up a new Lincoln in Detroit, handed Ford $25 and said, "Buy yourself something you can't afford otherwise." Then he left.

"Nothing could erase the image I gained of my real father that day, a carefree, well-to-do man who didn't really give a damn about the hopes and dreams of his firstborn son," Ford said. "When I went to bed that night I broke down and cried."

What added to his hurt was later learning that King had for years resisted court efforts to get him to pay child support. A few years after the disturbing encounter with King in Grand Rapids, when Ford was struggling to make expenses at college, he gave King a chance to make partial amends when he asked him for a loan. "I never received a reply."

Ford's ego was too healthy, his relationship with his new father too strong, for him to be shattered by these experiences. Nevertheless, he did seem determined to avoid making the sort of emotional commitment that would risk his being hurt again.

Though he claimed to be deeply in love with a beautiful young model named Phyllis Brown, whom he had met while at law school, he let that relationship dissolve without making a firm commitment. He was nearly thirty-five before he did get married, and in his relationship with his wife, his political career and ambitions served as a shield between him and her.

As a congressman and vice-president Ford traveled almost promiscuously. While part of it was useful to his role as Republican House leader, much of it was not politically significant. He seemed to prefer the bonhomie of the countless rubber-chicken dinners he addressed to the more emotionally demanding company of his wife. Ford rationalized that he had made up for his lack of companionship by achieving success in public service of which his children could be proud. But his absorption with travel on behalf of his congressional colleagues tended to reinforce his insular view of the world. Meanwhile, his wife clearly was in need of emotional support. Betty first sought psychiatric help during Ford's congressional days and then slipped into the nightmare of liquor and drugs that led to her public acknowledgment of alcoholism and her admission to a hospital for treatment.*

An additional negative influence on Ford's character was the tendency of others to undervalue his intelligence, reinforced by two oft repeated and oft published Lyndon Johnson wisecracks—"Jerry Ford played football too long without a helmet" and "Jerry Ford is so dumb he can't chew gum and walk at the same time."†

One cause of the derisive view of Ford's acuity was his plodding manner of speaking, an apparent aftereffect of a serious childhood stuttering problem. In addition, his concentration on the minutiae of Congress made him seem unaware of events and ideas outside of Capitol Hill. Finally, the notion that Ford was thick-witted fed on itself, as such things do in Washington, and became a standard component of cocktail party banter and of conventional journalistic wisdom.

Ford rarely complained about criticism in the press. He contended in

---

* Ford did not relax his travels even after he left the presidency. "Jerry's retirement was a fraud," Betty Ford complained in her memoirs. "He might as well have been campaigning. He was away teaching, lecturing, serving on the boards of ten or more business or charity organizations."

† What Johnson actually said, later bowdlerized in order to be printed in family newspapers, was: "Jerry Ford is so dumb he can't fart and chew gum at the same time."

his memoirs that his experience as a football player, dealing with "critics in the stands and critics in the press . . . helped me to develop a thick hide, and in later years, whenever critics assailed me, I just let their jibes roll off my back."

If Ford taught himself not to complain about criticism, though, the evidence suggests that he also taught himself to ignore it, so there was little opportunity for him to learn from mistakes. Having a "thick hide" was helpful to him in deflecting ridicule and unfair attacks. But the same reflex also cut him off from constructive criticism and inclined him to bull ahead regardless of what critics might say.

THE CHALLENGE

The disclosures of the abuses of power that came to be lumped together under the rubric of Watergate created the specter of a government out of control. For nearly two centuries the United States had relied on Constitutional institutions and processes to preserve the rule of law. Now the presidency appeared to be so swollen in arrogance that it was beyond these restraints. The Watergate scandal raised questions about whether the aggrandized presidency and the national security state that had come into being in the years after World War II were consistent with Constitutional government.

The challenge to Ford and other political leaders was to find answers to these questions and rebuild the credibility of government and of politics. To accomplish this it was necessary first to unearth the full story of the abuses of Watergate, then to establish responsibility and mete out punishment under the legal process. Just as important was the obligation to make clear that Watergate was a grave distortion of the political system that could not be tolerated by politicians regardless of party.

First as leader of his party in the House, then as vice-president and finally as president, Ford failed to meet this challenge. Because his outlook on politics was limited by his years as "a Congressman's Congressman" he did not grasp the broader implications of Watergate. Instead he viewed these crimes as a tactical political problem, an unfortunate episode best forgotten. Thus, when Nixon fired special Watergate prosecutor Archibald Cox in October 1973, an action that led to the so-called Saturday night massacre and outraged the nation, Ford did not join other Republicans in protesting. Instead he concluded, "What [Nixon] had done was politically dumb, but he had acted within his rights as Chief Executive in firing a subordinate."

This narrow ideology together with his adherence to the value of loyalty discouraged Ford from pressing for full disclosure of the Watergate abuses. And his ideology and values, combined with his characteristic stubbornness, led him to pardon Nixon without consulting his advisers or heeding the consequences, thus aborting the legal process and preventing both full disclosure and an assessment of responsibility.

With its damaging implications for the Republican Administration and the Republican party, Watergate confronted Ford with an awkward dilemma about Nixon's credibility. If Nixon's denials of wrongdoing could be believed, then the prudent course was to support him until the charges against him could be disproved. But if there was reason to doubt Nixon, then the wisest response, for the sake of the country and the party, was to maintain neutrality and urge the president to make full disclosure.

This dilemma faced all Republicans, but Ford had better reason than most to be skeptical of Nixon's denial of involvement. Knowing Nixon as he had for more than twenty-five years, Ford knew him well enough to realize that he exercised close control over his campaigns and would scarcely have left a problem as sensitive as dealing with the aftermath of the Watergate break-in solely to underlings. He also knew Nixon to be much given to deviousness, as he himself had observed after the 1960 convention charade Nixon had staged to make it seem that he was seeking advice on the selection of a running mate.

More than that, Ford also knew G. Gordon Liddy, mastermind of the Watergate break-in, having met him in a way that typified Ford's approach to politics. In 1968, Republican Congressman Hamilton Fish, Jr., of New York, who had just defeated Liddy in a bitter primary, asked Ford to find Liddy a job to keep him from running against Fish on the Conservative party line in the fall. Ford found Liddy "cocky and demanding," and "formed a bad impression of him." Nevertheless, he promised to help him. After Fish's victory, Ford made a "a pro-forma call" to the Treasury Department, where Liddy found work as a special assistant assigned to battle organized crime. "I didn't like him, but rationalized it was for the purpose of helping Hamilton Fish," Ford later explained.

When Ford learned Liddy had been involved in the Watergate break-in, "the case took on a new dimension," he said later. He expressed his concern to Jack Marsh, a former House colleague and longtime friend, a few days after the break-in. "I don't give a damn who's involved or how high it goes," Ford remembers telling Marsh. "Nixon ought to get to the bottom of this and get rid of anybody who's involved in it."*

* This concern with Watergate did not, however, prevent Ford from voting to block Congressman Patman's effort "to get to the bottom of it."

Ford did not repeat those bold words in public, though. Instead that very afternoon, at a meeting with John Mitchell to discuss 1972 campaign strategy, he asked Nixon's manager and confidant whether he or anyone else in the campaign had had anything to do with the break-in.

"He looked me right in the eye and said, 'Absolutely not.' " Ford then asked if Nixon had had anything to do with the affair and got the same response.

It is hard to imagine what other answer Ford expected to get from Mitchell under these circumstances. At any rate, Mitchell quickly changed the subject to one closer to Ford's heart, the 1972 congressional campaign, which Ford hoped would at last produce a Republican majority in the House of Representatives so he could achieve his longtime ambition of becoming speaker. In a generous mood, with his treasury overflowing with illegal campaign contributions, Mitchell promised significant help for congressional Republicans.

That, of course, was just what Ford wanted to hear and so his concern about Watergate was set aside. He got further encouragement from the president himself. After the Republican convention, over which Ford presided as chairman, Nixon wired him: "You looked so good on television. . . . that I became more convinced than ever that you would make a *great Speaker* [Nixon's emphasis]." But as it turned out, little help for the House campaign was forthcoming from Nixon's managers. "They wanted to reelect Nixon and didn't much care about helping anyone else," Ford finally realized. Though Nixon swept every state but Massachusetts against hapless George McGovern, Republicans gained only thirteen seats in the House, far short of the number needed to take control.

Convinced at last that he would never fulfill his quarter-century-old dream of becoming speaker, a disappointed Ford decided to bring his congressional service to a close. He promised his wife he would retire after the 1974 elections.

But in the fall of 1973 Ford's political career got a new lease on life. Spiro Agnew's resignation following revelations that he had received payoffs from state contractors during his tenure as governor of Maryland created an opening in the vice-presidency. Ford got the job for much the same reason that he had moved up the House leadership ladder. Of all the leading candidates, including John Connally, who was Nixon's first choice, Nelson Rockefeller, and Ronald Reagan, the favorites of most Republican leaders, Ford was the least objectionable.

In breaking the news to Ford, Nixon learned that his nominee still planned to retire after 1974. "That's good," Nixon told him. "Because John Connally is my choice for 1976."

As Ford must have known, though, Nixon was not likely to be in a position to dictate who the party should nominate at the next convention. At best, if he survived Watergate, he would be a wounded lame duck by the time the next presidential campaign got under way. In fact, if Nixon lasted out his term, Ford would undoubtedly have the gratitude of his party for helping rescue Nixon. If Nixon did not survive, then Ford as the incumbent chief executive would be difficult to beat for renomination. In other words, political realities dictated that one way or another the presidency was part of Ford's destiny.

During Ford's confirmation hearings, with each day bringing new Watergate revelations, the idea of a Ford presidency was increasingly viewed as a likelihood on Capitol Hill. One of the most provocative queries was raised by Senator Howard Cannon of Nevada, chairman of the Senate Rules committee. "If a president resigned his office before his term expired, would his successor have the power to prevent or to terminate any investigation or criminal prosecution charges against the former president?" Cannon asked. "I do not think the public would stand for it," Ford replied. His answer could hardly have been clearer, and no one in Congress saw the need to pursue that subject further.

Cannon's question and the portentous mood that pervaded his confirmation hearings should have made clear to Ford the profound impact Watergate was having on the political scene. The vice-presidency itself, which he assumed in December 1973, came to him only because the pressures of Watergate forced Nixon to choose him. Moreover, with each succeeding month it became increasingly apparent that Ford would succeed Nixon in the Oval Office.

Yet for all that, Ford could not untrack himself from the habits of a political lifetime. Nixon's weakness gave him strength—not to attack his chief but to put a certain distance between the president and himself while urging a thorough examination into Watergate. But instead of claiming the high ground, Ford spent the months of his vice-presidency hemming and hawing, zigging and zagging as if he were still back at the Appropriations committee trying to cut a deal on a defense budget.

At first he followed his natural instincts and defended Nixon in two key speeches. In November, even before he had been confirmed as vice-president, he blamed demands for Nixon's impeachment on "pressure groups that have always opposed the President and his Administration." He called on Nixon's silent majority to "speak up, speak now" in the president's defense.

Two months later, Ford returned to pounding Nixon's critics. He attacked "a few extreme partisans . . . bent on stretching out the ordeal of Watergate for their own purposes," which he contended were "to crush the President and his philosophy."

The reaction to the speech was, as Ford later acknowledged, so "overwhelmingly negative" that he resolved to soften his rhetoric. In his memoirs he blamed Nixon's speech writers for using him "to say what they wanted said about the President and his problems." But the words had come out of Ford's own mouth and they were not very different from what he had said two months earlier, presumably written by his own speech writers.

By March 1974 the issue of whether Nixon was obliged to release the White House tapes subpoenaed by the House Judiciary committee had become a raging public controversy. Ford offered two views.

First, he warned that "a totally adamant" refusal by the White House to cooperate with the impeachment inquiry would make Nixon's impeachment more likely. "He was sending a message to the White House," one of his advisers told me. But a few days later Ford sent a different message. He praised Nixon for "his great willingness to cooperate" with the House inquiry and criticized the Judiciary committee staff for being "overzealous."

Then the next week Ford declared his independence of Nixon. "I shall remain my own man," he asserted. "The only pledge by which I have bound myself in accepting the President's trust is the commitment by which we are all bound, before God and the Constitution, to do our best for America."

By then, however, Ford had shifted ground so often that he was having trouble getting the press or the public to take him seriously. "If you newsmen can make corrections and retractions, so can a Vice President," Ford joked at a press dinner in May. But this was no laughing matter, as Ford himself discovered in June. He had just finished telling a Republican dinner audience that "the preponderance of the evidence is that [the president] is innocent of any involvement in any cover-up" when word reached him that the federal grand jury probing into Watergate had named Nixon as an unindicted coconspirator.

Nixon tried to hold his vice-president in line with a note that he began by misspelling his name:

Dear Gerry: This is to tell you how much I have appreciated your superb and courageous support over the past difficult months. How much easier it would have been for you to try to pander to the press and others who

are desperately trying to drive a wedge between the president and the
Vice President. . . . History, I am sure will record you as one of the most
capable and courageous and honorable vice presidents we have ever had.

But history was now moving at a pace faster than either Nixon or
Ford could control.

Ever since Ford had become vice-president, he had worried that any
criticism by him of Nixon might appear disloyal, thus violating one of his
principal personal values. And as it became increasingly obvious that
Nixon's presidency was drawing to an end, Ford felt even more pressured
to seem loyal. "I couldn't abandon Nixon," he said, "because that would
make it appear that I was trying to position myself to be president." Yet
in a way this was just how Ford did position himself, not by making it
harder for Nixon to stay on as president, but rather by seeming to make
it easier for him to quit.

The agent who created this opportunity for Ford was Nixon's chief
of staff, Alexander Haig. When it came to wily manipulation, Haig was
a match even for Nixon and more than a match for Ford. On the morning
of August 1, as Nixon's presidency entered what would be its last week,
Haig phoned Ford and asked to see him on an urgent matter. Ford invited
him right over to the vice-presidential office on the second floor of the
Old Executive Office Building, next door to the White House.

Ford also took the precaution of asking his own chief of staff, Robert
Hartmann, to sit in on the meeting. A former Washington bureau chief
of the *Los Angeles Times*, Hartmann was a gifted speech writer whose
shrewd judgment was highly valued by Ford. Because he himself "was
not by nature suspicious of people or their motives," Ford "thought it
would be wise to have someone on my staff who was. Hartmann was
suspicious of everybody."

What Haig had to say was just as urgent as he had indicated. He had
learned from Nixon's lawyers that the Watergate tapes that Nixon had
been ordered to turn over to the federal court finally provided the "smoking gun" evidence long sought by investigators as conclusive proof of the
president's involvement in the cover-up conspiracy. "The whole ball game
may be over," Haig said.

After Haig left, Ford suspected that Haig had been inhibited by Hartmann's presence. Sure enough, that afternoon Haig called back and asked
for another meeting. This time he made clear, Ford later recalled, "that
he didn't want Hartmann there." At this second meeting Haig told Ford
he should be ready to assume the presidency within the next few days,

because Nixon was considering resigning. If he did resign, Haig explained, Nixon had several options. He could step aside temporarily under the Twenty-fifth Amendment. He could pardon himself and then resign. Or, as Ford recalled the way Haig put it, Nixon "could agree to leave in return for an agreement that the new President—Gerald Ford—would pardon him." Haig wanted to know Ford's assessment of the situation.

For a moment, as the two men sat in Ford's comfortable, high-ceilinged office, history stood still. When Haig first mentioned the pardon, Ford could have adhered to the conviction he had expressed during his confirmation hearings: "I do not think the public would stand for it." Had Ford made that response, the course of the next few weeks and indeed of Ford's entire presidency might well have been very different. But Ford instead asked Haig about the extent of presidential pardon authority and was told that a president had authority to grant a pardon even before any prosecution had begun. When Haig left, Ford told him, "Well, Al, I want some time to think."

When Ford reported this conversation to Hartmann, the latter exploded with indignation at Haig—and frustration at Ford. "You should have taken Haig by the scruff of the neck and the seat of the pants and thrown him the hell out of your office," he told Ford. Yet Hartmann realized that Ford "had not yet grasped the monstrous impropriety" of Haig raising the pardon issue—nor did Ford realize the impropriety of his own failure to object immediately.

Not until the next day, after he had been warned by two other long-time advisers—Jack Marsh and Bryce Harlow—"that the mere mention of the pardon option could cause a lot of trouble in the days ahead" did Ford call Haig to repair the damage. He told Haig that he had "no intention of recommending what the president should do about resigning" and added "that nothing we talked about yesterday afternoon should be given any consideration in whatever decision the President may wish to make."

That unexplicit, belated emendation, though, hardly undid what Ford had already done to weaken his position. His silence to what could only be considered to be a proposition from Haig had to be taken for a degree of assent or at least a willingness to think about what months before Ford had characterized as unthinkable. Ford had put himself in a position where if he did *not* pardon Nixon, his refusal would be construed by Haig and Nixon as a betrayal of his word and disloyalty to a friend. Just as important, in his own mind Ford might find it difficult to rebut such charges.

Meanwhile, even in these final hours of the Nixon regime, Ford did little to distance himself from the doomed president and thus shore up his own public credibility. The following day, Ford was asked at a press conference about a suggestion that the House of Representatives should censure Nixon as an alternative to impeachment. "If I had my druthers, I would rather have the House of Representatives vote as I think the facts justify, which is acquittal," Ford said.

Ford's assumption of the presidency on August 9 and his statement that "our long national nightmare is over" ushered in a period of national relief that approached euphoria. Yet while the public man seemed relaxed and confident, in private Ford was still struggling with the dilemma of Nixon's fate.

This tension was reflected in his awkward handling of the pardon issue at his first press conference, on August 28. He and his aides had agreed beforehand that he would refuse to comment on the possibility of a pardon for Nixon on grounds that this would be inappropriate while prosecutors were still delving into Watergate. But when the question did come up at the press conference, he muddied the waters by saying more than he had planned. *"Until the matter reaches me,"* Ford told the press corps, "I am not going to make any comment during the process of whatever charges are made." Ford had clearly left the impression that although he had the right to pardon Nixon, he would not act to forestall the criminal process.

He realized what he had done, and it troubled him. Also disturbing him was the number of questions about the pardon—five out of twenty-seven concerned Nixon or Watergate. Afterward, Ford asked his advisers how long reporters would continue to press him on the pardon issue. They told him the reporters would keep it up until Nixon's legal fate was resolved.

That was all Ford had to hear. Two days later, Ford met with Hartmann, Buchen, and Marsh and told them his mind was "about ninety-nine percent made up" to grant Nixon a pardon. He did not even pretend to seek their views. "It was very much his decision," recalled Phil Buchen, the White House counsel, who was given the assignment of researching Ford's legal authority to act. "He didn't invite any discussion."

The defects in Ford's decision were reflected in his inability to provide a clear and consistent explanation for what he had done. When Ford announced the pardon on September 8, the end of his first month as president, he claimed that he was acting to spare the American people bitterness and pain. After years of "bitter controversy and divisive national debate," Ford warned that if Nixon was forced to stand trial, there would be a prolonged period of delay during which "ugly passions would again be aroused." In fact, although Watergate had been a public controversy for the better part of two years, the country had shown no signs of being divided. The overall public reaction had been one of increased cynicism and alienation from the political process.

That mood had been alleviated by Ford's assumption of the presidency and his reassuring statement: "Our Constitution works. Our great Republic is a government of laws and not of men." The good he had accomplished, though, was swiftly undone by the pardon. And it was this damage to public confidence and renewal of cynicism that had to be weighed against the supposed divisiveness that would result from continued investigation of Nixon. As a number of the assistant Watergate prosecutors had argued to their chief, Leon Jaworski, before the decision on prosecuting Nixon was taken out of their hands: "The cost to the credibility of our institutions and government would be much greater if we *failed* to prosecute than if there were some public dismay over an indictment [original emphasis]."

The most direct damage done by the pardon was to the cherished principle of equality of justice, a point made by Ford's first presidential press secretary, J. F. terHorst, whose resignation in protest foreshadowed the torrent of public indignation that the pardon provoked. In his farewell letter terHorst told the president that he could not defend his actions "in the absence of a like decision to grant absolute pardon to the young men who evaded Vietnam military service as a matter of conscience and the absence of pardons of former aides and associates of Mr. Nixon who have been charged with crimes—and imprisoned—stemming from the same Watergate situation."

What made Ford's contention that he had acted to spare the country divisiveness unpersuasive was the impression he left that he was primarily concerned with sparing Nixon. Ford contended that he was much misunderstood on this point, even by his own aides. In his memoirs Ford noted that both terHorst and Buchen referred to the pardon as an "act of mercy." Yet Ford insisted that "compassion for Nixon as an individual hadn't prompted my decision at all."

It is easy to understand that many thought otherwise. For one thing there were Ford's own words when he issued the pardon. At the last minute he changed a sentence in his draft to add a reference to Nixon's health being threatened by the charges hanging over his head. Hartmann started to object that "adding the 'health' element at the last minute was like writing it in neon against a midnight sky," but Ford cut him off. Then there was Ford's testimony on October 17 before the House subcommittee that conducted a brief inquiry into the pardon. "Surely we are not a revengeful people," Ford said. "We have often demonstrated a readiness to feel compassion and to act out of mercy."

Ford's inability to provide a convincing explanation for his decision has inevitably led to continuing speculation about what his real motives were. One obvious possibility much discussed is that Ford and Nixon had reached an agreement under which Nixon would concede his presidency to Ford in exchange for Ford's promise to pardon him. Ford has denied that—"There was no deal, period," he told the House investigators—and no one has produced any hard evidence to the contrary. But as Watergate prosecutors Richard Ben-Veniste and George Frampton, Jr., have contended: "The real question is whether Ford subtly let it be known to Haig or Nixon that once he became president he would look favorably on exercise of the pardon power." Ford's solitary conversation with Haig on August 1 suggests this had happened.

But the significance of that conversation goes beyond what Nixon and Haig believed Ford to have promised to what Ford himself thought. Judging from his reaction, the main reason he pardoned Nixon was not for the country's sake, as he said, or for Nixon's sake, but for his own sake.

"The pardon was the *real* Jerry Ford," Hartmann observed. Ford's decision was consistent with the beliefs and values of his political lifetime on Capitol Hill.

Asked years afterward if he believed that a leader needs "to project a vision that inspires and directs," Ford replied in the negative: "Too often 'vision' is just a fancy word people use to justify spending a lot of money. You can spend an awful lot of money on some pretty unattainable goals. That's why I'm a firm believer in a pragmatic approach. I'm more concerned with the nuts and bolts of getting from here to there."

This was the voice of a politician whose vision of government was framed by long years of haggling over budget items on the Appropriations committee and quiet cloakroom compromises sealed with a handshake and who inhabited a world where the prize was often awarded to the least objectionable competitor. In that world the issues raised by Watergate about the abuses of presidential power seemed ethereal. The important thing for Ford, as he said, was the "getting from here to there"—to get on with the job in the Oval Office just as he had on the Hill.

In addition, his conversation with Haig impinged directly on his sense of loyalty. By withholding a pardon, might he be guilty of having misled and betrayed Nixon? That was a conundrum to vex Ford's conscience.

Finally, the stubborn streak in his character contributed to his decision. Under the pressures of his new job, he considered himself the best judge of his own interests and had no patience for the counsel of advisers.

Looking back on the pardon, Ford wrote: "It was an unbelievable lifting of a burden from my shoulders." And fifteen years later, when a high school student asked him why he had pardoned Nixon, Ford replied, "I finally decided that I should spend all my time on the problems of all Americans and not twenty-five percent of my time on the problems of one man." But not being able to concentrate on the nation's business was his problem, not the country's.

No matter what Ford's real motives were for the pardon, the results certainly torpedoed his stated objective—ridding the country of a distraction. The pardon touched off what one chronicler of Watergate called "a convulsive reaction that . . . seared the nation." Nearly 200,000 of the 270,000 or so letters and telegrams sent to the White House on the pardon objected to it. The majority of Americans who had gradually reached a guilty verdict on Nixon now much more swiftly condemned Ford. The new president, who had been riding high in the polls, dropped to nearly Nixon's Watergate levels. On his first post-pardon trip out of Washington, demonstrators in Pittsburgh chanted, "Jail Ford, jail Ford."

The public's anger was exacerbated by the realization that Nixon had escaped not only without any punishment, but without having to accept responsibility beyond the grudging acknowledgment: "I was wrong in not acting more decisively and more forthrightly in dealing with Watergate." Even Ford judged Nixon's statement to be "inadequate," complaining that "he didn't admit guilt and it was a good deal less than a full confession. I was taking one hell of a risk and he didn't seem to be responsive at all."

When Nixon had resigned the presidency, he had explained that "I no longer have a strong enough political base in the Congress to justify continuing" in office. Ford commented later: "The fact that he was linking his resignation to the loss of his Congressional base shocked me then and disturbs me still." But by granting the pardon Ford gave Nixon and his partisans a license to argue that Watergate was just another political vendetta against Nixon. By taking a firm stand against excesses of presidential power, Ford could have established a formidable moral and political precedent for the accountability of power. Instead, the point of Watergate seemed to fade in time. Ten years after the Watergate break-in, the Iran-Contra scandal produced disclosures about another administration in which presidential aides shredded documents and broke laws in pursuit of what they claimed was a higher purpose.

Ford's issuing the Nixon pardon reaffirms the earlier lesson of the Eisenhower presidency—weakness in one of the three major elements of leadership diminishes the potential value of the other two. In Ford's case his limited ideological background, defined by his years as "a congressman's congressman," left him insensitive to the broader implications of Watergate and of a pardon for the chief perpetrator of that scandal. Having had little experience with debate on a national scale, Ford was ill equipped to gauge the intensity of the public's reaction. Such broad controversies did not arise on Capitol Hill, where disputes could usually be smoothed over quietly in the normal course of legislative give-and-take between colleagues.

Because of this ideological blind spot, Ford thought of the pardon, as he himself said, mainly as a way of lifting a burden from his shoulders. In this state of mind he chose to interpret loyalty, the foundation of his value system, mainly in terms of his loyalty to Richard Nixon. Disregarded was the broader loyalty that he owed to his Republican colleagues in the House and to his political party, both of which suffered grievously as result of the pardon. Also obscured by his ideological shortcomings was his other basic value, integrity, an additional factor that should have weighed heavily against a hasty pardon.

Finally, Ford's narrow ideological perspective on the pardon brought out the stubborn side of his character, which reinforced his decision to act without prior consultation. This was particularly unfortunate since he had gained a host of friends in Congress in both parties who, if he had turned to them, could have given him constructive advice about the pardon.

Ford's lack of truly national political experience set him apart from all his recent predecessors, including Eisenhower. And for all these presidents, again including Eisenhower, it would have been out of character to have pardoned Nixon in the manner that Ford choose.

Eisenhower, judging from his response to the challenge of McCarthyism, would probably have persuaded intermediaries to negotiate a settlement behind the scenes between the Watergate prosecutor and Nixon, granting the latter a pardon in return for an explicit admission of guilt. Truman would have viewed a pardon for Nixon as an affront to the underdogs he championed, and he certainly would not have viewed Nixon as an underdog. For Kennedy, a pardon would have run counter to the leadership principles he had developed, which depended heavily on the thorough public airing of an issue. Johnson would have been loath to risk his consensus by acting abruptly; like Eisenhower, he probably would have sought a negotiated arrangement, though he would have been inclined to handle any such deal personally rather than rely on brokers. As for Nixon, he would have been quick to realize that to do for someone else what Ford did for him would outrage middle-class values.

Ford had no simple way out of the Nixon dilemma, but he did not need to create a national crisis. He could have taken some of the pressure off himself by announcing that he would take no action until the special prosecutor's office had completed its investigation. At the time of the pardon the prosecutors were exploring no fewer than ten areas of possible criminal conduct by Nixon, and Buchen said publicly that he believed it "very likely" that Nixon would have been indicted. If he had, Ford could then have pardoned him, on the condition that Nixon publicly acknowledge his responsibility for the crimes. The purpose of such a condition would not have been revenge but to uphold the Constitutional principle of accountability that Ford had so eloquently subscribed to on the day he took office.

In the meanwhile Ford could have used the time and the initial goodwill that his taking office had generated to build support for proposals addressing the nation's needs at home and its responsibilities abroad. The way to get the country to stop thinking of Nixon was not to pardon him but to give people something else to think about.

In the wake of the pardon, Ford's problems multiplied. He struggled vainly with the vicissitudes of the economy, first with inflation, then with the most severe recession since the Great Depression. In the 1974 congressional elections, public concern over the ailing economy and resentment of the Nixon pardon chewed up the ranks of Republican candidates. The GOP lost more than forty seats in the House and four in the Senate, confronting Ford with his next major challenge—dealing with huge Democratic majorities on Capitol Hill.

Once again his ideological limitations betrayed him. For all their numerical strength, the Democrats were divided as usual and lacking strong leadership. Ford, given his intimate knowledge of congressional operations and the strong relationships he had built over the years, could have used the moment to launch major policy initiatives. Even though he would have had difficulty getting his ideas adopted intact, he could at least have established an ideological bridgehead that would have served him well when he sought to develop a platform for his 1976 presidential candidacy.

In 1947, after Republicans took control of the 80th Congress, Harry Truman was in much the same predicament that Ford faced after the 1974 elections. Truman did use his veto power, most notably against the Taft-Hartley bill, but he also took the policy initiative, sending Congress bold proposals for civil rights, national health insurance, and an income tax credit. Though these measures did not become laws, they nevertheless were of immense benefit to the president in his 1948 campaign, helping him contrast the ideological differences between himself and the opposition party.

Gerald Ford, however, lacked the ideological depth for such proposals. He offered only a few bills of his own, mainly dealing with energy. Most of the time, recalled Ford's chief congressional liaison, Max Friedersdorf, the president was preoccupied with "legislation that the administration found objectionable, which included most of the other legislation that Congress was moving at that time."

Ford's main response to the challenge of the Democratic-controlled Congress was adopting what came to be called a veto strategy. "During his brief tenure," a Brookings Institution study concluded, "Ford undoubtedly vetoed more bills raising important substantive issues than any previous president."

The veto strategy, designed mainly to frustrate Democratic plans for spending on domestic programs, as Friedersdorf claimed, was "quite successful" in accomplishing that objective. But by concentrating on vetoing Democratic bills instead of backing his own, Ford was unable to compile much of a legislative record.

The sense of futility that gripped the Ford presidency can be judged by the fact that in 1975 when U.S. forces recovered the merchant ship *Mayaguez* after it had been seized by Cambodian patrol boats, Ford and his associates regarded it as the high point of his stewardship. "All of a sudden the gloomy national mood began to fade," Ford said later.

The recovery was illusory. Discontented conservatives rallied around Ronald Reagan, who challenged Ford for the 1976 Republican presidential nomination and failed only narrowly. Some Republicans blamed the divisive impact of Reagan's candidacy for causing Ford's defeat by Jimmy Carter in the general election. Others blamed the Nixon pardon.

Much has been written and said about the healing service Ford supposedly performed for the country. Ford called his memoirs *A Time to Heal,* and Jimmy Carter in his inaugural address said, "For myself and for our nation, I want to thank my predecessor for all he has done to heal our land." But Carter's success as a candidate was in itself a measure of Ford's failure of leadership. By his unwillingness to confront the legacy of Watergate, he paved the way for Carter—and then for Ronald Reagan—who based their candidacies on suspicion of government in Washington. "We still have to understand what effective leadership is in the presidency," Philip Buchen said. "But I think it has to be something more than what Ford brought to that office." Nonetheless, though Ford demonstrated the limitations of the insider's approach, the question that remained for Carter to answer was whether an outsider could do any better.

CHAPTER 8

Carter: The Road
to Malaise

Jimmy Carter's rise to the presidency in the wake of the scandal of Watergate and the ordeal of Vietnam stirred hope and belief among his supporters that, as one of them later wrote, Carter was destined to become a president "of towering significance at a critical time in American history." In much the same spirit, an idealistic journalist who had signed on with Carter as a speech writer after his nomination reminded his friends that the last state governor to win the White House had been Franklin Roosevelt. He contended that Carter "had at least the same potential to leave the government forever changed by his presence."

But such optimism was limited mainly to those close to Carter, whose judgment was colored by friendship and their own ambitions. Even at the moment of his triumph over Gerald Ford, apprehension was widespread among many of the voters who had just chosen him as their leader. "Fifty percent of the public still does not know where Carter stands on the issues," his campaign pollster, Patrick Caddell, wrote in a memorandum on political strategy for the new administration. "Voters can't establish a firm picture of him in their minds. Because he is an 'unknown,' whose actions and behavior can only be discerned when he is finally in office, many voters worry."

Having covered Carter's drive for the presidency, I shared some of these same hopes and misgivings. I had been collecting evidence on both sides since May 1975, when I first watched him campaign for the prize that he surprised everyone but himself by winning.

By that time the fifty-year-old Carter had been running for the White House for more than two years. He was a one-term Southern governor not widely beloved in his own state, with no significant experience in national affairs. Still, he could not be ignored, for no one had a clear advantage in the competition for the 1976 Democratic nomination. Moreover, Carter was running harder than anyone else. He was campaigning six days a week, and by the time I caught up with him he had already visited forty-five states.

On a plane ride to Concord, New Hampshire, the nation's first presidential primary state, Carter treated me, as he treated all other political reporters, as if we were longtime friends who shared a common interest in his success. Every question elicited a quick smile and a ready answer.

The most important issues of the campaign, he told me right off, would be trust and competence. "Americans want to know if their government can be decent and honest and purposeful and truthful and openhearted and compassionate and filled with love," Carter explained. Also, they want to know: "Can our government work, can it be competent, efficient, and economical?" Both questions could be answered affirmatively, Carter said, by electing him president.

Trust and competence were not really issues in an ideological sense. But they were Carter's principal values and he was more comfortable talking about them than about conventional issues, some of which he was unfamiliar with. Carter was a highly unconventional politician who had emerged from outside the closed universe that generally produces presidential candidates. This would prove to be an advantage in some ways and a handicap in others.

The unique circumstances of the 1976 campaign made Carter's background an important asset, at least in the beginning. Carter was insightful enough to understand that given the troubled mood of the country, voters would be more receptive to hearing about values than the sort of talk that normally dominated political debate. But he did not allow his unfamiliarity with the conventional political agenda to cramp his style. He was as assertive with the voters as he was with reporters, campaigning on his own terms, driving home his points about trust and competence.

"There's a lot of things I will never do to get elected," I heard Carter tell the crowd that greeted him in Concord. "I will never tell a lie, make a misleading statement, or betray a trust. If I should ever betray a trust, don't support me."

As for competence, Carter depicted himself as a sort of modern Renaissance man, capable of handling anything. "I'm a businessman, I'm a farmer, I'm a planner," he said. "I'm an engineer, I'm a nuclear physicist, I'm a politician, I'm a Christian."

Most politicians would hesitate to make such extravagant promises and unabashed boasts. But for Carter, these pledges and claims were a way of establishing how different he was from most politicians. It was this difference, a product of his ideology, values, and character, that excited Carter's admirers. Because he was different they saw in him the potential to lead the country away from the traumas of the past decade on to a new political road.

Apart from being businessman, farmer, planner, and the rest of the attainments he regularly reeled off in his stump speeches, Jimmy Carter was a Southerner. But he was a different sort of Southerner, too, from racist demagogues to whom Northerners had become accustomed. He was a Southerner who could appeal to black voters, thus enhancing the potential of his candidacy and offering hope after two decades of violent antagonism of reconciliation between the races.

"There is no good man like a good white Southerner," Eleanor Holmes Norton, who became one of the many blacks Carter appointed to his government,* told me during his campaign. "You can talk about a born-again Christian, but a man who's been born again to civil rights, who speaks with a Southern accent, and is good on civil rights issues, is the best form of civil rights advocate."

A white Southerner who could get black votes was the answer to a political dream. And it made his backers conceive of a broad new coalition taking the place of the tattered old New Deal alliance in which middle-class whites found common cause with working-class blacks, North and South.

Carter's admirers had the right to envision such dreams. The political turmoil of the times and Carter's freedom from the shibboleths of the past made possible a presidency that would be a watershed for the country and for his party, by creating a new electoral majority.

That chance had been bungled by his two immediate predecessors. After Lyndon Johnson's consensus leadership had foundered in Vietnam, the political future had seemed within Richard Nixon's grasp. But Nixon's Watergate folly had devastated him and his party and given Carter his opening.

This opportunity was also Carter's challenge. Although he was not burdened with stale ideas and old debts, he nevertheless needed to find fresh answers and form new alliances. He could not merely denounce the forces that had distorted the political system; he needed to demonstrate that he could make the system redeem the bold promises he made.

The tension between Carter's potential and his performance dominated his presidency, reaching its definitive moment during the so-called "malaise speech" of July 1979. It was his handling of that episode that

* She was the chairman of the Equal Employment Opportunity Commission.

chiefly determined whether history would regard him as the voice of a new political era or the victim of the high expectations he had created.

IDEOLOGY

When reporters asked during the 1976 campaign if Carter was a liberal or conservative, he told them he was a "fiscal conservative," but "quite liberal" on civil rights and the environment. "This was my political philosophy as governor of Georgia, as a presidential candidate and while I served in the White House," he later wrote. But this was just a commentary on his ideological inclinations, not a framework for governing. What served Carter as a political philosophy was really an antipolitical philosophy; it was the credo of the outsider.

This outlook reflected his background. Among the modern presidents up to that time, Carter came to office with the least familiarity with the national government and, with the sole exception of Dwight Eisenhower, with the least kinship with partisan traditions.

Though Carter acknowledged few links to the Democratic past, he did claim kinship between himself and Truman. "Of all the presidents who served during my lifetime, I admired Harry Truman most and had studied his career more than any other," he wrote. The Truman qualities he cited—his small-town roots and his willingness "to be unpopular if he believed his actions were best for the country"—were obviously traits he saw in himself.

Yet the two men differed significantly in ideological terms. Truman's political convictions were heavily grounded in old-fashioned Populism and latter-day interest-group liberalism. Carter's political outlook by contrast was far less substantive, far more personal, and was dominated by his self-image as an outsider.

Many factors contributed to Carter's outsider's view of the political world, including his small-town upbringing and his success as a businessman that preceded his political career. The most significant influence on his ideological outlook, though, was his political heritage as a Southerner, which made him an outsider by definition. He was the son of a region that when he began campaigning had been estranged from the mainstream of national politics for more than a century.

On the night of Carter's election, I recall waiting in his hotel headquarters while he delayed his victory statement as the late returns that would ensure his electoral majority trickled in. His press secretary, Jody Powell, asked the restive crowd of supporters for patience. "We have waited more than a hundred years for this moment," Powell said. "We can wait a few minutes more." I heard the crowd thunder back its exultation.

Yet even after he became the first president from the Deep South in more than a century, Carter did not find it easy to free himself and his beliefs from the tangled legacy of Southern politics. It was a web in which cause and effect were intermeshed. The South had been isolated because its politics was distorted and the isolation made the distortions worse.

"The South may not be the nation's number one political problem, as some Northerners assert, but politics is the South's number one problem," the revered political scientist V. O. Key wrote in 1950. Circumstances in the South changed dramatically in the next two decades, and these changes abetted Carter's rise to power. But some of the fundamental problems remained and shaped Carter's political career.

The most serious of these was, of course, the pervasive influence of race. The domination of race by foreclosing debate on other issues produced a political system controlled by the Democratic party and by an economic oligarchy based in those states, Carter's Georgia among them, with large black populations. The Democratic leadership and the business elite which controlled these states had a common interest in maintaining racial segregation as the key to maintaining political and economic control.

Instead of bipartisan competition as in the North, Southern politics was shaped "by transient and amorphous political factions within the Democratic party," Key wrote. Leadership devolved "on lone wolf operators, on fortuitous groups of individuals usually of a transient nature, on spectacular demagogues odd enough to command the attention of considerable groups of voters."

This system, which reigned supreme for more than a half century, began to be dramatically transformed in the postwar era. The civil rights revolution enfranchised the Negro. The Democratic party changed from being the bulwark of segregation to the champion of civil rights, opening the way for the emergence of the Republican party as a realistic competitor. The Supreme Court's one-man, one-vote doctrine broke the stranglehold of rural areas on governments in many Southern states, particularly Georgia, encouraging successful businessmen like Carter to enter politics.

For all these changes, though, much remained the same. Southern economic leaders now realized that their hitherto unyielding defense of legal segregation was not only ultimately futile but also created an atmosphere of instability harmful to business growth. Still, politicians in both parties continued to exploit racial fears to their advantage, although more subtly than in the past. Meanwhile, the Southern business elite, its ranks bolstered by an influx of entrepreneurs and managers from the

North, was revived by what one analysis of Carter's politics calls "the vanished tradition of Southern progressivism"—characterized by reliance on government by "expertise" rather than popular politics. It was this new climate that attracted Jimmy Carter to politics and defined his outsider's outlook.

Carter's views and experience were well suited to the managerial doctrines of progressivism. When he entered politics in 1962 by running for a Georgia state senate seat, he was no fresh-eyed stripling like Kennedy or Johnson. He was thirty-eight years old, well established as a successful businessman and clearly marked as an outsider not only by his mistrust of parties and other politicians but also his faith in so-called businesslike techniques. These attitudes were reinforced by his experiences in winning election to the legislature and by his service there. His candidacy met with the bitter opposition of old-line politicians, who sought to defeat him by stuffing the ballot box. By waging a prolonged and bitter legal battle, Carter won a recount and the election, an outcome that he later described as the triumph of "decency" over "corrupt public officials."

Once in the state senate, he found it a den of iniquitous special interests. "The confusion and complications of state government," he wrote, offered "many niches in which special interests could hide," making it "difficult for the common good to prevail." He had by now established the principal dialectic underlying his ideology, which would ultimately carry him to the presidency: Traditional politicians combined with "special interest groups" controlled and despoiled government. They could only be defeated if the victimized majority of citizens could find leaders from outside the political world whose sole objectives were efficiency and honesty—Carter himself being of course a prime example of such a paladin.

These themes helped him make the leap from the state senate to the governorship, on his second attempt in 1970. His outsider theme was made all the more potent when good fortune gave him as his chief opponent former Governor Carl Sanders, who because of his flossy style as much as the substance of his beliefs could be depicted as a creature of the establishment. "Cufflinks Carl" as Sanders's critics styled him, turned out to be the perfect foil for Carter.

In the governor's office, Carter's efforts to live up to his self-designated role as an outsider unwilling to do political business as usual yielded as many problems as solutions. By the time the four-year term to which he was limited by the state constitution had ended, his constant battles with the legislature over his reform proposals and unorthodox tactics had stirred so much antagonism that many politicians preferred to keep their distance from him. Indeed, the candidate he backed as his successor, Bert

Lance, who later became White House budget director, was soundly defeated.

Still, he had taken enough positive steps to enable him to use his one gubernatorial term as the foundation for his candidacy for the presidency. He made a start on prison reform and won friends among environmentalists by strengthening curbs against air and water pollution. Pushing through a much vaunted overhaul of state government took up more of his time than any other issue. The reforms did not give citizens more control over the government or significantly reduce the size of the bureaucracy or the state budget, as Carter had claimed they would. But enough changes were made to give him a paradigm for his later stress on procedures.

By far the most important step Carter took, though, was repudiating segregation and racism. Though he had made thinly veiled racist appeals during his campaign against Sanders, he realized that renouncing racism was an absolute necessity for any Southerner with national political ambitions. Moreover, doing so was consistent with the pattern set by Southern economic leaders who wanted to rid themselves of the distraction of bigotry so they could attract Northern capital and skilled managers and technicians.

"The time for racial discrimination is over," he declared in his inaugural address. In keeping with that spirit, he had Martin Luther King's portrait hung in the state capitol, a pantheon hitherto reserved for the state's Caucasian heroes.

In substantive terms, such as combating discrimination and segregation in schools, housing, and employment, Carter earned only mixed grades from civil rights leaders. But it was the symbolism of the inaugural rhetoric and the King portrait that had the most powerful impact on blacks and white liberals outside of Georgia. By decrying racism Carter not only made himself acceptable to these two potent groups in the Democratic party's nominating process, but he reinforced the most important potential strength of his candidacy, his outsider's ideology.

This asset took on additional value because of the widespread public alienation from government in the wake of Vietnam and Watergate. "The great stable middle class is becoming unhinged," Pat Caddell told a gathering of Democratic party leaders and activists I attended at the Flying Carpet motel in Chicago in March 1975. The numbers and the other pollsters in attendance backed him up.

Polls showed that the middle-class Americans that Nixon had rallied to his side had been fragmented by Watergate, inflation, and recession. Moreover, the public's suspicions extended beyond Nixon to all of government. Only 10 percent of Americans were optimistic about the nation's future, compared with 75 percent a decade earlier when the Great Society was still rich in promise.

Cynicism was rampant. Nearly 70 percent believed their government "consistently lies to the people," a view extending to political promises both left and right. The public attitude promised to cause most immediate damage to the Republicans because of Nixon's disgrace, Ford's pardon, and the hard economic times. But the long-range implications were more serious for liberal Democrats, simply because government activism is the basic tenet of liberalism. When people lose faith in government, liberals have a hard time staying in business.

"The old coalitions are breaking down," pollster Peter Hart warned at the Flying Carpet. The Democrats could no longer rely on majorities delivered by powerful blocs of interest groups held together by the shared confidence that government would benefit their lives.

On top of all that, the end of the Vietnam War had left liberal Democrats sharply divided. Many now argued that the war by its waste of resources and its inherent savagery had betrayed basic liberal beliefs. Others contended that the critics of the war were the betrayers, by undermining the nation's will to fight. These divisions had contributed to the downfall of the Democrats in the 1968 and 1972 presidential elections.

As Carter and his advisers realized early on, the divisiveness that gripped the Democratic party had favorable implications for Carter's candidacy. Under these circumstances, they reasoned, the party would be less concerned with finding a candidate who met certain ideological standards than with finding a way to return to the White House.

Another factor favoring Carter was the threat of a successful George Wallace candidacy. Wallace had demonstrated his powerful appeal not just to white Southerners but to working-class voters in the North when he ran as an independent candidate in 1968. In 1972, competing for the Democratic party nomination, he had already made a formidable showing by early spring when he was cut down by a would-be assassin's bullet.

The sector of the party—the liberals—that would have been ordinarily most concerned with ideological positions was the same group most worried about Wallace. Near panic, they sought a Southerner who could defeat Wallace in his home grounds. Carter, who had established his bona fides on civil rights by renouncing segregation as governor of Georgia, eagerly offered himself up for the job. No one was sure where he stood exactly on most issues, but Andrew Young, the black civil rights leader who had dealt with Carter in Georgia, assured the many liberal politicians who asked him that "Carter was all right on race."

Young usually added, "There are a lot of other questions I may have."

But the worried liberals heard only the reassuring "all right on race" and shut their ears to the "other questions." Meanwhile with strong liberal backing Carter swept to victory over Wallace in the Florida primary, a success that ensured him the nomination.

While the condition of the Democratic Party and the perceived threat from Wallace permitted Carter to avoid ideological definitions, he defined himself in broader terms as an outsider. This was equivalent to defining himself by what he was not. He was not from Washington, he was not a member of Congress, he was not a liberal, he was not a spokesman for any of the major interest groups in his party.

Under other circumstances these negative traits would have been seen as weaknesses. But during the 1976 campaign the things Carter had not done became virtues.

VALUES

In the spring of 1976, when Jimmy Carter was already well on his way to the nomination, he came to Washington to meet with a gathering of influential lobbyists for various liberal interest groups. When they pressed him for views on specific issues, the candidate fended them off by emphasizing his principal values—trust and competence—which he used as surrogates for issues. "I don't care how much you talk about issues, or how many numbers of Senate and House bills you name," he said, "if the people don't believe that when you're in the White House, you're going to do something about the problem and that they can trust what you tell them."

By stressing the importance of trust and competence, Carter diverted attention from his lack of Washington experience. But these values, which emerged naturally from his religious and business background, were not just a shield. They were also a sword that helped him to depict himself as a leader who could conquer the public cynicism that pervaded the political landscape.

Carter's emphasis on trust was grounded on morality and religion. When he asked voters to trust him, he was implicitly contending that he was worthy of that trust because he was a good man and a good Christian. "I'm a deeply religious person," he told the crowd in Concord on our excursion to New Hampshire two years later. "I have a deep commitment to my principles, based on my religious belief that would be unshakable."

His Southern Baptist faith had become closely linked to his political career. Though Carter had been a faithful churchgoer since childhood, his much discussed born-again experience significantly occurred as a direct consequence of his failed try for the governorship in 1966. "Emotionally devastated" by that defeat, he sought help from his sister, an evangelist who suggested that he could alleviate his depression if he took full advantage of his natural religious conviction. What followed, as Carter noted, "was no blinding flash of light," but instead a decision to "reassess my relationship with God." Carter became more personally involved in evangelical work, and as a result, he told his longtime adviser, Peter Bourne, "I've got a much more complete religious faith. It's personally satisfying to me. I'm at peace with myself and I can accept defeat."

Whatever other benefits his reaffirmed faith brought him, it certainly was an asset on the campaign trail, particularly in the post-Watergate political climate. In the ideological vacuum of the 1976 campaign, Carter used trust *cum* religion as a way to inspire his supporters. For him it served much the same purpose as the Vietnam protest and civil rights movements had served for other politicians. Moreover, it provided a striking contrast to the cynicism that dominated the electorate's mood. He often cited as his favorite definition of politics an aphorism taken from Protestant theologian Reinhold Niebuhr: "The purpose of politics is to establish justice in a sinful world."

When we talked on our trip to New Hampshire, Carter cautiously told me, "Religion is part of my life, part of my consciousness. It may or may not be politically significant." In actuality, however, Carter had a keen appreciation of the potential political benefits of his religious faith. He happened to be in Los Angeles with Peter Bourne when my story about the New Hampshire trip appeared in the *Los Angeles Times*, under a headline describing him as "The Moralist Candidate for President." The story made the point that Carter's highlighting of morality and religion set his candidacy apart from his rivals. Bourne, who read the article first, was worried that the stress on moral fervor would be damaging to Carter. But after Carter read the story he said flatly, "You're wrong. It will help me—even in Los Angeles."

In the White House, Carter continued to emphasize the moral standards that were the underpinning of the trust he sought from voters. But what had worked in helping to frame the promises of the campaign was much less effective in dealing with the realities of governing. Early in his presidency, addressing a group of federal employees, he felt called upon to urge, "Those of you who are living in sin, I hope you'll get married." Such behavior seemed to many Americans sanctimonious, which proved to be politically harmful, particularly after Carter later appeared insensitive to the financial indiscretions of his budget director and confidant, Bert Lance.

As he did with trust, Carter used the value of competence as a supplement to his outsider's ideology. His stress on competence came naturally from his experience as an Annapolis graduate, a naval officer, and a businessman, all of which focused on techniques and procedures and involved tangibles as contrasted with concepts.

In his campaign Carter vowed to bring a more businesslike approach to government by instituting a variety of reforms—from streamlining the federal bureaucracy to overhauling the tax code and the welfare system. This approach helped reinforce the impression of himself as an outsider opposed to the bureaucrats and special interests who Carter argued had created the existing system to serve their own purposes. "This is not a job for the fainthearted," he said about his promises to reform the government. "It will be met with strong opposition from those who now enjoy special privilege, those who prefer to work in the dark, or those whose personal fiefdoms are threatened."

Then, too, by focusing on changes in the machinery of government Carter was able to avoid controversy that would inevitably result were he to propose more substantive changes in the purpose and philosophy of government programs.

In fact, the principles Carter laid down for managing government, particularly his insistence on comprehensiveness as the sine qua non of efficiency, had inherent flaws. As he would find out in trying to push through his welfare and tax reforms, such sweeping changes, because they are so broad in impact, produce results that are extremely complex, hard to predict, and therefore unlikely rallying points for public support. Carter ignored this problem, because he feared that "incremental efforts at change," as he called them, would be blocked by his old nemesis, "the special interest groups" who would be able to focus their opposition to specific reforms better than to broad change. He was unwilling to accept the reality that the public is made up of a series of special interest groups and that the role of a leader is to forge a coalition of these groups to support his goals.

CHARACTER

During that New Hampshire trip Carter stopped at a factory gate to shake hands with workers at shift-changing time. A truck driver accosted Carter, bitterly complaining because Gerald Rafshoon, Carter's longtime adviser, had parked his car in the spot reserved for the driver. Carter tried to ignore the driver, but the man kept shouting, making an unpleasant scene. Finally, Carter glanced at Rafshoon, who had a camera dangling from a strap around his neck, because he had been taking photos for a Carter campaign brochure.

"He doesn't work for me," Carter told the driver. "He's a photographer."

The confused driver gave up and left. Carter might just as easily have apologized to him and given him a few dollars for his trouble. But he did not give ground to anyone, no matter how trivial the stakes, unless he had no other choice. Single-minded determination was as important a part of his character as of Richard Nixon's. The difference was that while Nixon's determination led to bitter conflicts with others, Carter's willfulness was manifested in a striking absorption with himself to the exclusion of others. This aspect of his character helped him reach the presidency, yet made it harder for him to succeed once he got there.

Carter had many exemplary character traits. In a trenchant critique of his political style, a former White House speech writer, James Fallows, described him as "a good man," adding: "If I had to choose one politician to sit at the Pearly Gates and pass judgment on my soul, Jimmy Carter would be the one."

In the political arena, however, other aspects of his personality rooted in his early upbringing tended to overshadow his virtues. Driven to prove that he was an exceptional human being, he was plagued by the fear that he would fail to achieve the goals he set for himself. His need to demonstrate that he was unusually gifted stemmed from a number of factors—being raised as an only child until he was thirteen, when his brother Billy was born, his remote rural hometown of Archery, where the Carters were one of only two white families, and the high expectations his keen native intelligence generated in those around him.

His relationships with his parents fueled his drive to stand out from the pack but also contributed to anxieties about his abilities. His father, Earl, had many admirable traits in his son's eyes. "My father was a natural leader in our community," Carter wrote. Yet Earl was not an entirely satisfactory role model for his son because in addition to his good qualities, he also was a living reminder of the limitations stemming from being raised in the rural South, handicaps that Jimmy knew he would have to overcome to fulfill his ambitions.

For one, the elder Carter had only gone as far as the tenth grade although, his son pointed out, this was "the most advanced education of any Carter man since our family moved to Georgia two hundred years ago." The son also recalled his father's effort to raise his sartorial standards by ordering, for the first time in his life, a tailor-made suit. But the tailor turned out to be lacking somewhat in skill. "All the family . . . gathered around the fireplace while Daddy began to put on his suit," which turned out to be twice Earl's size. "I remember that no one in the family laughed," Carter recalled, but he himself "felt desperately sorry" for his father.

Earl was not the sort of father who could provide reassurance to ease his son's anxieties. Nothing in Jimmy's generally positive description of him conveys any sense of intimacy. "He was a stern disciplinarian and punished me severely when I misbehaved." Using "a small, long flexible peach tree switch," Earl whipped his eldest son six times from the time he was four until he was fifteen, experiences that Jimmy never forgot.

In *Why Not the Best?* Carter also referred to his mother in admiring terms, unconsciously contrasting her with her husband, a comparison that usually worked to her advantage. He pointed out that his mother was a registered nurse, thus having attained a higher level of formal education than her husband. Moreover, "although my father seldom read a book, my mother was an avid reader, and so was I."

Just as the father–son relationship lacked warmth because of Earl's stern, aloof manner, Carter's relationship with his mother appears to have been inhibited by her preoccupation with her own life, particularly her vocation as a nurse. "She typically worked on nursing duty twelve hours per day, or twenty hours per day for which she was paid a magnificent six dollars" and also "served as a community doctor for our neighbors." Carter described her as "an extrovert, very dynamic, inquisitive in her attitude about life, compassionate toward others."

Strikingly, most of what Carter has to say about Lillian Carter has to do with her relationship to others rather than to himself. He devotes more space in his account of his childhood to the influence on his life of his grade-school superintendent, Julia Coleman, than to his mother. "As a schoolboy who lived in an isolated farm community, my exposure to classical literature, art and music was ensured by this superlative teacher." Evidently she also helped foster his faith in his own exceptionalism; at age twelve she gave Carter *War and Peace* to read. "It turned out to be one of my favorite books," he claimed, adding: "And I have read it two or three times since then."

As Carter grew to manhood, his "sense of being set apart was accompanied by a high degree of reclusiveness and shyness," writes Peter Bourne, who besides being Carter's friend had clinical training as a psychiatrist. At the Naval Academy he made few close friends and picked as a sport cross-country running, the most solitary of athletic pursuits. Carter devoted only two pages in *Why Not the Best?* to his Annapolis experience, and judging from his descriptions, his training there left him with few pleasant memories. He referred to "the homesickness and hazing" of his freshman year, various "punishments" for infractions of academy rules, the "stringent" academic requirements, and "the rigid engineering curriculum."

His hero worship of Admiral Hyman Rickover appears to have been an attempt to find a more satisfactory model for his drive to achieve exceptionalism than his father. As Carter acknowledges, this relationship meant much more to him than to Rickover, who though "he may not have cared or known it . . . had a profound effect" on Carter's life. "He was unbelievably hardworking and competent and he demanded total dedication from his subordinates." But Rickover, by Carter's account, gave very little in return. Though he never hesitated to criticize severely, "the absence of a comment" was the only compliment he usually offered.

Measured in some ways, Rickover's career was indeed "brilliant and remarkable." However, he served as an exemplar not only of great energy and intelligence but also of unconscionable egotism. It does not seem to have occurred to Carter that these traits gravely damaged Rickover's career, limited his effectiveness, and when adapted to political life could have disastrous results.

Carter's self-absorption was evidenced by the way he dealt with criticism of his public utterances and actions. Often he responded by charging bad faith on the part of his critics, thus making his own persona and ambitions rather than any substantive issue the center of political debate. Commenting on criticism of his 1970 gubernatorial candidacy by the Atlanta *Constitution*, years after the event, Carter asserted: "Since the newspaper strongly supported Gov. Sanders, I presume that the editors recognized me as his major potential opponent and wanted to destroy me early in the campaign." In May 1976, as his primary campaign met surprisingly resilient opposition, he charged in a campaign speech in Ohio: "My critics . . . want to stop the people of this country from regaining control of their government. They want to preserve the status quo, to preserve politics as usual, to maintain at all costs their own entrenched, unresponsive, bankrupt, irresponsible political power."

At the time, questions about Carter's political beliefs and his plans for the country were increasing instead of subsiding, a reflection of the vagueness of his candidacy. His response, by imputing to his opponents sinister motives, reflected not only his exaggerated sense of his own importance but also his disdain for political debate.

Nor did his character broaden or his outlook mellow after he reached the White House. Instead of his being reassured by his remarkable achievement in capturing the presidency, his elevation appeared to magnify his insecurity. For example, according to Bourne, Carter's concern that people he appointed might outshine him or his longtime aides from Georgia often seemed greater than his desire to recruit highly qualified people for his administration. "To succeed mightily is to be exposed mightily . . . and to be exceptionally vulnerable," Bourne wrote. "The personal insecurity which success engendered in Carter, aggravated by the burden of his Southern heritage, became his Achilles' heel."

THE CHALLENGE

"The time is ripe for a political realignment in America, for construction of a new political coalition," Patrick Caddell, Carter's pollster and also one of his chief political strategists, wrote in a memorandum to the president-elect a few weeks before inauguration day. But this was more than just an opportunity, it was an imperative. For the same turbulence that gave Carter and the Democrats the opening to create a new majority ensured that the president and his party would go down to defeat if they failed to seize the day.

In trying to exploit the momentous opportunity that history offered, Carter confronted some imposing difficulties not of his own making. Whether they were significantly harder or easier than those of his recent predecessors is, of course, difficult to measure. Clearly, though, Carter did not fully understand the problems he faced. Moreover, he did not fully exploit the assets that stemmed from the special nature of his presidency. His failure in both cases can be traced to deficiencies in the key ingredients for presidential leadership: ideology, values, and character.

His outsider's ideology and stress on the values of trust and competence had helped him win support for his candidacy from discontented voters. Now as president he needed to broaden his scope to take into account the complexities of governing and the varied needs of the electorate. This would have been a tall order for anyone, and Carter's characteristic self-absorption hindered his ability to learn from his new experiences and new political environment.

He was unwilling, James Fallows contended, "to convert himself from a good man into an effective one, to learn how to do the job." For example, as an orator his rhetoric was so pedestrian and his delivery so dull that his ability to communicate with the country was severely limited. After one Carter speech, Milton Gwirtzman, a Democratic speech writer, told me that if Carter had delivered Franklin Roosevelt's "nothing to fear but fear itself" address of 1933, "the Depression would still be going on." Yet Carter refused to make the extra effort of speech lessons that would have improved his performance.

This attitude made even more difficult a series of problems that would have daunted any president. The most fundamental and complex difficulty

Carter faced on taking office was economic. For more than a decade the tension between the perils of inflation and recession had dominated the thinking of presidential policymakers. The dilemma stemmed from Lyndon Johnson's guns-and-butter decision to escalate the Vietnam War without raising taxes, from the steady decline in productivity because of the nation's aging industrial base, and from intensified competitiveness abroad. As Carter campaigned for the presidency in the fall of 1976 the nation was still suffering from the impact of the 1974 recession, which had made a mockery of Ford's concern with inflation. But by the time Carter had settled into office, recovery had gone far enough that inflation once more was a threat.

On the political front, this economic conundrum was especially threatening to a Democratic president. Over the years the support of Democratic constituencies had been maintained by the largess of government made possible by steady economic growth. But this trend, Carter and others believed, had come to an end. That meant the rise in spending had to end, too. As Caddell advised Carter in his political strategy memorandum: "Our budget people must be made sensitive to spending what we have well, rather than thinking up new ways to spend."

Meanwhile the political landscape was littered with the debris from Watergate and Vietnam, sapping confidence in government, as had been made clear at the Flying Carpet motel in 1975. The pollsters' figures had showed that of the 38 percent of eligible voters who went to the polls in the 1974 election—the lowest turnout in more than thirty years—only a third thought their votes would make a difference. The electorate was so disturbed, one pollster claimed, "there would be a movement to socialistic action, except that the government is feared and disliked as much as big business."

As formidable as these problems were, Carter was in some ways well positioned to deal with them. Perhaps the single most significant achievement of his candidacy was the extent to which it helped heal the trauma of racial divisiveness that had crippled Democrats since 1948. With his dual identity as a bona fide white Southerner *and* the conqueror of racist George Wallace, Carter was freer than any president in two decades to address the real needs of both races.

Also an important asset for Carter was the high moral tone he had set as a candidate. Moreover, he expanded on his theme of trust even before he took office when he made a point of announcing that his appointees would have to meet rigid ethical standards. No other presidential candidate in modern times had so emphatically stamped himself as a man of God. And although it would take more than prayers and piety to alleviate public cynicism, Carter had worked hard to earn himself the benefit of the doubt.

Being an outsider not tied to the left or the right or to any element of the existing power structure was another potential advantage. "People still see Jimmy Carter as outside the traditional political establishment," Caddell wrote after reviewing poll results. "They feel he brings a new sense of doing business to the government and feel that he will staff it with a new generation of leaders."

Even with these factors on his side, Carter had his work cut out for him. With the traditional Democratic alliance of trade unionists, blacks, Catholics, and Southern whites collapsing, his political advisers recommended that while holding on to the support of the old cohorts as best he could, Carter should find a way to attract new groups. These would include in particular the upwardly mobile young professionals who would later become labeled as Yuppies.

"There needs to be some thought given to a better political definition of the issues and concerns that exist," Caddell wrote. What was required, he urged, was nothing less than "a fundamentally new ideology."

This was not a challenge that aroused Carter's interest, however. He regarded politics as a realm entirely distinct from governing. He mastered the tactics necessary to win nomination and the election, then lost interest in the subject. It did not occur to him that successful leadership in the White House required a continuing effort to convince voters that his objectives were in their best interests. Nor did he accept the responsibility of achieving the goals of those who had supported him because they believed he shared these same objectives.

"I feel deeply obligated to people but I'll do what I think is best for the country," he said after his election, adding proudly: "There are no strings on me."

So the advice about rallying interest groups into a coalition fell on deaf ears. When I asked him his plans for forging a new political alliance in the first spring of his presidency, he plainly saw no need for such an effort. Indeed, he claimed that his support was growing on all sides. "There has been a general increase in the number of people who consider me to be competent, who consider me to be in charge of the government," he told me. "There's been a substantial shift in my basic placement on the political spectrum by people of this country toward the conservative, and I think that's probably an accurate assessment on economic affairs."

Although Carter took comfort from these polls, his political advisers contemplated the same numbers with considerable distress. Caddell told his colleagues at a political strategy meeting I attended that the figures showed "enormous potential" for Carter to increase his strength across the political spectrum. The "but" was—and it was a highly significant "but"—Carter's support showed little intensity.

"His superficial popularity has increased, but his constituency is not defined," Caddell said. "There's a lot of long-run potential but right now there's no particular group to fall back on."

"What you're saying," interjected Mark Siegel, who had come to the White House political staff from a stint as executive director of the Democratic National Committee, "is that we don't have a political base."

For Carter's advisers this was ominous news indeed. Just as home is said to be the place from which you won't be turned away no matter what you've done, a politician's base is made up of supporters who will stick with him, no matter how badly things are going.

Carter's ratings showed that much of his backing came from conservatives and Republicans, voters who were probably pleased by his relatively conservative approach to economic policy in which he took such pride. But this support was not deeply rooted and it reflected the stable economic conditions of the first months of Carter's White House tenure. Experience had taught the president's political advisers that if hard times came, these voters would be quick to desert the president for someone with better established conservative credentials. And hard times did indeed threaten, because of the growing danger of inflation.

The clear leadership imperative for Carter, his advisers believed, was to take advantage of the relatively tranquil times to define himself and his beliefs in a way that would create a coalition to support his ambitious aims in the White House. But Carter saw himself as a problem solver guided by the twin verities of trust and competence, not a politician, certainly not as the founder of a new political coalition. So he forged ahead on all fronts heedless of political consequences, promoting the comprehensive solutions so close to his heart. If his policies seemed to other politicians to be disjointed and inconsistent, Carter was not disturbed. He was confident that he would prevail because the merit of his ideas would inevitably be recognized.

In the critical area of economic policy, Carter abruptly shifted gears in the first months of his presidency. Because of concern about inflation, he scrapped a prior proposal for a $50 tax rebate to spur the economy without warning to anyone, including his Treasury Secretary. The jarring move damaged his prestige and his relationships with Congress. Fellow Democrat Senator Edmund Muskie of Maine who later became Carter's Secretary of State called the rebate shift "a breach of promise to the people."

At the heart of Carter's domestic program were a series of sweeping comprehensive reforms characteristic of his thinking, covering the welfare system, tax code and energy crisis. But welfare reform failed to make progress because Carter had underestimated the cost of the reforms and the political roadblocks on the road to approval. Tax reform bogged down in part because of the ill will Carter had created by his abrupt abandonment of the $50 tax rebate. As for the energy program, it could serve as a paradigm for all the well-intentioned failures of his presidency. Energy policy appealed to Carter not only because the problem confronted the entire society rather than being the province of the "special interests" he resented but also because no other political leader had made a full-scale effort to solve it.

One major reason no one had offered a comprehensive energy package before was that any such solution was likely to offend more people than it would please. Another was that most Americans did not yet believe that the energy shortage had reached a critical stage. Before taking on this challenge Carter needed to consult the various interests most directly concerned with the problem, to persuade the public of its urgency, and then to develop grass-roots and leadership support of his answer.

Instead, Carter established an arbitrary deadline for developing a program by April 1977, only three months after his inauguration. Borrowing from William James, he proclaimed his proposals to be "the moral equivalent of war." Rhetoric aside, though, his proposals were not sufficiently drastic to rally the broad public support he needed. On the other hand, the package of tax increases and other conservation measures he called for were just burdensome enough to provoke the opposition of the "special interests" he had been hoping to defeat. Because Carter neglected his political homework, what he finally got out of Congress was only about half of what he had sought.

In the field of foreign policy, Carter's leadership exhibited a similar detachment from the demands of political reality. Abroad as at home, Carter demonstrated that it was not enough for a president to try to do the right thing unless he can convince a majority of citizens that success of his cause will serve their own and their country's best interests. He won high marks from history and foreign-policy experts with the Panama Canal treaty and the Camp David agreement between Israel and Egypt. But he was unable to generate strong public support for the Canal treaty, which turned out to be a better political issue for Ronald Reagan and other conservative opponents of the pact than it was for Carter. Even the Democratic National Committee balked at endorsing the accords with Panama. The 1978 Camp David agreement gave Carter a brief blip of public approval, which predictably vanished as public attention turned to problems closer at home and as new tensions emerged in the Middle East to overshadow Carter's success.

Meanwhile, Carter frittered away the initial advantages that had made his presidency seem so rich in potential. It soon became apparent that his appeal to his native South could not be sustained merely by the coincidence of his birth there. If Carter's victory had helped Southerners shed their parochial view of national politics, it also inclined them to judge Carter on the same basis other Americans did, and by these standards his performance fell short.

Carter's initial excellent rapport with black leaders also suffered during his presidency. This estrangement developed not just from Carter's resistance to supporting federal programs they deemed vital to their constituents, but also from his unwillingness to tolerate any dissent. When moderate black leader Vernon Jordan, director of the Urban League, complained that Carter was not doing as much as he could for poor people, Carter told Jordan, in a private conversation that the White House then pointedly released, that his criticism was "damaging to the hopes and aspirations of poor people."

As for Carter's image of unquestioned rectitude, that too was badly tarnished by his handling of the controversy surrounding Bert Lance, Carter's longtime confidante, whom he had named to head the Office of Management and Budget. Disclosure of Lance's slovenly conduct of his personal financial affairs as a Georgia banker, verging on illegality, stirred a public outcry, in the face of which Carter dug in his heels. Ultimately Lance was forced to quit, but the damage to the administration was lasting. "It made people realize that we were no different than anybody else," Carter's vice-president, Walter Mondale, told me.

Within his own party Carter succeeded in bringing together the diverse and fractious elements of the Democratic coalition—in unity against himself. Nearly every major interest group—blacks, unions, feminists, Jews—was vocal in its resentment.

Beleaguered on all sides, Carter and his advisers took hope from the enemies they had made. In early 1979 as the chorus of protests against the president's belt tightening mounted from Democratic constituencies, I visited the White House to talk to Gregg Schneiders, one of Carter's image manipulators. "If these people didn't exist, we'd have to invent them," Schneiders told me. "They're helping to make our point."

This point was that unlike past Democratic presidents, Carter was willing to stand up to pressures from "selfish" special-interest groups. Supposedly this perception would help Carter develop a new coalition that sounded strikingly similar to the silent majority that Richard Nixon had mobilized in defense of his Vietnam policies. But Carter's problem was that the war was a far more compelling rallying point than the greed of the so-called special interests. More to the point, after three years in the White House Carter had been unable to formulate any other clear message to develop a political base.

The course of the Carter presidency was by no means a toboggan ride to disaster. Rather, it followed an erratic pattern with declines occasionally broken by advances that offered the tantalizing hope for progress. For example, during one such hopeful interval in the fall of 1978 Carter was telling visitors that at last he had gotten a grip on the presidency. Two meetings at Camp David—the first in the spring to rally his cabinet, the second in the fall with Menachem Begin and Anwar Sadat that had produced the historic Middle East agreement—had given him hope for progress at home and abroad.

The president was forgetting, though, how fortunate he had been during his first two years in the White House in not being forced to confront a real crisis. This time he failed to use to build credibility with the public and a base of supporters who would bear with him through hard times. So when the hard times hit, the damage was devastating.

Starting late in 1978, a series of events hammered the Carter presidency at home and abroad.

In Iran, the shah fell and revolution erupted. Carter was blamed for not foreseeing and preventing the collapse of his regime.

In the U.S., oil prices shot up, boosting the cost of gasoline to unheard-of levels. Not only was the price exorbitant, the supply was short, and long lines formed around gas stations.

On Capitol Hill, there was defiance. In April 1979 Carter announced he would lift controls on oil to encourage oil companies to increase production—but failed to make this decision contingent upon congressional enactment of a windfall profit tax. Suspicious that the oil companies would simply reap bigger profits without easing the fuel scarcity, House Democrats, in a slap in the face to Carter, went on record against decontrol. Then Congress added to the president's humiliation by refusing to grant his request for standby authority for gas rationing.

On the economic front, inflation rocketed to 14 percent and a federal judge ruled that Carter could not deny government contracts to violators of his wage-price guidelines, emasculating his anti-inflation program.

In June 1979, when the president was at an economic summit in Tokyo, his troubles came to a head. The gasoline shortage appeared to dominate national life. Millions of Americans were sweating it out on gasoline lines and being forced to scrap their vacation plans. Domestic policy adviser Stuart Eizenstat sounded the alarm with a memo dispatched from Washington. "Nothing which has occurred in the administration to date has added so much water to our ship," Eizenstat wrote. "Nothing else has so frustrated, confused, angered the American people—or so targeted their distress at you personally."

That got Carter's attention. He canceled a planned post-summit Hawaii vacation and came home to face the music. His first decision was to schedule a speech to the nation on energy, the fifth of his presidency.

But then he heard from pollster Caddell, who considered the roots of the current crisis to be much deeper than the gasoline shortage, vexing as that was. Instead, Caddell set forth a thesis that would largely define Carter's controversial approach to this critical moment in his presidency. Caddell's thinking was based on polling figures going back to 1975 that showed increasing pessimism among citizens about their own and their country's future. Caddell argued that Carter's performance as president was just an incidental factor in contributing to the national gloom. The principal causes, he claimed, were such dramatic traumas as the assassinations of the Kennedy brothers and Martin Luther King, Jr., the Watergate scandal, and the Vietnam War.

After studying these surveys of the national mood over a period of years, Caddell told me, "I began to understand that the political process is not the leading indicator, but rather the lagging indictor in reflecting political trends. We are at a particular point in our society where cultural changes and social changes that are at work are more dominant than the political ones."

This thesis held obvious attractions for Carter, because it tended to minimize the impact of his own deficiencies as president and because it appealed to his inclination to moralize. Besides, Americans were tired of hearing Carter talk about energy, as even Carter had come to understand.

At Camp David, where he had gone to prepare for his energy address, Carter studied Caddell's latest poll findings and then sent for the draft of his proposed energy speech, which he shared with his wife. "After Rosalynn and I read it over, I told her I couldn't deliver it, that I had already made four speeches to the nation on energy and that they had been increasingly ignored," Carter wrote in his diary. "I had to do something to get the attention of the news media and the public."

He certainly accomplished that. Carter canceled the energy speech with little notice and no explanation. Then he called for a sort of summit conference of political leaders at Camp David while he prepared for a broader speech.

The curtain rose on a presidential melodrama that epitomized Carter's principal shortcomings as a leader. With the exception of Caddell, whose gifts as a political conceptualizer were on this occasion blurred by his theatrical tendencies, none of Carter's advisers had any enthusiasm for the idea. Vice-President Mondale, who Carter had said right after his inauguration would be his closest adviser, was "distraught," as Carter later wrote. By far the most politically seasoned of Carter's inner circle, Mondale was convinced that Carter was on a course bound for "political catastrophe" and told the president so. But Carter plunged ahead anyway.

Here was self-absorption carried to its ultimate extreme. First of all, Carter ignored the counsel of those he supposedly trusted. Moreover, his actions inevitably focused attention not on the energy problem, but rather, as he must have known would happen, on Carter himself. For nearly a week the so-called summit dragged on, during which period more than one hundred prominent Americans from all walks of life trooped to Camp David to speak their minds to the president. As the deliberations continued without any clear pattern or purpose, speculation mounted about the president's intentions, his state of mind, and his political future. Republican Senator Ted Stevens of Alaska wondered aloud if the president was "approaching some sort of mental problem" and suggested he "ought to go off and take a rest."

At a governors' conference in Louisville, which coincided with the energy summit, I found that Carter's behavior had added to the doubts about him among his fellow politicians, even those committed to support him politically. In a candid chat, Governor Bill Clinton of Arkansas said that most people in his state "felt almost empty about the White House. They don't feel any sense of movement or involvement." One reason, Clinton said, was the president's well-known lack of oratorical skill, which he refused to attempt to improve. Another was his bleak moralistic approach to problems. "When the president said the energy program was the moral equivalent of war, he sounded almost like a seventeenth-century Puritan bringing bad news to the country," Clinton said. "What people are looking for is someone who will say that this is the moral equivalent of a war of independence—and that everybody has some role and some mission to play."

This was not what the country was to hear from its president, though, when he finally delivered his speech on July 15, ten days after he had originally planned to speak. Instead he announced to the country that it was suffering from "a crisis of confidence . . . that strikes at the very heart and soul and spirit of our national will."* Though this threat was "nearly invisible," the president said, it could be seen "in the growing doubt about the meaning of our own lives and in the loss of a unity of purpose for our nation."

For this sorry state of affairs the American people were mostly to blame. They had lost faith not only "in their ability as citizens to serve as the ultimate rulers and shapers of our democracy" but also in their values and traditions. "In a nation that was proud of hard work, strong families, close-knit communities and our faith in God, too many of us now tend to worship self-indulgence and consumption," Carter complained.

He himself accepted some responsibility but not much. "I've worked hard to put my campaign promises into law and I have to admit with just mixed success," he said. He made clear, though, that he was not as much at fault for this as was the Congress, which he described as "twisted and pulled in every direction" by his favorite target—"hundreds of well-financed and powerful special interests."

Carter conceded there was no quick way out of this sorry predicament, or malaise, as it came to be called. But he suggested that Americans could begin rebuilding their unity and confidence by conquering the energy problem. And so ultimately his speech turned back into what had been originally planned—yet another proposal for making the nation less dependent on foreign fuels and more committed to conservation of energy supplies.

Because Americans initially react to almost any national crisis by rallying around their president, the early response to Carter's speech was mildly positive. But that mood changed swiftly afterward when Carter decided to follow up his address by demanding that all the members of his cabinet submit their resignations and actually firing four of them. "I handled the cabinet changes very poorly," Carter himself later admitted in what was a vast understatement. The shakeup destroyed whatever inspirational thrust the speech had achieved, drove down the price of the dollar, rocked the stock market, bewildered the public, and further battered the president's prestige.

The purge also antagonized the many influential friends of its victims. "They're cutting down the big trees and keeping the monkeys," Democratic Congressman Charles Wilson of Texas said. "It's unprecedented, and it couldn't have come at a worse time," said Senator Henry M. Jackson of Washington, who had been in Congress since the start of Franklin

* This was the phrase that gave rise to the use of the word "malaise" to describe the speech.

Roosevelt's third term. "We need a sense of confidence in the country and you don't create confidence by announcing that all those people who have been running the details of the country are out."

But the malaise speech was bound to fail anyway. By his response to the challenge created by the energy crisis, Carter transformed it into the crisis of the Carter presidency. This gained him the attention he sought, but it also built unrealistically high expectations. Given the advance ballyhoo, Carter needed a strong message that outlined a clear answer to the problems confronting the country, something similar to what Governor Clinton had suggested. The speech Carter delivered was an exercise in self-indulgence in which he invited the country to wallow in guilt and share his frustration. Rather than an expression of leadership, it was a tacit admission that after three years of trying to govern he had lost his way.

At the time, Ronald Reagan was gearing up for his 1980 presidential candidacy. Pollster Richard Wirthlin, who was Reagan's counterpart of Caddell, told me later that he was "absolutely ecstatic" when Carter gave his malaise speech. "He completely misread the perception of what people wanted a leader to be," Wirthlin said. "He set us up with a perfect foil. It made him sound impotent. It was the most important political speech in the last four years."

The malaise crisis, which Carter invented, was a prelude to the Iran hostage crisis in the fall of 1979, which he exacerbated. The failure of his efforts to use the shortage of gasoline to revive his presidency left Carter a political cripple. In this condition he was ill equipped to deal with a new challenge—the November 1979 seizure of the U.S. embassy in Tehran and about fifty-two Americans by followers of Muslim leader Ayatollah Khomeni, who since the fall of the shah earlier in the year had become the dominant figure in Iran.

For Carter this was a personal blow. First of all, he had gravely underestimated Iranian discontent with their imperial ruler. In a well-remembered toast to the shah on New Year's Eve of 1977, the president had referred to Iran, which for years had seethed with economic and religious unrest, as "an island of stability in one of the more troubled areas of the world." In addition, Carter had allowed himself to be persuaded by former Secretary of State Henry Kissinger and banker David Rockefeller to allow the ailing shah into the U.S. for medical treatment, an action that predictably outraged Khomeni and his extremist cohorts.

No wonder, then, that Carter was deeply shaken. "I spent most of the day, every spare moment, trying to decide what to do," he wrote in his diary two days after the hostages were taken. Unable to decide on a clear course of action, he fell back on the same melodramatic strategy that he had used to deal with the energy challenge: he declared a new national crisis.

Political calculation combined with Carter's natural tendencies to shape this decision. The crisis atmosphere engendered by the malaise speech had given Carter's popularity a temporary boost before that strategy ultimately failed. Carter badly needed such a quick fix again—particularly since Senator Edward M. Kennedy was preparing to challenge him for the 1980 Democratic presidential nomination. More basically, the crisis strategy fit in with Carter's characteristic self-absorption. Since he was deeply troubled, he deemed it appropriate to share this mood with the rest of the country.

He set the tone in the official announcement of his candidacy for re-election in December, a month after the embassy fell. "At the height of the Civil War, Abraham Lincoln said, 'I have but one task and that is to save the Union,' " Carter declared. "Now I must devote my considered efforts to resolving the Iranian crisis."

Two weeks later, Carter sought to darken further the country's mood by deciding not to light the huge national Christmas tree. "The dark tree was symbolic of that holiday season," Carter later wrote. "In spite of the uplifting religious theme, it was a sad time." What was really sad was that Carter exaggerated the importance of the hostage episode to the point that freeing the hostages became the national purpose, and he made himself personally the center of the drama. The seizure of the hostages was an outrageous affront to the U.S. government, but it scarcely compared to the Civil War. It was in reality an event whose impact was mostly symbolic, and Carter by his response enlarged that impact and thus added to the damage done.

The president was in distress. He later told an interviewer that the predicament of the hostages gave him the same sinking feeling in the pit of his stomach he had had in his early years in business when he feared that the bank might foreclose on him. As presidential scholar James Barber has pointed out, Carter was obsessed with the hostage problem. "But he was not obsessed with a particular solution."

Several options offered themselves. At one extreme, Carter might have gone to war against Iran; at another, he might have shipped the shah back to his native land in return for release of the embassy prisoners. Or more logically, he might have addressed the nation, accepted his share of the responsibility for the episode, pledged to do everything in his power to gain the hostages freedom, and then gone about the business of governing the country and running for re-election.

Instead he continued to brood publicly about the hostages and to lament their fate at every opportunity. This was all to no practical purpose, except for the political benefits it brought Carter in his defense of his incumbency against the challenge of Edward Kennedy. The hostage crisis gave Carter an excuse to avoid debating the Massachusetts senator and allowed him to cloak himself in patriotism as a defense against Kennedy's attacks. By spring, however, Kennedy's chances of winning the nomination had faded, and so had the political benefits of the hostage crisis.

Yet Carter remained absorbed by the plight of the hostages, in part because it offered an escape from what he liked least about the presidency—politics. "It made the political job and the job of the politicians much more difficult," one staff member later told an interviewer. "This was something that [Carter] was almost exclusively involved in. Everything else got shunted aside. People in the White House, particularly as this issue grew, suffered from a myopia on the subject. Nothing else, including politics, could get through the doors."

Indeed, just as in the case of the energy crisis, Carter's response to the hostage challenge ultimately caused him more harm than good. Throughout the rest of that election year, it underlined his weakness and inability to deal with events. Carter's hopes of political recovery crashed along with the abortive hostage rescue mission's helicopter in the desert.

The death throes of Jimmy Carter's presidency began with his malaise speech in the summer of 1979. That address, and the events immediately following, reflected and reinforced Carter's failures to develop a coherent political vision and to build a coalition to support his programs.

Carter did not believe that any such effort was necessary. In the White House, as two scholarly biographies have suggested, outsider Carter saw himself as a trustee for the public good, acting on behalf of the average citizen as opposed to the interest groups he despised. His rationale, developed as a state legislator in Georgia, was that it was necessary to propose "comprehensive solutions," because, he later wrote, "in the absence of clear or comprehensive issues it is simply not possible to marshal the interests of the general public."

This theory did not work well in practice in the Oval Office. Convinced that he knew what the public good was, he did not make a sufficient effort to persuade the public of the merits of his various comprehensive objectives or to bargain with other political interests to get their backing. "We had a very heavy agenda of items that I thought would be beneficial for our country," he later told an interviewer. "I can tell you with complete candor we didn't assess the adverse political consequences of these goals.

I thought eventually our good efforts would be recognized and our achievements would be adequate to justify my re-election."

Carter's failure to build support during the relatively tranquil first two years of his presidency left him vulnerable in 1979 when things went drastically wrong. No single event that year, not even the energy shock or the hostage seizure, was necessarily disastrous, and a president with a strong political base and ideological message would have been able to withstand their impact until his luck changed or he could win support for new policies.

Carter's outsider ideology had been effective in gaining him the White House, but the outsider theme wore thin as his tenure in the presidency lengthened. He tried to bolster his vague ideology by relying on his values of trust and competence. As his difficulties multiplied, though, Carter found it increasingly difficult to make a credible claim to competence. That left him with only one element of leadership to use—his character— which led him into the crisis of his own self-absorption.

Whether they are responsible for it or not adversity always tests presidents severely, but some of Carter's predecessors were better suited than he to deal with it. Harry Truman, the chief executive Carter said he most admired, was helped by his firm ideological foundation to bounce back from the drubbing his party suffered in the 1946 election to launch new legislative initiatives and eventually to win the White House in his own right. John Kennedy, who suffered a humiliation at the Bay of Pigs that was at least as serious as the fall of the embassy in Teheran, was pragmatic enough to profit from his mistakes and prepare for the next challenge. But Carter indulged himself in the melodrama of the hostage crisis until it was too late to save his office. He became the first elected incumbent president since Herbert Hoover to fail to win re-election.

The failure of his leadership paved the way for Ronald Reagan. In his malaise speech Carter said, "Our people have turned to the Federal government and found it isolated from the mainstream of our nation's life." In essence, Reagan won the 1980 presidential campaign by reminding people that it was his opponent, Carter, whom they had chosen to head that government.

CHAPTER 9

Reagan: The Half Revolution

The winter of 1975 was a bleak season for the Republican Party yet bright with opportunity for Ronald Reagan. The previous November, in the aftermath of Gerald Ford's pardon of Richard Nixon, Republicans had suffered a crushing defeat in the congressional elections, and as long as Ford remained at the helm of their party, they had little hope for recovery. The president had lost control of the economy, lost the respect of the public, and, many Republicans feared, would ultimately lose the presidency.

In these grim circumstances conservative Republicans turned inevitably to Ronald Reagan. He had been their hero in the Goldwater debacle of 1964. Now they believed he might be able to turn the impending defeat in 1976 into a conservative victory.

Reagan, who had just turned sixty-four, had become the man of the hour. This made it difficult for me to get the time I needed for a conversation with him about his political future. I had been trying for weeks when finally his aides informed me that the governor, as they still referred to him, though he had been out of that office for months, would be in Washington in late February. Reagan's time was short and the demands on him great, I was told; my interview could not go beyond thirty minutes.

I found him in his suite at the Madison Hotel, hunched over a coffee table, riffling through a pack of five-by-seven index cards on which he was scribbling barely decipherable notes. As always, he was cordial; he was also evasive about whether he would challenge Ford for the presidential nomination.

Yes, he felt that Americans were becoming increasingly receptive to his view of the country and the world. "There's certainly a polarization taking place among people, and philosophical differences are becoming pretty clear-cut," he told me.

But no, his own plans were not yet set. He mentioned "a checkpoint down the road someplace" at which he would have to make up his mind. After chatting for about thirty minutes, conscious of Reagan's aides staring at me and their watches, I started to put away my notes. Just then, though, a question I had asked about foreign policy touched Reagan's interest.

He launched into a lengthy recounting of the kidnapping in Morocco early in this century of a wealthy American* named Perdicaris by the Berber bandit Raisuli. A forerunner of contemporary Arab terrorists, Raisuli vowed he would hold Perdicaris hostage until the United States pressured the sultan who ruled Morocco to make certain concessions to Raisuli. President Theodore Roosevelt, Reagan related, would have none of this. Instead he ordered the fleet to battle stations and issued the still celebrated response of the United States to this threat of extortion: "This government wants Perdicaris alive or Raisuli dead."

"Perdicaris alive or Raisuli dead," Reagan said, relishing the phrase. "That's what this country should tell other countries today," he concluded firmly, his eyes blazing with patriotic zeal.

It had taken him more than half as long to tell this story in all its elaborate detail as we had spent on the rest of the interview. As I thanked him for his time and hurriedly beat a retreat, I noticed his aides glowering at me.

Reagan himself, though, seemed to consider the time well spent. I could not think of any other politician who under those circumstances would have spoken at such length and with such fervor about such a remote incident from American history. That foreign-policy lesson from Reagan served to demonstrate the intensity of his convictions. The intensity came naturally to him because his ideology was formed far more by his personal experience than by the exercise of his intellect. It gave him an aura of credibility that helped inspire supporters, confound critics, and for a time return the presidency to the forefront of political leadership.

His credibility helped him combine his ideology, values, and character into a powerful force for presidential leadership. After losing his challenge

---

* Actually Perdicaris, though a native-born American, was not a citizen of the U.S. because he had become a naturalized Greek subject some forty years earlier. An embarrassed State Department suppressed this information at the time and Reagan certainly seemed unaware of it, though this was not the sort of distinction that generally mattered to him anyway. (See "Perdicaris Alive or Raisuli Dead," by Barbara Tuchman, *American Heritage*, August, 1959.)

to Ford in 1976, he rebounded in 1980, ousting an incumbent Democratic president. Taking office at a time of economic distress, he won a great victory for his beliefs. The enactment of his sweeping economic proposals restricted the federal government's ability to meet commitments made over the past half century and undercut the will and resources for taking on new obligations.

For all his appeal, however, his qualities as a leader were inadequate for facing the complex consequences of his early triumphs as president. As a result his leadership and success, like his beliefs, were incomplete and flawed. He was unable to exploit the historic opportunity created by the early impetus of the Reagan Revolution, and his legacy thus fell short of the expectations he had created and the opportunity history offered him.

IDEOLOGY

Reagan's central belief was that individual freedom is the highest good and that government is its enemy. This was the idea he began with when he first made his mark on presidential politics. In 1964, speaking on behalf of Barry Goldwater, he declared, "Either we believe in our traditional system of individual liberty, or we abandon the American Revolution and confess that an intellectual elite in a far distant capital can plan our lives for us better than we can plan them ourselves." It remained the core of his ideology, as was evinced in his first inaugural speech: "In this present crisis government is not the solution to our problem. Government is the problem."

This credo led to two major imperatives that defined Reagan's leadership. At home he was committed to checking the power of the federal government by cutting taxes, and either eliminating its responsibilities or turning them over to local government. Abroad, he was equally determined to check the threat from foreign communist regimes, which embodied the evil of unrestrained government power in its ultimate form. It was true that warding off the peril from "the evil empire" could only be accomplished by a strong federal government, but that was an advantage because if the government's resources were expended on national security, they could not be squandered on domestic programs.

More than any other president since Truman, Reagan presented himself as holding a strong ideological position. Yet his ideology was largely based on his personal circumstances rather than on any body of scholarship or, as in Truman's case, on the traditions of his political party. The strength of Reagan's beliefs greatly enhanced his public appeal, helping him gain the presidency under circumstances that opened broad horizons for change. But the lack of a broad intellectual or political foundation for his ideology in the long run deprived his leadership of the focus and discipline needed to confront economic and political realities.

His views shifted with the changing conditions of his life and occasionally according to political expediency. Following his disillusionment with the New Deal, his earliest ideological lodestar, he absorbed the conventional conservatism of the businessmen he increasingly associated with during the twilight of his Hollywood career. His economic outlook was typified by an observation I heard him make in his speech to that conservative conference in 1975.

"The painful fact is we can only halt inflation by undergoing a period of economic dislocation—a recession, if you will," Reagan said. That contention turned out to be all too true, as Reagan's presidency unfortunately demonstrated. But it was a hard sell. Even the ardent Reagan supporters in his audience that night did not applaud the sobering assessment their hero offered them. Within three years Reagan no longer uttered such unpleasant truths in public. Instead he became an apostle of the much cheerier and more fashionable supply-side doctrines espoused by New York Congressman Jack Kemp and other new conservative theorists who maintained that inflation could be cured without sacrifice by reliance on a massive tax cut. With a tax revolt sweeping the country in 1978, the supply-side approach would help Reagan get support for his forthcoming presidential candidacy. Besides, the notion of cutting taxes had always appealed to Reagan. The longer-run implications of this theory for the country's fiscal stability he left to others to calculate.

This shift to supply side, which would have fateful consequences for his presidency, paralleled other ideological changes Reagan made during his career in response to changes in his personal life or in the political environment. The remarkable aspect of these adjustments was not how much Reagan's thinking changed, but how fervent a believer he was in whatever particular faith he happened to hold at the time.

The homemade nature of Reagan's creed helped make him convincing. The plight of the kidnapped Perdicaris was not related to the national debate on foreign policy when Reagan recounted that tale in 1975. It was simply a story that he had stumbled upon in his reading, had incorporated into his own set of beliefs, and recounted with as much passion as if he had actually gone through it all himself. This was the key to his persuasiveness. To a public hesitant to buy a Reagan argument, what often clinched the political sale was his listeners' belief that Reagan himself truly believed what he was saying.

Rather than spouting the rhetorical baggage of a traditional politician, Reagan spoke in the idiom of the sports announcer and movie actor that he had been, with directness and simplicity. "You have the ability of putting complicated, technical ideas into words everyone can understand," Richard Nixon had written him in 1959 after reading a set speech Reagan was giving to business groups as a spokesman for General Electric.

This trait impressed me as well in my first encounter with Reagan. This was early in 1973 when he was still governor of California. I had just joined the Washington bureau of the *Los Angeles Times* and had come out to California to meet Reagan and other West Coast politicians. As it happened, the day I interviewed Reagan in his office in Sacramento, the *Times* carried an analysis I had written of the resurgence of conservatism. Reagan had read the story and told me that he was bothered by the use of the terms "left" and "right" in political discourse.

He drew a horizontal line on a scratch pad, wrote *L* and one side and *R* on the other, and shook his head. "That's not the way I look at things," he said. "There is no left or right, only up and down." Then he drew a vertical line. "Up is freedom," he said. "Down is slavery."

I found out later that Reagan had been using that metaphor for ten years, and he would continue to use it for years afterward. Reagan's vertical line did not explain anything, but like his other simplifications, it was not intended to explain as much as to get the attention of people who do not ordinarily pay attention to politics. As the record shows, these gambits did their job.

As politically successful as Reagan's ideology was, some of his admirers nevertheless sought to enhance its intellectual origins. While he conceded that Reagan did not know "the latest nuances of economic theory," Martin Anderson, Reagan's chief domestic policy adviser, nevertheless claimed in his memoir of Reagan's White House days that the president "had his basics down as well as any of his economic advisers." He added: "The essence of the comprehensive economic program he has pursued in the 1980s was derived from the classical economic principles he learned almost sixty years ago as a young man." At Eureka College, from which Reagan graduated in 1932, Anderson wrote, "The economics he was taught was the old classical variety, straight from the works of Adam Smith, Alfred Marshall, Irving Fisher, Eugene Boem-Barwek, David Ricardo and Jean Baptiste Say."

It is true that Reagan did major in economics at Eureka College. But it is hard to find evidence that this experience made much impression on him. Reagan devotes fourteen pages to his years at Eureka in his auto-biography, *Where's the Rest of Me?*, describing the walls "covered with friendly ivy" and recounting his adventures as a football player and as a leader of a student strike against a threatened cutback in the academic program. But he does not make a single reference to a single class he attended in economics or any other subject. He later identified his student enthusiasms as drama, sports, and politics, though not necessarily in that order. Eureka's only professor of economics recalls that Reagan got through college without ever cracking a book, though he earned good grades by cramming before exams.

The first experience in Reagan's life to significantly influence his political thinking was the Great Depression. The national economic collapse caused him to resent big business and later to worship Franklin Roosevelt and inspired in him the liberalism that dominated the first stage in his ideological development.

Like many other middle-class Americans in the 1920s, the Reagan family enjoyed a comfortable small-town existence, but lacked the economic resources to withstand hard times. "Our family didn't exactly come from the wrong side of the tracks," he later recalled, "but we were certainly always within the sound of the train whistle." In the 1930s, it was as if the train itself came crashing in on their lives.

Reagan's father, Jack, had dreamt of owning his own business. The Depression killed that dream and also cost him his job. Reagan's mother, Nell, was forced to find work in a dress shop at $14 a week. Reagan, still in college, worked part-time so he could send money home for groceries and found job opportunities drying up. Wealthy people he had met through his summer job as a lifeguard who had promised to help him find work after graduation "weren't making those noises now," he recalled. "Again, it was the mark of the Depression with every man, no matter how high his station, worried about keeping his own job," he wrote.

Reagan's father, a volunteer in Roosevelt's 1932 election campaign, was rewarded by being put in charge of the local Works Progress Administration office in Reagan's hometown of Dixon, Illinois, about ninety miles from Chicago. "Practically all the unemployed were able bodied and capable and they besieged him for chances at working for their keep, even calling on him at home." The problem was, Reagan later wrote, that "those in charge of direct relief resisted releasing their charges to WPA." This occurred despite the fact that, as Reagan points out, Roosevelt himself had called direct relief "a subtle destroyer of the human spirit" and declared that "the Federal government must and shall quit this business of relief."

"He said that," Reagan wrote in 1965, "but it didn't work out that way. Wheels were turning in Washington and the government was busy at the job it does best—growing."

This conflict between relief and work infuriated Jack Reagan, his son wrote. "However, his rage was directed only at his local tormentors. Being a loyal Democrat, he never criticized the administration or the government."

Neither did his son, until many years later. The acerbic comments about the follies of big government in *Where's the Rest of Me?* seem intended to blur the contradiction between Reagan, the new conservative voice of 1965, and the earlier Reagan who memorized portions of Roosevelt's first inaugural address, tuned in faithfully to his fireside chats, and worked up a convincing imitation of the founder of the New Deal, managing even to evoke his trademark cigarette holder.

In part this behavior reflected his personal admiration for Roosevelt. But, for Reagan, as for millions of other Americans at the time, the personal magic of Roosevelt fostered a broader political faith.

"I was a near-hopeless, hemophilic liberal," Reagan wrote later of the beliefs he held during the New Deal era. "I bled for 'causes'; I had voted Democratic, following my father, in every election. I had followed FDR blindly, though not without some misgivings." These views were bolstered in his early Hollywood years by his involvement in the Screen Actors Guild, which was like the rest of organized labor, a trusty ally of the New Deal, and by the outbreak of World War II, which surrounded Roosevelt with an aura of patriotism and made it seem almost seditious to criticize the commander-in-chief.

During the 1940s, when Roosevelt was beginning his third term in the White House, Reagan and his older brother, Neil, an early defector from the family's Democratic tradition, used to argue about politics so vociferously that they drove other people away at social occasions. As Neil recalled the battles: "His statement to me always was: 'That's the trouble with you guys. Anybody who voted for Roosevelt is a Communist,' and I used to agree with him heartily at which point he'd get the screaming meemies."

Reagan's disillusionment with liberalism began in the postwar era; he later claimed that his idealistic hopes inspired by the global struggle against the Axis were dashed by postwar realities. "Like most of the soldiers who came back I expected a world suddenly reformed," he recalled. "I was wrong. I discovered that the rich had got just a little richer and a lot of the poor had done a pretty good job of grabbing a quick buck. I discovered that the world was almost the same and perhaps a little bit worse."

Apart from the overall state of the world, practical problems directly threatening Reagan's financial well-being contributed to his change of heart. One was the income tax. During the war the maximum marginal rate soared to 91 percent, which meant a huge bite out of the $3,500 weekly salary Reagan was earning from Warner Brothers. The tax code would become a prime target for the antigovernment fulminations he delivered when he later became a roving spokesman for General Electric. "The entire structure was created by Karl Marx," Reagan would say. "It simply is a penalty on the individual who can improve his own lot."

Meanwhile, Reagan's career was running into trouble because of his wartime absence from the screen and the postwar audience's yearning for new faces. "I was a star, but I had a sneaking suspicion that a lot of people across America hadn't stayed in a breathless state of palpitation for three and a half years waiting for my return," he wrote.

More generally, the motion picture industry was having economic difficulties. The main reason, of course, was the surging new entertainment medium television, which could do everything Hollywood could and deliver it into the nation's living rooms. But there were other difficulties, and Reagan blamed these on Washington. He was angered by President Truman's refusal to intervene with the restriction imposed by foreign countries on Hollywood filmmakers, preventing them from taking their earnings back to the U.S. On top of that, when the Truman Administration's Justice Department forced the studios to relinquish their holdings in theater chains, the movie industry's stability was "literally destroyed." As Reagan saw it, "The studios were in the position of a candy manufacturer who had no store to peddle his product."

In addition to economic problems, increasing concern about the threat of communism at home and abroad cast a shadow over his early liberal beliefs. In his liberal salad days, Reagan had spent little time worrying about the danger of communism. "I was not sharp about Communism," he later wrote. "The Russians still seemed to be our allies. The American Communists were high on the Hollywood hog. . . . Most of us called them liberals and, being liberal ourselves, bedded down with them with no thought for the safety of our wallets."

Ideological turmoil in the movie capital in the postwar era, though, drastically altered that perception. A communist-controlled group moved to take over the Hollywood trade unions, and Reagan as leader of the Screen Actors Guild was pitted against them in a bitter jurisdictional dispute. Meanwhile, the House Un-American Activities Committee began its probe of communist influence on Hollywood. Called to testify, Reagan was relatively restrained in the context of the near hysteria stirred by the investigation. Asked if a communist clique had tried to "dominate" the union, Reagan, perhaps recalling his arguments with his brother over red baiting, replied, "Well, sir, by attempting to put over their own particular views on various issues, I guess in regard to that you would have to say that our side was attempting to dominate, too, because we were fighting just as hard to put over our views."

Nevertheless, Reagan ultimately became persuaded that the communists had intended to seize control of the movie industry so that it could be used as "a worldwide propaganda base." He concluded that "like the measles," communism "will always be with us." His remedy for this disease, which became a hallmark of his ideology and of his rhetoric, was "that each American generation must be re-educated to the precariousness of liberty."

The clashes with communists at home coincided with the rise of Cold War tensions abroad, bringing to an end the benign era of Soviet–American friendship to which Reagan's hero Roosevelt had been committed. Reagan later claimed that not only did his battle with communist labor leaders awaken him to the danger from Moscow, it also made him personally unpopular in the Kremlin. In a 1980 campaign interview he contended that Soviet leaders probably preferred President Carter to him as leader of the Free World because "they remember back to those union days when . . . I was very definitely on the wrong side for them."

At any rate, by 1951 he was fully alert to the Soviet threat. "The so-called Communist party is nothing less than a Russian–American bund," he wrote, "owing allegiance to Russia and supporting Russia in its plan to conquer the world."

Out of all this emerged Reagan's conservative creed, which like his Depression-born liberalism had been shaped by experiences that directly and indirectly influenced his own life. From the economic difficulties that plagued the movie industry and his own career came his resentment of government. The Cold War, the film industry labor disputes, and congressional investigations of Hollywood fostered Reagan's hostility to communism, which was the other chief component of his ideology.

Reagan's turn to the right occurred gradually over the first postwar decade. In 1948 he campaigned for Harry Truman and for Hubert Humphrey's senate campaign, and in 1950 he backed Helen Gahagan Douglas when the so-called "pink lady" was defeated by Richard Nixon. Though he supported Eisenhower on the Republican ticket in 1952, he did not actually change his party registration until the 1962 campaign. That year Reagan backed Nixon when he ran for governor of California and lost. As it turned out, by the time the next California gubernatorial campaign came around, the Republican ticket was topped by Reagan himself.

In the meantime, though, Reagan made a significant job change, abandoning his faltering Hollywood career to go to work as a spokesman for General Electric. From 1954 to 1962 Reagan served the industrial giant as host of a televised series of dramas and as a sort of corporate ambassador of goodwill to GE employees and to civic and business groups around the country. It was this latter part of the job that increasingly crystallized Reagan's views and prepared him for his entry into politics.

Reagan's motive for taking the job was largely financial. He and his second wife, Nancy, needed money badly. But he performed at a pace and with a zeal that ensured GE more than its money's worth, sometimes making a dozen or more appearances a day. His talks, initially just lighthearted reminiscences of Hollywood's Golden Age, grew more serious as he used Hollywood's misfortunes to illustrate the folly of big government and the threat of communism. The movies had suffered, he claimed in one typical talk, because the studios had allowed "the planners and regulators to get a foot in the door. This superstructure of government imposed on our original form is composed of bureaus and departments and is unchanged by an election. This hierarchy threatens to reverse the relationship of citizen and civil servant."

Reagan steadily broadened his scope to cover a wide range of national issues. Though he had left Hollywood, he was once again playing a role, as the voice of a huge business enterprise, but this time he was writing his own scripts. Testing out his still developing conservative ideology on audiences sympathetic to such arguments, his confidence was greatly reinforced in what he had to say and also in his own skills at saying it.

As time went on, Reagan became more committed to his newfound faith than his employer had bargained for, even attacking such relatively sacrosanct New Deal institutions as the TVA, which happened to be a $50-million-a-year GE customer. Ultimately he dropped his references to TVA to spare his employer embarrassment.

By 1962, when his arrangement with General Electric ended, Reagan claimed that he already had speeches booked as far ahead as 1966. "It would be nice to accept this as a tribute to my oratory," Reagan wrote. "But I think the real reason had to do with a change that was taking place all over America. People wanted to talk about and hear about encroaching government control, and hopefully they wanted suggestions as to what they themselves could do to turn the tide."

If that was what people were ready to hear, Reagan was ready to tell them. The style and tone of his rhetoric was much the same as it had been in his liberal days. Only the targets of his indignation had changed, and this was a dramatic change. The liberal Reagan in a 1948 campaign address for Truman lamented the fact that corporate profits had soared four times faster than the wages of working people. The conservative

Reagan, in his memorable 1964 "time for choosing" campaign address for Goldwater, decried the fact that since the beginning of the century the government had increased in size 234 times while the gross national product had grown only 33 fold. Reagan had transformed himself, biographer Lou Cannon wrote, "from an adversary of big business into one of its most ardent spokesmen."

Of greater potential political significance than Reagan's championship of business, which many Americans still viewed with suspicion, was his antagonism to government, which increasingly was blamed for a range of grievances, foreign and domestic. The 1960s had started out hopefully with the promise of John Kennedy and the civil rights movement. By the time the decade was half over the Vietnam War abroad and a series of economic and social dislocations at home had made it an era of discontent for the middle-class majority.

Reagan's ability to express that discontent in terms that commanded attention and yet remained on the safe side of demagoguery made him the leading conservative spokesman in the country after 1964. And two years after that it helped make him governor of the nation's largest state and a plausible contender for the presidency.

In eight years in Sacramento, Reagan's ideology was not expanded as much as it was tempered in the crucible of governing. To a considerable degree his performance in the corner office in the state house foreshadowed his stewardship in the Oval Office. In the governorship, as he would be in the presidency, he was confronted with problems that were easier to make speeches about than solve. Also the opposition was formidable in both jobs. In California the Republicans controlled the state's legislature for only two years of Reagan's eight-year tenure while during his two terms as president his party never controlled both houses of Congress.

In some ways, though, the governorship was an even bigger challenge to Reagan's hopes of implementing his ideology because it was his first public office and he was wholly unprepared for it. "Ronald Reagan materialized out of thin air with no political background, no political cronies and no political machine," Lyn Nofziger, Reagan's gubernatorial press secretary, said at the time of his election. "His campaign was run by hired people who then walked away and left it. Therefore, when he was elected, the big question was, 'My God, what do we do now?' "

What Reagan did, whenever the political seas got too stormy, was to tack into unfavorable winds and then try to resume his original course. Out of guile, and sometimes simply because he had no other choice, he displayed a tendency to compromise that belied his rhetoric and demonstrated his underlying adaptability. In his first term he signed into law a tax bill notable not only for its size—the largest in the state's history—but because it drastically increased the burden on corporations and the wealthy, infuriating many of Reagan's allies on the right. By contrast, his initiative to shrink the size of government by slashing taxes failed dismally at the ballot box.

Governor Reagan did succeed in pushing through a long-promised reform of the welfare system, but this "proudest achievement" of his governorship was nowhere near as draconian as his unrelenting harangues against abuses of the welfare system had led people to expect. As part of the compromise that got the program enacted, Reagan gave up his most cherished goal, a permanent limit on yearly welfare appropriations, and also yielded on his objective of legislating tighter controls on establishing eligibility for welfare.

Reagan was able to make such concessions without losing his conservative followers because they put more stock in his words than in his actions. Convinced by his rhetoric, they concluded that he gave ground only because his ideological adversaries gave him no choice. His rhetoric also worked to Reagan's advantage with his opponents. In the course of political bargaining they sometimes gave up more than they needed to because they overestimated Reagan's intransigence.

Whatever Reagan actually accomplished, political professionals complained, he got more than his share of the credit. "He did some important things, but not as much as he said he would do and not as much as he said he did," a California legislative specialist said of Reagan's performance. In Sacramento, as would be the case in Washington, it sometimes seemed that what mattered more to Reagan than the practical results of his efforts was the appearance of success.

VALUES

It was no casual decision on Ronald Reagan's part to stage his first inaugural on the west front of the Capitol, the first time in history that site had been chosen. From the west front he was able to point during his address to the monuments to Washington, Jefferson, and Lincoln, "those shrines to the giants on whose shoulders we stand." A few months later in an address at Notre Dame, he paid tribute to the Founding Fathers as "a group so unique we've never seen their like again. . . . They brought to all mankind for the first time the concept that all men were born free."

Reverence for past values was central to his presidency and a concept he returned to again and again. This was a theme Reagan had been sounding since he first started thinking seriously about politics. It was one of the two major premises underlying his value structure, the other being the primacy of the individual as opposed to the encroachments of government, especially the federal government. Values and ideology thus marched in step to Reagan's cadence, with the chief distinction being that the values he espoused were more symbolic and personalized than his ideological goals.

The political significance of the values of America's past for Reagan's leadership was encapsulated by one appreciative biographer, William K. Muir, who wrote that the Reagan Administration "was organized to achieve a moral revolution . . . moral in the sense of affecting the character shaping ideas of the American people, a revolution in the sense of returning the nation to its starting point."

This was exactly the perception Reagan was trying to establish. "We here in the United States often fail to realize that we were born free in 1776, long before the rest of the world started talking about it," he wrote in *Where's the Rest of Me?* Moreover, to quash any possible liberal claim to the American past, Reagan added: "The original government of this country was set up by conservatives, as defined years later by Lincoln, who called himself a conservative with a 'preference for the old and tried over the new and untried.' "

Reagan had no doubt which value had suffered most from the nation's recent tendency to stray from Lincoln's preference: rugged individualism, a timeworn but still honored concept made up of such strands as the belief that individuals are the best judge of their own interests, the celebration of private effort, and the presumption against enlarged government authority. This value, Reagan believed, went a long way toward defining the distinction between liberals and conservatives. "The liberals believe in remote and massive strong-arming from afar, usually Washington, D.C.," he wrote. "The conservatives believe in the unique powers of the individual and his personal opinions."

This conviction stands in opposition to another value held by many Americans, that of mutual responsibility. This value is based on the belief that the individual has distinct obligations to the community while the community bears some responsibility to protect the rights and welfare of the individual. As political scientist Hugh Heclo points out, "The American public philosophy has always been a series of trial balances struck between those two opposing views of individualism and communitarianism." Starting in the 1960s, Reagan would argue vigorously that the value balance had shifted too far away from individualism. As president he would push hard to force it in the other direction.

Reagan's faith in individualism and his other values were shaped first by his formative years in a Midwestern small town where the institutions of family and church, along with such virtues as hard work and patriotism, were held in high esteem, and later reinforced by his experience as movie actor.

Because Dixon had a population of only about ten thousand, others might have found coming of age there a limiting experience, but not Reagan. "It was a good life," he recalled many years later. "I never have asked for anything more, then or now."

That comment seriously understates Reagan's ambition and acquisitive instinct, which carried him to stardom in Hollywood and ultimately to the presidency. Nevertheless, Reagan clearly viewed his Dixon years as a rich experience and often expressed his values by drawing on his experiences there. For example, he put a higher value on work and opportunity than on security, a view shaped by the benefits he had gotten as a young man from summer jobs that he claimed changes in society later denied to young people. "We have taken jobs away from teenagers," he told an interviewer. "We have taken them away in some instances by way of unions, but more by way of our own social legislation." Reagan recalled that for one teenage job he had held, remodeling old houses, "the boss paid you out of his pocket in cash. He didn't have to sit down and do a lot of paperwork for Social Security and all of those things. I'm not criticizing it for the legitimate work force, but for the kids who have to go through school, it seems to me we could make some exceptions."

In small towns of those days, an atmosphere of goodwill prevailed; townspeople were expected to look after each other, and many of them did. This old-fashioned standard of conduct, Reagan's admirers suggest, allowed Reagan to oppose government aid to the less fortunate without feeling that he was being callous.

Yet other, harsher mores were operative in Dixon that Reagan chose to overlook or to interpret in a positive light. "The American dream," he wrote in his autobiography, is "that each individual has the right to fly as high as his strength and ability will take him." But in Dixon life at times seemed to be a test of strength in which might made right.

Reagan recalled being involved in a schoolyard fight when his father arrived unexpectedly. "He stopped the fight, tongue lashed the crowd— then lifted me a foot in the air with the flat side of his boot."

" 'Not because you were fighting,' he said, 'but because you weren't winning.' "

"That was my first sample of adult injustice," Reagan complained. "I *had* been winning."

At Eureka College, where small-town values also prevailed, Reagan was impressed by the efficacy of athletic competition in solving racial problems. He recalled a football game in which a Negro teammate named Franklin Burkhardt was being physically victimized by an opponent, who was pounding away at Burkhardt's bad knee. Burkhardt fought back using his hands on his tormentor "with devastating effect."

When the game was over, Burkhardt's antagonist, who had been "literally beaten to his knees by Burky's hands" and had called him "a black bastard" on nearly every play, shook hands with his victim and remarked, "You're the whitest man I ever knew." Meanwhile Burkhardt's teammates had to cut his pants to get them over the young man's swollen knee.

Apparently oblivious to the racism explicit in the apology and the brutality pervading the entire episode, Reagan recounted the incident in his autobiography, referring to "the trouble going on today, and the bitter feelings engendered by extremists, both Negro and white." He was convinced, he wrote, "that among the extremists you'll find no one who ever participated in athletics on a team that numbered among its personnel both Negroes and whites."

Reagan's tendency to sentimentalize the harsh edges of reality helped make him comfortable in Hollywood, site of an entire industry devoted to make-believe and, in Reagan's time, to the enshrinement of traditional values. "Film is forever," Reagan, newly inaugurated as president, told the Academy of Motion Picture Arts and Sciences on Oscar night. "It is the motion picture that shows all of us not only how we look and sound but—more important—how we feel." This suggestion, that motion pictures instead of simply inducing feelings on the part of audience reflect the audience's real feelings, helps explain why for Reagan as a public man, the distinction between movie life and real life often was blurred.

His use of dialogue from old movies was varied and effective. At times he uttered lines whose origin was well known, thus benefiting from the association with the original version. Thus he dared Congress to enact a tax increase so he could veto it by mimicking Clint Eastwood's challenge to a hoodlum threatening to shoot a hostage: "Go ahead. Make my day."

On other occasions Reagan borrowed from a script without attribution, giving the appearance of spontaneity. "Where do we find such men?" he asked about the Americans who gave their lives in D-Day. This was the same line delivered by Fredric March, portraying the commander of an aircraft carrier in the 1953 Korean War film *Bridges at Toko-Ri*.

Both tactics served the same purpose. They helped Reagan dramatize the traditional values of America's past—the boldness of its quick-drawing, straight-shooting lawmen and the heroism of its soldiers and sailors—and thus make his ideological goals more appealing.

The first major test of the political potency of Reagan's values came during the 1966 California gubernatorial campaign. The outbreak of student unrest at the University of California, Berkeley, the forerunner of the campus disorder that was to spread across the country in protest against the Vietnam War, provided him with an ideal opportunity to make his case for tradition. The Berkeley demonstrations were intended to dramatize a student demand for academic freedom, a cause Reagan readily dismissed. Labeling the leaders of the movement "a small minority of beatniks, radicals and filthy speech advocates," Reagan asked: "What in heaven's name does academic freedom have to do with rioting, with anarchy, with attempts to destroy the primary purpose of the University which is to educate our young people?"

By the time Reagan ran for the presidency in 1980, the campus protest movement had long since run out of steam and the accompanying surge of social change had also subsided. The reaction was a sort of national quest for values that would provide spiritual support for an enervated citizenry.

Carter had tried to address this unease himself, but the clumsy presentation of his "malaise" address mainly called attention to his own inadequacies. Nevertheless, polling data did support pollster Caddell's contention that Americans were unusually distressed about the condition of society and prospects for the future. One survey around that time found more than two thirds of Americans believing that families are weaker than they used to be and a similar number acknowledging that things had changed so quickly they often had trouble "deciding what rules to follow."

The preoccupation with self-gratification that had marked the 1960s and early 1970s had been replaced, according to pollster Daniel Yankelovich, with "a tremendous yearning for escape from the prison of the self—a desire for bonds that aren't remote. There is emphasis on couples and on family. There is emphasis on local community. The nation state is remote; your community is not."

The climate could hardly have been better suited to the message Reagan wanted to preach. In his acceptance speech to the 1980 convention, he appealed to "all those across the land who share a community of values embodied in these words: family, work, neighborhood, peace and freedom." He called upon the electorate to make a commitment "to teach our children the virtues handed down to us by our families; to have the courage to defend those values and virtues and the willingness to sacrifice for them."

His party's platform used many of the same emotionally charged words, pledging to "reemphasize the vital communities like the family, the neighborhood, the workplace and others which are at the center of our society."

To be sure, Reagan himself hardly was a paradigm for the values he propounded. Instead, with his divorce, his uneasy relationships with his children, and his offsprings' unorthodox life-styles, Reagan seemed more like a victim of the social turbulence that preceded his election.

During the 1980 campaign "there was a lot of talk about how to handle the Patti [Davis] problem," because of Reagan's daughter's association with the acid-rock culture "and the Ron problem" because of Reagan's son dropping out of college to become a ballet dancer, recalls Richard Williamson, a campaign adviser and later a member of the White House staff.

> In the end it was felt that the voters having lived through the sixties and seventies would find RR more humanized because he too had experienced these things. His words offered a vision of America we wanted to believe in. His experiences showed that his feet had walked the same difficult trail as other American parents.

This calculation turned out to be correct. But there was an even broader conflict between the values that Reagan preached and those he practiced. The president offered his values, in William Muir's phrase, as the catalyst for "a moral revolution" that would presumably elevate standards for individual and public behavior. Yet by their nature, Reagan's values fostered individual acquisitiveness and aggrandizement often at the expense of public needs and responsibilities, results that made their promise of a general uplifting seem hypocritical.

Despite these conflicts, the same persuasiveness that contributed to the effectiveness of his ideology made his values a net asset to his leadership throughout his presidency. Reagan himself seemed unembarrassed by the contradictions. It was an example of his ability to shut out uncomfortable parts of reality, which was a significant aspect of the other force shaping his leadership, his character.

CHARACTER

In 1975 Reagan was holding a press conference when he found himself pressured to define himself in ideological terms. One reporter recalled Barry Goldwater's disastrous statement that "extremism in the defense of liberty is no vice" and "moderation in the pursuit of justice is no virtue," and he asked Reagan where he stood on moderation versus extremism.

"Well, it sort of depends on the circumstances," Reagan said softly, grinning. "If you were an airplane passenger on a stormy night, you wouldn't want a pilot who was only moderately safe, would you?"

"Now he has finally done it to himself," I thought as I listened to that exchange. In my mind's eye I could see headlines blaring the news: "Reagan Backs Goldwater's Extremism." But as I looked around, I noticed that none of my colleagues were paying much attention to Reagan's response. A few made some notes, but no one followed up and Reagan was immediately asked a question about another subject.

Goldwater's defense of extremism, delivered during his acceptance speech at the 1964 Republican convention, shocked the country and ensured the doom of his candidacy. Reagan had made much the same point and barely an eyebrow was raised. Of course, the circumstances were different; Goldwater made his remarks in a more dramatic setting. But the point is that Reagan's escaping unscathed from his press conference defense of extremism illustrated his ability to maintain hard-line ideological positions without causing outrage except among his most dedicated enemies. His genial smile, his soft voice, his apt analogy, all had taken the threatening edge off his comments and deflected criticism.

This facility was a function of Reagan's character, which, like his values, greatly bolstered his ideology and his leadership. The difference was that while his values dovetailed with his ideology, Reagan's character, or more precisely the style derived from his character, represented a seeming contradiction with his ideological agenda. As political scientist Bert Rockman observed in a retrospective essay, Reagan's style, reflecting his character, "mostly appears as soft and comforting," while his ideological agenda "mostly appears as clear and polarizing."

Instead of undercutting his ideology, though, Reagan's character and style abetted it. His "soft and comforting" character was the spoonful of sugar that helped the "polarizing" ideological medicine go down.

Reagan's mellow demeanor reflected the optimism and self-confidence that marked his personality and allowed him to avoid much of the controversy that surrounds politicians with less even tempers and less sense of security. Whatever faults Reagan may have had, his close associates agree that he was easy to get along with. Richard Wirthlin has described his tenure in the White House as characterized by "humor, optimism and the resilience that allowed him to rebound from adversity." The operative word used by his advisers to describe his disposition is "sunny"; even Donald Regan in his astringent memoir of his White House service refers to "the president's sunny and open personality."

One major reason for Reagan's relaxed manner was that he made things easier for himself by depending heavily on other people. He learned to pass on to others—his wife and his aides—tasks that were distasteful or seen by him as unsuitable to his talents and disposition. This practice, his admirers claimed, helped him to act decisively on selected matters that were most important to him and to give the impression of strength that was a positive part of his appeal.

But evidence indicates that as president, Reagan tended to rely on others even in matters that concerned him directly. When James Baker, then White House chief of staff, and Donald Regan, then Treasury Secretary, came to ask him about the switch that would put Regan in Baker's job, a shift that would be portentous for the last years of his presidency, Regan observed that the president "seemed to be absorbing a fait accompli rather than making a decision." Similarly, though White House press secretary Larry Speakes was pilloried for faking a Reagan quote at the Geneva Summit in 1985, it seems clear that the president's trusted spokesman was varying only slightly from his customary role, with which the president himself was quite content.

In an ordinary citizen this trait is usually regarded as irresponsibility; in the nation's chief executive it was called "delegation of authority." Understandably, this tendency invited criticism from those who contended that Reagan was too lazy or too dumb to run the country. Certainly it caused him difficulties, notably in the Iran-Contra case that soiled the image of his presidency. Even the restrained language of the special review board headed by former Republican Senator John Tower appointed to investigate the affair could not mitigate the gravity of the president's nonfeasance: "With such a complex, high risk operation and so much at stake, the President should have ensured that the [National Security Council] system did not fail him. . . . Had the president chosen to drive the NSC system the outcome could well have been different."

Reagan's early years offer clues to the development of both his congeniality and dependency. His mother was a far stronger figure in the household than her alcoholic husband. When Lou Cannon first asked Reagan about his family, "he talked non-stop about his mother for several minutes without even mentioning his father." In his autobiography, Reagan recalled that when he was five, his mother taught him and his brother, Neil, to read, "following each word with a finger, while we watched over her shoulder."

The late Wilbur J. Cohen, whose judgment was seasoned by service under six presidents, contended that the best way for a president to develop the balanced, secure personality required for White House success is "to have a mother who loves you and nurtures you." Cohen cited the maternal care and affection lavished on Franklin D. Roosevelt and

John F. Kennedy. Similarly the warmth and affection bestowed by Nell Reagan appears to have fostered her son's pleasant temperament.

His father, a very different figure, cast a far different influence. Reagan recalled coming home at age eleven to find his father "flat on his back on the front porch and no one there to lend a hand but me. He was drunk, dead to the world." Nevertheless, Reagan claimed he felt no resentment of his father because of his mother. "She told Neil and myself over and over that alcoholism was a sickness—that we should love and help our father and never condemn him for something that was beyond his control." Being raised in a matriarchal household with a father who could not control his own behavior but was nevertheless loved and cared for likely contributed to Reagan's inclination toward dependency.

Another factor fostering Reagan's dependency was his experience in Hollywood. "Reagan was an actor, not a producer, he follows a script," Howard Phillips, a onetime Reagan speech writer once told me. Don Regan also made the point that Reagan's years in films either instilled or reinforced a tendency to depend on others to be responsible for all but a relatively few tasks to which he dedicated himself:

> As president Ronald Reagan acted on the work habits of a lifetime. He regarded his daily schedule as being something like a shooting script in which characters came and went, scenes were rehearsed and acted out, and the plot was advanced one day at a time and not always in sequence. The Chief of Staff was a sort of producer, making sure that the star had what he needed to do his best; the staff was like the crew, invisible behind the lights.

Not surprisingly Reagan disavowed the notion that he was a passive president. Told by a reporter that presidential scholar James David Barber had classified his character in the Oval Office as passive-positive (the former referring to assertiveness, the latter to temperament), Reagan brooded overnight. Then he called the reporter to argue "that those things that are the Federal government's responsibility we do damn well."

The president missed the point, which concerned his personal traits as chief executive, not the policies of his administration. That is not to say that Reagan was dumb or lazy. Richard Williamson told me that he believed Reagan's supposed indolence was in part "staff induced":

> When we gave President Reagan briefing material he always read it and returned it the next day, with notes. But Nancy Reagan terrorized the staff to ease off, and not to burden the president. The staff was scared of her and did just that. The striking thing to me was his lack of curiosity.

If given information, he devoured it; if not given it, he seldom asked for it.

As president Reagan chose to save his energy for the things that mattered most to him, and jibed most with what he believed. This highly selective mindset allowed him to maintain his generally good disposition.

He was always able to find a bright side to even the darkest news. After his operation for cancer, he told a reporter, "I didn't have cancer. I had something inside of me that had cancer in it, and it was removed." And while denying his dependency he flaunted his optimism. He loved to tell the story of the child who when he is presented with a mound of manure insists, "There must be a pony hidden here someplace."

The support and forbearance of his staff helped preserve his good humor. "You can't have people rushing in [on Reagan] and talking about mistakes," said Reagan's attorney general and longtime adviser Edwin Meese. "The people around you can get you down," he said, adding that Reagan's aides had "a responsibility not to create self-doubt."

By setting aside unpleasant, difficult tasks that tended to cause discouragement and frustration, Reagan found it easier to maintain his confident good nature and to deflect the criticism stirred by his ideology. In this way his character added a certain strength to his leadership. Yet it also shielded him from an awareness of his shortcomings, self-knowledge that in the long run might have strengthened his presidency.

THE CHALLENGE

The challenge facing Reagan when he took office as the fortieth president was to repair the damage done to the nation's economy during the Carter presidency. The new president's response reflected the combination of his ideology with his values and character and was foreshadowed by his conduct of the campaign that won him the White House.

As that campaign got under way, Carter had clearly lost his long struggle to maintain a balance between inflation and recession. The country was now suffering from both. Median family income had declined, the proportion of families below the poverty line had increased, inflation had skyrocketed—a 1960 dollar was worth 36 cents—and because of inflation, effective marginal tax rates had soared. Candidate Reagan offered a biting one-liner that summed up the national mood: "A recession is when your neighbor loses his job; a depression is when you lose yours—recovery is when Jimmy Carter loses his."

Carter had all but destroyed himself. "We came out of the primaries with the posture that the American people simply did not want Jimmy Carter as their president if they could possibly avoid it," pollster Caddell said later. In addition to its economic problems, the administration was "suffering grievously" from the Iranian hostage crisis. Polling data showed not only low standings for Carter but deep public pessimism in general and low regard for the presidency as an institution.

Given this setting, Carter's advisers saw no way their man could *win* the election. The only real question was whether Reagan could lose it.

For a time the Republican candidate seemed to be doing just that. In the late summer weeks immediately following the Democratic convention, Reagan became involved in pointless controversies about such peripheral matters as "creationism," the merits of the Vietnam War, and the Ku Klux Klan, which diverted public attention from Carter's problems to Reagan's judgment, a shift that was bound to hurt the challenger.

The future significance of these episodes was the difficulty Reagan was having in sorting his strong convictions into a cohesive structure during a campaign, where his views were subjected to continuous and intense examination. More immediately, Reagan's advisers now faced the possibility that their candidate would destroy himself before he could defeat Carter. Some had seen the potential for this problem in advance. In late spring, after Reagan had assured himself of his party's nomination, Richard Wirthlin urged that planning begin for a post-convention speech on economic policy. Such a speech was critically needed, he contended, to bring "direction, focus and coherence" to Reagan's economic position and to protect him from the charge, first made by one of his Republican rivals, George Bush, that what Reagan was preaching amounted to "voodoo economics." In early September Reagan delivered the definitive economic speech that Wirthlin had recommended. It turned out to be vital indeed to the success of his candidacy by blunting criticism of his economic proposals. But Reagan's speech did not really reconcile the contradictions of these proposals; it merely camouflaged these inconsistencies behind layers of rhetoric and misleading statistics that in the heat of the campaign neither the press nor his Democratic rival was able to penetrate.

The basic message of the speech, which had far-reaching implications for Reagan's presidency, was the decision to promise relief and ignore the pain. Reagan pledged to cut taxes, boost defense spending, and balance the budget by 1983. This would be made possible, the candidate explained, by economic growth and by the tens of billions he would save by trimming "waste, extravagance, abuse and outright fraud." Then he made this key promise, which was to haunt his budget director, David Stockman, for the next four years: "This strategy for growth *does not require altering or taking back necessary entitlements already granted to the American people*. The integrity of the Social Security system will be defended" (emphasis added). With the economic speech out of the way, Reagan's strategists decreed that he should avoid ideology and stress instead his personality, which was far more appealing than Carter's, and his values. The good-natured, optimistic Reagan who now appeared on the campaign stage quickly overshadowed not only the fretful persona of the incumbent, but also the image of the right-wing-extremist bogeyman whom Carter had been trying to depict.

In his rhetoric Reagan underlined the value themes that had been a major part of the convention, promising in one climactic televised address to launch "an era of national renewal" that "will revitalize the values of family, work and neighborhood." The successful climax of this strategy came in the televised debate during the closing days of the campaign. Carter had prepared himself to demonstrate Reagan's weakness on a broad range of issues and the president spent the ninety minutes of air time cutting Reagan's positions to ribbons.

For his part, Reagan continued to stress his faith in the value of individualism. In his closing statement, he promised "to lead a crusade . . . to take government off the backs of the great people of this country and turn you loose again to do those things that I know you can do so well, because you did them and made this country great." In one of his most effective moments he drew on the strength of his character, shattering Carter's aggressive strategy by responding to one of the president's attacks with a typically wrath-deflecting soft answer: "There you go again."

The clincher came in Reagan's closing statement when he brilliantly linked his beliefs to the electorate's self-interest by asking voters to ask themselves "Are you better off than you were four years ago?" and then to cast their ballots accordingly.

The fuzzy campaign brought Reagan a sweeping victory but also an inevitably fuzzy mandate, which reflected the intellectual limitations of Reagan's ideology. In the first summer of the Reagan presidency Wirthlin told me that Reagan had "a general mandate" for change, involving "a leap of faith" that the new president could accomplish what he had set out to do. Rather than endorsing a specific set of policies, Wirthlin said, the votes for Reagan represented a commitment to "the personality of the man who would provide strong leadership."

In one sense, that meant that Reagan was free to develop his own mandate as president. But in another sense, that freedom was seriously restricted. Since he had not suggested to the voters during the campaign that sacrifice and restraint would be required to cure the economy, he was in poor position to do so as president.

In the event, he did not even try. First he declared the nation's economy to be in crisis—"We're in the worst economic mess since the Great Depression," he told the country. Then he proceeded to outline just the sort of solution he had promised during the campaign—one without pain, at least for the white middle-class Americans who had supported Reagan.

Reagan's three-pronged strategy fully reflected his ideology and values.

First, he called for a giant tax cut, which was in accord with his belief that the federal government was the greatest threat to freedom.

Then he demanded budget reductions, embodied in two congressional resolutions that reduced benefits to low-income Americans and others dependent on the federal government. Among the programs cut back were food stamps, Medicare, public-service jobs, unemployment compensation, urban mass transit, student loans, and child nutrition.

Finally, Reagan called for a huge increase in defense spending. This jibed with his ideological imperative to curb the threat of communist aggression and also dramatized his allegiance to the traditional value of patriotism. "Defense is not a budget issue. You spend what you need," Reagan told his budget director.

Somewhat to their surprise, Reagan and his advisers found the opposition to these measures disorganized and ineffective. "Everyone was giving Ronald Reagan his head, more so than we had anticipated," recalled Richard Williamson of the early months of 1981.

Reagan helped his own cause greatly by quickly grasping the various dimensions of his office, exploiting the strengths of his character to gain access to the full range of presidential power. Wounded by a would-be assassin's bullet early on, he had the grace and wit to say to his doctors as they were preparing him for the surgery that saved his life: "Please tell me you're Republicans."

That Reagan's approval ratings soared in the opinion polls following the shooting was an inevitable reflection of public sympathy. But by his command of the personal powers of the presidency, underlined by his conduct when his life was in peril, he was able to channel public response into the debate over his economic policy proposals then in full swing, and use it to help overcome his Democratic opponents on Capitol Hill.

Even so, Reagan's program ran into difficulty. Instead of opposing the idea of tax reduction, the Democrats proposed reductions of their own. Caught in a log-rolling competition in order to get its version enacted, the administration wound up sponsoring cuts that cost the Treasury far more than originally contemplated.

To avoid the Niagara of red ink this would produce in federal fiscal affairs, budget director Stockman proposed a revised approach: delay the income-tax cuts in return for an agreement with Congress to make more spending cuts, particularly in the entitlement programs such as Social Security, Medicare, and veterans benefits. Together these accounted for more than half of the government's domestic spending.

In the long run, Stockman's approach, with its reductions in entitlement programs, would have been more consistent with Reagan's own ideological goals of reducing government than the original timetable for tax reduction. But this sort of reasoning was too complex for Reagan; he turned Stockman down.

"Delay would be a total retreat," he said. "We would be admitting that we were wrong."

When Stockman pressed his case, Reagan exploded, "Well, damn it, Dave, we came here to attack deficit spending, not put more taxes on the people," he said.

As for entitlements, as Stockman ultimately came to realize, the president had little appetite for taking on the political challenge that cutting them involved. This was a manifestation of Reagan's homemade ideology. "Reagan's body of knowledge is primarily impressionistic," Stockman observed. "He registers anecdotes rather than concepts." Because of his unwillingness to reduce entitlements, Reagan lost his opportunity to implement fundamental, equitable cuts in spending that would have completed his revolution against big government. It turned out, as Stockman later wrote, that the progenitor of the so-called Reagan Revolution only "had a half-revolution in his mind."

The enactment of Reagan's economic program in the first six months of his presidency represented a signal success for his leadership. But both the glow from that triumph and its full implications were obscured for some time, because soon after this prescription for recovery was adopted, the country plunged into a severe recession, the worst since the Great Depression. Starting in the fall of 1981, unemployment rates soared to the highest levels of the post–World War II era, and Reagan's popularity declined accordingly. Yet the president stood his ground. Backed by the strength of his ideological convictions and his values, aided by the underlying optimism of his character, he blamed the plunge of the economy on the excesses of liberal spending in the past and contended that recovery was certain and not far off.

Although remaining firm on fundamentals, Reagan once again displayed the ability, as he had as governor, to make what he regarded as temporary and ancillary adjustments in his ideological plans. Thus, in the midst of the recession, with the 1982 midterm elections in the offing, only a year after pushing through the largest tax *cut* in the nation's history, the president signed into law what critics claimed was the largest tax *increase* ever. The three-year $100 billion measure was authored by Republican senators who feared that without this additional revenue the deficit would reach uncontrollable proportions and damage prospects for an economic recovery.

Reagan sought to pass off the bill as merely a loophole-closing, compliance-enforcement measure. "This bill only collects taxes we are owed already," he told House Republican leaders. In fact, though the new law preserved the 1981 reductions in income taxes, it boosted levies on cigarettes and phone service as well as on insurance companies, defense contractors, and construction firms.

Having made this concession to fiscal prudence, Reagan rallied his party for the congressional elections behind the slogan: "Stay the course." Republicans suffered severe losses, turning over 26 House seats to the Democrats, but by holding to his basic beliefs—he managed to gloss over the tax increase—Reagan maintained control of the political agenda. Democrats in the new Congress were reluctant to press their own solutions to the recession. More important, when the economic indicators headed up again in the fall of 1983, Reagan claimed full credit for the recovery. The good times would extend throughout his presidency and on into the next, keeping the opposition party on the defensive.

To a significant degree, Reagan had successfully met his first challenge, alleviating the economic ills he had inherited from Carter. But his overall conduct of economic policy, notably his unwillingness to complete his revolution by cutting middle-class entitlements, also demonstrated the inconsistencies and oversimplifications inherent in his ideology, which would cloud the legacy of his leadership.

On the economic front, the Reagan program's most immediate impact was to relieve the short-term complaints of those Americans who were already the best off economically—the upper middle class—by reducing taxes. It also eased inflation, which had become a problem for the entire middle class. Reagan's preservation of the entitlement programs, in which middle-class Americans had a huge stake, was the price for their support, or at least acquiesence in his policies which brought great benefits to the upper-income groups.

But by protecting middle-class benefits while cutting government help to the poor, Reagan exacerbated existing societal inequities. The rich got substantially richer; the poor fell further behind. The "unabashedly regressive" tax reductions totaled $360 billion from 1982 to 1985; during that same period cuts in human service programs amounted to about $112 billion. Low-income Americans, particularly the working poor, were hurt because of cuts in government programs that many of them depended upon.

As the most vulnerable group in the population, low-income citizens also suffered disproportionately from the 1982 recession, brought on at least in part by Reagan's economic policies. The recession was the price paid for curbing inflation, as Reagan had forecast in his 1975 speech to the conservative conference, before he converted to supply-side economics.

Over the long run, though, by increasing the disadvantages of low-income Americans, Reagan's policies compounded problems that middle-class Americans had to confront—drugs, the homeless, the accelerating collapse of the cities. Moreover, the deficit created by Reagan's tax cuts left the federal government in poor position to help deal with these problems.

Though Reagan's economic program was first on his leadership agenda, he also had a strong commitment to foreign policy, where he took on another formidable challenge—to strengthen the U.S. role in the world without plunging the nation into full-scale war. To achieve that overall goal he followed two policy routes: one the so-called Reagan Doctrine, which committed the U.S. to support insurgencies against communist regimes, and the other the buildup of the country's military establishment. Both approaches reflected Reagan's ideological commitment to checking the threat of communism and his emphasis on the values of the nation's past, when its dominance in the world had been unquestioned. As in the economic arena his character aided his leadership by making his proposals seem less threatening. Once again Reagan succeeded to a significant degree in meeting the challenge he took on, but in the process also exposed the gaps between his ideology and reality.

The Reagan Doctrine, for example, failed to recognize the dramatic changes in international power relationships in the previous two decades that limited the scope of effective U.S. intervention in other countries. It also failed to take sufficient account of the continuing reluctance of Americans to support such interventions for fear of becoming bogged down in another Vietnam-like morass. Thus the president was unable to mobilize a majority of the public to back what became the centerpiece effort of the Reagan Doctrine—support for the contra insurgency against the Sandinista regime in Nicaragua.

Yet even if Reagan fell short of majority support, by using his leadership skills he did generate enough backing in Congress and the country to maintain the contras and the threat of increased U.S. intervention as a thorn in the Sandinista side for the duration of his presidency. Thus, he arguably deserves credit for helping pressure Sandinista leader Daniel Ortega to agree to the democratically conducted elections that led to his loss of power in February 1990, a year after Reagan had left the White House.

Unfortunately for Reagan and for the country, that long-run result did not come soon enough for some of his top aides, who were obsessed with the goal of overturning Ortega's regime one way or another. Unwilling to accept congressional refusal to provide the contras with assistance on the scale they deemed necessary, these zealots, notably Reagan's national security adviser, John Poindexter, and one of his aides, Oliver North, took matters into their own hands. The result was the Iran-Contra debacle, which was to leave a permanent stain on the Reagan presidency.

Reagan would claim later to have been unaware of the clandestine operation North and Poindexter mounted to smuggle arms to the contras in violation of federal law. He was equally ignorant, he insisted, of this operation's most bizarre aspect—its funding with proceeds from the sale of arms to Iran, another murky and duplicitous enterprise. Reagan also at first contended that he did not realize that the purpose of the arms shipments to Iran was to gain the release of American hostages seized in Lebanon by Shiite terrorists with ties to the Ayatollah Khomeni. But after months of investigation and controversy he qualified that denial at a White House press conference: "A few months ago I told the American people I did not trade arms for hostages. My heart and my best intentions still tell me that's true, but the facts and the evidence tell me it is not."

Having acknowledged error, the president told the nation it was time to move on to other concerns. But the matter was not so readily dismissed. The image of Reagan that emerged from the many inquiries into Iran-Contra hardly squared with the picture he had sought to present of himself. The president who had now admitted bargaining with the terrorists who held American captives was the same one who a week after his inauguration, at a Rose Garden ceremony welcoming back the hostages held in the Teheran embassy, had declared: "Let terrorists beware: when the rules of international behavior are violated, our policy will be one of swift retribution." Personally, I could not help thinking how different Reagan now sounded from the politician who had proudly echoed Theodore Roosevelt's fiery battle cry: "Perdicaris alive or Raisuli dead!"

Along with showing Reagan to be somewhat lacking in the firm resolve in which he prided himself, the Iran-Contra affair focused attention on one of the less appealing aspects of his character, his dependency on aides and others close to him. The Tower commission appointed by Reagan himself put the matter as gently as possible. "President Reagan's personal management style places an especially heavy responsibility on his key advisers," its report said. The select committees established by the House and Senate to probe into the affair used harsher language to deal with Poindexter's claim that he had taken responsibility on his own shoulders to shield the president. "This kind of thinking is inconsistent with democratic governance," their joint report said. "The ultimate responsibility for the events in the Iran-Contra affair must rest with the president. If the president did not know what his National Security advisers were doing, he should have."

For Jimmy Carter, Ronald Reagan's predecessor, generally adjudged a failure in the presidency, it would have been far out of character to have allowed such a fiasco as Iran-Contra to happen. Carter was absorbed with procedures and methods, reflecting his emphasis on the value of competence, which he considered the secret of governing. Carter's eyes brightened when he talked of such reforms as zero-based budgeting and standardized benefits; he even kept track of the use of the White House tennis courts. He would certainly have known what Poindexter and North were up to and put a stop to it.

Ronald Reagan on the other hand, was committed to the advocacy of large political ideas. Details, even when they touched on matters of great consequence, were least among his concerns.

At the 1976 Republican convention, Reagan's managers concocted an elaborate stratagem intended to break incumbent Gerald Ford's hold on the party by requiring him to make known his choice for vice-president before the roll-call vote on the presidential nomination. When I asked Jeff Bell, one of Reagan's lieutenants, what the candidate himself thought about this scheme, he seemed startled at the notion that Reagan might think anything about it at all.

"That's not what he was hired for," Bell said. "His job is to perform."

To call Reagan a performer is not to dismiss him, as many of his critics did, as nothing more than an erstwhile Hollywood hack. But Bell's offhand remark acknowledged that Reagan's leadership depended mainly on the public projection of his persona, his values, and his ideology, not on his private deliberative processes. Reagan concentrated much more on the former than on the latter, and the net result was a certain slackness of mind, a resistance to focusing on matters that did not immediately command his interest. Reagan was talented enough and surrounded by enough staff support so that most of the time he got away with this flaw. Iran-Contra was one time he got caught.

If the Iran-Contra debacle underlined Reagan's weaknesses as a leader, another foreign policy development—his success at arms negotiations with the Soviets—reflected mainly his strengths and helped him to leave office with the highest ratings of any president since the end of World War II. In this field of endeavor, he again displayed the commitment to principle and willingness to make tactical adjustments that made his other leadership successes possible.

Reagan entered the presidency breathing fire about Soviet–American relations. Convinced that the Soviets had engaged in an unrestrained strategic buildup while the U.S. had slid far behind, lulled by its unilateral pursuit of detente, Reagan dramatically escalated Pentagon spending while seeming to reject even the idea of negotiations with Moscow. "The only morality they recognize is what will further their cause," he said of the Soviets in 1981. "They reserve unto themselves the right to commit any crime, to lie, to cheat, in order to attain that." For most of his first term Reagan adhered to this view of the conflict between the two superpowers as one of good versus evil, reiterating it most emphatically in a 1983 address to the National Association of Evangelicals. He used that occasion to denounce the nuclear-freeze proposals then drawing increasing attention and to characterize the aims of the Soviet Union as "the aggressive impulses of an evil empire."

Despite the ideological purity of his rhetoric, Reagan had already realized that he could not totally ignore public interest in the much ballyhooed idea for a "freeze" on nuclear weaponry and support for some form of arms control. In late 1981 he began laying out his own arms control proposals—starting with the so-called zero-option plan for removing all intermediate missiles in Europe and following that up with a proposal for deep cuts in strategic weapons. Both proposals were sharply criticized by arms control experts as being so one-sided in favor of the United States that they were unlikely to achieve any progress toward agreement.

Still Reagan would make no concessions, even after the Soviets broke off negotiations. Then in March 1983, he complicated matters by unveiling an entirely new approach to strategic weaponry—the Strategic Defense Initiative, or Star Wars system. Reagan presented SDI as a step toward peace—a defensive measure that would make the long-existing dependence on the fear of mutual assured destruction to prevent nuclear war obsolete. But the Soviets saw SDI as a threat to their very existence, and prospects for any sort of agreement seemed bleak. U.S.–Soviet relations appeared to be at their lowest point since the Cuban missile crisis.

The dramatic turnabout four years later, marked by the historic agreement to ban medium-range missiles concluded by Reagan and Soviet leader Mikhail Gorbachev in their Washington summit meeting, obviously owed much to the presence of Gorbachev at the helm of the Soviet state. Gorbachev clearly had plans for domestic reform and thus also had a natural interest in disarmament, but the evidence suggests that Reagan's leadership formula of ideological consistency tempered with a dash of flexibility and imagination helped to shape events. By bolstering U.S. arms, by making his own stringent arms-control proposals, and by calling for dramatic technological innovation in strategic weaponry, he forced Gorbachev to give ground. What seems clear, as Soviet scholar Condoleezza (cq) Rice points out, is that it was the Soviets who "made their peace with Reagan's arms control agenda" and not the other way around.

Whatever advantage Reagan gave his country in international affairs, though, has to be balanced against the long-term economic problems he left behind. Surveying the "twin peaks" of deficit—the balance of trade and the federal budget—which both reached record highs in his administration, Thomas Mann of Brookings Institution declared: "We are today probably more vulnerable economically than we have been at any time in our recent history."

Reagan not only aggravated these problems, mainly by reducing taxes and not reducing middle-class entitlements, but he also failed to inspire the realism that could have reduced public expectations for a continuing stream of government benefits. "The President has permitted his relentless optimism to blind him to a unique opportunity," wrote the Urban Institute's John Palmer. "The American people apparently found Reagan's personality so appealing they would have swallowed some unpleasant truths from him."

Reagan's failure to limit the growth of middle-class entitlements, including Social Security, parallels Lyndon Johnson's refusal to ask for a tax increase needed to pay for his decision to continue to wage both the war on poverty and the war in Vietnam simultaneously. In Johnson's case, his obsession with consensus blinded him to the need to make a choice. As for Reagan, what was within his reach as a leader was outside the vision of his simplistic ideology. Just as Johnson's decision triggered the inflation that burdened his successors, Reagan's unwillingness to confront the cost of entitlements contributed to the deficits that cast a long shadow over the nation he had governed.

"For decades we have piled deficit upon deficit, mortgaging our future and our children's future for the temporary convenience of the present. To continue this long trend is to guarantee tremendous social, cultural, political and economic upheaval." The somber words are from Ronald Reagan's first inaugural address, intended as a battle cry for the Reagan Revolution. In the light of the ensuing eight years they serve better as an epitaph for his presidency—and as a warning to his successor.

CHAPTER 10

Bush: "The Way I Was Brought Up"

It was the morning after the Iowa Republican precinct caucuses in 1980, and to all intents and purposes George Bush had taken over the main dining room at the musty old Fort Des Moines hotel, turning everyone's breakfast into a celebration of his own triumph the night before. Bush seemed to be everywhere at once, sweeping from table to table, shaking hands and slapping backs.

The Iowa caucuses were the first official event of the 1980 campaign and Bush, then fifty-five, whom no one had previously considered a serious contender for the Republican presidential nomination, had defeated the overwhelming favorite, Ronald Reagan. Any candidate would have been pleased with himself under those circumstances. But most whom I had known would have made some attempt to restrain the expression of their feelings.

Bush let his joy reign unchecked. Spotting me on my way in to breakfast, he called me over. "There are some people I want you to meet," he said.

I shook hands with his friends who had worked for his success and congratulated him.

"I've got the momentum," the victorious candidate told me, smiling broadly. "I'm on my way."

"But now you're the front runner," I reminded him. "People are going to take you more seriously. What are you going to tell them?"

He looked a little puzzled, but he never stopped smiling. "I'm just going to keep going," he said. "I've got Big Mo."

As it turned out, momentum was most of what Bush had to offer and

257

that soon ran out. In a few weeks Reagan recovered from his Iowa setback and defeated Bush decisively in the New Hampshire primary. By May Bush was forced to drop out of the race.

His fundamental problem was, he had never given Republicans a good reason to vote for him. His staff had seen disaster coming and tried to warn him. "You're trying to substitute energy for ideas," his political director, David Keene, told Bush after his Iowa victory. "It would help if you could try to think of two or three things that you want to do when you're president."

Bush thought for a moment. "When I'm elected I'll bring in the best people and put them in charge of the government," he said.

"But what will you tell them to do?" Keene asked.

Bush just shrugged off the question, as he did similar advice from others on his campaign staff.

His advisers urged him to be more substantive, Bush recalled afterward. "And I would argue with them: 'I think I'm being substantive. I'm answering questions every day.'

"I just didn't see it," he acknowledged. "I'll readily concede at this point I might have been wrong. But I didn't feel any great need to do something different."

Something different meant, as his aides had suggested, formulating issues, policies, and ideas. Ronald Reagan, the front runner, was not considered to be any great intellect. Nevertheless he tied his candidacy to an idea—slashing taxes to spur the economy and curb government.

But Bush neither in 1980 nor any time since has felt "any great need" to dwell on ideas. And despite occasional setbacks, one of the most remarkable aspects of his political career is how far he has come without them.

For his first eighteen months in the White House, conciliation and congeniality were the watchwords of George Bush's presidency. Good times, and his determination not to give offense, brought him high ratings in the polls. But in the face of profound change abroad, and growing unease at home, the country seemed adrift.

Suddenly, in his second summer as chief executive, Bush was galvanized into action, not by any of the great issues that confronted the nation at home or abroad but rather by the actions of a Third World despot. Within a week after dictator Saddam Hussein of Iraq had conquered tiny Kuwait, the previously passive Bush had set in motion a massive U.S. military buildup, the largest since the Vietnam War. More than that, with minimal debate or explanation he had, in effect by default, made the reversal of Iraq's aggression the central purpose of a presidency that previously had lacked any overrriding goal at all.

Despite the drama surrounding Operation Desert Shield, the code name given to the U.S. military response to Hussein, Bush's failure to respond to the broader challenges facing the country has made his presidency hard to define or measure. This in itself may well turn out to be a revealing clue as to what he will have achieved when his presidency concludes. At any rate, as this is written, in October 1990, the threshold challenge Bush faces in his tenure is much the same as the one that has dogged him throughout his career—to establish a firm political identity for himself. Meanwhile, even in the absence of any such clear profile, it is still possible to delineate the three chief components of his leadership potential.

IDEOLOGY

Since the start of his political career Bush has strenuously avoided ideological labels and definitions. Pressed during his 1980 presidential campaign to define himself as either a conservative or a moderate, Bush replied, "I don't want to be perceived as either."

"Well, you can't be both," a reporter contended.

"How do you know I can't?" Bush retorted.

After Reagan's triumph in 1980, Bush as his vice-president was willing to accept having his views placed under the conservative rubric that by now dominated his party. "I am a conservative," he told the Ripon Society, one of the last strongholds of moderate Republicanism, in July 1985. "I voted along conservative lines when I was in Congress. I took conservative positions before assuming this job. I take conservative positions now."

But as even Ripon's leaders acknowledge, nearly everyone of consequence in the Republican party today is a conservative. The question that Bush's remarks did not address is: Which kind of conservative is he—the traditional establishmentarian or the more contemporary neopopulist? The answer is that he is a bit of both.

Bush has links to the two main branches of modern Republicanism—the Eastern establishment traditionalism of his birthplace and the fast-emerging Sunbelt neopopulism of his adopted political base in Texas. These competing forces have pulled him in different directions and contributed to the vagueness of his beliefs.

On the economic front, establishment conservatives worry about deficits while neopopulist conservatives consider supply-side tax cuts the remedy for most of the nation's economic ills. On civil rights, education, health care, and other social-welfare issues the establishment is willing to accept the federal government's responsibility established by the New Deal; the neopopulists fervently believe in the principle of the less government the better.

On matters having to do with morals and individual behavior, however, attitudes are reversed. The neopopulists want government to ban abortion and suppress pornography while establishmentarians defend individual prerogatives.

Rather than trying to resolve this conflict, Bush has mainly tried to ignore it and to avoid ideological commitments. In his political life he has tended to choose the course that appeared to offer the greatest opportunity for advancement with the least risk, and which was consistent with his principal value, his loyalty to organizations and the people associated with them.

Bush's oldest political roots are in New England, a stronghold of traditional Republicanism. His father, Prescott, a pillar of the Northeast establishment, served the state of Connecticut as a U.S. Senator. Bush himself was graduated from two of the establishment's favored training grounds, Phillips Andover Academy and Yale University.

The Northeast establishment is not a fixed entity, as Kevin Phillips has pointed out, but rather "a changing aggregation of vested interests" that tends in turn to change the shape of Northeastern politics. From the Civil War until the New Deal the Northeast had been strongly Republican and conservative, with its banking and industrial leaders giving support to the laissez-faire economics of the Republican party that advanced their interests. The triumph of the New Deal in 1932 overthrew the old establishment, and different vested interests took power in its place.

The new Northeast establishment that gradually emerged was tied to public policies of social spending and internationalism, and thus closely linked to the power structure of political liberalism. The Democrats, who now dominated the Northeast, set the liberal tone for the region. Republican political and business leaders, responding to the same economic and social problems and changes that affected their Democratic counterparts, also shifted to the left, supporting the expansion of the welfare state and the advances of the civil rights revolution. Elected to the Senate in 1952, Prescott Bush hewed to the establishment line, opposing Senator Joe McCarthy and voting for civil rights.

Meanwhile, though, his son George was being propelled in a different direction in Texas, where he was exposed to the neopopulist Republicanism of the Sunbelt. Two sets of issues have spurred the spread of neopopulism, one having to do with economics and the other with race and morals.

Economics came first. Indeed, the origins of Sunbelt Republicanism can be traced back to the booming twenties, when middle-class citizens, many of them migrants to the new cities of Texas and Florida from the North, viewed the GOP as the party of economic growth. After being stifled during the Depression, Republicanism revived there when the economy recovered during World War II and then boomed more vigorously than ever after the war, linked to the headlong growth of energy and high-tech industries.

This was the side of neopopulism Bush encountered early and adjusted to readily. Fresh out of Yale, young Bush got off to a fast start in the oil business with its freewheeling, growth-oriented economic doctrines of Sunbelt conservatism.

He settled first in Midland, a west Texas town then in the midst of an oil boom that had drawn young, ambitious men like him from all around the country. Bush, his wife, and their first two children lived in a neighborhood that he later said would nowadays be referred to as "Yuppieland West."

"The time, the place and the prospects for the future were all bright," he recalled. "There wasn't anything subtle or complicated about it. We all just wanted to make a lot of money quick."

As a young man on the make, Bush's circumstances and outlook on the world were very different from his establishment heritage. "Class warfare has many fronts in the United States," observes Nelson Aldrich, himself the scion of a politically powerful patrician family. "But none is so rhetorically lively as the front between the patrimonial haves, or Old Money, and the entrepreneurial haves and would-haves, or Market Man."

Prescott Bush, managing partner of Brown Brothers Harriman, was clearly prototypical Old Money. Old Money took the long view. It was worried about balancing books, but also concerned with preserving the political and social peace. In order to do that, Old Money was willing to make an effort to listen to the grievances of the less fortunate.

George was just as plainly a specimen of entrepreneurial Market Man. The entrepreneurs had little patience for book balancing and little interest in alleviating injustice. They were in a big hurry to catch up with the Old Money crowd and could not afford to play the game safely. If disharmony resulted from their haste, they were prepared to take their chances.

As if to emphasize this contrast, Bush and his partner decided to name the oil-exploration company they founded after the Mexican revolutionary hero Emiliano Zapata, whose violent exploits were celebrated in a Marlon Brando film then playing in downtown Midland. Zapata's slogan, Bush pointed out, was "Tierra y Libertad"—"Land and Liberty"—adding: "We couldn't afford a public relations counsel, but if we had had one he would have told us that was exactly the corporate image we were looking for."

Soon thereafter Bush decided to splurge on a newfangled drilling barge for offshore oil exploration that cost $3 million. This was a huge gamble for a young company, but Bush writes, "We hadn't named our company Zapata in order to be gun-shy about going into revolutionary high risk ventures."

It is questionable, to say the least, that this was the kind of revolution that the radical reformer Zapata had in mind. But Bush's high-roller attitude did represent a revolution of sorts against the economic thinking that had prevailed in his father's house. This contradiction had significant political implications. An electorate geared to go-for-broke economics turned out to have little resources to spare to support the benign social policies of the establishment that Prescott Bush sought to further in the Senate.

This conflict was heightened by the other major component of neo-populism, which had racist and fundamentalist overtones. The appeal of these issues was demonstrated by Barry Goldwater's 1964 presidential candidacy. Goldwater did not go over well in the fast-growing urban South, where his seeming opposition to Social Security and willingness to wage nuclear war made middle-class voters uneasy.

By contrast, Goldwater ran well in the Deep South, carrying five states. There the race issue was more important than in the urban South, where the Negro population was small. And there Goldwater's opposition to the 1964 civil rights bill helped lay the base for the new Republican Sunbelt strength that emerged in the 1968 election to rival and at times surpass the old power bases in the Northeast and the Midwest.

But the appeal of Goldwater, reinforced in subsequent elections by Nixon and Reagan, went beyond race and beyond the black belt of the Deep South. In the Rocky Mountain West as well as in the rural South these Republican leaders mined a vein of discontent as deep as the resentments that fanned the populist rebellion of the late nineteenth century. Instead of farm folk hard-pressed by the "vested interests" of big business, these were middle-class businessmen and wage earners who looked to the Republican party to shield their livelihoods and their families against the intrusions of government and the threatening wave of social permissiveness.

In the 1964 election, Theodore White described the core of Goldwater's support as citizens in ferment. "Intensely moral people who hated and despised . . . Communism, waste, weakness, government, bureaucracy and anarchy." Unlike the Taft conservatives of the 1940s, who were concerned mainly with preventing further advances of liberals, these neopopulist conservatives demanded that the country be turned around.

This hard core, still a minority in 1964, expanded over the years, giving the Republicans a solid majority in the Sunbelt. While their views varied somewhat from state to state and issue to issue, by and large they were dead set against the establishment and therefore opposed to most of what George Bush had been brought up to believe. Their attitudes were bound to clash with Bush's legacy of establishment positions on such issues as civil rights, the Equal Rights amendment, and abortion.

Bush's response to this conflict was to seek neutral ground that would shelter his political career from substantive controversy. In this respect he resembled his father. Prescott Bush's entrance into politics was divorced from passion, motivated instead by a sense of noblesse oblige. In 1950, when the elder Bush made his first try for the Senate, the Democrats had controlled the White House for eighteen years and Congress for sixteen of those years. "Dad was concerned about the future of the two-party system," Bush wrote.

During his ten years in the Senate, though he stood by his principles on controversies such as McCarthyism and civil rights, Prescott Bush never fought hard enough for anything to make any enemies. He was widely respected for his conscientiousness and integrity, but he was remembered for the strength of his personality more than for his accomplishments.

The reasons George Bush gives for beginning his own career in politics are strikingly similar to the motives he ascribed to his father. He decided to seek the Republican party chairmanship in Harris County, Texas, in 1962, he wrote later, because he viewed "a new generation" of Texans as "the voters who could turn Texas into a genuine two-party state."

Until that time Bush had never given much thought to political issues and beliefs. At Yale in the mid-1940s "there was just a trace of political activism on campus," Bush recalled. "But aside from following the front-page news . . . I wasn't politically involved. I came back to civilian life feeling that I needed to get my degree and go into the business world as soon as possible. I had a family to support."

By the late 1950s Bush had developed a "growing interest in going into politics." He had done "grass-roots work" in Midland during Eisenhower's two presidential campaigns, but he offered no explanation for his interest except that he had already achieved financial security and was "young enough to look for new challenges."

When Texas Democrats urged him on practical grounds to switch parties, young Bush rejected their advice. "Philosophically, I was a Republican," he explained. "Privately my own political philosophy had long been settled," Bush asserted. "I considered myself a conservative Republican." Yet he also added: "I didn't have much chance to get into any deep ideological discussions during my early years in Texas."

He continued to avoid "ideological discussions" when he ran for Harris County chairman. He had been recruited for the post by local party leaders to forestall a takeover by ultra right-wing members of the John Birch Society. But in his successful campaign for the post and his two-year tenure as county chairman, Bush avoided criticizing the Birch Society's extremist positions. "There was no point trying to resolve the deep ideological differences in the membership," he explained, "so I shifted the emphasis to the nuts and bolts of building the party organization."

Once he moved beyond intraparty contests and sought public office, Bush could no longer wholly avoid ideology. The result was a series of ideological switches back and forth, each of which was driven by short-term political convenience.

Thus in 1964, in his first try for public office, challenging liberal Democratic Senator Ralph Yarborough, he turned his back on his moderate legacy and tied himself closely to the ill-fated presidential candidacy of Barry Goldwater. Bush denounced the landmark 1964 Civil Rights Act as "politically inspired and destined to failure." And he opposed Medicare and the nuclear test-ban treaty. His candidacy was overwhelmed by the Lyndon Johnson landslide.

Years later Bush's opponent recalled that his initial strategy had been to stress his record in the Senate. But then Yarborough's aides told him, "All you have to do is quote Bush, who had already called himself one hundred percent for Goldwater and the Vietnam War. So that's what I did and it worked very well."

Bush bounced back from that drubbing to run for the House of Representatives in 1966. This time the field of battle was Texas's seventh congressional district, with upper middle-class neighborhoods not very different from the Connecticut environs where Bush had been raised, and also with a fair percentage of black voters. His Democrat opponent was Frank Briscoe, the county district attorney, from the right wing of his party.

The situation called for a shift back to the center, particularly on civil rights. Bush began with his own Episcopalian minister in Houston. "You know, John, I took some of the far right positions to get elected," he said of his 1964 campaign. "I hope I never do it again. I regret it."

Having thus absolved himself, Bush promised the voters "to work with the Negro and white leadership" to get at the root causes of racial violence and also pledged "not to appeal to the white backlash." He took

34 percent of the Negro vote, compared with 10 percent for the Republican candidate for governor, and easily defeated Briscoe.

In his 1964 Senate campaign Bush had opposed the Civil Rights Act, but mindful of his 1966 campaign promises he voted for the 1968 Fair Housing Act. This was not excessively bold; the law had the support of a majority of House Republicans and eight other congressmen on the twenty-three-member Texas delegation. Nevertheless sentiment in his district turned against him because of the vote, and he went home to face his critics at a mass meeting. Only two years before, campaigning for Senate on the ticket with Goldwater, Bush had called Martin Luther King, Jr., "a militant" and declared segregation to be a problem "better handled by moral persuasion on the local level" than by federal action. Now, though, he reminded his listeners that Negro troops were fighting in Vietnam, and said, "Somehow it seems fundamental that a man should not have the door slammed in his face because he is a Negro or speaks with a Latin American accent." The audience gave him a standing ovation.

He seems, however, to have remembered their initial disapproval better than their applause. In the twenty years since he backed the 1968 Fair Housing Act he has rarely risked political damage on behalf of the cause of civil rights.

When he ran for the Senate again in 1970, Bush prepared to campaign against Ralph Yarborough, who had defeated him in 1964. Instead he found himself pitted against conservative Lloyd Bentsen, who had defeated Yarborough for the Democratic nomination. Bush professed to be unworried. "If Bentsen is going to try to go to my right, he's gonna step off the edge of the Earth," he boasted. But Bush, who had moved right in 1964, then left in 1966, found it hard to turn himself around again in 1970. He had the backing of a fair number of liberal Democrats, who were determined to reject Bentsen as too conservative. But there were too many other Democrats in Texas and most of them voted for Bentsen.

After the returns were in, Nixon aide Charles Colson wrote a memo to the president stating that Bush was defeated because he "tried to be more liberal than Bentsen." Nixon, who had persuaded Bush to give up his House seat to make the race, scribbled on the margin: "Probably true."

The error of excessive liberalism was a mistake Bush sought to avoid when he sought the presidency in 1980. On the other hand, he also tried to present himself as a moderate alternative to Reagan. The combined burden was not easy to carry.

To forestall conservative criticism, Bush early on resigned his post on the board of the Council of Foreign Relations, claiming the organization, a favorite target for right-wing conservatives, was too liberal. Yet he could not prevent right-wing attacks on his establishment background. In the critical New Hampshire primary William Loeb, arch conservative publisher of the *Manchester Union Leader*, denounced Bush as the candidate of "the self-appointed elite of this country." And Gerald Carmen, Reagan's campaign manager, described the contest between Bush and Reagan as "old school tie and inherited influence against the working middle-class Americans." Such arguments helped defeat Bush in New Hampshire and destroy his chances for the nomination.

For the most part, Bush tried to soft-pedal his differences with Reagan during the campaign for fear of offending his supporters and because of his distaste for ideological debate. Though he disagreed with the slash in personal income tax rates that was the centerpiece of Reagan's economic proposals, he was restrained in his criticism until the Pennsylvania primary campaign in April. By then he had his back against the wall. Unless he could turn the tide by defeating Reagan in that state, his candidacy would soon collapse.*

His speech writer and press secretary, Peter Teeley, wrote an insert for Bush's standard stump speech, labeling Reagan's proposals as "voodoo economics," and Bush delivered Teeley's indictment at a campaign rally in Pittsburgh. He only uttered the phrase once, but he never heard the end of it. The Democrats made it a rallying cry against Reagan for eight years.†

Bush had other disagreements with Reagan, too, on issues that were more visceral than economic policy. For one, he had always opposed a Constitutional amendment to ban abortion, which Reagan favored. For another, he had always supported the proposed Equal Rights Amendment, which Reagan opposed. But all that went out the window when Reagan called him in Detroit to invite him to be his running mate.

"George, is there anything at all about the platform or anything else, anything that might make you uncomfortable down the road?" Reagan asked gently but pointedly.

He saw no problems, Bush replied. The important thing, he told Reagan, was to win the election in November.

In his autobiography Bush marveled at Reagan's tact in phrasing the question. "The question generally asked of vice presidential prospects

---

* As it turned out, Bush did win the Pennsylvania primary, but his candidacy was too far gone for even this success to salvage it.

† After Bush became vice-president he even tried to deny uttering the notorious words, but NBC news correspondent Ken Bode unearthed and broadcast a television tape of the Pittsburgh speech.

these days is: 'Is there anything about *you* that might make *me* uncomfortable down the road?' " Bush wrote.

But Reagan knew exactly what might cause him discomfort: what Bush professed to believe. He wanted assurances from Bush that those beliefs would be shunted aside during his vice-presidency, and he got it. For the next eight years, if Bush ever disagreed with his president, the country never knew about it.

By the time he became vice-president, Bush had become accustomed to holding his tongue. "George has never had a job in which he was required to take definitive positions," Mary Louise Smith, a longtime friend who succeeded him as chairman of the Republican National Committee, told me that spring. In this respect the vice-presidency was like every other public position Bush had held since he had left Congress in 1970—U.S. ambassador to the United Nations, Republican national chairman, envoy to China, and chief of the Central Intelligence Agency.

In Reagan's second term, as Bush's anticipated candidacy for the presidency drew closer, pressure from the press and other politicians for him to establish his own positions increased. But Bush resisted, insisting that the loyalty he owed Reagan prevented him from speaking out. "I'm going to have to discipline myself and not talk to the press about what I believe and what my views are," he told his staff in 1985. "I'm going to show you discipline and I want you people to do the same thing."

Bush seemed troubled not at all by this self-imposed inhibition. "I don't feel under-appreciated or under-identified," he told me after nearly six years in the vice-presidency. "I don't feel any compulsion to have a dramatic announcement or unveiling, to jump out of a cake and say: 'Here's the real me.' I think it's very good to be Ronald Reagan's vice president."

Bush's second campaign for the presidency in 1988 was as barren of content as the one in 1980. His advisers regarded the Reagan era's peace and prosperity as Bush's greatest assets. Beyond promising to continue Reagan's policies, Bush offered some modest proposals of his own—a tax-credit program to finance child care and an agenda for cleaning up the environment. But he avoided making the spending commitments that would make such measures significant, instead repeatedly insisting— "Read my lips," he declared—that no matter what, he would not raise taxes.

His advisers concluded that besides stressing prosperity, their best chance for success was to attack the Democratic nominee, whose wooden personality and self-absorption made him highly vulnerable. Their rationale was summed up for me by one senior party consultant, Eddie

Mahe: "We can't elect George Bush, but we can defeat Michael Dukakis."

The campaign became notable for its negativeness. By focusing on a half-dozen or so aspects of Dukakis's gubernatorial record—such as his veto of the law requiring the pledge of allegiance, his opposition to capital punishment, and the weekend furlough granted to convicted killer Willie Horton under a Massachusetts program Dukakis had defended—Bush sought to define his opponent as outside the mainstream of American beliefs and values. Bush and his strategists put particular stress on the case of Horton, who brutally assaulted a Maryland woman and her fianceé while on furlough. "Clint Eastwood's answer to violent crime is: 'Go ahead, make my day,' " Bush told a campaign rally in Fort Worth. "My opponent's answer is slightly different. His motto is: 'Go ahead, have a nice weekend.' "

Despite Bush's nearly thirty years in politics, a cloud of ambiguity surrounded his beliefs when he entered the White House. This uncertainty reflected not just Bush's service in the vice-presidency, whose occupant is expected to submerge his private convictions, but also the new chief executive's long previous record of ideological noncommitment. "Within whatever context he's been in, George Bush always emerges as without any sharp edges," Stephen Hess, a Nixon aide, told me. "The man has a sort of bland and wishy-washy quality." It remained to be seen whether under the pressures of the presidency, George Bush's ideology would come more clearly into focus.

VALUES

In his autobiography, George Bush contends that while he was serving as Republican national chairman during the Watergate scandal, Richard Nixon's aides wanted to use him as "point man in a counterattack against investigators leading the Watergate charge." He rejected that idea, Bush wrote. "My feeling was that the RNC chairman's job wasn't to be a rubber stamp for wild political charges drawn up by White House staffers."

Significantly, Bush does not mention an episode in midsummer of 1973 in which he played just such a role. To demonstrate his allegiance to his president, Bush plunged into the morass of Watergate, risking serious damage to himself and to his party. His behavior was a measure of the loyalty that is the talisman of his political career.

At the time Nixon was taking a pounding; almost every day appeared a new Watergate revelation, keeping the president on the defensive. In desperation Nixon's strategists devised a scheme to strike back. Aware that the thrust could not come from the White House because its credibility had been badly damaged, they turned instead to Bush, whom Nixon had made chairman of the Republican National Committee six months earlier. Despite what Bush later contended, he did their bidding.

He called a press conference to charge that electronic surveillance such as the bugging of Democratic party headquarters at the Watergate was nothing new in American politics. Back during the 1960 presidential campaign, Bush claimed, the Democrats themselves had conducted electronic surveillance of key aides to Richard Nixon. The chief culprit, Bush asserted, was Carmine Bellino, former aide to President John Kennedy and now chief investigator for the Senate committee probing into Watergate. I asked Bush if he meant to imply that this supposed spying by Bellino justified the Watergate break-in.

Absolutely not, he said, he just wanted to put Watergate into proper perspective. "It is a gross distortion to microscopically analyze one campaign and totally ignore what others have done in other campaigns," he said.

A few days after Bush's press conference, twenty-two Republican senators signed a statement urging that Bellino be suspended while the charges were investigated. Then John Ehrlichman, who had been forced by Watergate disclosures to resign as Nixon's chief domestic adviser, claimed that Bellino had improperly investigated income-tax returns in 1960 when he had been an aide to President Kennedy.

This well-orchestrated assault was intended to support the White House argument, central to Nixon's defense, that Watergate was just another example of hard-boiled political tactics that had been used by both parties in the past. But for all the machinations of the White House, the evidence produced was flimsy and the case against Bellino soon collapsed.

In the importance Bush placed on loyalty he resembled Gerald Ford, except that Ford's loyalty focused on his relationships on Capitol Hill. Bush's loyalty was both more personal and yet more far-reaching. The core of his loyalty was his relationship to his family. These early personal ties served as a model for his attitude toward the professional "families" with whom he became identified during his career, namely the Nixon and Reagan administrations, the Republican party, and the Central Intelligence Agency.

Bush always had the supportive bonds of his childhood in mind. Answering charges that his vice-presidential loyalty to Reagan was excessive, Bush told an interviewer, "I think it's good for the country and I think it's good for the office of the vice presidency itself, and, if it isn't good, well, that's just too bad because that's the way I was brought up." His upbringing was bound to make a lasting impression. His childhood home was a richly textured setting, blending comfort, discipline, and wealth, providing a nurturing cocoon for his early years and a power base that would serve him well later.

Bush and his three brothers and sister were raised in Greenwich, Connecticut, one of New York City's most fashionable bedroom communities. Their spacious house was sited on a hillside, a long driveway curved into a canopied entrance in front, a broad veranda circled the house, and there was a brook in back. Inside were quarters for the cook, the maid, and the chauffeur. The children spent their Christmases in a lodge in the South Carolina woods; they summered on the beach in Maine. "Our childhood was like a beautiful dream," recalled Bush's sister, Nancy.

Six-feet four, broad shouldered, and ruggedly handsome, Prescott Bush was the dominant figure in his household and a cynosure of the Northeast establishment. At Yale he had made Skull and Bones and captained the baseball team. In World War I he had fought in the Meuse-Argonne and earned captain's bars and a chestful of decorations.

Above all else Prescott Bush was well connected. After the war, old grads at Yale helped place him with Winchester Arms and U.S. Rubber. When he was ready for his big move, opportunity awaited him at Averell Harriman's new investment company, where it just so happened that his father-in-law, George Herbert Walker, was president. Before long that firm had become Brown Brothers, Harriman, and not very long after that Prescott Bush became its managing partner.

Even with his workload on Wall Street, Prescott Bush made a point of being home for family dinner every night. Afterward there was always a swirl of civic club meetings and charitable functions to attend. As a sportsman and philanthropist, his scope was not just local but national. He was president of the U.S. Golf Association and during World War II headed up the USO. "Our father had a powerful impact on the way we came to look at the world," Bush remembered. "Dad taught us about duty and service."

In the late 1940s, Prescott Bush's community activities, plus his fundraising for the Republican party, led to an opportunity to run for Congress. In his world, though, the concept of noblesse oblige did not extend as far down as the House of Representatives. His partners at Brown Brothers, Harriman told him that he could not be spared merely for a House seat. It took an opening in the Senate for them to release him to politics.

George Bush's mother, Dorothy, was a match for her husband. Just as he won championships at golf, she excelled in tennis. Just as her husband's father, Samuel P. Bush, had made his mark in the business world as a management consultant, so had her father, George Herbert

Walker, for whom George Bush was named, as a partner with Averell Harriman. Also a sportsman of note, Grandfather Walker founded amateur golf's Walker Cup. Dorothy herself is remembered by her son as "a first rate athlete" who encouraged her children in sports. She also enforced discipline and supervised religious training, quoting the Bible at breakfast and insisting on regular attendance at the Episcopal church. "Mother taught us about dealing with life on a personal basis, relating to other people," Bush wrote later.

Bush refers to his decision to move to Texas following the war as an act of bold independence. "After three years in the navy I'd come home with my own ideas about what I wanted out of life," he wrote. Bush claimed that his uncle Herbie Walker, an investment banker, offered to find a place for him on Wall Street, but that was not what he and Barbara wanted. "Breaking away meant just that—living on our own. We were young, still in our early twenties, and we wanted to make our own way, our own mistakes and shape our own future."

Yet his move was not nearly as daring as he suggests, thanks to the long arm of his family's connections. While he was still in his senior year at New Haven, uncertain of his future, Neil Mallon, "a close family friend," and "surrogate uncle and father confessor to all the Bush children," offered the young man some advice and some help to go with it. "What you need to do is head out to Texas and those oil fields," Mallon suggested. "That's the place for ambitious young people these days." As it happened, Mallon controlled an oil-equipment company that had an opening for a traince in west Texas. This was enough to get Bush started in the oil business.

When the young entrepreneur decided to go out in his own, starting an oil-exploratory firm, Uncle Herbie helped raise $300,000 to get him under way. Recalling his uncle's assistance, Bush wrote that "in business as in politics you can only go so far relying on the backing of relatives and friends." But the capital was critically important to Bush in developing his enterprise. One oil field veteran, J. C. Williamson, told a journalist: "George would've been just another carpetbagger if he hadn't rode in on a silk carpet."

His start in Congress was family-assisted, too. When he arrived in Washington to take his newly won House seat after the 1966 election, it was no secret that he was the son of the widely liked Prescott Bush, who had retired from the Senate only four years before. That helped the new man on the Hill get invitations to the best cocktail parties, and encouraged the most sought-after guests to accept his invitations in return. Perhaps most important, Bush got a post on the Ways and Means committee, rivaled only by the Appropriations committee for power and influence in the House. Gerald Ford had to hustle to get placed on Appropriations after one term in the House, yet Bush got Ways and Means at the beginning of his first term. "His father asked me to help," recalled Democrat Wilbur Mills, who then chaired the committee.

The advantages Bush gained from his family connections served as a base from which he diligently built his own network. He behaved as if every one of his far-flung relationships were very important, and Nicholas Brady, a Bush confidant, said that Bush's pals joke about being among "George Bush's one thousand closest friends."

"I make friends," Bush once told me. "I believe in 'hands on.' I believe in staying in touch with people. And I learn from them. Loyalty goes two ways, to them and from them. I pride myself on that."

When Bush talks about political action he speaks in terms of personal relationships, not in terms of issues. "I know for a fact certain how I got where I am," he told a Republican rally midway through his second term as vice-president. "I got there through a lot of help from people who weren't afraid to roll up their sleeves and get behind a candidate and do grubby precinct work."

Indeed, most of the significant moves Bush has made in his political career have resulted from important doors being opened by friendly hands. Some of these ventures have not worked out well. Bush gave up his House seat in 1970 because Nixon persuaded him to make a run for the Senate. But all was not lost. Nixon then appointed him as ambassador to the United Nations. This saved Bush from fading out of the public scene, and, particularly important in the long run, gave him an initial claim to experience in foreign affairs, a credit essential to his subsequent effort to seek the presidency.

The U.N. post also provided Bush with an opportunity to show the White House it could depend upon him. He had been on the job for only six months when Charles Colson took note of his performance in a memo to White House scheduler, Pat O'Donnell, urging that Bush be used more often as a "speaking resource." Colson noted that Bush was "very good on his feet" and "generally can get media attention," and added what to Colson, who was fanatical in his loyalty to Nixon, was the highest praise of all: "He takes our line beautifully."

Bush's involvement in diplomacy was interrupted after the 1972 election, when Nixon named him chairman of the Republican National Committee. Because of Watergate, this turned out to be a fiasco. Nevertheless, Bush dutifully stuck to his post until Nixon resigned. He was then rewarded for his service to the party by the newly installed President Ford, who named him envoy to China. A year later, Ford appointed him chief of the Central Intelligence Agency.

His stewardship there provided another demonstration of the extent to which his strong sense of loyalty overrode other values. As CIA director Bush felt "growing frustration" about pressure from Congress and the press seeking information about suspected abuses of authority by the agency. "I believed in cooperating with Congress and the press," he said, "but unless CIA sources were protected, the agency couldn't carry out its national security assignment."

Bush stood up for the CIA even when it meant preventing violations of the law from being exposed and punished. In one instance, involving charges that CIA officials had lied under oath to Congress about the agency's operations in Chile, Bush fought against Justice Department and White House officials to restrict a criminal investigation of the suspected officials. Bush contended that declassifying documents and calling agency officials to testify before the federal grand jury looking into the charges would threaten national security. Finally President Ford overruled Bush and ordered him to let the investigators have what they needed. The result was that former CIA director Richard M. Helms pleaded no contest to charges of failing to testify accurately to the Congress.

Both the CIA and China posts allowed Bush to add to his experience in international affairs and his circle of friends, both of which helped him reach the White House. In addition, because his service in these jobs was shielded by the confidentiality required by diplomacy and intelligence work, he was able to continue to steer clear of what he had long sought to avoid—taking public positions on controversial issues.

CHARACTER

The traits that have contributed most to George Bush's approach to political leadership are his determination to be liked and his ambition. As with Gerald Ford, Bush's congeniality, reflected in his ingratiating manner, his optimism, and his enthusiasm, has helped him to make his way in the political world. But Bush's personality has also been a drawback. The mannerisms that some times seem congenial at other times seem contrived and artificial, rendering Bush as insincere and weak.

Bush's behavior is largely a product of his patrician upbringing with its emphasis on self-restraint. Because of the negative political connotations of the word "patrician," the very mention of it makes Bush uncomfortable. "I don't even know what the word means," he claimed during the 1980 campaign. "I'll have to look it up."

Whether Bush acknowledges it or not, the word, defined as "a person of breeding and cultivation," is an apt description of his childhood rearing. Bush's parents, according to one member of their set, "did everything right and expected the same from people around them," certainly from their children. Attending a party at which one of the speakers told a joke with a barnyard epithet, the Bushes simply bundled themselves up and walked out. One of George Bush's younger brothers, Jonathan, once told friends that he had never heard his father break wind.

Life was no less demanding at Phillips Academy, where Bush literally became a "preppie." Such boarding schools for the children of the establishment, according to Nelson Aldrich, is to provide exposure "to a simulated real world, sink or swim America." By inculcating its offspring in the same principles of self-reliance and aggressive competitiveness that inspired the founders of their family fortunes, the establishment hopes to maintain its advantageous position in society.

The reactions of youngsters growing up in such an exacting environment at home and school obviously will vary greatly. In the case of George Bush this background endowed him with traits such as self-discipline and perseverance that helped him fulfill his ambition. But by repressing his personality, it also produced an individual whose excessive body language, tendency to speak in sentence fragments, and use of euphemisms like "doo-doo" have made him vulnerable to the most devastating weapon that can be used against a public man, ridicule.

"I think created Texans are just as good as birth Texans," Texas journalist Molly Ivins wrote of Bush's perpetual yearning to be accepted in his adopted state. "Most of those who died at the Alamo had come from somewhere else. But Bush has to know that there are three things a Texan does not do. We do not use summer as a verb. We do not wear blue ties with little green whales on them. And we do not call trouble 'doo-doo.' "

Such rules are, of course, somewhat arbitrary, devised in this case by someone obviously unsympathetic to Bush. But at times his behavior has disturbed even those who admire him. During his 1984 campaign debate against Democratic vice-presidential candidate Geraldine Ferraro, Bush's enthusiasm for President Reagan seemed boundless. "The President is calling the shots," he said at one point, and at another: "I'll be honest with you, it's a joy to serve with a President who does not apologize for the United States of America." His high-pitched, quavery voice and his spastic gestures caused one close friend to remark afterward that Bush looked like he was being electrocuted.

He made matters even worse the morning after the debate when he told a group of longshoremen that "we tried to kick a little ass last night." Then, noticing that his voice was being picked up by a boom microphone, he exclaimed, "Whoops! Oh God, he heard me! Turn that thing off!" Bush claimed that "kicking ass" was just a standard expression of sports and politics, but the general impression was of a preppy candidate trying to sound macho.

In his autobiography, written with longtime associate Victor Gold, Bush contended that what his critics deride as affectations are really manifestations of his natural qualities, such as optimism. Looking back on the criticism of his behavior in the 1980 campaign after his upset victory in Iowa, Bush wrote: "Optimism in my case meant, among other things, enthusiasm, talking about 'big Mo' and America's being 'Up for the Eighties.' "

Advised by friends that these were preppy phrases that would make voters suspect that his campaign lacked substance, Bush complained that the charge of elitism was unfair. "I hadn't worn a button down shirt in twenty years," he said, adding as further proof of the baselessness of the accusation that he liked country and western music. Later he would profess a liking for bacon rinds. Nevertheless, Bush claimed that one media specialist advised him that he could do little to rebut the charge since it had something to do with "perceptions."

Of course it does. Because of how he was raised, and how he has presented himself to the public, Bush's persona is linked in the minds of many people with deep-rooted, almost primordial suspicions of the Old Money patrician class. This group was characterized by one early twentieth-century muckraker as hopelessly effete and "self-intoxicated, stupid and pretentious." Though these attitudes go back many years, they still persist today, as Bush found out during his first campaign for the presidency. After it was over he concluded, with an attempt at light-heartedness, that "the charge that I was part of a preppy conspiracy to take over the government was just something that I'd have to live with."

Whatever difficulties the public attitude toward his character caused, it did not block his steady advancement in his chosen profession. Indeed, Bush made his congeniality the instrument of the other major facet of his character, his ambition.

"He was such a congenial guy," recalls Thomas L. Ashley, a fellow member of Skull and Bones with Bush and later a Democratic congressman from Ohio. "If anyone was predicting success, Bush was at the forefront. He had this specialness about him."

Ashley did not define what made George Bush so special. But if anything set him apart, it was his enthusiasm for making new friends and his determination to please the ones he had. This feature of his character, combined with his loyalty, accounted for the reluctance to question authority that has been one of the hallmarks of his career.

Bush's character traits tending toward subservience and self-denial reinforced his adherence to the value of loyalty. The result of this combination was exemplified from start to finish by his experience as national party chairman. When his wife heard that President Nixon wanted Bush to take the national chairman's job in 1972, she argued against it. "Do anything but that," she pleaded.

Meanwhile, Bush was asked by Treasury Secretary George Shultz to be his deputy. Because this was a far more substantive job than the party chairmanship, Bush was intrigued. But he told Shultz he first had to learn what Nixon wanted him to do.

He soon found out. "The job I really want you to do, the place I really need you, is over at the National Committee, running things," Nixon told him. "This is an important time for the Republican Party, George. We have a chance to build a new coalition in the next four years, and you're the one who can do it."

Bush needed to hear no more. When he broke the news to his wife, she protested bitterly. But Bush stood firm. "Boy, you can't turn a president down," he explained.

Within a few months the hopes of building a new Republican coalition had been buried under the wreckage of Watergate, and Bush was trapped. "Most national party chairmen, Republican or Democrat, visit state and local party workers in the role of cheer leader," Bush lamented later. "My job was to serve as a bandage carrier, traveling the country to wrap up party wounds."

His aversion to questioning authority made him willing to accept Nixon's claims of innocence until the last hours of Nixon's presidency. At a Republican meeting a few weeks before Nixon's final collapse I had a drink with Bush and took the opportunity to ask him if he did not think it would be prudent to put more distance between himself and the GOP on one hand and Nixon on the other hand.

Not yet, he insisted. "I know a lot of people disagree," he told me, "but I believe the president is telling the truth."

On August 5, 1974, the White House released the "smoking gun" transcript of a taped Nixon conversation. Two days later, Bush wrote Nixon recommending that he resign. "This letter is much more difficult because of the gratitude I will always feel toward you," he said.

Bush's character was well suited to the vice-presidency, an office where self-effacement is a prime requirement. But even given that standard, Bush's dedication to subservience attracted attention. He abandoned any previous positions that differed from Reagan's, refused to discuss substantive issues, and sought to win favor among his old adversaries on the right. Once I even heard him make a point of disparaging his presidential candidacy in 1980.

"When I ran against Ronald Reagan the smartest thing that ever happened was that people elected him and not me," he told a Republican fund-raiser in Philadelphia.

If he had been so unqualified in 1980, I asked him, how could he justify seeking the presidency again in 1988, which it was already clear he intended to do.

"I've learned a lot since then," Bush replied.

Not surprisingly, Bush's behavior invited ridicule. Doonesbury cartoonist Garry Trudeau depicted him as having "put his manhood in blind trust." Conservative columnist George Will likened him to "a lap dog" for pandering to the right wing.

His image as a wimp became a matter for public debate and friends rushed to defend him. Nicholas Brady told me of the time he and Bush were caught in heavy seas aboard a launch off Florida. "The damn waves were eight feet high and everybody else's eyes were big as saucepans. But it didn't seem to bother Bush at all."

In Michigan, where the first skirmishes of the 1988 presidential campaign were being fought, Bush supporters began wearing tiny replicas of Bush's Avenger torpedo bomber, shot to pieces under him when as a World War II navy pilot he won the Distinguished Flying Cross. Pointing to the plane pinned to his lapel, Brooks Patterson, a leader of the Bush forces, told me: "This is my answer to those who try to write George Bush off as a preppy."

As Patterson realized, Bush's home life and schooling provided him, along with his preppy mannerisms, a measure of steel to bolster his ambition. No one could deny his tenacity, most dramatically demonstrated when he took his plane through heavy antiaircraft fire to strike at his target, bailed out over the Pacific, and waited for hours alone in a rubber boat until a submarine picked him up.

Under very different circumstances he demonstrated his resolve after the tide turned against him in the 1980 presidential campaign. "His campaign was living on one lung," recalled friend and ally, Victor Gold. "He kept getting knocked down in six or seven states. But he kept getting back up and that's how he got to be vice president."

Despite his spells of obsequiousness, Prescott Bush's son is not lacking in self-confidence; indeed, underneath the shield of politesse there is a touch of arrogance. I first realized that soon after the 1980 election at a party at the vice-presidential residence.

As I shook hands with Bush on the reception line I noticed he was wearing a striking suede blazer.

"That's a handsome coat," I said. "What poor animal was sacrificed to make it?"

Bush never blinked an eye. "We don't bother with animals anymore," he said. "We use humans."

Since this riposte was intended as jest, perhaps it is wrong to attach much significance to it. Nevertheless, I heard Bush display the same cavalier attitude in a more serious context after he had become president. At a press conference Bush was asked about the widely heard contention that the negativism marking the 1989 gubernatorial campaigns in Virginia and New Jersey was a product of the emphasis on negativism in his own campaign the year before.

"I don't have to stand here and defend the campaign of 1988," Bush replied. "I'd be perfectly prepared to do it, but I was elected."

Bush had a point. The campaign was over and he had won. Now, however, he would have to defend his presidency.

THE CHALLENGE

History will judge Bush on his management of the two great issues of his time—the huge budget deficit which has crippled the federal government's ability to meet long-neglected domestic needs, and the changing nature of the post-Cold War world. His response will, of course, depend in part on events outside his control and on the outcome of the Persian Gulf crisis which can only be guessed at this time.

Given his ideology, values, and character as reflected by his previous record in politics, however, his prospects for success are dubious. This conclusion is reinforced by his start in the presidency, which left the country with only a hazy impression of his beliefs and the direction in which he wanted to lead.

His inaugural address offered him an obvious opportunity to begin defining himself as a political leader, but equivocation pervaded his speech. At some points Bush sounded vigorous and commanding. "A new breeze is blowing—and a nation refreshed by freedom stands ready to push on," he declared. "There is new ground to be broken and new action to be taken."

He had scarcely sounded this clarion call, however, when he in effect retracted it. "Our funds are low," he warned. "We have a deficit to bring down. We have more will than wallet," he said, a puzzling contention since with sufficient will presumably the money could be found to fatten the wallet.

The temporizing tone of the inaugural set the theme for the presidency that has followed. Bush's proposed budget for 1991 included an essay by his budget director, Richard Darman, who painted a bleak picture of a nation with abysmally low savings rates and an inadequate education system, facing the need for tens of billions in additional future revenues to pay for what Darman called "the hidden Pac-Men of government," such as soaring health costs. Yet the budget itself made little attempt to address the realities sketched in Darman's rhetoric.

Contributing to the presidential reluctance to act boldly was his continued inability to resolve the conflict between his establishment heritage and the neopopulist credos to which he committed himself as Reagan's vice-president.

The establishment attitude, with its sense of noblesse oblige, was evident in his inaugural rhetoric. "America is never wholly herself unless she is engaged in high moral principle. We as a people have such a purpose today. It is to make kinder the face of the nation and gentler the face of the world."

But for all this high-mindedness, the neopopulist political realities had significant impact on both Bush's utterances and his actions. When the Supreme Court ruled that protestors burning an American flag were protected by the First Amendment, Bush returned to the patriotic themes he had emphasized in his presidential campaign. He called upon Congress to amend the constitution by banning flag burning, insisting that the symbolic importance of the flag justified the infringement of free speech. Positioning himself in front of the bronze memorial to the marines who raised the stars and stripes on Iwo Jima in World War II, he declared to television cameras: "If the debate here is about liberty, then we cannot turn our backs on those who fought to win it for us."

Though the campaign promises Bush made as a candidate were modest, they were more than a match for his actions as president. The one promise he seemed most determined to keep was his "read my lips" campaign pledge not to raise taxes. Many economists contended that a tax increase was badly needed to restore the federal government to fiscal health. What is more, they contended financing was needed for the problems Bush himself cited in his inaugural and in his budget proposal. But Bush rejected that view and instead called for a new tax cut, this one on capital gains. Though he had pledged to make himself "the education president," the education budget proposal he introduced in his first year in office did not keep pace with inflation. He had vowed in his first major presidential address to put a stop to the "scourge" of drugs. But when Bush finally unveiled his drug program, he called for a spending increase of less than $1 billion, and he emphasized law enforcement to punish drug traffickers rather than longer-term measures such as treatment and prevention.

Not until nearly halfway through his second year in the White House did Bush acknowledge the seriousness of the budget-deficit problem that he had faced from the beginning of his presidency, calling upon Democratic congressional leaders to join with him to devise a solution. What made this appeal notable was that for the first time in his tenure he allowed for the possibility of a tax increase.

In a generally admiring analysis of Bush during his first year in the White House, Michael Duffy wrote in *Time*: "Bush generally feels more at home with foreign policy than domestic issues." That preference is easy to understand, since presidents are generally granted more freedom of action with problems abroad than at home. Even so, in international affairs Bush's major actions have been mainly reactions.

Thus his proposal at the 1989 NATO summit to reduce U.S. conventional forces in Europe was a response to the disarmament proposals Soviet leader Mikhail Gorbachev had been putting forward for months. Also reactive in good part was Bush's order to U.S. troops to invade Panama just before his first Christmas in the White House. The decision to attack, the *Washington Post* reported, was spurred by the heavy criticism Bush had received for his failure to take advantage of the abortive military coup launched against Panamanian ruler Manuel Noriega in October 1989. The invasion succeeded in toppling Noriega, but raised a host of unanswered questions about the future of Panama and about future U.S. relations with other Latin American countries aggrieved by the assault on Panama.

Bush's action on Panama by contrast underlined his passivity in facing the far more profound problem facing the U.S. as a result of the dissolution of the Soviet empire in Eastern Europe. Bush's slowness to develop U.S. initiatives in these countries, his haste in making diplomatic overtures to China only a month after the slaughter of pro-democracy demonstrators in Tiananmen Square, and his adventure in Panama were all part of a pattern. They reflected a management of foreign affairs that, as in domestic policy, appeared driven by short-term, narrow considerations rather than any broad overview.

The Panama invasion gave Bush's already high poll ratings another boost, raising them above that of any other post–World War II presidents at a comparable point in their terms. But a *Washington Post* survey taken at the same time showed that while approval support for Bush was widespread, it was also shallow.

Perhaps the most striking measure of how little impact the public believed Bush was having on the government he headed was that when asked who has the most power in Washington, 53% of those interviewed said Congress, only 15% the president.

In his first eighteen months in the White House, as polling results indicated, Bush had succeeded in lowering public expectations to the level where he could easily meet them. However, this relativist attitude toward presidential leadership could last only so long. By failing to establish a clear ideological identity for himself and a direction for his presidency, Bush had forfeited the chance to take command of the country. Instead he coasted on a tide of good fortune, buoyed by economic stability at home and the collapse of the communist threat abroad. But it was inevitable that sooner or later the force of events would expose the leadership vacuum surrounding Bush's presidency, and remind him and the country of the problems he had sought to avoid.

Bush's luck began to turn in the second summer of his presidency. First, the economy dipped alarmingly. A growing number of economists concluded that the country was either in a recession or certainly headed there, and opinion polls showed that this bleak perception was shared by a majority of the citizenry.

On top of that, the costly convulsions of the savings and loan industry, first labeled a mess and then a scandal, now reached crisis proportions. The lax hand of government regulators during the booming eighties, overspeculation, and the collapse of energy and real estate industries in the Southwest had wrought havoc with the savings and loan industry as the Reagan presidency came to an end.

Once in office, Bush proposed a plan to close or sell hundreds of institutions and revamp the federal regulating system, but estimates of the costs skyrocketed beyond his initial predictions. Although Democrats were themselves vulnerable on the issue because many of their congressmen had taken fat campaign contributions from the savings and loan industry, their leaders seized the initiative, accusing Bush of bungling the cleanup of the crisis by paying off uninsured depositors and failing to prosecute savings and loan malefactors. Adding to Bush's embarrassment, his son Neil emerged as a culprit, having been accused of conflict of interest in his role as a director of a failed thrift institution in Denver.

With the thrift-industry bailout adding tens of billions to federal expenses, Bush came to realize that he had no choice but to retract his "read my lips" opposition to any increase in taxes that had been the centerpiece of the "progrowth" economic policies he had relied on during his presidential campaign. Democrats immediately charged that the president's real reason for raising taxes was to ensure that the Treasury had enough funds to pay off his wealthy friends in the savings and loan industry. "We have found the one cause for which George Bush is willing to break his 'no new taxes' pledge—the bankers and speculators who ran the savings and loan industry into the ground," contended Democratic National Chairman Ronald Brown.

Vociferous protests also came from within Bush's own party. Many Republicans complained that Bush should have stood fast against the Democrats, forcing them to accept the sequestration of funds threatened under the Gramm-Rudman deficit-reduction law, rather than yield to the pressure for added revenue. By giving ground on taxes, they charged, Bush had thrown away the one issue which more than any other served to define the two parties' differences to the GOP's advantage.

In defiance of the president's new position, a majority of the Republican members of the House of Representatives went on record against a tax increase. And in a number of states Republican candidates who had been running on a no-new-taxes platform stuck to their guns, even making a point of declaring their independence from their president and his newly declared position on tax increases.

This train of negative events had a cumulative impact on public attitudes, causing anxiety for Republicans as the midterm congressional elections approached. A survey by Market Opinion Research, a respected Republican polling form, showed that by a margin of roughly two to one, Americans believed that the country was heading down "the wrong track," a figure that one Republican congressional campaign strategist said was "horrendous." Though the president still got high marks in opinion surveys, criticism from influential journalists was increasing. "Bush is sailing without a rudder and a map," Fred Barnes wrote in the *New Republic*. "His presidency has no definition, no political purpose in the short run other than averting a serious fight."

Then, more than six thousand miles from the White House, came the event which suddenly energized Bush's hitherto lethargic presidency. Saddam Hussein, despotic ruler of Iraq, seeking to aggrandize his oil wealth to rebuild his country after its prolonged war with Iran, sent his battle-seasoned legions to conquer neighboring Kuwait, a task they accomplished within twenty-four hours. Frustrated by the complex problems that faced him, Bush seized upon this aggression not only as an outlet for the ambition which was one of the dominant features of his character but also as a welcome distraction from domestic issues. By his response Bush sought to transform the perception of himself from that of a temporizing caretaker, a weak and indecisive figure who was in danger of losing his grip on his own party, into that of a dynamic and forceful world leader.

To Bush, the Gulf crisis appeared to represent what the *Wall Street Journal* described as a "crucial opportunity to define his presidency," a belief widely expressed at the time by a press corps caught up in the drama of events. But this view overlooked what Bush had demonstrated about himself during the first eighteen months of his stewardship. By the time Iraq marched against Kuwait, the Bush presidency had already been well defined. In fact, both the makings of the Gulf crisis as well as Bush's response to it reflected the reactive leadership pattern Bush had established not only in the Oval Office but throughout his public career.

The threat to the country's economic and political security that did not become apparent to the president until the Iraqi seizure of Kuwait was not an overnight development. Rather, it had its roots in Bush's failure during the previous months to come to terms with the new global realities spawned by the collapse of the old order behind what was once the Iron Curtain.

As Strobe Talbott recalled, during the Cold War era U.S. policy in the Mideast had consisted of "regarding the Gulf as a giant gas station in a rough part of town threatened by pro-Moscow gangs and the Soviets themselves." U.S. determination to resist Soviet intrusion in the region served to maintain the status quo by a sort of balance of deterrence. But the reality to which Bush failed to respond was that in the Mideast, as elsewhere in the world, the removal of the Soviet threat created new dangers—and also new opportunities for developing alliances based on mutual interests with regional powers.

This realization should at the least have brought about a cold-eyed assessment of Saddam Hussein's regime and his goals. Instead the Bush Administration, transfixed by Iraq's enmity against Iran, America's decade-long antagonist in the Middle East, persisted in relying on the short-sighted notion that "the enemy of my enemy is my friend," a guideline left over from the Cold War.

Moreover, Bush valued Hussein not only as a bulwark against the Islamic extremism preached in Teheran, but also as a multi-billion-dollar trading partner, particularly as a big customer for American grain. Thus as late as July 31, with 100,000 of Saddam Hussein's troops already massed for the seizure of Kuwait that would take place two days later, the State Department opposed congressional attempts to end U.S. trade credits to Iraq as punishment for its human-rights abuses and as a curb on its increasing aggressiveness, arguing that American farmers and other exporters would suffer the most from such sanctions. The reasonable inference for Hussein to draw was that the U.S. would not come to the defense of Kuwait.

Much the same impression had been given directly to Hussein a week earlier when he summoned the U.S. Ambassador to Baghdad, April Glaspie, to a meeting in which he asserted that his demands upon Kuwait constituted a matter that should be left for Arab countries to resolve without U.S. interference. The ambassador appeared to accept that contention by telling her host, "We have no opinion on Arab-Arab conflicts like your border disagreement with Kuwait."

The lack of understanding and imagination on foreign policy was matched on the domestic side. The Iraqi aggression dramatized the long-standing need for a federal energy policy placing heavy emphasis on conservation. This requirement Bush had almost entirely overlooked, while U.S. oil production dropped and U.S. imports of oil rose sharply.

When the Mideast crisis erupted, the Energy Department, at the president's request, had been going about the business of developing a new energy policy at a markedly leisurely pace—delivery to Congress was not scheduled until the spring of 1991. Following the seizure of Kuwait, Energy Secretary James D. Watkins declared that the administration would follow a "short-term strategy" for encouraging conservation rather than expedite the timetable for developing a full-scale policy. Watkins said the administration was not yet prepared to answer such critical questions as whether the government should press for higher auto mileage standards, nuclear power, or energy taxes.

The president himself plainly had little interest in conservation measures. When a reporter pointed out that he had not called upon Americans to conserve energy, he replied limply, "I call upon Americans to conserve." Asked about whether conservation should extend to his speedboat, *Fidelity*, in which he had been tooling around the waters off his summer vacation retreat at Kennebunkport, Bush said, "I'm going to keep using my boat. And I hope the rest of America will prudently recreate."

What he lacked in ideological forethought he sought to make up for by falling back on the network of personal connections that were the expression of his value structure. In this case the connections extended around the world and reached to the highest levels of power. In this realm, where he could operate behind the scenes one-on-one, where he did not have to explain his actions in terms of his beliefs, Bush was supremely confident, and notably effective in forging a global alliance against Iraq.

Once having done this, the president might well have waited for the economic sanctions backed by the United Nations to work against Hussein, while dispatching only a minimal force to Saudi Arabia as an earnest of the U.S. intention to protect that country against invasion. Instead he called up the reserves and ordered a deployment the scale of which greatly increased the danger of outright hostilities.

Once again Bush's preference for the foreign-policy side of the presidency was evident. This was the arena in which U.N. Ambassador Bush and C.I.A. Director Bush had wielded far more responsibility and had far more experience than Congressman Bush or Vice-President Bush had had in domestic policy. But Bush had another reason at least as important to feel uninhibited to act in foreign affairs. He was confident that in a confrontation with a foreign power, with national honor and security at stake, he would not face the challenging questions from the press and Congress that would hound his actions on the domestic front.

This confidence was borne out by the early reaction to his response to the Iraqi thrust into Kuwait. When a reporter asked the president, right after his assertion that the conquest of Kuwait "will not stand," how he proposed to force Saddam Hussein to dismantle the puppet government he had just set up and withdraw from the country he had just annexed, Bush's only reply was "Just wait, watch, and learn." It soon became evident that Bush himself had no clear idea of how he would accomplish this objective either. But the press did not pursue the question, which was of course the central conundrum underlying the American adventure in the Gulf. Instead, many of the same writers and publications which had been disdainful of Bush to the point of contempt now changed their tune and joined in a hymn of praise to the commander-in-chief.

Time, which not so many months before had bemoaned "The Can't Do Government" headed by Bush, now pictured the president next to the nuclear-powered U.S.S. *Dwight Eisenhower* on its way through the Suez Canal under the headline "Read My Ships." Meanwhile *Newsweek* attributed Bush's conduct to "the values of the old WASP establishment," which "prized not only good breeding and proper manners but martial virility and moral certitude." In the *New Republic*, Fred Barnes, only two weeks after he had dismissed Bush as a president "without a rudder and a map," lauded his "dazzling performance," hailing his response to the invasion as "the finest moment" of the Bush presidency.

As for Congress, the critical faculties of most of its members seemed at least initially deadened by polling figures showing that more than 70 percent of Americans, manifesting reflexive patriotic impulses, supported the president's response to the Iraqi aggression. In ordering the U.S. troop buildup in Saudia Arabia, Bush had disregarded the War Powers Resolution that Congress had enacted as a result of Vietnam to force presidents to consult with Congress before deploying U.S. forces in harm's way. But when I asked Democratic Senator Dale Bumpers of Arkansas, a vigorous supporter of the law in the past, whether he would challenge Bush on that issue, he candidly replied, "I am not going to lead the charge because anybody who does that will get his brains beat out."

Congressman Robert Torricelli of New Jersey did try to press Secretary of State Baker on the Administration's decision to ignore the War Powers Resolution during Baker's testimony at the House Foreign Affairs Committee. But committee chairman and fellow Democrat Dante Fascell of Florida cut him off, saying, "We need to get on to our questioning."

"After Vietnam there was this deep feeling that never again would the nation face combat without our people understanding our objectives," Torricelli said later. "The evidence is that in modern America, 'never again' comes very soon."

Bush's own interest in the past did not seem to extend beyond his obvious determination not to follow the dismal example Jimmy Carter had set in responding to the seizure of American hostages in Teheran. Thus, in the critical first weeks of the crisis, as Bush faced critical decisions at home and abroad, he insisted on completing his vacation at Kennebunkport, as if to demonstrate that, unlike Carter, he would not himself become a hostage to the crisis.

He ignored other more salient lessons, however. The most important conclusion to be drawn from Johnson's and Nixon's Vietnam experiences, from Kennedy's handling of the Cuban missile crisis, from Truman's response to the invasion of Korea, is that success in meeting foreign-policy challenges to presidential leadership requires a clear statement of goals and principles to rally and sustain public support. But such a response required the sort of firm ideological framework that Bush clearly lacked and indeed to which he had always had a strong aversion.

Behaving more like the director of central intelligence than the president, Bush was notably reluctant to explain himself, as his early "wait, watch, and learn" response had suggested. Moreover, the explanations he did offer were unconvincing and inconsistent. At times he justified the American commitment in the Mideast on grounds of high principle. "America stands where it always has, against aggression, against those who would use force to replace the rule of law," he told the Veterans of Foreign Wars.

Yet the post-war world had seen a host of other aggressions, ranging from the Indian seizure of Goa in 1961 to the Soviet thrust into Afghanistan in 1979, to which the U.S. had not responded on a scale comparable to Operation Desert Shield. As far as international law was concerned, the U.S. had flouted its claims whenever it seemed convenient—under President Reagan when it had invaded Grenada and mined Nicaraguan waters, and under Bush himself only a few months prior to Operation Desert Shield by invading Panama.

Further undermining the assertion of principle was the hasty alliance formed with Syrian President Hafez Assad, whose regime is believed to have instigated the suicide bombing in Beirut that killed more than two hundred Marines and is notorious for sheltering the most ruthless of terrorists. This relationship suggested that Desert Shield is being driven not by principle but by the same sort of expediency that led the U.S. earlier to consort with Saddam Hussein himself.

In more practical terms, the president described the Iraqi threat to "the world's great oil reserves" as endangering "our way of life, our own freedom, and the freedom of friendly countries." As justification for such a far-reaching national commitment, this seemed crass even to political leaders who were trying to help Bush rally support. "I think that the American people are not willing to have their children in harm's way to protect cheap oil prices in the U.S.," said Democratic House Majority Leader Richard Gephardt of Missouri, who was chosen by his party to publicly pledge its support for Bush's Gulf policies.

In addition, on close scrutiny the threat to oil supplies posed by Iraq appears considerably overdrawn. As Douglas Bandow, a former policy adviser in the Reagan White House pointed out, even if Hussein were to seize all the current oil supplies in the Gulf, it would do him no good to hold it off the market, since the price increases that would result would only benefit his competitors. The most Hussein can do to satisfy his greed is to cut production marginally and try to convince other oil producers to do the same. That means the U.S. would pay more for oil, but that burden would hardly be as great as the expense of Operation Desert Shield. As far as oil reserves are concerned, the known total has increased by 30 percent in the past five years and seems likely to continue to expand rapidly, particularly if higher prices create additional incentive.

No wonder the public seemed confused. Asked what was the main reason for U.S. Mideast involvement, about half of those interviewed in a *Los Angeles Times* poll while the buildup was in full swing cited protecting oil interests, while 45 percent gave preventing aggression as the answer.

During the congressional recess that followed the Iraqi invasion, lawmakers returning home to campaign found their constituents staunch in their support of the president for the time being but uneasy about what the future would bring. Mostly they hoped the Gulf crisis would soon be over. Republican Congressman Howard Coble of North Carolina noted that voters in his district wanted Bush to make a major address offering a clear definition of the country's goals in the Mideast. "I don't want to be presumptuous enough to pick up the phone to tell him that, but I think he needs to do that soon," he said. "I think it's fireside chat time."

Not until September 11, nearly six weeks after Bush had committed the U.S. to hold "a line in the sand," did he make a full-scale address to the American people. In a way his speech was reminiscent of Lyndon Johnson's rhetoric on the Vietnam War, relying on glittering generalities that glossed over the complex realities of the crisis. The president promised a joint session of Congress and an anxious public that "out of these troubled times . . . a new world order can emerge," but offered no specifics on how that world would differ from the old. He warned that "at home the material cost of our leadership can be steep," but did not say what that price might be or who would pay it. One analyst pointed out that although Bush's rhetoric sought to evoke memories of Winston's Churchill's stand against aggression, "Churchill went on to promise blood, sweat, and tears. Bush promises a cut in the capital-gains tax."

Bush fervently asked for support—"If there ever was a time to put country before self and patriotism before party, the time is now"—and reiterated his goal of forcing the Iraqis out of Kuwait—"We will not let this aggression stand." But he did not clarify the means he would use to achieve this end or how he would deal with the far-reaching consequences of his actions.

Bush's adventure in the Gulf represented both an enormous distraction from the nation's fundamental problems and a dangerous gamble. The most obvious risk is that the U.S. could become involved in a shooting war under circumstances which reminded even Bush's long-time supporters of the quagmire that Vietnam became. "If Bush is planning on a land war in the Mideast, count me out," said Iowa Congressman Tom Tauke, an early and active supporter of Bush's candidacy for his party's nomination in 1988.

Bush has contended that the Iraqi invasion of Kuwait threatens the national interest. But the national interest is multifold, and Bush's decision to make the thwarting of Iraq the first priority of U.S. foreign policy in itself creates other perils. In the course of aligning the coalition against Hussein, Bush has drawn the Soviet Union into a prominent role in Mideast power politics, established an alliance of convenience with Hafez Assad of Syria, and committed his own country to maintaining its influence in the region for an indefinite period under unknown conditions. Separately and together these decisions would have implications for U.S. interests abroad that will take years to unfold.

The risks at home are fully as serious. The commitment to Desert Shield has not only diverted attention from critical domestic problems, it threatens to aggravate them. The more than $40 million-a-day cost of the U.S. military buildup, falling on a federal government already desperately strapped by the savings and loan bailout and a slowing economy, threatens to send the budget deficit soaring into the fiscal stratosphere.

"We really can't afford to spend that kind of money," Jay White, a scrap dealer in Monticello, Iowa, near Cedar Rapids, and a county coordinator for a Republican House candidate told me. "I'm already paying twenty-five to thirty percent of my income in taxes and I don't want to pay any more."

Meanwhile, as the *Wall Street Journal* pointed out, the jump in oil prices as a result of the Gulf crisis "continued pushing the U.S. economy toward recession at a time when unprecedented corporate debt and a weak financial system make recession far more perilous than usual." Moreover, the huge budget deficit limits the president's ability to use the standard weapons of increased spending or tax cuts to spur the economy.

Not only is the Mideast effort out of proportion, but by dealing with it purely in military rather than political terms, Bush is ignoring the change in international competition which has made economic power more important than military. With the supremacy of economic forces, as one analyst noted, "Disposable capital displaces firepower, product innovation counts more than military research, and development and systematic market penetration replaces garrison bases."

Pointing to the unwillingness of Japan and other prosperous countries more dependent on Mideast oil than the U.S. to share equitably in the burden of confronting Hussein, the columnist anad erstwhile Democratic political operative Mark Shields wrote:

> Toward the Japanese we are in no position to impose a levy; we can only submit a plea that is the relationship between a debtor, us, and our principal creditor, Japan. Events in the Persian Gulf cannot be divorced from our continuing budget deficits at home and the sad reality that the United States government cannot meet its own payroll and obligations with our borrowing from Japanese bankers.

Some believe that Bush can guarantee his re-election in 1992 by achieving success or at least the appearance of success in the Mideast. Typical of such thinking was the advice offered in a newsletter to his clients by a stock market analyst for a major securities firm:

> What if the Middle East economic sanctions or military actions are successful? George Bush may be able to claim the 1992 election by acclamation. He also may claim to have brought about a major improvement in the economy. Consumer confidence has been weakening for months. Confidence in the banking system has fallen because of problems with the

thrift industry and to a lesser degree in commercial banks. A successful resolution of the Middle East situation could easily make Americans believe that we have regained some of our lost international clout. That would make us all feel better—and when we feel better we spend more.

Such forecasts, however, reflect mainly the pseudo-sophisticated view of politics held among the communications and business elite. They believe that the media age offers a president an unlimited potential for manipulating symbols and images into artful concoctions that the public will accept as substitutes for reality. Such faith has been founded in part on a misunderstanding of the successes of the Reagan presidency. Reagan's support was not based on his vaunted skills of political prestidigitation, as some suppose. Rather, it was derived from his strong convictions and ultimately on his ability to persuade a substantial majority that his leadership was in their best interests.

Bush will be held to no less rigorous a standard. In the 1992 election voters are bound to ask the same question Reagan raised in the 1980 campaign: "Are you better off than you were four years ago?" and their answer is likely to be decisive as to the result.

Driving Iraqi forces from Kuwait, either by force of arms or economic pressure, would certainly greatly enhance Bush's prestige and popularity, and present him with an enviable opportunity to muster backing for his goals at home and abroad. Given such an opportunity by his success in the Cuban missile crisis, John Kennedy forged the historic agreement with the Soviet Union on nuclear-test-ban treaties. If the Middle East crisis is brought to a swift and successful conclusion, Bush's leadership will be tested by his ability to exploit that success. If on the other hand, the confrontation is prolonged, his leadership will be tested even more severely by his ability to maintain public support for the commitment he has made.

Whatever the outcome of Desert Shield, the success or failure of the forty-first president will still depend on how he responds to the two major challenges facing his presidency. At home, he needs through fiscal discipline to restore the federal government's ability to meet its responsibilities, in particular the reinvigoration of the economy; while abroad he must define a new role for his country in a changing world. In both instances, if Bush is to rally public support he must establish a strong identity for himself and a clear direction for his presidency, so that he can govern by actions, not reactions.

CHAPTER 11

A Leadership Primer

In the fall of 1972, as Richard Nixon headed toward his sweeping re-election victory, Vice-President Spiro Agnew was already being widely discussed as a likely Republican candidate for the presidency in 1976. Agnew himself was glad to encourage such talk and took the time to explain to me why he had no misgivings about his ability to handle the presidency:

"You have to evaluate not yourself against the job as much as yourself against the people who can fill the job," said Agnew, whose chief qualification for the White House, aside from fulfilling the limited demands of the vice-presidency, consisted of two years as governor of Maryland. "And I don't feel that I have any worries in that respect."

Within a year of that conversation Agnew's prospects for the presidency had been destroyed by the trail of graft and corruption he left behind in Maryland. But the winner of the 1976 election turned out to be another former governor, Jimmy Carter, who after meeting some of the presidential contenders had reacted much as Agnew had. "I lost my feeling of awe about presidents," Carter wrote later. "This is not meant as a criticism of them, but it is merely a simple statement of fact."

The prospect that every four years any politician with a healthy ego can offer himself for the presidency and stand a fair chance of success is a relatively recent phenomenon. This development underlines the importance to the average citizen of being able to make his own measurement of candidates for the White House. In the early years of the modern presidency the leaders of political parties still controlled the selection of presidential contenders, relying heavily on an informal system of peer

291

review. The party bosses were not necessarily possessed of the loftiest motives or the best judgment, but they could base their choices on first-hand knowledge of the beliefs, values, and character of presidential prospects, and were thus able to screen out candidates who had little to offer beyond their ambition.

But both of our major political parties have steadily lost power in recent years because of social and economic change—and this has cost party bosses their control of the presidential selection process. Instead of candidates being chosen by their peers, they choose themselves, as Agnew and Carter did. The result is that the ordinary voter facing a crowded field of self-selected contenders urgently needs enough information about the presidency to do his own screening.

The presidential successes and failures recounted here can help the voter be his own political boss. These episodes illuminate the leadership choices of incumbent chief executives. More than that, applying the lessons of these experiences to the combination of leadership elements a presidential candidate would bring to the White House can help predict his performance as chief executive.

The four presidents who achieved some measure of success in meeting their challenges were not without defects in ideology, values, and character. But all followed one fundamental principle—they established clear objectives and fought for them. They were able to do this because they had strong ideological foundations, which aided them to identify their goals. Just as important, they were able to use their values and character to support their ideology by mobilizing public support for these goals. Moreover, in each case a conscientious voter would have been able to detect their potential strengths when they first sought the White House.

As Harry Truman whistle-stopped around the country in 1948, he pledged to protect the gains made by the New Deal. Time and again the underdog president spelled out what Democrats had done for unions, workers, farmers, and the elderly—and what they stood to lose if the Republicans captured the presidency.

Well before the 1948 campaign Truman had made plain his commitment to the Democratic party's deep-rooted tradition of government activism. In the Senate he had denounced the malefactions of the railroad holding companies; as an unelected president, his activist ideas led Republicans to charge him with "out New Dealing the New Deal."

Truman's identification with the underdog, which was at the heart of his value system, was well suited to the populist themes of his ideology. Similarly, his assertive character fit well with the activism inherent in his political beliefs and bolstered the loyalty of his supporters.

But Truman's aggressive manner also hardened his opposition and sometimes alienated potential supporters. This contributed to his low poll standings at the end of his presidency, when the country was divided over his handling of the Korean War.

Operating under the shadow of nuclear holocaust, John Kennedy aimed at slowing the arms race. Even as he announced the blockade of Cuba in the midst of the 1962 missile crisis, he held out hope for an eventual accord on nuclear arms. Later, seeking support for his test-ban treaty, he called peace "the necessary rational end of rational men."

Despite the skepticism that marked his early career, Kennedy drew on the same activist ideological tradition as Truman did. "This contest is not between the vice president and myself," he declared running against Richard Nixon in 1960. "This contest is between the Democratic Party and the Republican Party and in that regard there is no contest."

The rationalism underlying Kennedy's values, along with his disciplined character, aided his ability to adjust his ideology to changing political realities. He had demonstrated this skill when he was still in the Senate by criticizing France's vain effort to crush the Algerian rebellion, a speech betokening a fresh approach to the emerging nations of the Third World.

Kennedy had two flaws that were the other sides of his values and character. His drive for success caused him him to seek power before he was fully ready for it, and his streak of self-indulgence led to sexual excesses and macho behavior.

Early in his presidency, Richard Nixon fought for the chance to wage successful diplomacy with the two communist giants—China and the Soviet Union. Confronting the powerful Vietnam protest movement head-on, he called upon the silent majority to help him "win the war in a way we can win the peace."

Unlike Democrats Truman and Kennedy, Republican Nixon's ideology was derived not so much from his party as from his socioeconomic stratum. As spokesman for the middle class he was a man of the center, a position best described by its relationship to the ideological extremes. "What this country needs is not an adm [sic] which will represent big business, nor one which will represent big labor," he wrote in drafting his first campaign speech in 1946, "but one that will stand for the interests of *all* the people of the country."

This made sense to the middle-class voters Nixon was trying to reach. And Nixon's middle-class values and his strong-willed character at first meshed well with the polarizing strategy he developed to champion middle-class interests. But the frictions he generated, which had marked his career from the start and which were aggravated by the intensity of his character, ultimately offended middle-class sensibilities and brought him down.

With inflation rampaging across the land, Ronald Reagan promised Americans in the closing days of his 1980 campaign that he would get government off their backs and revive the economy.

Reagan's ideology was largely homemade, and for that reason more persuasive to many citizens. "There is no left or right, only an up or down," Reagan contended. "Up to the maximum of individual freedom consistent with law and order, or down to the ant heap of totalitarianism." From the time he uttered those words, on behalf of Barry Goldwater's doomed presidential candidacy in 1964, Reagan became the undisputed leader of the right.

Inconsistencies in his reasoning—"He was not one for fine theory spinning or jesuitical hairsplitting," wrote one presidential scholar—later produced flaws in his policies. But Reagan's simplistic thinking was an asset in helping him pull together the intellectually diverse threads of the conservative movement.

His reverence for the values of the past helped to dramatize the antigovernment creed that was fundamental to his ideology. His character, unlike Truman's, was conciliatory, which served the purpose of moderating the harshness of his values and ideology.

But Reagan's character, like Truman's, also created problems. His lack of self-discipline was reflected in the inconsistencies of his ideology, which left their mark on his economic legacy to the nation. His negligence in tending to his responsibilities allowed his aides to run amok in the Iran-Contra affair.

By contrast with the successful leaders, the failed presidents were unable to establish meaningful objectives the public could understand. Their ideological defects could not be redeemed by their characters and values. Like the strengths of the successful presidents, these weaknesses also could have been detected by discerning voters.

Eisenhower in responding to the civil rights revolution articulated no goal except a negative one—the avoidance of controversy. His ideological approach, shaped by his military experience, was to operate behind the scenes. "Everyone who's yapping now would be cheering," he once said about criticism of his self-imposed restraint, "if only I would do my 'leading' in public—where they could *see* me. Well, I can't do that."

His congressional testimony against military integration before he officially entered politics and his decision to woo Southern whites while ignoring Negroes in the 1952 campaign were among the actions and utterances that foreshadowed his passive response to the crisis over school desegregation.

In the White House, Eisenhower's emphasis on teamwork as a value, and his determination to be liked, both lifelong attributes, reinforced his tendency to inaction.

"On this issue, there must be no delay, no hesitation, no compromise with our purpose," Lyndon Johnson told Congress in calling for passage of the Voting Rights Act in 1965. But Johnson approached nearly every issue with this same unrelenting urgency. He needed an unending stream of results to fuel his ideological strategy of consensus.

His emphasis on consensus grew out of his experience in Texas politics and in the Senate. His manipulative tactics as majority leader and his unwillingness to discuss Vietnam in the 1964 campaign presaged his refusal to choose between waging the war in Vietnam and pressing the Great Society reforms.

Johnson's character and values compounded his problems. His value system, with its goal of success, drove his ideology in one direction—toward the vigorous use of government. But from the start of his career, his anxiety to avoid conflict impelled him away from the contentiousness that government activism inevitably begets and led him down the enervating path of consensus.

Ford's reasons for pardoning Nixon, his most critical leadership challenge, were so confused he could not convey them to the public.

By the time voters had the chance to decide for the first time whether to vote for him for president in 1976, Ford had already made plain his inability to outgrow the ideological limits of the House of Representatives. Just as his pardon of Nixon revealed a lack of sufficient understanding of the implications of Watergate to deal effectively with the aftermath of the scandal, his so-called veto strategy against the Democratic-controlled Congress demonstrated his intellectual barrenness.

Rather than ideology, Ford relied on his value system, with its stress on personal loyalty, in making his fateful decision to pardon Nixon.

Instead of concentrating on one feasible objective in facing the challenges of his presidency, Carter at times reached for goals beyond his grasp and other times drove himself and his aides in several directions at once.

Having resisted adopting any coherent ideological approach during his career in Georgia politics, Carter could hardly have been expected to shift his stance once he gained the White House—and he did not. His self-absorbed character worked against it.

Carter fell into much the same trap as Ford. Lacking a coherent ideology, he sought to substitute his values, his belief in faith and competence, and tried to rely on them as an approach to politics. As a consequence, he was never able to build the political base a president needs.

As formidable as the challenges faced by these eight chief executives were, the task of presidential leadership is likely to become even more difficult in the years ahead. One major reason is the continuing decline in political parties, which has been both cause and consequence of an ideological vacuum in the political system. This void threatens to deprive future presidents of support for the one element of leadership in which outside support is both appropriate and most needed. The condition affects both parties, but its impact is particularly striking in the Democratic party, which for so long relied on the New Deal philosophy of Franklin Roosevelt to maintain itself as the nation's majority party.

When the band struck up "Happy Days Are Here Again" at the 1988 Democratic national convention, it was a poignant reminder of those days of ideological glory. The cheerful ditty had been Roosevelt's anthem when he forged the coalition of interest groups that swept him and his party to four presidential victories. The trouble was that the old marching song has stood the test of time better than the old Democratic coalition.

In Roosevelt's day, the Democrats constructed seemingly invincible majorities by mustering behind the New Deal banner whites in the then Solid South and blue-collar workers, Catholics, blacks, and Jews in the cities of the North and West. And even after Roosevelt's death, the formula continued to work; it helped both Harry Truman and John Kennedy win election and govern afterward. But when Jimmy Carter entered the White House after the 1977 election, it was already clear that the ideological appeal behind the coalition needed refurbishing.

This Carter was unable to do. And so by the time Michael Dukakis rose to accept the 1988 nomination, a good many Southern whites, Catholics, and blue-collar workers had turned their backs on the Democratic party. As for blacks and Jews, while most remained in Democratic ranks, the rising tensions between them over such issues as big-city crime and affirmative action are straining the bonds of what remains of Roosevelt's old alliance.

As Berkeley political scientist and old-line Democratic activist Austin Ranney put it: "The old fault lines of American politics—when you tapped hard, that's where the cleavages would fall—those fault lines have reformed."

The reasons for these shifts in loyalties go far beyond the limitations of Dukakis or any other presidential candidate. Rather, they are the result of the social and economic revolutions that transformed the United States in the half century since Roosevelt forged the Democratic coalition and made the New Deal ideology dominant. A flood tide of change—the rise in personal income, proliferation of the suburbs, advent of television, growth of high-technology enterprises and white-collar employment, decline of smokestack industries and blue-collar jobs—all of these and more have been sweeping the New Deal constituencies away from their traditional roots.

Fewer and fewer voters now think of themselves as members of one of the traditional blocs—whether Catholics, union members, or Southerners. Instead they consider themselves as belonging to categories that were either too broad or too narrow to meld into the old-style coalitions— as consumers or commuters, for example, or as gun owners or condominium owners. Moreover, the issues that excite interest nowadays— abortion and capital punishment, for example—tend to increase fragmentation of the citizenry and hinder efforts to form a broad coalition.

In a sense the Democrats have been victims of their own success. By conquering the Depression and reducing economic insecurity, they had eroded the cement that held their coalition together. Instead of reaching out to the family of underprivileged voters who huddled together in the 1930s, the Democrats have to face a myriad of disparate groups competing for favors of government in a zero-sum economy.

So it was only to be expected that in the wake of their string of presidential defeats—they have lost five out of the last six contests for the White House—Democrats have been seeking a fresher, more relevant vision to offer the electorate. To start with, the party is trying to moderate its reliance on government activism. "Government often does good things badly," Democratic Governor Mario Cuomo of New York has been telling party leaders striving to find new directions. But even though they now agree that government is no longer the only answer to the nation's society's needs, Democrats have yet to agree on any other answer.

Just as the Democrats are floundering, Republicans are plagued by their own contradictions. Although they can take some satisfaction in the inability of the Democrats to roll back the Reagan Revolution, Republicans concede they have themselves been unable to devise a sequel to that political star turn.

"Whoever follows Ronald Reagan can't be just someone who exists within the shadow of Ronald Reagan," former Republican national chairman Frank Fahrenkopf told me before George Bush replaced Reagan in the White House. "He must have his own philosophy and tell the country where he wants to take it."

But so far Bush has been no more successful at accomplishing that than Carter was at finding a substitute for the New Deal. In part, of course, Reagan's successor has been hindered by the huge budget deficit that was part of Reagan's legacy. But Republican problems go beyond the deficit. They still suffer from the perception of being the party of the wealthy. Though they have struggled to change that image, it was revived during the Reagan presidency by Reagan's cuts in federal help for the poor and by the disproportionate benefits reaped by affluent Americans from his extravagant tax cuts.

Moreover, just as the Democrats face a dilemma over the uses of government, so do the Republicans. In the modern era Republicans have usually won the presidency by exploiting dissatisfaction with the Democrats, as Reagan did against Carter in 1980, rather than by offering a new vision of their own for government. But with Bush's victory in 1988, the Republicans extended their hold on the White House for more than two terms for the first time since the 1920s, a success that has forced them to confront the burdens of incumbency.

Increasingly Republicans now tell themselves they must address the country's problems. "If you are going to take power, you are going to have to take responsibility," points out House Republican Whip Newt Gingrich, founder of the Conservative Opportunity Society. Yet most conservatives retain their inherent opposition to activism of any kind by government, particularly the federal government, and still search for ways to contract out the obligations of government to the private sector. This makes it difficult for the Republicans to formulate a constructive political philosophy and leaves them on the defensive. In that posture their chief concern is that the long economic recovery that began under Reagan will finally collapse under Bush, that their party will bear the blame, and that in the next presidential election the Democrats will borrow an old GOP battle cry and persuade the voters to "throw the rascals out."

The import of this ideological confusion is that a president must now work harder than ever to achieve success. Without an ideological construct from his party to lend shape and substance to his political creed, a president must rely solely on his own intellectual resources and experience to define his ideology. The loss of vitality by the parties, which are our principal political institutions, also makes it more urgent that a president examine himself so that he can synthesize his value and character to help him gain public support.

First a president must help himself. Then, if he is to succeed, he must get the public to help him. The public's initial role is to judge. Based on that judgment the public can then become the president's most potent ally or his most formidable adversary. Just as the times require great discipline and imagination from a president, they demand more vigilance and concern for politics and government from the citizenry, more willingness at the very least to vote, and also, when the opportunity arises, to march, to write letters, to sign petitions in praise or in protest.

Presidential leadership is not a spectator sport. It should be an enterprise in which both the president and the public participate together, for it is certain that they will succeed or fail together.

Bibliography

For the reader's convenience I have made separate source lists for each chapter. Sources used in more than one chapter are starred.

To Be As Big a Man As He Can Be

Berman, Larry. "Lyndon Johnson: Paths Chosen and Opportunities Lost." In Fred I. Greenstein, ed., *Leadership in the Modern Presidency*. Cambridge, Mass.: Harvard Univ. Press, 1988.

Burns, James MacGregor. *The Power to Lead*. New York: Simon and Schuster, 1984.

Cloud, Stanley W. "The Can't Do Government." *Time*, October 23, 1989.

Goldman, Peter. "The Presidency: Can Anyone Do the Job?" *Newsweek*, January 26, 1981.

Hargrove, Erwin C. *The Power of the Modern Presidency*. New York: Knopf, 1974.

Hodgson, Godfrey. *All Things to All Men*. New York: Simon and Schuster, 1980.

Leuchtenburg, William E. "Franklin D. Roosevelt: The First Modern President." In Fred I. Greenstein, ed., *Leadership in the Modern Presidency*. Cambridge, Mass.: Harvard Univ. Press, 1988.

Neustadt, Richard E. *Presidential Power*. New York: Wiley, 1980.

Shogan, Robert. *None of the Above: Why Presidents Fail and What Can Be Done About It*. New York: New American Library, 1982.

Wilson, Woodrow. *Constitutional Government in the United States*. New York: Columbia Univ. Press, 1917.

* Princeton Conference on Leadership in the Modern Presidency. This conference at Princeton University on April 3, 1987, organized by Fred I. Greenstein, brought together associates of each president from Truman to Reagan, along

with scholars specializing in each presidency. The scholars' papers prepared for the conference have been published in *Leadership in the Modern Presidency*, cited above. Material drawn from the conference discussions is cited here and in the notes to the Reagan chapter as Princeton conference.

TRUMAN: The Underdog

BOOKS AND PERIODICALS

Appleton, Sheldon. "Public Perceptions of Truman." In William Levantrosser, ed., *Harry S Truman*, New York: Greenwood Press, 1986.

Bernstein, Barton J., and Alan J. Matusow, eds. *The Truman Administration*. New York: Harper, 1966.

Daniels, Jonathan. *Man of Independence*. Philadelphia: Lippincott, 1950.

Donovan, Robert. *Conflict and Crisis: The Presidency of Harry S Truman, 1945–1948*. New York: Norton, 1977.

*———. *Nemesis: Truman and Johnson in the Coils of War in Asia*. New York: St Martin's Press, 1984.

———. *Tumultuous Years: The Presidency of Harry S Truman, 1949–1953*. New York: Norton, 1982.

Douglas, Paul. *In the Fullness of Time*. New York: Harcourt Brace, 1971.

Ferrell, Robert, ed. *Dear Bess: The Letters from Harry to Bess Truman, 1910–1959*. New York: Norton, 1983.

———. *Off the Record: The Private Papers of Harry S Truman*. New York: Harper & Row, 1980.

Hamby, Alonzo. "Harry S Truman: Insecurity and Responsibility." In Fred Greenstein, ed., *Leadership in the Modern Presidency*. Cambridge, Mass.: Harvard Univ. Press, 1988.

Hofstadter, Richard. *The Age of Reform*. New York: Vintage, 1955.

Keyserling, Leon H. "Truman, the Man and the President." In William Levantrosser, ed., *Harry S Truman*. New York: Greenwood Press, 1986.

Kluger, Richard. *Simple Justice*. New York: Knopf, 1976.

Landecker, Manfred. "Harry S Truman, Leadership, and Public Opinion." In William Levantrosser, ed., *Harry S Truman*. New York: Greenwood Press, 1986.

*Leuchtenburg, William E. *In the Shadow of FDR*. Ithaca, N.Y.: Cornell Univ. Press, 1983.

Miller, Merle. *Plain Speaking*. New York: Berkley, 1986.

Phillips, Cabell. *The Truman Presidency*. New York: Macmillan, 1966.

Poen, Monte. " 'Rose, File It.' " In William Levantrosser, ed., *Harry S Truman*. New York: Greenwood Press, 1986.

Ross, Irwin. *The Loneliest Campaign*. New York: New American Library, 1968.

Shogan, Robert. "1948 Election." *American Heritage*, June 1968.

Slosson, Preston W. *The Great Crusade and After*. Chicago: Quadrangle, 1971.

Smith, Richard Norton. *Thomas E. Dewey and His Times*. New York: Simon and Schuster, 1982.

Steinberg, Alfred. *The Man from Missouri*. New York: Putnam, 1962.

Truman, Harry S. *1945: Year of Decisions*. New York: New American Library, 1965.

——. *Years of Trial and Hope*. New York: Doubleday, 1956.

Truman, Margaret. *Harry S Truman*. New York: Morrow, 1973.

Warren, Robert Penn. *All the King's Men*. New York: Harcourt, Brace, 1974.

HARRY S TRUMAN LIBRARY

Diary of Eban A. Ayers, May 23, 1948. Papers of Eban A. Ayers.

Memorandum for the President, Nov. 19, 1947. Papers of Clark M. Clifford.

Medical Records, 1937, 1942, Box 2, Personnel file of Harry S. Truman, U.S. Adjutant General's Office. Department of the Army.

Oral History Interviews: Clark Clifford, George M. Elsey, James H. Rowe, Jr.

EISENHOWER: Fatal Flaw

Ambrose, Stephen E. *Eisenhower the President*. New York: Simon and Schuster, 1984 (cited in notes as Ambrose, Vol. II).

——. *Eisenhower: Soldier, General of the Army, President-Elect*. New York: Simon and Schuster, 1983 (cited in notes as Ambrose, Vol. I).

Branch, Taylor. *Parting the Waters*. New York: Simon and Schuster, 1988.

Brendon, Piers. *Ike: His Life and Times*. New York: Harper & Row, 1986.

Burk, Robert F. *The Eisenhower Administration and Civil Rights*. Knoxville: Univ. of Tennessee Press, 1984.

Davis, Kenneth S. *Soldier of Democracy*. New York: Doubleday, 1946.

Durham, James C. *A Moderate Among Extremists*. Chicago: Nelson-Hall, 1981.

Eisenhower, Dwight. *At Ease: Stories I Tell to Friends*. New York: Doubleday, 1967.

——. *Mandate for Change*. New York: Doubleday, 1963.

——. *Waging Peace*. New York: Doubleday, 1965.

Ewald, William Bragg, Jr. *Eisenhower the President*. Englewood Cliffs, N.J.: Prentice Hall, 1981.

Flemming, Arthur S. "Perspective on Eisenhower's Values." In Kenneth W. Thompson, ed., *The Eisenhower Presidency*. Lanham, Md.: University Press, 1980.

Greene, John Robert. *The Crusade: The Presidential Election of 1952*. Lanham, Md.: University Press, 1985.

Greenstein, Fred. *The Hidden-Hand Presidency*. New York: Basic Books, 1982.

*Hughes, Emmet John. *The Ordeal of Power*. New York: Atheneum, 1975.

Kempton, Murray. *Part of Our Time*. New York: Dell, 1955.

Lyon, Peter. *Eisenhower: Portrait of the Hero*. Boston: Little, Brown, 1974.

Manchester, William. *The Glory and the Dream*. Vol. II. Boston: Little, Brown, 1974.

Mayer, Michael S. "Eisenhower and Race." In Joann P. Krieg, ed., *Dwight D. Eisenhower*. Westport, Conn.: Greenwood Press, 1987.

Morrow, E. Frederic. *Black Man in the White House*. New York: Coward-McCann, 1963.

Moskos, Charles. "Racial Integration in the Armed Services." *The American Journal of Sociology*, September 1966.

Parmet, Herbert S. *Eisenhower and the American Crusades*. New York: Macmillan, 1972.

Rovere, Richard. "Eisenhower Revisited." In Robert D. Marcus and David Burner, eds., *America Since 1945*. New York: St. Martin's Press, 1977.

Shogan, Robert and Tom Craig. *The Detroit Race Riot*. Philadelphia: Chilton, 1964.

Stevenson, Adlai. *Speeches of Adlai Stevenson*. New York: Random House, 1952.

Taylor, Allan. *What Eisenhower Thinks*. New York: Crowell, 1952.

Truman, Margaret. *Bess W. Truman*. New York: Macmillan, 1986.

KENNEDY: Rules of Reason

Briggs, Philip J. "The Nuclear Test Ban Treaty, 1963." In Paul Harper and Joann Krieg, eds., *John F. Kennedy: The Promise Revisited*. New York: Greenwood Press, 1988.

Bundy, McGeorge S. "Kennedy and the Nuclear Question." In Kenneth S. Thompson, ed., *The Kennedy Presidency*. Lanham, Md.: University Press, 1988.

Burner, David. *John F. Kennedy and a New Generation*. Boston: Little, Brown, 1988.

Burns, James MacGregor. *John Kennedy: A Political Profile*. New York: Avon, 1961.

Halberstam, David. *The Best and the Brightest*. New York: Fawcett, 1973.

Hilsman, Roger. *To Move a Nation*. New York: Doubleday, 1973.

Kennedy, John F. "The Speeches, Remarks, Press Conferences and Statements of Senator John F. Kennedy, August 1 through November 7, 1960." In *Freedom of Communications: Part I*. Washington, D.C.: U.S. Senate Commerce Committee, 1961 (cited in notes as Kennedy Campaign Speeches).

———. *Profiles in Courage*. New York: Harper & Row, 1964.

Kennedy, Robert F. *Thirteen Days*. New York: New American Library, 1969.

Manchester, William. *The Death of a President*. New York: Harper & Row, 1967.

Nevins, Allan, ed. *The Burden and the Glory*. New York: Harper & Row, 1964.

O'Brien, Lawrence. *No Final Victories*. New York: Doubleday, 1974.

O'Donnell, Kenneth P. and David F. Powers. *"Johnny, We Hardly Knew Ye."* Boston: Little, Brown, 1970.

Parmet, Herbert. *Jack: The Struggles of John F. Kennedy*. New York: Dial, 1980.

———. *JFK: The Presidency of John F. Kennedy*. New York: Dial, 1983.

Riccards, Michael P. "The Dangerous Legacy." In Paul Harper and Joann Krieg, eds., *The Kennedy Presidency: The Promise Revisited*. New York: Greenwood Press, 1988.

*Schlesinger, Arthur M., Jr. *Kennedy or Nixon: Does It Make Any Difference?* New York: Macmillan, 1960.

———. *Robert F. Kennedy and His Times*. Boston: Houghton Mifflin, 1978 (cited in notes as *RFK*).

———. *A Thousand Days*. Boston: Houghton Mifflin, 1965.

———. "What the Thousand Days Wrought." *New Republic*, November 21, 1983.

Sorensen, Theodore C. *Kennedy*. New York: Harper & Row, 1965.

Whalen, Richard F. *The Founding Father*. New American Library: New York, 1964.

Wofford, Harris. *Of Kennedys & Kings*. New York: Farrar, Straus & Giroux, 1980.

JOHNSON: LBJ vs. LBJ

BOOKS AND PERIODICALS

Broder, David. *The Party's Over*. New York: Harper & Row, 1972.

Busby, Horace. "Reflections on a Leader." In Kenneth W. Thompson, ed., *The Johnson Presidency*. Lanham, Md.: University Press, 1986.

Caro, Robert. *The Years of Lyndon Johnson: The Path to Power*. New York: Knopf, 1982.

Dugger, Ronnie. *The Politician*. New York: Norton, 1982.

Evans, Rowland and Robert Novak. *Lyndon B. Johnson: The Exercise of Power*. New York: New American Library, 1968.

Fulbright, J. William. "The Johnson Presidency and Vietnam." In Kenneth W. Thompson, ed., *The Johnson Presidency*. Lanham, Md.: University Press, 1986.

Goldwater, Barry. *With No Apologies*. New York: Morrow, 1979.

Halberstam, David. *The Best and the Brightest*. New York: Fawcett, 1973.

Johnson, Lyndon. *The Vantage Point*. New York: Holt, Rinehart and Winston, 1971.

Kearns, Doris. *Lyndon Johnson & the American Dream*. New York: New American Library, 1976.

Lambert, William. "How LBJ's Family Amassed Its Fortune." *Life*, August 21, 1964.

*Lemann, Nicholas. "The Unfinished War." *Atlantic*, December 1988.

McPherson, Harry. *A Political Education*. Boston: Little, Brown, 1972.

Rostow, Walt Whitman. "Lyndon Johnson and Vietnam." In Kenneth W. Thompson, ed., *The Johnson Presidency*. Lanham, Md.: University Press, 1986.

Steinberg, Alfred. *Sam Johnson's Boy*. New York: Macmillan, 1968.

White, Theodore. *The Making of the President: 1964*. New York: Atheneum, 1965.

LYNDON B. JOHNSON LIBRARY

Memo, Horace Busby to the president. ND. Office files of Bill Moyers.

Memo, Bill Moyers to the president. October 3, 1964. Office of the President Files, Box 8.

*Oral history interview with Douglass Cater.

Oral history interview with Harry McPherson.

Roundtable discussion with Harry Middleton, Dean Rusk, John Gronouski, Wilbur Cohen, Robert Hardesty, George Christian, and Larry Temple.

NIXON: Us Against Them

BOOKS AND PERIODICALS

Abrahamsen, David. *Nixon vs. Nixon.* New York: Farrar, Straus and Giroux, 1977.

Allen, Frederick Lewis. *Only Yesterday.* New York: Harper & Row, 1964.

———. *The Big Change.* New York: Bantam, 1961.

*Ambrose, Stephen E. *Nixon: The Education of a Politician.* New York: Simon and Schuster, 1987.

Brodie, Fawn M. *Richard Nixon: The Shaping of His Character.* New York: Norton, 1981.

Chester, Lewis, Godfrey Hodgson, and Bruce Page. *An American Melodrama.* New York: Viking, 1969.

Evans, Rowland, Jr., and Robert D. Novak. *Nixon in the White House.* New York: Random House, 1971.

Hersh, Seymour M. *The Price of Power.* New York: Summit Books, 1983.

Hoff-Wilson, Joan. "Richard M. Nixon: The Corporate Presidency." In Fred I. Greenstein, ed., *Leadership in the Modern Presidency.* Cambridge, Mass.: Harvard Univ. Press, 1988.

Kempton, Murray. *Part of Our Time.* New York: Dell, 1957.

Kronitzer, Bela. *The Real Nixon: An Intimate Biography.* Chicago: Rand McNally, 1960.

Kraus, Sidney, ed. *The Great Debates.* Gloucester, Mass.: Peter Smith, 1968.

Mazo, Earl and Stephen Hess. *Nixon.* New York: Popular Library, 1967.

Morris, Roger. *Richard Milhouse Nixon.* New York: Holt, 1990 (cited in notes as Morris).

———. *Uncertain Greatness.* New York: Harper & Row, 1977.

*Nixon, Richard. *RN: The Memoirs of Richard Nixon.* New York: Grosett & Dunlap, 1978 (cited in notes as Nixon).

———. *Six Crises.* New York: Doubleday, 1962.

*Parmet, Herbert S. *Richard Nixon and His America.* Boston: Little, Brown, 1990.

*Reichley, A. James. *Conservatives in an Age of Change.* Washington: Brookings Institution, 1981.

Safire, William. *Before the Fall.* New York: Doubleday, 1975.

Shogan, Robert. *A Question of Judgment: The Fortas Case and the Supreme Court.* New York: Bobbs-Merrill, 1972.

Steel, Ronald. *Walter Lippmann and the American Century.* New York: Vintage, 1981.

Stelzner, Herman. "The Quest Story and Nixon's Nov. 3, 1969 Address." *Quarterly Journal of Speech,* April 1971.

Whalen, Richard J. *Catch the Falling Flag.* Boston: Houghton Mifflin, 1972.

Wills, Gary. *Nixon Agonistes.* New York: New American Library, 1969.

Witcover, Jules. *The Resurrection of Richard Nixon.* New York: Putnam, 1970.

NIXON PRESIDENTIAL MATERIALS PROJECT, NATIONAL ARCHIVES

Haldeman Notes, Box 40, Staff Member and Office Files, White House Special Files.
President's Speech File, Box 53, President's Personal Files.

FORD: The Congressman's Congressman

Ben-Veniste, Richard and George Frampton, Jr. *Stonewall.* New York: Simon and Schuster, 1977.
Buchen, Philip. "Reflections on a Politician's President." In Kenneth W. Thompson, ed., *The Ford Presidency.* Lanham, Md.: University Press, 1988.
Burns, James MacGregor. *Deadlock of Democracy.* Englewood Cliffs, N.J.: Prentice-Hall, 1963.
Cannon, James M. "Domestic Issues and the Budget." In Kenneth W. Thompson, ed., *The Ford Presidency.* Lanham, Md.: University Press, 1988.
Casserly, John J. *The Ford White House.* Boulder: Colorado Univ. Press, 1977.
Ford, Betty. *Betty: A Glad Awakening.* New York: Doubleday, 1987.
Ford, Gerald. *A Time to Heal.* New York: Harper & Row, 1979.
Greene, John Robert. "The Dilemma of the Ford Image." Hofstra University Conference on the Ford Presidency, April 1989.
Griffin, Robert P. "The Man Who Happened to Become President." In Kenneth W. Thompson, ed., *The Ford Presidency.* Lanham, Md.: University Press, 1988.
Hartmann, Robert T. *Palace Politics.* New York: McGraw-Hill, 1980.
Kutler, Stanley I. *The Wars of Watergate.* New York: Knopf, 1990.
Lukas, Anthony J. *Nightmare.* New York: Viking, 1973.
McElroy, S. C. "Gerald R. Ford." Ralph Nader Congress Project. Washington: Grossman, 1972.
Nessen, Ron. *It Sure Looks Different from the Inside.* Chicago: Playboy, 1978.
Reeves, Richard. *A Ford Not a Lincoln.* New York: Harcourt, Brace, Jovanovich, 1975.
Schapsmeier, Edward L. and Frederick H. "President Gerald R. Ford's Roots in Omaha." *Nebraska History,* Summer 1987.
Speakes, Larry. *Speaking Out.* New York: Avon, 1988.
TerHorst, J. F. *Gerald Ford and the Future of the Presidency.* New York: Third Press, 1974 (cited in notes as terHorst).
———. "President Ford and the Media." In Kenneth W. Thompson, ed., *The Ford Presidency.* Lanham, Md.: University Press, 1988.
United States Senate, Committee on Rules and Administration. Nomination of Gerald R. Ford of Michigan to Be Vice President of the United States. Hearings, Nov. 1, 5, 7, and 14, 1973 (cited in notes as Senate hearings).
Vestal, Bud. *Jerry Ford: Up Close.* New York: Coward, McCann & Geoghegan, 1974.
Webber, Alan M. "Gerald R. Ford: The Statesman as CEO." *Harvard Business Review,* September-October, 1987.
Witcover, Jules. *White Knight.* New York: Random House, 1972.

GERALD R. FORD LIBRARY

Oral history interviews with Philip Buchen.
Oral history interview with Neil A. Weathers.
Syers Papers (transcripts of research interviews with former White House and congressional associates of Gerald Ford, conducted by William Syers).
White House staff files: Philip Buchen files, John Marsh files.

CARTER: The Road to Malaise

Barber, James David. *The Presidential Character*, 3rd ed. Englewood Cliffs, N.J.: Prentice-Hall, 1985.

Bass, Jack and Walter DeVries. *The Transformation of Southern Politics*. New York: Basic Books, 1976.

Bourne, Peter. "Jimmy Carter: A Profile." *Yale Review*, 1982.

Carter, Jimmy. *Keeping Faith*. New York: Bantam, 1982.

*————. *Why Not the Best?* New York: Bantam, 1976 (cited in notes as *WNTB?*).

*Fallows, James. "The Passionless Presidency." *Atlantic*, May 1989.

Gladd, Betty. *Jimmy Carter: In Search of the Great White House*. New York: Norton, 1988.

Hargrove, Erwin. *Leadership and the Politics of the Public Good*. Baton Rouge: Louisiana State Univ. Press, 1988.

————. "The Politics of Public Goods." In Fred Greenstein, ed., *Leadership in the Modern Presidency*. Cambridge, Mass.: Harvard Univ. Press, 1988 (cited in notes as Hargrove).

Heineman, Ben, Jr. and Curtis A. Hessler. *Memorandum for the President*. Random House: New York, 1980.

Johnson, Haynes. *In the Absence of Power*. New York: Viking, 1980.

Jones, Charles O. *The Trusteeship Presidency*. Baton Rouge: Louisiana State Univ. Press, 1988.

Key, V. O., Jr. *Southern Politics in State and Nation*. New York: Knopf, 1950.

Knott, Jack and Aaron Wildavsky. "Jimmy Carter's Theory of Governing." *Wilson Quarterly*, Winter 1977.

Kuttner, Robert. *Revolt of the Haves*. New York: Simon and Schuster, 1980.

Polmar, Norman and Thomas B. Allen. *Rickover: Controversy and Genius*. New York: Simon and Schuster, 1982.

Schram, Martin. *Running for President 1976*. New York: Stein and Day, 1977.

Shogan, Robert. *Promises to Keep: Carter's First 100 Days*. New York: Crowell, 1977.

REAGAN: The Half Revolution

Anderson, Martin. *Revolution*. New York: Harcourt, Brace, Jovanovich, 1988.

Barber, James D. *The Presidential Character*, 3rd ed. Englewood Cliffs, N.J.: Prentice-Hall, 1985.

Barrett, Laurence I. *Gambling With History*. New York: Penguin, 1984.

Boyarsky, Bill. *Ronald Reagan*. New York: Random House, 1981.

Cannon, Lou. *Reagan*. New York: Perigree, 1982.

Ceaser, James. "The Reagan Presidency and American Public Opinion." In Charles O. Jones, ed., *The Reagan Legacy: Promise and Performance*. Chatham, N.J.: Chatham House, 1988.

Dallek, Robert. *Ronald Reagan: The Politics of Symbolism*. Cambridge, Mass.: Harvard Univ. Press, 1984.

Destler, I. M. "Reagan and the World: An Awesome Stubbornness." In Charles O. Jones, ed., *The Reagan Legacy: Promise and Performance*. Chatham, N.J.: Chatham House, 1988.

Drew, Elizabeth. *Portrait of an Election*. New York: Simon and Schuster, 1981.

*Erickson, Paul D. *Reagan Speaks*. New York: New York Univ. Press, 1985.

Evans, Rowland and Robert Novak. *The Reagan Revolution*. New York: Dutton, 1981.

FitzGerald, Frances. "Memoirs of the Reagan Era." *New Yorker*, January 16, 1989.

Greider, William. "The Education of David Stockman." *Atlantic*, December 1981.

Heclo, Hugh. "Reaganism and the Search for a Public Philosophy." In John L. Palmer, ed., *Perspectives on the Reagan Years*. Washington, D.C.: Urban Institute, 1986.

Layne, Christopher. "Requiem for the Reagan Doctrine." In David Boaz, ed., *Assessing the Reagan Years*. Washington: Cato Institute, 1988.

Mann, Thomas E. "Thinking About the Reagan Years." In Larry Berman, ed., *Looking Back on the Reagan Presidency*. Baltimore: Johns Hopkins, 1990.

Mayer, Jane and Doyle McManus. *Landslide*. Boston: Houghton Mifflin, 1988.

Moore, Jonathan, ed. *The Campaign for President: 1980 in Retrospect*. Cambridge, Mass.: Ballinger, 1981.

Muir, William K., Jr. "Ronald Reagan: The Primacy of Rhetoric." In Fred I. Greenstein, ed., *Leadership in the Modern Presidency*. Cambridge, Mass.: Harvard Univ. Press, 1988.

Palmer, John L. "Philosophy, Policy and Politics." In John L. Palmer ed., *Perspectives on the Reagan Years*. Washington, D.C.: Urban Institute, 1986.

Reagan, Ronald, with Richard C. Hubler. *Where's the Rest of Me?* New York: Duell, Sloan & Pearce, 1965.

Regan, Donald T. *For the Record*. New York: St. Martin's Press, 1988.

Rice, Condoleezza. "The Reagan Legacy and U.S.–Soviet Relations." In Larry Berman, ed., *Looking Back on the Reagan Presidency*. Baltimore: Johns Hopkins, 1990.

Rockman, Bert A. "The Style and Organization of the Reagan Presidency." In Charles O. Jones, ed., *The Reagan Legacy: Promise and Performance*. Chatham, N.J.: Chatham House, 1988.

Rogin, Michael. *Ronald Reagan: The Movie*. Berkeley: Univ. of California Press, 1987.

Speakes, Larry. *Speaking Out*. New York: Avon, 1988.

Stockman, David. *The Triumph of Politics*. New York: Harper & Row, 1986.

Tower Commission Report. The President's Special Review Board. New York: Bantam and New York Times Books, 1987.

Von Damm, Helene, ed. *Sincerely, Ronald Reagan*. New York: Berkley, 1980.

Weatherford, M. Stephen and Lorraine McDonnell. "Ideology and Economic Policy in the Reagan Years." In Larry Berman, ed., *Looking Back on the Reagan Presidency*. Baltimore: Johns Hopkins, 1990.

White, John Kenneth. *The New Politics of Old Values*. Hanover, N.H.: Univ. Press of New England, 1987.

Wills, Gary. *Reagan's America*. New York: Doubleday, 1987.

Yankelovich, Daniel. "American Values: Change and Stability." *Public Opinion*, December/January, 1984.

BUSH: "The Way I Was Brought Up"

Aldrich, Nelson W. *Old Money*. New York: Knopf, 1988.

Apple, R. W. "Panama Invasion Costly in a Far Wider Theater." *New York Times*, January 25, 1990.

Baltz, Dan. "For Bush, Next Phase of Confrontation Likely to Be More Difficult." *Washington Post*, September 12, 1990.

Baltz, Dan, David Broder, and Paul Taylor. "Introspective Electorate Views Future Darkly." *Washington Post*, January 21, 1990.

Baltz, Dan and David Hoffman. "Bush Under Pressure to Better Explain Deployment in Gulf." *Washington Post*, August 29, 1990.

Bandow, Doug. "The Myth of Iraq's Oil Stranglehold." *New York Times*, September 17, 1990.

Barnes, Fred. "Hour of Power." *New Republic*, September 3, 1990.

———. "Standing Soft." *New Republic*, August 20 & 27, 1990.

Bass, Jack and Walter DeVries. *The Transformation of Southern Politics*. New York: Basic, 1976.

Bearak, Barry. "Team Player Bush." *Los Angeles Times*, November 22, 1987.

Blustein, Paul. "When Politics Induces Paralysis." *Washington Post*, February 21, 1990.

Bush, George. *Looking Forward*. New York: Doubleday, 1987.

Dickey, Christopher. "A 'Common Purpose'—Or a Common Enemy." *Newsweek*, September 24, 1990.

Drahuschak, Gregory M. "Saddam Hussein and the Stock Market." "Investors Spectrum, Wheat Butcher & Singer." Vol. 12, no. 9, September 1990.

Duffy, Michael. "Mr. Consensus." *Time*, August 21, 1989.

"Excerpts from Iraqi Transcript of Meeting With U.S. Envoy." *New York Times*, September 23, 1990.

Evans, Rowland and Robert Novak. "Jordan in a Lose-Lose Situation." *Washington Post*, September 3, 1990.

Germond, Jack W. and Jules Witcover. *Blue Smoke & Mirrors*. New York: Viking, 1981.

———. *Wake Us When It's Over*. New York: Macmillan, 1985.

Goldman, Peter and Tony Fuller. *The Quest for the Presidency 1984*. New York: Bantam, 1985.

Goshko, John and R. Jeffrey Smith. "State Department Assailed on Iraq Policy." *Washington Post*, September 19, 1990.

Green, Fitzhugh. *George Bush: An Intimate Portrait*. New York: Hippocrene, 1989.

Gugliottta, Guy, et. al. "At War Iraq Courted U.S. into Economic Embrace." *Washington Post*, September 16, 1990.

Hoffman, David and Bob Woodward. "President Launched Invasion With Little View to Aftermath." *Washington Post*, December 24, 1989.

House Foreign Affairs Committee Hearings. Persian Gulf Crisis, September 4, 1990. Federal News Service Transcript.

Krauthammer, Charles. "The Road to War . . ." *Washington Post*, September 21, 1990.

Lane, Charles. "The Making of a Monster." *Time*, August 20, 1990.

Lewis, Flora. "Between-Lines Disaster." *New York Times*, September 19, 1990.

Luttwak, Edward N. "Bush Has the Momentum, But What about His Mess at Home?" *Washington Post*, September 9, 1990.

Mann, Jim. "As CIA Director, Bush Sought to Restrict Probe of Agency Officials." *Los Angeles Times*, September 30, 1988.

McWilliams, Wilson Carey. "The Meaning of the Election." In Gerald Pomper, ed., *The Election of 1988*. Chatham, N.J.: Chatham House, 1989.

Nelson, Jack. "Conflict in Gulf Is a Make-or-Break Test for President." *Los Angeles Times*, August 9, 1990.

Oreskes, Michael. "Nearly Six Out of Ten Americans Say Nation Is in a Recession." *New York Times*, August 24, 1990.

Oudes, Bruce. *From: The President*. New York: Harper & Row, 1989.

Pennar, Karen. "Are We in a Recession?" *Business Week*, August 13, 1990.

Phillips, Kevin B. *The Emerging Republican Majority*. Garden City, N.Y.: Doubleday, 1970.

"Press Stakeout With Congressman Richard Gephardt et. al." September 5, 1990. Federal News Service Transcript.

Schneider, Keith. "U.S. Energy Policy to Stress Output and Conservation." *New York Times*, August 30, 1990.

Sciolino, Elaine and Michael R. Gordon. "Before Invasion, U.S. Spoke Little of Defending Kuwaitis." *New York Times*, September 23, 1990.

Seib, Gerald F. and Murray Alan. "Expensive Gulf Action Is about to Collide With Domestic Needs." *Wall Street Journal*, September 7, 1990.

Shields, Mark. "The Free-Lunch Countries." *Washington Post*, September 3, 1990.

Shogan, Robert. "Democrats Offensive Targets Tax Switch." *Los Angeles Times*. June 30, 1990.

Shribman, David. "Iraq Crisis Presents Bush Crucial Opportunity to Indelibly Define His Presidency." *Wall Street Journal*, August 7, 1990.

Silk, Leonard and Mark Silk. *The American Establishment*. New York: Basic, 1980.

Skelton, George. "Americans Support Bush But Are Split on Gulf Goals." *Los Angeles Times*, August 31, 1990.

Talbott, Strobe. "The Deterrence Vacuum." *Time*, August 13, 1990.

Thomas, Evan. "The Code of the WASP Warrior." *Newsweek*, August 20, 1990.

White, Theodore. *Making of the President: 1964.* New York: New American Library, 1965.

Wills, Gary. "The Ultimate Loyalist." *Time,* August 22, 1988.

Wines, Michael. "U.S. Aid Helped Hussein's Climb." *New York Times,* August 13, 1990.

Woodward, Bob and Carl Bernstein. *The Final Days.* New York: Simon and Schuster, 1976.

Woutat, Donald. "Policy on Oil: A Continuing U.S. Dilemma." *Los Angeles Times,* August 13, 1990.

Yang, John and Ann Devroy. "Poll Finds Increasing Pessimism about Economy." *Washington Post,* September 11, 1990.

Reference Notes

The following abbreviations are used in the notes:

PPP   *Public Papers of the Presidents*
LAT   *Los Angeles Times*
NYT   *New York Times*
WP   *Washington Post*

Full titles of sources below are listed in the preceding bibliographies for each chapter.

To Be As Big a Man As He Can Be

PAGE

1   "Can anyone do the job?": Goldman.
2   "Can't do government": Cloud.
3   "Turn the stomach": *LAT*, May 7, 1990.
4   "As big a man as he can": Wilson, p. 70. This view of the presidency, presented in a book first published in 1908, represented a departure from Wilson's earlier view, presented in *Congressional Government* (Baltimore: Johns Hopkins, 1981), written in 1884, in which he contended that Congress was the dominant force in the American political system. Wilson's own presidency ended with his notable failure to "get the people behind him" and his plan for the League of Nations.
5   Constitutional checks: Shogan, pp. 27–44. See also James M. Burns *The Deadlock of Democracy* (Prentice-Hall, 1963).
5   Paradox of the presidency: Hodgson, p. 13.
5   "Weakness is what I see": Neustadt, p. xi.
5   "The only power is nuclear": Goldman.
6   Equality vs. opportunity: Hargrove, pp. 177–85.
6   "This isn't about ideology": *NYT*, July 22, 1988.

313

7 Psychoanalyzed by God: Leuchtenburg, citing editors of Time-Life books, *This Fabulous Century*, Vol. 4. *Time*, 1969, p. 141.
7 Piano player in whore house: Princeton conference, remarks by Kenneth Hechler.
7 Fear of informal approach: Princeton conference, remarks by Larry Berman.
9 Reagan's high poll ratings post–Iran-Contra: *NYT*, March 29, 1989.

Truman: The Underdog

12 Johnston's vacant table: Shogan
13 No one had planned for Truman to be president: Although Democratic party leaders were aware of Roosevelt's failing health, their chief concern in picking Roosevelt's running mate in 1944 was the impact of their choice on the November election rather than his qualifications to succeed Roosevelt. As Cabell Phillips writes, even Roosevelt conceded that incumbent vice-president Wallace would be "a drag on the ticket" because of his reputation as an ultraliberal; the other leading candidate, Southerner James Byrnes, was too conservative to suit organized labor. Truman was selected as a compromise, with an eye on the 1944 electorate, not on his fitness for the Oval Office (Phillips, 42–48).
13 "Not an ordained New Dealer": Donovan, 127.
13 "I was a New Dealer": Truman, *Year of Decisions*, 171.
13 Two historical traditions: Hofstadter, 9.
14 It also helped: Daniels, 113.
14 Populist and progressive upbringing: Hamby, 72.
14 Failure in haberdashery: Truman, 154 and Hamby, 48.
15 Farm depression in twenties: Slosson, 205–15.
15 Republican policies: Daniels, 102–10.
15 Working in local government: Hamby, 49–50.
16 Some roads better than none: Daniels, 142–50.
16 "Unimpeachable character": *Ibid.*, 172–73.
16 "Beliefs into action": Ferrell, *Dear Bess*, 307.
16 Railroad robbery: Margaret Truman, 105–07.
16 Truman-Wheeler Act: Ferrell, *Dear Bess*, 307.
17 Informal inspection: Phillips, 32.
17 Big companies getting bigger: Truman, *Year of Decisions*, 189.
17 Expansion of New Deal: *Ibid.*, 530–32.
17 Out New Dealing FDR: Steinberg, 262.
18 Settled strike and angered labor: Donovan, 208–18.
18 Overriding Taft-Hartley veto: Donovan, 299–304.
18 Initial thinking on civil rights: *Ibid.*, 30–33.
18 Backing down and FEPC demise: *Ibid.*, 173.
18 Establishment of President's Committee: Kluger, 250.
19 Revival of civil rights measures: Shogan.
19 Unveiling the Marshall plan: Ross, 17.
19 Postwar problems: Shogan.

19 Taft accusations (fn.): Donovan, 216.

20 "Glasses seldom prescribed": Margaret Truman, 47.

20 "They called me four-eyes": Miller, 23.

20 Not the favorite son: Hamby, 45.

20 Love of reading: Margaret Truman, 47.

21 "My stomach turned over": *Ibid.*, 302.

21 Midwestern values: Truman, *Year of Decisions*, 134.

21 Victorian morals: Hamby, 45; Phillips, 11.

22 Target of special interests: Truman, *Year of Decisions*, 174.

22 "Heart and soul" campaigning for FDR: Leuchtenburg, 4.

22 "Message for the president": Margaret Truman, 111–12.

22 "Tell them to go to hell": *Ibid.*, 120.

22 "Like a battered document": Truman, *Year of Decisions*, 185.

22 "Grudging" decision by FDR: Leuchtenburg, 7.

23 "That's all there is": Miller, 196–97.

23 Truman's hospital visit: Donovan, *Nemesis*, 9–10.

24 Achieving goals: Hamby, 44.

25 "Men make history": Truman, *Year of Decisions*, 138–39.

25 Likened to a "hick": *Ibid.*, 165.

25 "The moon, stars, and all the planets": Shogan.

25 Not burdened by self-doubts: Donovan, 15.

25 Not too much "soft soap": Ferrell, *Off the Record*, 51.

25 Low poll ratings: Appleton, 169.

26 "Kept press": Poen, 372.

26 Pressures of politics: Hamby, 53.

26 Welcomed medical attention: Medical records, Truman personnel file. Although Truman's hospital visits were briefly noted in the Missouri newspapers at the time, no reporters delved into the reasons for his treatment as later-day journalists almost certainly would have done, particularly after Truman was nominated for vice-president. But if journalists had been more aggressive about such matters in the 1940s they would also have raised many more questions about the health of Franklin Roosevelt, whose physical condition was rarely even mentioned openly in the 1944 campaign.

26 Treatment "like a king": Ferrell, *Dear Bess*, 402.

27 A hick's: Warren, 94–95.

28 Attitude of liberals: Shogan.

28 Alternatives to Truman candidacy: Ross, 74.

28 Liberal campaign tactics: *Ibid.*, 19.

29 Marching to a liberal beat: Bernstein and Matusow, 86–157; Donovan, 271–72.

29 Clifford's influence: *Ibid.*, 270.

29 Clifford's ideas rejected: Ross, 26.

29 Clifford lacked "political acumen": Ayers Diary, May 23, 1948. Whatever Clifford lacked in political experience he made up for in public relations skill, which he exercised adroitly on his own behalf. He saw to it that his

own reputation benefited as much from the 1948 election results as Truman did.

29   Authorship of memorandum (fn): Rowe oral history interview.
29   Ignore the South: Clifford memorandum.
29   States Rights Party: Ross, 125–33.
30   Tax-cut credit scheme: Bernstein and Matusow, passim, and Donovan, 352, 392.
30   "Many respectable Americans": *Ibid.*
30   Government witch hunt: Bernstein and Matusow, 357.
30   Truman "stole their thunder": Clifford memorandum.
31   Good marks for vetoes: Bernstein and Matusow, 143–47, 386–97.
31   "Sick or out of town": Ferrell, *Off the Record*, 145.
31   "Step aside": Shogan.
31   Improbable results: *Ibid.*
32   Attempt to block plank: Douglas, 132–35.
32   Credit for strong plank: Truman, *Years of Trial and Hope*, 179–84.
32   "Eighty years behind": Ferrell, *Off the Record*, 146–47.
32   Defeatism prevailed: Ayers Diary, Oct. 7, 1948.
33   "Not putting on a show": Elsey oral history interview.
33   The making of a martyr: Donovan, *Conflict and Crises*, 397.
33   "Off the cuff" a success: Ferrell, *Off the Record*, 134.
33   Informality set the tone: Elsey oral history interview.
34   Ten talks a day: Shogan.
35   Republicans voted to override veto: Donovan, *Conflict and Crises*, 392.
35   "When the farmers have to sell": *Ibid.*, 392.
35   "Private power benefits": Ross, 187.
35   "A man on casters": Smith, 526. Just as Dewey's personality was a hindrance to his candidacy, so was his party. Indeed, the 80th Congress may have been as hard for Dewey to get along with as it was for Truman. Dewey sent his close adviser, and Eisenhower's future attorney general, Herbert Brownell, to Washington to plead with the GOP leadership to adopt a "responsible program" during the special post-convention session Truman had called. But Bob Taft, in command of the Senate, turned him down, arguing accurately but irrelevantly that Truman was trying to use the Congress for partisan purposes (Smith, 512). Said Taft: "We're not going to give that fellow a thing" (*Ibid.*, 33). After the returns were in, Pennsylvania Congressman and GOP National Chairman Hugh Scott said of his colleagues on the Hill: "Now maybe those sons of bitches will go out and pass some social legislation" (*Ibid.*, 48).
35   Roper poll findings: *Ibid.*, 523.
36   Truman jabbed back: Shogan.
36   Dewey's grace in defeat: Shogan.
36   Truman shielded himself: Bernstein and Matusow, 385–86.
37   Truman's kind of courage: Steinberg, 332.
37   Preservation of the New Deal coalition: Ross, 264.
37   Proposals served to educate: Bernstein and Matusow, 86.

37 His most important decision: Donovan, *Tumultuous Years*, 408, and *PPP*, Jan. 15, 1953.
38 "Most leaders have been such men": Landecker.
38 All right in the long run: *Ibid.*
39 Eisenhower's views on Korea: Bernstein and Matusow, 485, and *NYT*, Oct. 25, 1952.
39 "Acceptable solution": Eisenhower, *Mandate for Change*, 190.

Eisenhower: Fatal Flaw

40 "An enthusiastic reception": *Providence Journal*, Sept. 5, 1957.
40 "Never did I feel so good": *PPP*, 1957, 176.
41 He complained: Ambrose, *Vol. II*, 414.
42 A spacious vacation home: *Providence Journal*, July 10, 1957.
43 Concealed leadership: Greenstein, 5.
43 "Nothing so distasteful": Ambrose, *Vol. I*, 414.
43 Contempt for politicians: *Ibid.*, 96.
44 "I'll just confuse them": Kempton, 20.
44 "Indirect methods": Nixon, *Six Crises*, 161.
44 "The only leadership I know": Hughes, 123–24.
44 Inflict more damage: Ambrose, *Vol. II*, 619–20.
45 Truman's boyhood in Independence: Margaret Truman, *Bess W. Truman*, 4–5.
45 Abilene background: Ambrose, *Vol. I*, 25.
45 Mennonite beliefs: Davis, 10–11.
45 "Closely knit community": Lyon, 33.
45 Rewards for the good life: Davis, 49.
46 A profound influence: Brendon, 28.
46 David Eisenhower's failure: Ambrose, *Vol. I*, 17.
46 Grin and bear it: Davis, 47.
46 Little interest in ideas and the abstract, *Ibid.*, 67, 83–84.
46 "An event like Arbela": Eisenhower, *At Ease*, 39.
46 Cut off from social forces: Rovere.
46 Cadet contempt for politics: Ambrose, *Vol. I*, 53.
47 An extension of experience: Greenstein, 11.
47 "A better politician": Ambrose, *Vol. I*, 96.
47 The Bonus March: Ambrose, *Vol. I*, 96–98.
47 "A broader education": Greenstein, 12.
48 Planning division service: *Ibid.* The distinction between political and military responsibilities was driven home to Eisenhower by no less an authority than Franklin Roosevelt during a White House conversation the two men had in January 1944, after Eisenhower had been named to command Overlord, the invasion of Europe. When Eisenhower ventured to raise the subject of postwar occupation zones of Germany for the U.S. and the Soviet Union, Roosevelt cut him off, as Eisenhower later recalled, and told him "to let the political authorities make decisions of this kind" (Eisenhower, *At Ease*, 267–68).

48   Readily gave credit: Ambrose, *Vol. I*, 34–35.
48   Hard work in Abilene: Eisenhower, *At Ease*, 80–81.
49   "A standard of values": Ambrose, *Vol. I*, 27.
49   The tool of the body: Davis, 86–87.
49   "Unquestioning lives": Ambrose, *Vol. I*, 23.
49   Teamwork at home: Eisenhower, *At Ease*, 32.
50   Seeking combat: *Ibid.*, 151, 155.
50   Encouraging the cabinet: Flemming.
51   "Remarkably few decisions": Hughes, 133–34.
51   "Calculating dexterity": Brendon, 30.
51   The wrong side of the tracks: Davis, 48.
52   Glossing over poverty: Eisenhower, *At Ease*, 36.
52   "Us against the odds": Davis, 73.
52   Not lacking in confidence: Ambrose, *Vol. I*, 37.
52   Knee injury: Brendon, 33–37.
52   Doing his duty: Eisenhower, *At Ease*, 117–18.
52   The other brothers (fn): Ambrose, *Vol. I*, 69.
53   Liking to be liked: Brendon, 13.
53   "A tragic flaw": Ewald, 240.
53   Eisenhower and Roosevelt: Ewald, 25.
54   Eisenhower reneged: Ambrose, *Vol. I*, 370.
55   Campaign strategy on race: Lyon, 468 fn; Burk, 16–17.
55   Others flatly opposed: Eisenhower, *Mandate for Change*, 55.
55   "The highest test": Eisenhower, *Waging Peace*, 148.
56   "A group of darkies": Mayer.
56   "Equality before the law": Eisenhower, *Waging Peace*, 148.
56   "Rest of the team was ashamed": Ambrose, *Vol. I*, 35.
56   The Dirk Tyler episode: Davis, 142–43.
57   Only 13 blacks: Ambrose, *Vol. I*, 47.
57   He told Morrow: Mayer.
57   He asked for forgiveness: Mayer. Patience was the key to Eisenhower's
       view of civil rights. "There is no race in the history of man that in eighty-
       five years has come so far . . . as the American Negro race," he said in
       a 1949 address to the Harlem branch of the YMCA. "Now if you have
       come all that way in eight-five years in terms of history, think of what a
       great moment that is." Taylor, 85.
57   "A sacred obligation": Eisenhower, *Mandate for Change*, 235.
57   An overt gesture (fn): Morrow, 216.
58   Importance of Negro votes: Ambrose, *Nixon*, 414. (See Nixon bibliography.)
58   Warning on the platform: Duram, 133.
58   Other civil rights areas: Lyon, 589; Burk, 45–47, 68–76.
58   Warren a mistake: Ewald, 85.
59   "Not bad people": Ambrose, *Vol. II*, 190; Ewald, 80–82.
59   No advice to offer: Burk, 145.
59   Views on court decisions: Eisenhower, *Waging Peace*, 150.
59   "The whole issue set back": Duram, 133.
60   Only fuel the controversy: Burk, 162.

60 "Extremists on both sides": *Ibid.*, 167–68.
60 Reassuring Southerners: Parmet, 464.
60 Claiming credit in the North: Burk, 169.
60 "A job well done": Morrow, 106.
60 "I can't imagine": *NYT*, July 18, 1957.
61 The school board plan: Burk, 176.
61 Letter to Gruenther: Ambrose, *Vol. II*, 419.
61 The golf course awaited: *Providence Journal*, Sept. 5, 1957.
61 Eisenhower's schedule: *Ibid.*, Sept. 7, 1957.
61 "Need to act calmly": Ambrose, *Vol. II*, 419.
62 Information from Russell: *Ibid.*, 414–15.
62 Faubus had "soiled" himself: Durham, 146.
62 If Faubus would go along: Ferrell, 347–48.
63 Mann's telegram: Durham, 154–56.
63 Eisenhower's speech: *PPP*, 1957, 689–94.
64 Detroit riot toll: Shogan and Craig, 89.
65 Nixon's view: Ambrose, *Nixon*, 438. (See Nixon bibliography.)
65 "A lot of good in Houston": Hughes, 201.
66 No evidence of Negro votes: Ambrose, *Vol. II*, 529.
66 "To leave things undone": Hughes, 244–45.
67 The Marshall tribute: *Ibid.*, 42.
68 "This he cannot stand": Ferrell, 234.
68 "Easy to hate Americans": *Ibid.*, 242.
68 The president held his fire: Greenstein, 182.
68 "They do not realize": Ferrell, 270.
69 "If anybody believes that": *PPP*, 1960, 198–99.
70 Farewell address: *PPP*, 1960, 1035–40.

Kennedy: Rules of Reason

73 New Democratic party in the twenties: Burner, 2.
73 Irish-American attitudes: *Ibid.*, 3.
73 Irish cut off from Western liberalism: Burns, 31.
74 Dedication to neutrality: *Ibid.*, 102.
74 "We all have fathers": Parmet, 55.
74 Legacy of activism: Whalen, 425.
74 Lessons from Laski: Schlesinger, *RFK*, 19.
75 Harvard seething: Burns, 46.
75 Kennedy "fiddles" at Choate: Sorensen, 27.
75 "Young scientist": Burner, 16.
75 Analysis of Snell: Whalen, 221.
75 Publication of thesis: Burns, 54–57.
75 Promise of government activism: *Ibid.*, 76.
76 Family ties and wealth: Whalen, 393–99.
76 Logical party "stream": Keyserling.
76 Attacks loss of China: Burns, 89.
76 Support for McCarthy: Burner, 24–25; Whalen, 425.

76 Father's move to right: Whalen, 342–52.
76 Fair-Dealish record against Lodge: Burns, 119.
77 Matching Lodge's "snob appeal": O'Brien, 29.
77 Warning the West: Wofford, 33–36. Two years after that address, Kennedy in trying to recruit Wofford told him: "The key thing for this country is a new foreign policy that will break out of the confines of the cold war." Wofford later wrote: "His arguments were obviously honed to my interests; nevertheless, by the time we finished I was impressed by his apparent candor, conviction and determination" (Wofford, 37).
77 Address provokes and answers criticism: Burns, 187–88.
77 More balanced foreign policy: *Ibid.*
78 "Not just any Senator": Sorensen, *Kennedy*, 105.
78 Democrats vs. Republicans: Kennedy campaign speeches, 170.
78 "The ice of indifference": *Ibid.* 205.
78 Need for social reform: *Ibid.*, 397.
79 "Nixon lacks taste": Schlesinger, *Kennedy or Nixon*, 13.
79 Stress on activism: In evaluating Kennedy's ideology at that stage, Richard Whalen wrote: "Though he attracted intellectuals Jack Kennedy did not share their conviction that ideas are the moving force of politics. Asked once why he wanted to be President he replied: 'Because that is where the power is.' . . . He was in politics not to advance an ideology but to derive personal satisfaction" (Whalen, 426). This was a judgment many liberals would have agreed with at the time. But Kennedy demonstrated in his presidency that he knew how to use power to advance ideas.
80 "Like nuns talking about sex": Schlesinger, *RFK*, 10.
80 Bias against Irish: Burns, 36.
81 Second not good enough: Burner, 10; Whalen, 168.
81 "Do the best you can": Burns, 43.
81 "No political ambitions": *Ibid.*, 12.
81 Joseph Kennedy's ambitions: Whalen, 15.
81 "It was his responsibility": Burner, 19.
81 His father's example: *Ibid.*, 10.
82 "Utter detachment": Sorensen, 13.
82 Uncertainty about religion: Schlesinger, *RFK*, 17.
82 "Events and conditions change": Sorensen, 25.
82 Doubts about commitment: Burns, xiii.
82 "Unless somebody shouts": Sorensen, 13.
83 Pressure from father's letters: Schlesinger, *RFK*, 15–16.
83 Disappointment builds character: *Ibid.*, 17.
83 Physical problems, emotional manifestations: John Kennedy, xii; Burner, 25–26.
83 Learning the political ropes: Sorensen, 101.
84 "What did you expect?": O'Donnell and Powers, 296.
84 "It did not interfere": Schlesinger, "What the Thousand Days Wrought."
85 Making the most of life: Burner, 26.
85 "Limited number of days": Sorensen, 27.
85 Bay of Pigs ceremony: Burner, 72.

85 "Much happier frame of mind": O'Donnell and Powers, 277.
86 Dulles's rhetoric bored him: Schlesinger, *A Thousand Days*, 279.
86 Hard line against communism: Parmet, 65.
86 Taunting Nixon: Riccards.
87 Khrushchev favors nationalist uprisings: Schlesinger, *A Thousand Days*, 283.
87 Kennedy's inaugural pledge: *PPP*, 1961, 1.
87 Personal involvement: Sorensen, 306.
87 Lure of early victory over communism: Parmet, 159, 179.
88 Public ratings soar: *Ibid.*, 179.
88 CIA plots against Castro: *Ibid.*, 215–21.
88 "Not primarily nuclear": Bundy.
89 Promise to "act" in Cuba: Parmet, 282–83.
89 "Keating the next president": O'Donnell and Powers, 310.
89 Threat to credibility: Riccards.
89 Balance of power at stake: Sorensen, 678.
90 ExCom activity: Riccards.
90 "Maybe our mistake": *Ibid.*
90 Makeup of ExCom: Hilsman, 550.
90 Kennedy in command: *Ibid.*, 213.
90 Curbing ExCom: Riccards.
91 "The no's have it": O'Donnell and Powers, 319–20.
92 Leaving the door open; Parmet, 296.
92 "Many months of sacrifice": *PPP*, 1962, 806–09.
92 Khrushchev's retreat: Kennedy, *Thirteen Days*, 107–10.
93 Magnanimity in victory: *Ibid.*, 279.
93 Closer to accord: Hilsman, 224.
93 Criticism from left and right: Burner, 91.
93 The idea survived: Briggs.
94 Testing resumes: *Ibid.*
94 Hotline debate: Sorensen, 727.
94 American University speech, man-made solutions: *PPP*, 1963, 459–64.
95 Soviets enthusiastic: Sorensen, 733.
95 Eisenhower on treaty: Parmet, 315; Briggs, 41.
95 Address on treaty signing: *PPP*, 1963, 601–06.
95 Endorsement in tax-cut speech: *Ibid.*, 687.
95 Sorensen's complaint: Sorensen, 733.
96 Power of the pen: Sorensen, 480.
96 No sleepless nights: Wofford, 481.
96 No "great innovations": Broder, 30.
96 Avoiding attention: Sorensen, 482.
97 Impetus of Birmingham: *Ibid.*, 489.
97 As helpful as Lincoln: *Ibid.*
97 Equal treatment: *PPP*, 1963, 468–71.
98 Negotiating a compromise: Sorensen, 501.
98 "Motivated by justice": Sorensen, 472.
99 Kennedy told Heller: Lemann (see Johnson bibliography.)

100   A limited commitment: Hilsman, 536.
100   No more advisers: Parmet, 336.
100   "Make damn sure I'm reelected": *Ibid.*, 329.
100   Rusk's view: *Ibid.*, 336.

Johnson: LBJ vs. LBJ

101   Just to keep his hand in: Lemann.
102   "I think they were right": McPherson oral history interview.
104   "Make 'em work": *NYT*, July 23, 1968.
104   Flaw in consensus: Broder, 69–70.
105   "A happy nation": *PPP*, 1963–64, Vol. I, 729.
105   Always front and center: Johnson, 28.
105   Hill Country description: Caro, 39.
106   Views of Sam Ealy and Lyndon Johnson: *Ibid.*, 80, 137.
107   The 1960 Texas convention: Broder, 64–66.
107   Limits of consensus in 1960: *Ibid.*
107   Johnson's campaign posters: Caro, 404.
108   Johnson's performance in the House: *Ibid.*, 546–50; Evans and Novak, 22.
108   Views of Douglas and Cole: *Ibid.*, 550.
108   Johnson's wealth: Lambert.
109   "He never said a word": Caro, 31.
109   "Landslide Johnson": Evans and Novak, 33–35.
110   Hedging the hedge: *Ibid.*, 43.
110   Johnson's fears on civil rights issue: Kearns, 154.
110   Working both sides of the fence: McPherson oral history interview.
110   Easing seniority rules: Kearns, 400.
111   "The only president we have": Goldman, 414.
111   Johnson's fears of "endless debate": Kearns, 149.
111   "Will over adversity": Kearns, xi.
111   Johnson's childhood: Caro, 78, 67, 72; Steinberg, 31.
112   "Direction behind force": Dugger, 119–19.
112   He attacked every task: Caro, 169, 211.
112   Johnson's views on demagoguery: Kearns, 96–97.
113   Childhood tensions: *Ibid.*, 385, 24, 27
113   Impact of business reverses: Caro, 85–97.
113   Seeking power and control: *Ibid.*, 111, 72, 77.
114   Ear popping: *Ibid.*, 77.
114   Response to conflicts: Kearns, 386.
114   Rusk's comment: Roundtable discussion.
115   Johnson's surrogate fathers: Caro, 146–47, 333–34.
115   Relationship with Russell: Kearns, 398–400, 109.
115   Corcoran's claim: Caro, 501.
115   "Not very likeable": Halberstam, 531.
116   College comparisons: Roundtable discussion.
116   Response to McPherson: McPherson oral history interview.
116   Preoccupied with the press: Cater oral history interview.

116 "They take me like I am": Busby.
116 Torn up withdrawals: Kearns, 397.
116 Had to be hospitalized: Caro, 704.
117 "A martyr's cause": Kearns, 185.
117 Conversation with Dirksen: Johnson, 29.
118 Goldwater's pledge: Goldwater, 192–93.
118 "We're for a lot of things": White, 747.
118 Brandishing a poll: Broder, 68–69. Johnson relied so heavily on polls, which
        reinforced his faith in consensus, and talked about them so much that one
        of his aides, Horace Busby, advised him during the 1964 campaign that
        "the newsmen are both tired of and negative about your interest in the
        polls." Busby suggested that "in press plane-talk or other meetings polls
        be left unmentioned for a week or so. The newsmen are . . . interested
        in your views and personality and don't like the polls" (Busby memo).
118 Moyers argued against: Moyers memo.
118 Talk to the lobbyists: Evans and Novak, 514.
119 Something for everyone: Shogan, *None of the Above*, 102. (See Ch. 1
        bibliography.)
119 Voting rights controversy: Evans and Novak, 516–18.
119 "We shall overcome": *PPP*, 1965, 2830.
120 Califano's phone: O'Brien, *No Final Victories*, 182. (See Kennedy bibliog-
        raphy.)
120 84 of 87: *Ibid.*
120 "Quite a few means": McPherson oral history interview.
121 "No longer possible": Cater oral history interview.
121 "Give the president my regards": Johnson, 210.
122 "All my programs": Kearns, 263.
122 Johnson's Chicago speech: *PPP*, 1966, Vol. I, 288.
123 "Liberal Democrats suspect": McPherson, 390.
123 Johnson's fears: Busby.
123 "Peace for all Americans": *PPP*, 1963–64, Vol. II, 727.
123 Opposition to the war: Goldman, 441–42.
124 Johnson's plan from the start: Johnson, 115.
124 Fulbright's complaint: Fulbright.
124 The Bundy-McNamara memo: Berman, 38–39.
125 Black's appointment: Goldman, 406–09.
126 Three choices: Berman, 100–05.
127 The decision to lose slowly: *Ibid.*, 124.
127 Not the victim of his advisers: Johnson had initially attempted to rely on
        Kennedy's foreign-policy advisers, but his domineering nature, linked to
        the personalization necessary for consensus, made this difficult. In con-
        trast with Kennedy, whose style was "to have men around who had
        opinions of their own, and to encourage them to articulate their positions
        vigorously," Roger Hilsman thought that "President Johnson seemed to
        have a more hierarchial way of handling the job." Hilsman left government
        soon after Johnson became president (Hilsman, 535; see Kennedy bib-
        liography).

127   Humphrey shut out: Berman, 145.
127   McPherson's memo: McPherson oral history interview.
127   Aspects of a charade: Berman, 106, 145, 107.
128   The denouement: Halberstam, 728.
128   What the polls showed: Rostow.
129   Truman's State of the Union: *PPP*, 1951, 12.
130   Funding the Korean War: Donovan, *Nemesis*, 164–65. (See Truman bibliog-
        raphy.)

Nixon: Us Against Them

133   Middle-class erosion: Ambrose, *Nixon*, 510.
134   Uneasy environment: Morris, 46–48.
134   Early employment: Mazo and Hess, 11.
134   Far from easy street: Ambrose, 16–34, 43.
134   Missing out on oil: Mazo and Hess, 11.
134   Financial troubles: *Ibid.*, 16.
135   Populist strain: Nixon, 6–7.
135   "A lawyer they can't bribe": *Ibid.*, 29.
135   A vote for Roosevelt: *Ibid.*, 7.
136   Arguing politics: Abrahamsen, 100.
136   Support for Wilkie: Nixon, 25.
136   OPA experience: *Ibid.*, 26.
136   Not rights but privileges: Morris, 105.
136   California anti-red statutes: Murray, 234–35.
136   Firing school teachers: Morris, 105.
137   "Wave of indifference": *Ibid.*, 106.
137   End of big government: Parmet, 91.
137   Faith in individual freedom: *Ibid.*, 94.
137   Voorhis thrown on defensive: *Ibid.*, 110–12.
137   The PAC endorsement (fn): Parmet, 110–11.
138   Backing the Marshall plan: Nixon, 51.
138   Middle-class economic interests: Reichley, 46.
138   Appeal to middle-class voters: Ambrose, 220.
138   Anticommunism made him national figure: Nixon was quicker to exploit
        this issue than most other politicians. In the 1948 presidential campaign,
        when the outcome of the Hiss case was still uncertain, Nixon tried to
        prevail on John Foster Dulles to persuade Dewey to use the threat of
        communism in general and the charges against Hiss in particular as a
        weapon against Truman, who had dismissed the charges against Hiss as
        a red herring. But Dulles was reluctant because of his ties to Hiss, whom
        he had hired as president of the Carnegie Endowment. And Dewey was
        gun-shy after an ill-fated attempt to tie Roosevelt to Communist Party
        leader Earl Browder in 1944 (Ambrose, 186).
139   Communist "smears": Nixon, *Six Crises*, 83.
139   Red baiting on both sides: Parmet, 195.
139   "Pink lady": Morris, 179.

139 "Down to her underwear": Brodie, 24.

139 "If she had her way": Morris, 584.

139 Nixon "ideal" for vice-president: Mazo and Hess, 80.

140 Eisenhower on Hiss case: Nixon, 88.

140 Eisenhower's misgivings: Ambrose, 300.

140 "I was carried away": Nixon, 112.

140 Attacking Acheson: *Ibid.*, 349.

141 Lambasting the Democrats: *LAT*, May 12, 1958.

141 "To answer the attack": Ambrose, 500.

142 Nixon's polarizing strategy: One major drawback to his divisive tactics was that they made it hard for him to present himself as a centrist, which would be the natural position for a middle-class champion and which was where Nixon generally claimed to be ideologically. "On the race issue I'm a liberal; on economics I'm a conservative," he told interviewers during the 1968 campaign. "If there is one thing that classifies me it is that I am a non-extremist" (Mazo and Hess, 316).

143 Life in Whittier: Reichley, 42.

143 "Neatly paved": Morris, 69.

143 "Family church and school": Nixon, *Ibid.*, 13.

143 From groceries to tires: Morris, 72.

143 Social shifts: Reichley, 42–43.

143 The evangelical appeal: Allen, 176; Nixon, 14; Morris, 86–87.

143 One reason: Ambrose, 10.

144 "Confusion and distress": Allen, *Only Yesterday*, 99–101.

144 "Virtuous and irresponsible": Allen, *The Big Change*, 131.

144 "The idea of college": Nixon, *Six Crises*, 14–15.

145 "We never thought of ourselves as poor": Morris, 98.

145 Nixon's Model A: *Ibid.*, 137–38.

145 Vow to keep Checkers: Nixon, *Six Crises*, 115.

145 "The most demeaning experience": Steel, 483.

146 Verdict favors Nixon: Parmet, 249.

146 "You would give it to the Ambassador": Kempton, 20.

146 "Hook line and sinker": Nixon, 110.

147 "There is a man": Kraus, 397.

147 Someone should stand up: Nixon, 354.

147 Winning the battle: Nixon, *Six Crises*, xv.

148 "Very cunning": Brodie, 107–08.

148 "I'm gonna win": Morris, 319–20.

148 Nixon would deny: Nixon, 42.

148 Saturnine impressions: McGinnis, 31–32.

148 Nixon's self-consciousness: Morris, 67, 99.

148 Heaping praise: Brodie, 65.

149 Frank Nixon's temperament: Nixon, 6.

149 Contrast with Frank Nixon: *Ibid.*, 39.

149 Relationship with mother: Ambrose, 24–25, 51; Morris, 55, 61.

149 Arthur's death: Nixon, 10.

149 Three sons in one: Brodie, 100.

150 No play fellow: Abrahamsen, 49.
150 Biggest thrill: Morris, 74–75.
150 Nixon's college personality: Ambrose, 63, 72, 75; Morris, 108, 154–57; Brodie, 116.
150 Punching bag: Ambrose, 64.
151 Analytical, not philosophical: Morris, 123–24.
151 Plans to end the war: Nixon, 298, 349.
151 Prisoners in the White House: Safire, 172.
152 Johnson's supposed error: Nixon, *Ibid.*, 289.
152 Problem of public support: Reichley, 107.
152 "No way to win": Whalen, 137.
152 This historic fissure: Nixon, 344.
152 Discussed with speech writers: Safire, 121.
153 "If there's war": Nixon, 58.
153 "Lift to the American dream": Witcover, 357–58.
154 Why not win?: McPherson oral history interview. (See Johnson bibliography.)
154 Decision to withdraw: Evans and Novak, 80–85.
154 Mutual withdrawal: *PPP*, 1969, 369–75.
154 Suffocating peace: *Ibid.*, 1969, 432–37.
155 To drive a wedge: Safire, 138.
155 Ultimatum to the North: Nixon, 399, 405.
155 "They can't break us": *Ibid.*, 404.
155 No ghost writers: Safire, 172.
155 Drafting the speech: Nixon, 408.
156 Two choices: Safire, 173–74.
156 Loss of confidence: *PPP*, 1969, 369–75.
156 "Silent majority": President's speech file.
157 "Shrill America": Stelzner.
157 Reaction to speech: Haldeman notes.
158 Aggressive and sure: Hersh, 130–31.
158 "Emasculation": Morris, *Uncertain Greatness*, 170–71.
158 "Win their approval": Safire, 178.
158 "An honorable conclusion": Nixon, 410.
158 Dealing from strength: Reichley, 120–21.
160 Nixon's conduct: Hoff-Wilson, 190.
160 "What would best bring peace": Nixon, 514–15.
160 Campaign in Dixie: Nixon, *On the Issues*, 80–87.
160 No debts to blacks: Chester, Hodgson and Page, 625.
161 Defiance of court: Evans and Novak, 150–58.
161 Trying to change the court: Shogan, 270–73.
161 "Character assassination": *PPP*, 1970, 345–46.
161 "New majority momentum": Nixon, 669.
161 Tearing up the pea patch: *Ibid.*, 761, 768.
162 "The kind of tricks": Nixon, 476.
162 Reckless aggressiveness: Safire, 315.
163 Bogus tax deductions: Lukas, 357–61.

163 Undermining confidence: Nixon, 967.
164 History will judge: *Ibid.*, 515.
164 Cut and thrust: Nixon, 111.

Ford: The Congressman's Congressman

166 The story that upset Ford: *LAT*, May 8, 1974.
168 Nixon's anger: Ford, 120.
168 Buchen's view: Buchen.
169 The minority view: Syers papers.
169 "Practical pacifism": Buchen oral history interview.
169 Impact of military experience: Ford, 61.
170 Jonkman's attacks: terHorst, "President Ford and the Media."
170 "Ought not go unchallenged": terHorst, 15.
170 Ford won easily: Ford, 67.
170 Milanowski's view: Vestal, 100.
171 Ford's early career in the House: terHorst, 55–60; McElroy.
171 Snapping visitors: Vestal, 105.
172 "My seat seemed safe": Ford, 71.
172 "The only guy who could do you good": Griffin.
172 "He didn't have enemies": Reeves, 6.
173 Hoeven's warning: Ford, 74.
173 "He had no enemies": Griffin.
173 Ford's record: McElroy.
173 Jefferson's axiom: Ford, 66.
173 The Great Society steamroller: Syers papers.
173 "Congressman's congressman": terHorst, 78.
174 "Ford learned the essence": Cannon.
174 "Too many arguments": Buchen.
174 The successful coup: Ford, 72.
176 Wholesome Grand Rapids: terHorst, 32; Ford, 51.
176 Parental influence: terHorst, 34; Ford, 44–45.
176 Milanowski talked him out of it: Ford, 70.
176 The Winter-Berger case: terHorst, 159–60; Senate hearings, 52–62, passim.
176 "As clean as anyone": McElroy.
177 "Truth is the glue": Senate hearings, 18.
177 "A Nixon trait": Ford, 73.
177 "You owe it to the team": Ford, 52.
177 Ward's comments: Vestal, 62.
177 "He knew everybody": Weathers oral history interview.
178 "A compulsive joiner": Ford, 62.
178 The Chowder & Marching Club: terHorst, 69.
178 The 20th anniversary (fn): *WP*, April 10, 1974.
178 Private White House dinner (fn): *WP*, March 13, 1969.
179 Ford's warning to Nixon: Ford, 118–19.
180 "We love him": Reeves, 28.
180 Getting along with others: Ford, 46.

180 O'Donnell's view: Syers papers.

180 "The only father I knew": Schapsmeier and Schapsmeier.

181 Keeping the business afloat: Vestal, 50–51.

181 "I owe it to them": Ford, 45.

181 Ford's record at Michigan: terHorst, 43.

181 Ford at Yale: Ford, 56.

181 Navy record: *Ibid.*, 48.

181 "I broke down and cried": Ford, 49.

181 King resisted paying child support: Schapsmeier and Schapsmeier.

182 King never replied: Ford, 51.

182 The Phyllis Brown romance: Ford, 56–57.

182 Ford's travel rationale, Betty Ford's problems: Nessen, 23–24.

182 Childhood stuttering: Ford, 43.

182 Ford did not relax (fn): Betty Ford, 40–41.

183 Nixon within his rights: Ford, 109.

184 Ford's reactions to Watergate: *Ibid.*, 94–96.

185 Nixon's wire: terHorst, 136.

185 Ford's disappointment: Ford, 98.

185 The least objectionable: Nixon, *RN*, 926. (See Nixon bibliography.)

185 Breaking the news: Ford, 105.

186 "The public would not stand for it": Senate hearings, 124.

186 "Speak up, speak now": *LAT*, Nov. 14, 1973.

187 Negative reaction: Ford, 115–16.

187 Ford shifts ground: *LAT*, March 17, 1974; May 15, 1974.

187 "Dear Gerry": Ford, 122.

188 Ford's dilemma: *Ibid.*

188 The meeting with Haig: Ford, 6.

189 "Time to think": Ford, 4.

189 Hartmann's objection: Hartmann, 131.

189 Trying to repair the damage: Ford, 13.

190 In favor of acquittal: Ford press conference, Hattiesburg, Miss., Aug. 3, 1974, John Marsh files, Box 25.

190 "Our long nightmare": *PPP*, 1974, 2.

190 "Until the matter reaches me": *PPP*, 1974, 65.

190 Ford's troubled mind: Ford, 159.

190 Watergate questions: *PPP*, 1974, 56–66.

190 The reporters would keep it up: Ford, 158.

190 His mind made up: Hartmann, 258–59.

190 "He didn't invite discussion": Buchen.

190 Fear of a Nixon trial: *PPP*, 1974, 102.

191 "The cost would be greater": Ben-Veniste and Frampton, 305.

191 TerHorst's protest: terHorst, 236.

191 Compassion not a factor: Ford, 179.

191 Ford cut him off: Hartmann, 266.

191 "Not a revengeful people": *PPP*, 1974, 363.

192 "The real Ford": Hartmann, 239.

192 "Vision a fancy word": Webber.

192 "Lifting a burden": Ford, 178.
193 High school speech: *LAT*, April 8, 1989.
193 Public reaction: Kutler, 572, 566.
193 "Jail Ford": Ford, 171–72.
193 Nixon's statement: *NYT*, Aug. 9, 1974.
193 "Ford's shock": Ford, 37.
195 Nixon indictment likely: Buchen press conference, Sept. 8, 1974, Box 33, Philip Buchen files.
196 Ford's vetoes: Reichley, 323–25. (See Nixon bibliography.)
196 "The gloom began to fade": Ford, 284.
196 "Carter's thanks": *PPP*, 1977, 1.
196 "Something more than Ford brought": Buchen.

Carter: The Road to Malaise

197 "Towering significance": Bourne.
197 Carter's potential: Fallows.
200 "Fiscal conservative": Carter, *Keeping Faith*, 74.
200 Admired Truman: *Ibid.*, 65–66.
201 Worth the wait: Bourne.
201 Southern political problems: Key, 3.
201 Domination of race: *Ibid.*, 4.
201 Political factions: *Ibid.*, 11.
201 Leadership devolved: *Ibid.*, 16.
201 The changing Southern political system: Bass and DeVries, 3–5, 13–14; Carter, *WNTB?*, 87–89.
201 Shift on segregation: Shogan, 33.
202 Vanished progressivism: Hargrove.
202 Carter's political start: Glad, 87.
202 The triumph of decency: Carter, *WNTB?*, 96.
202 "Difficult for the common good": *Ibid.*, 99–101.
202 Carter's record in Atlanta: Glad, 202–03, 180–86, 133–35, 15.
204 Worried liberals: Shogan, 45.
206 Highlight on morality: *LAT*, May 25, 1975.
206 "At peace with myself": Bourne.
206 Advice to get married: Shogan, 135–36.
207 Not for fainthearted: Shogan, 34.
207 Sweeping change: Knott and Wildavsky.
207 Carter feared incremental efforts: *Ibid.*
208 "A good man": Fallows.
208 His need to prove he was gifted. Carter, *WNTB?*, 32.
208 Parental relationships: *Ibid.*, 9–13, 80, 30.
209 Life at Annapolis: *Ibid.*, 41–47.
209 Rickover's example: Polmar and Allen, 294–316.
210 Responding to press criticism: Glad, 496.
210 Lashing out: Schram, 159.
210 Personal insecurity: Bourne.

211 Unwilling to become better: Fallows.
212 End of economic growth: Hargrove.
214 No political base: Indeed, Carter seemed to have succeeded in uniting the traditional Democratic base *against* him. Feminists objected to Carter's opposition to federal aid for abortion (*LAT*, Jan. 14, 1979). Jews complained about his "evenhanded"—they thought heavy-handed—treatment of Israel (*LAT*, July 23, 1978). The elderly protested his plan to cut Social Security benefits (*LAT*, Jan. 20, 1979). And as the fateful year of 1979 got under way more than sixty liberal groups active in the Democratic party established a new coalition called the Progressive Alliance with its avowed goal a rollback of $600 million in cuts Carter had proposed in domestic social programs (*LAT*, Jan. 16, 1979).
214 Merit of his ideas would prevail: *Ibid.*
215 Democrats balk at Panama treaty: *LAT*, Oct. 8, 1977.
217 Getting a grip at last: Johnson, 272.
217 Events hammered Carter's presidency: *Ibid.*, 270–81.
218 Speech preparation: Carter, *Keeping Faith*, 114–15.
219 Speculation about "summit": *Facts on File*, July 20, 1979, 531.
220 "I handled it poorly": Carter, *Keeping Faith*, 121.
220 "Keeping the monkeys": *LAT*, July 20, 1979.
221 Toast to the Shah: *PPP*, 1977, 2220–21.
221 Carter deeply shaken: Carter, *Memoirs*, 458.
222 "I have but one task": *PPP*, 1979, 2192–93.
222 "A sad time": Carter, *Memoirs*, 470.
222 Sinking feeling: Hargrove.
222 Hostage obsession: Barber, 454.
223 Trustee for the public: Hargrove and Jones, passim.
223 Comprehensive solutions: Carter, *WNTB?*, 101.
223 "We didn't assess the consequences": Hargrove.

Reagan: The Half Revolution

227 Reagan's 1964 speech: Barrett, 52.
227 Reagan's inaugural: *PPP*, 1981, 1.
228 "The painful fact": *LAT*, March 16, 1975.
228 Reliance on a massive tax cut: Stockman, 72.
228 Cutting taxes always appealed: Cannon, 236.
228 He left others to ponder: Barrett, 130–32.
229 Nixon's praise: Ambrose, *Nixon*, 541. (See Nixon bibliography.)
229 From Adam Smith to Baptiste Say: Anderson, 171–72.
230 Not a single reference: Reagan, 24–38.
230 Student enthusiasms: Edwards, 95.
230 Without cracking a book: Cannon, 39.
230 Reagan's early years: Reagan, 39–41.
230 Jack Reagan's reaction: *Ibid.*, 49–51.
231 Mimicking FDR: Cannon, 32.
231 Blindly, with misgivings: Reagan, 126.

231 Neil Reagan's recollections: Edwards, 254, quoting UCLA oral history interview.
232 "Created by Marx": Barrett, 55.
232 "I was a star, but": Reagan, 167.
232 Blaming the Truman Administration: Barrett, 56.
232 Like a candy maker: Reagan, 259.
232 The threat of communism: *Ibid.*, 128.
233 "We were fighting just as hard": Boyarsky, 68.
233 Reagan's remedy: *Ibid.*, 149.
233 Unpopular in the Kremlin: Barrett, 57.
233 Alert by 1951: Cannon, 87.
234 Reagan's need for money: *Ibid.*, 92.
234 Why the movies suffered: Boyarsky, 78.
234 Dropping attacks on TVA: Reagan, 240.
234 "A change all over America": *Ibid.*, 238.
235 The ardent spokesman: Cannon, 99.
235 "What do we do now?" *Ibid.*, 119.
236 The welfare compromise: *Ibid.*, 182–84; Boyarsky, 137–38.
236 "Not as much as he said": Cannon, 185.
236 "Shrines to the giants": *PPP*, 1981, 3.
237 "All men born free": *PPP*, 1981, 433.
237 "A moral revolution": Muir.
237 "Preference for the old": Reagan, 265.
237 "The conservatives believe": Reagan, 263.
237 Celebration of private effort: Heclo.
238 "A good life": *Ibid.*, 20.
238 Taking jobs from teenagers: Boyarksy, 32.
238 Small-town goodwill: Cannon, 24.
238 "The flat side of his boot": Reagan, 11.
239 No athletes among extremists: *Ibid.*, 59.
239 "Film is forever": Rogin, 3.
239 "Where do we find such men": *Ibid.*, 7.
240 Attack on radicals: Erickson, 63.
240 "What rules to follow": White, 41.
240 Stress on local communities: Yankelovich.
241 An even broader conflict: Heclo.
242 Rebounding from adversity: Princeton conference.
243 Speakes's role: Speakes, 170.
243 Some thought him lazy: Ceaser.
243 Reagan's management style: *Tower Commission Report*, 79–80.
243 Reagan's early years: Cannon, 25; Reagan, 15.
243 Wilbur Cohen's view: Princeton conference.
244 "Beyond his control": Reagan, 10–11.
244 "Habits of a lifetime": Regan, 252–53.
244 Passive-positive: Barber, 463; Barrett, 23–25.
245 "I didn't have cancer": Speakes, 237.
245 Staff support: Princeton conference.

245 Defining a recession: Barrett, 126–27.
246 Caddell's view of campaign: Moore, 90.
246 Pointless controversies: Cannon, 279–89.
246 Wirthlin's view of campaign: Drew, 371–72.
246 The economic speech: *NYT*, Sept. 10, 1980.
247 Underlining values: White, 50.
247 Reagan's closing statement: *NYT*, Oct. 29, 1980.
248 Defense not a budget issue: Stockman, 283.
248 Reagan's wit: Cannon, 404.
249 Reagan exploded: Stockman, 319.
249 Only a half revolution: *Ibid.*, 276.
250 Reagan on tax bill: *Ibid.*, 356.
250 The rich got richer: Weatherford and McDonnell.
251 Reagan Doctrine's failings: Layne.
252 The qualified denial: *PPP*, 1987, 209.
253 As gently as possible: *Tower Commission Report*, 80.
253 Joint report of Select Committees: *NYT*, Nov. 19, 1987.
253 Carter's eyes brightened: Fallows. (See Carter bibliography.)
254 Reagan's high poll ratings: *NYT*, Jan. 18, 1989.
254 Moralistic view of Soviets: *PPP*, 1981, 57; 1983, 363–64.
254 Criticism of Reagan's arms-control proposals: Rice, Destler.
254 Soviet view of SDI: Rice.
255 Economic vulnerability: Mann.
256 Lost opportunity: Palmer. One measure of Reagan's appeal was the kid-
      glove treatment he got at the 1988 Democratic convention. Not only did
      the Democrats refrain from attacking the outgoing president, but their
      choice to succeed him, Michael Dukakis, in accepting his party's nomi-
      nation, hailed Reagan as having "set the stage for deep cuts in nuclear
      arms," adding: "I salute him for that" (*NYT*, July 22, 1988). Reagan also
      won praise from another prominent Democrat, Edward M. Kennedy, for
      his successful summit conference with Gorbachev in Moscow. Kennedy
      went on to contrast Reagan favorably with George Bush: "At least Ronald
      Reagan accepts the blame as well as the credit for the policies of the past
      eight years" (*NYT*, July 19, 1988).

Bush: "The Way I Was Brought Up"

258 Bush just shrugged: Author's interview with David Keene, July 1980.
258 No need to change: Germond and Witcover, *Blue Smoke and Mirrors*,
      120–21.
259 "How do you know?": Bearak.
260 Northeast establishment: Phillips, 44.
261 Republican sunbelt revival: *Ibid.*, 270–77.
261 Quick money: Bush, 58.
261 Class warfare: Aldrich, 106.
261 Zapata's slogan: *Ibid.*, 67.
262 High-risk ventures: *Ibid.*, 72.

262 Goldwater's core support: White, 113.
263 Concern for the two-party system: Bush, 25.
263 Prescott Bush made no enemies: Green, 9.
263 Bush wanted a two-party state: Bush, 84.
263 Back to reality: *Ibid.*, 44.
263 Early politics: *Ibid.*, 81–91.
264 The roots of racism: Bass and DeVries, 323.
265 "It seems fundamental": Bush, 92.
265 "Off the edge of the Earth": Bearak.
265 "Probably true": Oudes, 169.
265 Quitting Council on Foreign Relations: Silk and Silk, 220.
266 Reagan vs. Bush: *Ibid.*, 308.
266 Voodoo economics: *LAT*, April 11, 1980.
267 "Anything down the road?": Bush, 15.
267 "I'll show you discipline": Author's interview with Marlin Fitzwater, April 1986.
268 "Have a nice weekend": *LAT*, Oct. 17, 1988.
268 Not a rubber stamp: Bush, 124.
269 Chief culprit: *LAT*, July 25, 1973.
269 Urging suspension of Bellino: *LAT*, July 31, 1973.
269 "The way I was brought up": Bearak.
270 "Like a beautiful dream": *Ibid.*
270 Working with Harriman: Green, 4.
270 Duty and service: Bush, 23–26.
271 Breaking away: *Ibid.*, 23.
271 The place for ambition: *Ibid.*, 46–47.
271 Only so far: *Ibid.*, 65.
271 Help from Mills: Bearak.
272 Brady's remark: Author's interview, April, 1986
272 "He takes our line": Oudes, 302.
273 Protecting the CIA problems: Bush, 175; Mann.
273 "I don't know what the word means": Aldrich, 129.
274 "They did everything right": Green, 3.
274 Maintaining the establishment's position: Aldrich, 146.
274 "It's a joy to serve": *NYT*, Oct. 12, 1984.
274 Like he was being electrocuted: Goldman and Fuller, 320.
274 "Kicking ass": Germond and Witcover, *Wake Us When It's Over*, 522.
275 All in the perception: Bush, 203.
275 Old money image: Aldrich, 107.
275 A preppy conspiracy: Bush, 203.
276 "Anything but that": Bearak.
276 Building a new coalition: Bush, 121.
276 No turning it down: Bearak.
276 The bandage carrier: Bush, 123.
276 Letter to Nixon: Bush, 122.
277 A smart choice: *LAT*, April 14, 1986.
279 "Hidden Pac-Men": Blustein.

279   "Kinder and gentler": *NYT*, Jan. 21, 1989.
279   No turning back on liberty: Presidential Documents, Vol. 25, No. 26, June 30, 1989, 1007.
279   The education president: *NYT*, Feb. 10, 1989.
279   "Stop the scourge": *NYT*, Jan. 21, 1989.
280   Stress on enforcement: *NYT*, Sept. 6, 1989.
280   More at home with foreign policy: Duffy.
280   Decision to attack: Hoffman and Woodward.
280   Panama implications: Apple.
280   Poll ratings rise: *WP*, Jan. 18, 1990.
280   Congress has most power: Baltz.
280   That bleak perception: Pennar, Oreskes, Yang and Devroy.
281   Savings and loan figures: *Encyclopedia Americana Annual*, 1989, 132; 1990, 512.
282   "The one cause": Shogan.
282   "No political purpose": Barnes, "Standing Soft."
283   Opportunity to define: Shribman, Nelson.
283   "Pro-Moscow gangs": Talbott.
283   Opposing sanctions: Lane, Gugliotta et. al.
284   "We have no opinion." Sciolino and Gordon, Lewis, excerpts. Accounts of the meeting are based on a transcript made available by the Iraqi government, on whose accuracy the State Department declined to comment.
284   Oil imports rose: Woutat.
284   Short-term energy strategy: Schneider.
284   "Prudently recreate": *NYT*, August 22, 1990.
284   Supremely confident: Baltz and Hoffman.
285   "Wait, watch, and learn": *LAT*, August 6, 1990.
285   "Read My Ships": *Time*, August 20, 1990.
285   Old WASP values: Thomas.
285   "A dazzling performance": Barnes, "Hour of Power."
286   Fascell cut him off: House Foreign Affairs.
286   VFW speech: *NYT*, August 21, 1990.
287   Gephardt's views: "Press Stakeout," *WP*, September 12, 1990.
287   Considerably overdrawn: Bandow.
287   *Los Angeles Times* poll: Skelton.
288   Bush's speech: *NYT*, September 12, 1990.
288   Contrast with Churchill: Krauthammer
289   Economic burden: Seib and Murray.
289   Recession threat: *Ibid.*
289   Economic power more important: Luttwak.
289   Borrowing from Japan: Shields.
289   "When we feel better": Drahuschak.

A Leadership Primer

291   "A simple statement of fact": Carter, *WNTB?*, 158–59. (See Carter bibliography.)

293   Nixon's first speech: Parmet, 95–96. (See Nixon bibliography.)

294   "No left or right": Erickson, 125. (See Reagan bibliography.)

294   "Not one for fine theory": James MacGregor Burns, *The Crosswinds of Freedom* (Knopf, 1989), 628–29.

295   "I can't do that": Hughes, 124–25. (See Eisenhower bibliography.)

295   "On this issue": *PPP*, 1965, 283.

297   Ranney's view: Author's interview, June 1984.

298   Gingrich's view: Author's interview, March 1987.

INDEX